D1431666

A Dictionary of
Political Quotations

A Dictionary of Political Quotations

COMPILED BY ROBERT STEWART

LONDON
EUROPA PUBLICATIONS LIMITED
1984

Europa Publications Limited
18 Bedford Square
London, WC1B 3JN

British Library Cataloguing in Publication Data
Stewart, Robert
  A dictionary of political quotations
  1. Politics, Practical — Quotations, maxims, etc.
  I. Title
  320   PN6084.P6
  ISBN 0-905118-81-2

Printed and bound in England by
STAPLES PRINTERS ROCHESTER LIMITED
at The Stanhope Press

Contents

Preface   vii

Quotations   1

Key-word index   179

Supplementary index   225

Preface

Like any anthology compiled by one person, this book will undoubtedly betray the personal tastes of its begetter. What I think constitutes a 'political' statement, *a fortiori* what I think makes it an interesting or memorable one, cannot be expected to win universal consent. I have, nevertheless, endeavoured to make of the collection something more than a mere commonplace book of mine, and it is well, at the outset, to inform readers of the principal considerations which have governed my selection.

There are, in the first place, quotations whose title to admission seems to me to be incontrovertible. These fall into two categories. There is the quotation in which appears for the first time (at least, so far as I have been able to establish) a word or phrase, such as 'cold war' or 'splendid isolation', that thereafter passed into the language of a nation or the world. Second, there is the quotation which, whatever the intrinsic merit of its content or language, has nevertheless become so well known that a person who wishes to settle a bar-room bet has the right to expect to find it here. I have tried to compile as full a list of such quotations as possible, but readers will no doubt discover the omission of some personal favourites.

For the rest, my selection was governed by my belief that a political statement is interesting chiefly to the extent that it leads outwards to general considerations, that is, to the degree to which it invites us to reflect upon the general forms which political activity takes, or upon the temper of an age in which it was possible to say certain things, or upon the kind of man or woman who felt able to say them. Political theorists and men of letters are, accordingly, amply represented. Professional historians, whose comments on the past cannot properly be called political, have been left out. I have, however, in the spirit of Clausewitz, included remarks about war which seem to me to bear a political, not simply a military, significance.

When a person is represented by only one or two quotations, it is not to be thought that I have judged those remarks to be the best or wisest that he ever made, far less that they somehow characterize his political position. For the major figures, theorists like Adam Smith or Marx and political leaders like Lincoln or Metternich, I have attempted to give quotations which are, in the brief space available, representative of their main beliefs.

I have been led by a number of considerations to exclude certain kinds of statement. Attributed remarks which it is not possible to verify have not been included. Louis XIV does not assert his identity with the state in these pages. On the other hand, remarks made in conversation and recorded by an ear-witness, even if not *verbatim*, have gained entry. After all, before the age of electronic recording, all spoken words, even those delivered in parliament, were reported only more or less accurately. In the second place, amusing or epigrammatic remarks, of no political reference, have not gained entry simply because they were uttered by a politician. Of this kind is Disraeli's famous jest that when he wanted to read a book he wrote one. Of this kind, too, are personal remarks about politicians which are nevertheless not about politics. Finally, I have left out those quotations, however admirable they may be in other respects, which would require extensive annotation in order to make their gist understood by the English-speaking reader of today.

Some readers may find the collection unbalanced in two ways. The first imbalance is artificial and deliberate. It was thought that a largely English-speaking readership would not object to a substantial bias in favour of quotations of a Western, and even a British and American, provenance. The second is entirely natural. Politics is the fruit of a mature civilization; it is the activity, and the mark, of a society which has progressed beyond the use of merely customary judicial instruments to resolve its conflicts. A political society is one which recognizes that power and influence are constantly passing from one set of institutions, one class, or one group of individuals to another. The more open, dare one say the more democratic, a society, the more it is able to nurture and sustain political activity. It is for this reason that the bulk of the statements in this dictionary were made in the last 250 years.

Finally, a note of apology to the constitutional purists: for the sake of convenience the phrase 'member of parliament' has been used to describe a 'member of the House of Commons'.

Robert Stewart
August 1984

A

Abū Yūsuf (*fl.* 9th century)
EGYPTIAN JUDGE

1 'Rulers are a scourge through whom God punishes those whom He decides to punish. Therefore do not meet God's scourge with hot temper and anger, but with humility and submission.'
KITAB AL-KHARA

Acheson, Dean (1893–1971)
AMERICAN DEMOCRATIC POLITICIAN,
SECRETARY OF STATE, 1949–1953

2 'The greatest mistake I made was not to die in office.'
In conversation with Luke Battle, 27 May 1959. After listening to the eulogies of his successor as secretary of state, John Foster Dulles, at the latter's funeral

3 'Great Britain has lost an Empire and has not yet found a role.'
Speech at West Point Military Academy, 5 December 1962

Acton, Ist Baron (John Dalberg-Acton) (1834–1902)
ENGLISH HISTORIAN AND WHIG
MEMBER OF PARLIAMENT, 1859–1864

4 'Liberty is not a means to a higher political end. It is itself the highest political end.'
Lecture at Bridgnorth, 26 February 1877,
THE HISTORY OF FREEDOM IN ANTIQUITY

5 'If there is a free contract, in open market, between capital and labour, it cannot be right that one of the two contracting parties should have the making of the laws. . . Before this argument, the ancient dogma that power attends on property broke down. Justice required that property should – not abdicate, but – share its political supremacy.'
Letter to Mary Gladstone, 24 April 1881. On the democratic implications of classical economic theory

6 'Power tends to corrupt and absolute power corrupts absolutely. Great men are almost always bad men, even when they exercise influence, and not authority . . . There is no worse heresy than that the office sanctifies the holder of it.'

Letter to Bishop Mandell Creighton, 3 April 1887
SEE ALSO *William Pitt, Earl of Chatham*

7 'The principles of public morality are as definite as those of the morality of private life; but they are not identical.'
IBID.

Adams, Henry (1838–1918)
AMERICAN HISTORIAN

8 'Politics, as a practice, whatever its professions, has always been the systematic organization of hatreds.'
THE EDUCATION OF HENRY ADAMS *(1906), Chapter 1*

9 'Practical politics consists in ignoring facts.'
IBID., *Chapter 22*

Adams, John (1735–1826)
AMERICAN FEDERALIST POLITICIAN,
PRESIDENT, 1797–1801

10 'The Thought that we might be driven to the sad Necessity of breaking our Connection with G[reat] B[ritain], exclusive of the Carnage & Destruction which it was easy to see must attend the separation, always gave me a great deal of Grief. And even now, I would chearfully retire from public life forever, renounce all Chance for Profits or Honours from the public, nay I would chearfully contribute my little Property to obtain Peace and Liberty. But all these must go and my life too before I can surrender the Right of my Country to a free Constitution.'
Letter to his wife, 7 October 1775

11 'Democracy is Lovelace and the people is Clarissa.'
Letter to William Cunningham, March 1804

12 'Brutus and Cassius were conquered and slain, Hampden died in the field, Sidney on the scaffold, Harrington in jail etc. This is cold comfort. Politics are an ordeal path among red-hot ploughshares. Who then would be a politician for the pleasure of running about barefoot among them? Yet somebody must.'
Letter to James Warren, undated

Adams, John Quincy (1767–1848)
AMERICAN REPUBLICAN POLITICIAN,
PRESIDENT, 1825–1829

1 'Wherever the standard of freedom and independence has been or shall be unfurled, there will be America's heart, her benedictions and her prayers. But she goes not abroad in search of monsters to destroy. She is the well-wisher to the freedom and independence of all. She is the champion and vindicator only of her own.'
Address, 4 July 1821

Adams, Samuel (1722–1803)
AMERICAN REVOLUTIONARY LEADER
AND STATESMAN

2 'A nation of shopkeepers are very seldom so disinterested.'
Speech at Philadelphia, 1 August 1776
SEE ALSO *Adam Smith*

Addison, Joseph (1672–1719)
ENGLISH ESSAYIST AND WHIG
POLITICIAN, SECRETARY OF STATE,
1717–1718

3 'There is nothing so bad for the Face as Party-Zeal ... I never knew a Party-Woman that kept her Beauty for a twelvemonth.'
SPECTATOR, *No. 57, 5 May 1711*

4 'There cannot be a greater Judgment befall a Country than such a dreadful Spirit of Division as rends a Government into two distinct People, and makes them greater Strangers and more averse to one another, than if they were actually two different Nations ... A furious Party-Spirit, when it rages in its full Violence, exerts itself in Civil War and Bloodshed; and when it is under its greatest Restraints naturally breaks out in Falsehood, Detraction, Calumny, and a partial Administration of Justice. In a Word, it fills a Nation with Spleen and Rancour, and extinguishes all the Seeds of Good-Nature, Compassion and Humanity.'
IBID., *No. 125, 24 July 1711*

Adler, Victor (1852–1918)
AUSTRIAN POLITICIAN, FOUNDER OF
THE AUSTRIAN SOCIAL DEMOCRATIC
PARTY

5 'The Austrian government ... is a system of despotism tempered by casualness.'
Speech to the International Socialist Congress, Paris, 17 July 1889
SEE ALSO *Carlyle*

Aksakov, Sergei (1791–1859)
RUSSIAN NOVELIST

6 'The Russian people is not a political people, that is, it does not aspire to political power, does not want political rights, does not contain in itself even the germ of the love of power.'
Manuscript fragment. Quoted in M Cherniavsky, TSAR AND PEOPLE, *Chapter 6*

Alcuin (c. 735–804)
ENGLISH CHURCHMAN AND SCHOLAR

7 'Nor should we listen to those who say, "The voice of the people is the voice of God", for the turbulence of the mob is always close to insanity.'
Letter to Charlemagne, undated

Allen, (Charles) Grant (1848–1899)
CANADIAN-BORN ENGLISH
PHILOSOPHICAL WRITER AND NOVELIST

8 'Aristocracies, as a rule, all the world over, consist, and have always consisted, of barbaric conquerors or their descendants, who remain to the last, on the average of instances, at a lower grade of civilisation and morals than the democracy they live among ... the barbaric invaders have seldom or never learned the practical arts and handicrafts which are the civilising element in the life of the conquered people around them.'
POST-PRANDIAL PHILOSOPHY *(a collection of essays first published in the* WESTMINSTER GAZETTE, *1894), 'In the Matter of Aristocracy'*

9 'Patriotism is one of the Monopolist Instincts. And the Monopolist Instincts are the greatest enemies of the social life in humanity. They are what we have got in the end to outlive. The test of a man's place in the scale of being is how far he has outlived them. They are surviving relics of the ape and tiger. But we must let the ape and tiger die. We must begin to be human.'
IBID., *'The Monopolist Instincts'*

10 'Conservatism, I believe, is mainly due to want of imagination. In saying this, I do

not for a moment mean to deny the other and equally obvious truth that Conservatism, in the lump, is a euphemism for selfishness. But the two ideas have much in common. Selfish people are apt to be unimaginative: unimaginative people are apt to be selfish. Clearly to realise the condition of the unfortunate is the beginning of philanthropy. Clearly to realise the rights of others is the beginning of justice. "Put yourself in his place" strikes the keynote of ethics. Stupid people can only see their own side of a question: they cannot even imagine any other side possible. So, as a rule, stupid people are Conservative.'
IBID., *'Imagination and Radicals'*

Allen, William (1803–1849)
AMERICAN DEMOCRATIC POLITICIAN, SENATOR, 1837–1849

1 'Fifty-four-forty or fight!'
Speech to the Senate, 1844. On the need to occupy Oregon to that latitude. The phrase was adopted by the Democrats as their chief slogan in the 1844 presidential election.

Allende Gossens, Salvador (1908–1973)
CHILEAN SOCIALIST POLITICIAN, PRESIDENT, 1970–1973

2 'Between 3 September and 4 November, Chile is going to feel like a football being kicked about by a Pele.'
Campaign speech, 1970. Quoted in R Debray, CONVERSATIONS WITH ALLENDE, *Part I. Predicting the struggle which would follow Socialist victory at the election*

3 'We are a canal, not a dam.'
Often-repeated statement. IBID. *Part II*

Ames, Fisher (1758–1808)
AMERICAN FEDERALIST POLITICIAN, MEMBER OF CONGRESS, 1789–1797

4 'A monarchy is a merchantman, which sails well, but will sometimes strike on a rock, and go to the bottom; a republic is a raft, which will never sink, but then your feet are always in the water.'
Speech to the House of Representatives, 1795

5 'The people of France ... find their cap of liberty a soldier's helmet.'
Eulogy of George Washington, Massachusetts state legislature, 8 February, 1800

6 'The agents that move politicks, are the popular passions; and those are ever, from the very nature of things, under the command of the disturbers of society.'
PALLADIUM, *November 1801, 'No Revolutions'*

7 'Our country is too big for union, too sordid for patriotism, too democratick for liberty ... Its vice will govern it, by practising upon its folly. This is ordained for democracies.'
Letter to a congressman, 26 October 1803

8 'Of all despotisms a democracy, though the least durable, is the most violent.'
THE DANGERS OF AMERICAN LIBERTY *(1805)*

9 'Though justice might possibly support a democracy, yet a democracy cannot possibly support justice.'
IBID.

10 'It is indeed a law of politicks as well as of physicks, that a body in action must overcome an equal body at rest.'
IBID. *On the handicap of conservatism*

Amis, Kingsley (1922–)
ENGLISH NOVELIST AND POET

11 'Growing older, I have lost the need to be political, which means, in this country, the need to be left. I am driven into grudging toleration of the Conservative Party because it is the party of non-politics, of resistance to politics.'
SUNDAY TELEGRAPH *2 July 1967*

Anthony, Susan (1820–1906)
AMERICAN SUFFRAGETTE

12 'The true Republic: men, their rights and nothing more; women, their rights and nothing less.'
Motto of her newspaper, REVOLUTION

Aquinas, St Thomas (c. 1225–1274)
MEDIEVAL SCHOLASTIC THEOLOGIAN

13 'For a war to be just, three conditions are necessary – public authority, just cause, right motive.'
SUMMA THEOLOGICA *(1267–73)*

Arbuthnot, John (1667–1735)
SCOTTISH PHYSICIAN AND MAN OF
LETTERS, MEMBER OF THE SCRIBLERUS
CLUB

1 'All political parties die at last of
swallowing their own lies.'
Epigram, c. 1735

Argyll, 1st Marquis of (Archibald Campbell) (1598–1661)
SCOTTISH SOLDIER AND LEADING
COVENANTER

2 'Toleration is the cause of many evils,
and renders diseases or distempers in the
State more strong and powerful than any
remedies.'
MAXIMS OF STATE *(1661). On religious
toleration*

Aristotle (384–322BC)
GREEK PHILOSOPHER

3 'If the earlier forms of society are natural,
so is the state, for it is the end of them
and the nature of a thing is its end. For
what each thing is when fully developed,
we call its nature ... Hence it is evident
that the state is a creation of nature and
that man is by nature a political animal.'
THE POLITICS, *Book I*

4 'For few, or many, to have power is an
accidental feature of oligarchies and
democracies, since the rich are few
everywhere, and the poor numerous ...
The real point of difference is poverty
and wealth; and it follows that wherever
the rulers owe their power to wealth,
whether as a minority or as a majority,
this is oligarchy; and where the poor
rule, it is democracy.'
IBID.

5 'Revolutions are not about trifles, but
they spring from trifles.'
IBID.

6 'Poverty is the parent of revolution and
crime.'
IBID., *Book II*

7 'The law is reason free from passion.'
IBID., *Book III*

8 'Those who live in a cold climate and in
Europe are full of spirit, but wanting in
intelligence and skill; and therefore they
keep their freedom, but have no political
organisation, and are incapable of ruling
over others. Whereas the natives of Asia
are intelligent and inventive, but they
are wanting in spirit, and therefore they
are always in a state of subjection and
slavery. But the Hellenic race, which is
situated between them, is likewise
intermediate in character, being high-
spirited and also intelligent.'
IBID.

Arnold, Matthew (1822–1888)
ENGLISH POET AND CRITIC

9 'He who administers governs, because he
infixes his own mark and stamps his own
character on all public affairs as they pass
through his hands; and, therefore, so long
as the English aristocracy administers the
commonwealth, it still governs it.'
1861. Quoted in W L Guttsman, THE
BRITISH POLICIAL ELITE, *Chapter 2*

10 'Culture is the eternal opponent of the
two things which are the signal marks of
Jacobinism, – its fierceness, and its
addiction to an abstract system.'
CULTURE AND ANARCHY *(1869), Chapter 1*

11 'There are many things to be said of this
exclusive attention of ours [the English]
to liberty, and of the relaxed habits of
government which it has engendered ...
In the first place, it never was part of our
creed that the great right and blessedness
of an Irishman, or, indeed, of anybody on
earth except an Englishman, is to do as
he likes; and we can have no scruple at
all about abridging, if necessary, a non-
Englishman's assertion of his liberty.'
IBID., *Chapter 2*

12 'Thus we have got three distinct terms,
Barbarians, Philistines, Populace, to denote
roughly the three great classes into
which our society is divided.'
IBID., *Chapter 3*

13 'We may regard this energy driving at
practice, this paramount sense of the
obligation of duty, self-control, and work,
this earnestness in going manfully with
the best light we have, as one force. And
we may regard the intelligence driving at
those ideas which are, after all, the basis
of right practice, the ardent sense for all
the new and changing combinations of
them which man's development brings
with it, the indomitable impulse to know
and adjust them perfectly, as another
force. And these two forces we may
regard as in some sense rivals, – rivals not

by the necessity of their own nature, but as exhibited in man and his history, – and rivals dividing the empire of the world between them. And to give these forces names from the two races of men who have supplied the most signal and splendid manifestations of them, we may call them respectively the forces of Hebraism and Hellenism.'
IBID., *Chapter 4*

1 'First and foremost of the necessary means towards man's civilisation we must name *expansion*. The need of expansion is as genuine an instinct in man as the need in plants for the light, or the need in man himself for going upright ... And the one insuperable objection to inequality is the same as the one insuperable objection to absolutism: namely, that inequality, like absolutism, thwarts a vital instinct, and being thus against nature, is against our humanisation.'
MIXED ESSAYS *(1879), Preface*

2 'Nations are not truly great solely because the individuals composing them are numerous, free, and active; but they are great when these numbers, this freedom, this activity are employed in the service of an ideal higher than that of an ordinary man, taken by himself.'
IBID., *'Democracy'*

Arnold, Thomas (1795–1842)
ENGLISH SCHOLAR, HEADMASTER OF RUGBY, 1828–1842

3 'To do national injustice is a *sin*, and ... the clergy, whilst they urge the continuance of this injustice, are making themselves individually guilty of it.'
Letter to the Rev. J Lowe, 16 March 1829. On the opposition of the Established Church to Roman Catholic emancipation.

4 'It seems to me a most blessed revolution, spotless beyond all example in history, and the most glorious instance of a royal rebellion against society promptly and energetically repressed, that the world has yet seen.
Letter to the Rev. G Cornish, 24 August 1830. On the 'July Revolution' in France and the abdication of King Charles X, 1830

5 'There is nothing so revolutionary, because there is nothing so unnatural and so convulsive to society, as the strain to keep things fixed, when all the world is by the very law of its creation in eternal progress; and the cause of all the evils of the world may be traced to that natural but most deadly error of human indolence and corruption, that our business is to preserve and not to improve.'
Letter to J T Coleridge, 1 November 1830

6 'When an aristocracy is not thoroughly corrupted, its strength is incalculable; and it acts through the relations of private life, which are permanent, whereas the political excitement, which opposes it, must always be short-lived.'
Letter to J C Platt, 6 December 1837

7 'Aristocracy as a predominant element in a government, whether it be aristocracy of skin, of race, of wealth, of nobility, or of priesthood, has been to my mind the greatest source of evil throughout the world, because it has been the most universal and the most enduring. Democracy and tyranny, if in themselves worse, have been, and I think ever will, be, less prevalent, at least in Europe; they may be the Cholera, but aristocracy is Consumption; and you know that in our climate Consumption is a far worse scourge in the long run than Cholera.'
Letter to J T Coleridge, 18 May 1838

8 'The principle of Conservatism has always appeared to me to be not only foolish, but to be actually felo de se: it destroys what it loves, because it will not mend it.'
Letter to James Marshall, 23 January 1840

Asquith, Herbert, 1st Earl of Oxford and (1852–1928)
ENGLISH LIBERAL STATESMAN, PRIME MINISTER, 1908–1916

9 'The first duty, if not the whole duty, of a private member of the House of Commons is to speak as little and to vote as often as he can.'
Speech at Cambridge, 3 May 1890

10 'I still regard him – measured by his opportunities and his achievements – as one of the half-dozen great men of action of this century. Napoleon stands by himself ... But the only others of this age that I would rank higher than

Parnell are Abraham Lincoln, Bismarck, and (perhaps) Cavour.'
Letter to Margot Tennant, October 1891. Of Charles Stewart Parnell

1 'This new-fangled Caesarism which converts the House of Lords into a kind of plebiscitory organ is one of the quaintest inventions of our time.'
House of Commons, 1909

2 'I am afraid we must wait and see.'
House of Commons, 4 April 1910. On whether the government would make changes in its budget

3 'The Army will hear nothing of politics from me, and in return I expect to hear nothing of politics from the Army.'
Speech at Ladybank, 4 April 1914. During the crisis of the Curragh episode

4 'Happily there seems to be no reason why we should be anything more than spectators.'
Written on 24 July 1914. Quoted in Roy Jenkins, ASQUITH, *Chapter 20. On the impending European war*

5 'In public politics as in private life, character is better than brains, and loyalty more valuable than either; but, I shall have to work with the material that has been given to me.'
In conversation with his wife, 31 July 1914

6 'There is nothing to be got by being a Liberal today. It is not a profitable or a remunerative career.'
Speech to the National Liberal Federation, 26 November 1920

7 'Nothing is so demoralising to the tone of public life, or so belittling to the stature of public men, as the atmosphere of a Coalition.'
FIFTY YEARS OF PARLIAMENT *(1926), Part VI, Chapter 2*

Asquith, Margot (1864–1945)
ENGLISH SOCIETY LADY, SECOND WIFE OF HERBERT

8 'Life in the House [of Commons] is neither healthy, useful nor appropriate for a woman; and the functions of a mother and a member are not compatible.'
AUTOBIOGRAPHY *(1920–1922), Chapter 13*

Astor, Nancy (1879–1964)
AMERICAN-BORN ENGLISH CONSERVATIVE POLITICIAN, MEMBER OF PARLIAMENT, 1919–1945

9 'I am a Virginian, so naturally I am a politician.'
Speech at Plymouth, 1919. Accepting the nomination to stand as a Conservative candidate

Atatürk (Mustapha Kemal) (1881–1938)
TURKISH POLITICIAN AND GENERAL PRESIDENT, 1923–1938

10 'It was necessary to abolish the fez, which sat on the heads of our nation as an emblem of ignorance, negligence, fanaticism and hatred of progress and civilisation, to accept in its place the hat, the headgear worn by the whole civilised world.'
Speech to the Turkish assembly, October 1927

Attlee, Clement, 1st Earl (1883–1967)
ENGLISH LABOUR POLITICIAN, PRIME MINISTER, 1945–1951

11 'The people's flag is palest pink,
It is not red blood but only ink.
It is supported now by Douglas Cole,
Who plays each year a different role.
Now raise our Palace standard high,
Wash out each trace of purple dye,
Let Liberals join and Tories too,
And Socialists of every hue.'
Published anonymously in the DAILY HERALD, *22 February, 1939. On the Popular Front*

12 'I could not consent to the introduction into our national life of a device so alien to all our traditions as the referendum, which has only too often been the instrument of Nazism and Fascism.'
Letter to Winston Churchill, 21 May 1945

13 'The voice was the voice of Churchill, but the mind was the mind of Beaverbrook.'
Speech on BBC radio, 5 June 1945. In reply to Winston Churchill's charge that Labour in power would establish a Gestapo

14 'You have no right whatever to speak on behalf of the Government. Foreign affairs are in the capable hands of Ernest Bevin

'... a period of silence on your part would be welcome.'
Letter to Harold Laski, chairman of the Labour party's National Executive Committee, 20 August 1945

1 'I believe that the foundation of democratic liberty is a willingness to believe that other people may perhaps be wiser than oneself.'
Speech to the Labour party annual conference, October 1948

2 'I have none of the qualities which create publicity.'
In conversation with Harold Nicolson, 14 January 1949

3 'I think the British have the distinction above all other nations of being able to put new wine into old bottles without bursting them.'
Quoted in TIME *magazine, 6 November 1950*

4 'Just when we were beginning to win the match, our inside left has scored against his own side.'
Quoted in P Williams, HUGH GAITSKELL, *Chapter 11. On Aneurin Bevan's*

resignation from the shadow cabinet, over Indo-China, April 1954

5 'Few thought he was even a starter
There were many who thought
  themselves smarter
But he ended PM
CH and OM
An earl and a knight of the garter.'
Lines written on 8 April 1956. On his forthcoming installation as a Knight of the Garter

Azaña y Días, Manuel
(1880–1940)
SPANISH REPUBLICAN POLITICIAN, PRESIDENT OF THE REPUBLIC, 1936–1939

6 'Always I had been afraid that we would come back to power in bad conditions. They could not be worse. Once more we must harvest the wheat when it is still green.'
Quoted in Hugh Thomas, THE SPANISH CIVIL WAR, *Book I, Chapter 10. On becoming prime minister at the head of the Popular Front government, February 1936*

B

Babbitt, Irving (1865–1933)
AMERICAN CRITIC AND WRITER

1 'Commercialism is laying its greasy paw upon everything (including the irresponsible quest of thrills); so that, whatever democracy may be theoretically, one is sometimes tempted to define it practically as standardized and commercialized melodrama.'
DEMOCRACY AND LEADERSHIP *(1924)*, *Chapter 7*

Bacon, Francis, 1st Viscount St Albans (1561–1626)
ENGLISH PHILOSOPHER AND STATESMAN, LORD CHANCELLOR, 1618–1621

2 'Nothing doth more hurt in a state than that cunning men pass for wise.'
ESSAYS *(1625)*, '*Of Cunning*'

3 'Men in great place are thrice servants: servants of the sovereign or state; servants of fame; and servants of business. So as they have no freedom; neither in their persons, nor in their actions, nor in their times. It is a strange desire, to seek power and to lose liberty: or to seek power over others and to lose power over a man's self.'
IBID., '*Of Great Place*'

4 'All rising to great place is by a winding stair.'
IBID.

5 'Above all things, good policy is to be used that the treasure and monies in a state be not gathered into a few hands. For otherwise a state may have a great stock and yet starve. And money is like muck, not good except it be spread.'
IBID., '*Of Seditions and Troubles*'

6 'No body can be healthful without exercise, neither natural body nor politic; and certainly to a kingdom or estate, a just and honourable war is the true exercise.'
IBID., '*Of the True Greatness of Kingdoms and Estates*'

7 'In the youth of a state arms do flourish; in the middle age of a state, learning; and then both of them together for a time; in the declining age of a state, mechanical arts and merchandise.'
IBID., '*Of Vicissitude of Things*'

Bagehot, Walter (1826–1877)
ENGLISH POLITICAL THEORIST

8 'A constitutional statesman is in general a man of common opinions and uncommon abilities . . . If we wanted to choose an illustration of these remarks out of all the world, it would be Sir Robert Peel. No man has come so near our definition of a constitutional statesman – the powers of a first-rate man and the creed of a second-rate man.'
NATIONAL REVIEW, *July 1857, "The Character of Sir Robert Peel'*

9 'The great political want of our day is a *capitalist conservatism*.'
IBID., *January 1859, 'Parliamentary Reform'*

10 'The rarity of great political oratory arises in great measure from this circumstance. Only those engaged in the jar of life have the material for it; only those withdrawn into a brooding imagination have the faculty for it.'
IBID., *July 1860, 'Mr Gladstone'*

11 'No one can approach to an understanding of the English institutions, or of others which, being the growth of many centuries, exercise a wide sway over mixed populations, unless he divides them into two classes. In such constitutions there are two parts (not indeed separable with microscopic accuracy, for the genius of great affairs abhors nicety of division): first, those which excite and preserve the reverence of the population – the *dignified* parts, if I may so call them; and next, the *efficient* parts – those by which it, in fact, works and rules.'
THE ENGLISH CONSTITUTION *(1867), Chapter 1*

12 'The Crown is, according to the saying, the "fountain of honour"; but the Treasury is the spring of business.'
IBID.

13 'So long as the human heart is strong and the human reason weak, Royalty will be strong because it appeals to diffused feeling, and Republics weak because they appeal to the understanding.'
IBID., *Chapter 2*

1 'The sovereign has, under a consitutional monarchy such as ours, three rights – the right to be consulted, the right to encourage, the right to warn.'
IBID.

2 'So long as many old leaves linger on the November trees, you know that there has been little frost and no wind: just so while the House of Lords retains much power, you may know that there is no desperate discontent in the country, no wild agency likely to cause a great demolition.'
IBID., *Chapter 4*

3 'The old-world diplomacy of Europe was largely carried on in drawing-rooms, and, to a great extent, of necessity still is so. Nations touch at their summits.'
IBID.

4 'The whole life of English politics is the action and reaction between the Ministry and the Parliament.'
IBID., *Chapter 5*

5 'The House of Commons lives in a state of potential choice: at any moment it can choose a ruler and dismiss a ruler. And therefore party is inherent in it, is bone of its bone, and breath of its breath.'
IBID.

6 'The mass of the English people are politically contented as well as politically deferential.'
IBID., *Chapter 8*

Bakunin, Michael (1814–1876)
RUSSIAN ANARCHIST, CO-FOUNDER OF THE FIRST INTERNATIONAL

7 'Intellectual slavery, of whatever nature it may be, will always have as a natural result both political and social slavery. At the present time Christianity, in its various forms, and along with it the doctrinaire and deistic metaphysics which sprang from Christianity and which essentially is nothing but theology in disguise, are without doubt the most formidable obstacles to the emancipation of society.'
FEDERALISM, SOCIALISM AND ANTI-THEOLOGISM *(1868)*

8 'The State ... is the most flagrant negation, the most cynical and complete negation of humanity.'
IBID.

9 'Where the State begins, individual liberty ceases, and *vice versa.*'
IBID.

10 'Every State must conquer or be conquered.'
IBID.

11 'It is impossible to arouse the people artificially. People's revolutions are born from the course of events.'
LETTER TO NECHAYEV *(1870)*

12 'A revolutionary idea is revolutionary, vital, real and true only because it expresses and only so far as it forms popular instincts which are the result of history.'
IBID.

13 'We wish, in a word, equality – equality in fact as corollary, or, rather, as primordial condition of liberty. From each according to his faculties, to each according to his needs; that is what we wish sincerely and energetically.'
Anarchist declaration, 1870. Written (with others) after the failure of the anarchist uprising at Lyons
SEE ALSO *Louis Blanc*

14 'Everywhere, in short, religious or philosophical idealism ... serves today as the banner of bloody and brutal material force, of shameless material exploitation. On the contrary, the banner of theoretical materialism, the red banner of economic equality and social justice, is unfurled by the practical idealism of the oppressed and famished masses.'
THE KNOUTO-GERMANIC EMPIRE AND THE SOCIAL REVOLUTION *(1871)*

15 '*To exploit* and *to govern* mean the same thing ... Exploitation and government are two inseparable expressions of what is called politics.'
IBID.

16 'Property is a god. This god already has its theology (called state politics and juridical right) and also its morality, the most adequate expression of which is summed up in the phrase: "That man is worth so much!".'
IBID.

17 'Idealism is the despot of thought, just as politics is the despot of will.'
A CIRCULAR LETTER TO MY FRIENDS IN ITALY *(1871)*

18 'There are but three ways for the populace to escape its wretched lot. The

first two are by the route of the wine-shop or the church; the third is by that of the social revolution.'
GOD AND THE STATE *(1882)*

1 'If there is a human being who is freer than I, then I shall necessarily become his slave. If I am freer than another, then he will become my slave. Therefore, equality is an absolutely necessary condition for freedom ... That is the entire programme of revolutionary socialism, of which equality is the first condition, the first word. It admits freedom only after equality, in equality and through equality, because freedom outside of equality can create only privilege.'
COLLECTED WORKS *(German edition), II, 74*

Baldwin, James (1924–   )
AMERICAN NOVELIST AND ESSAYIST

2 'Freedom is not something that anybody can be given; freedom is something people take and people are as free as they want to be.'
NOBODY KNOWS MY NAME *(1961), 'Notes for a Hypothetical Novel'*

3 'Perhaps the whole root of our trouble, the human trouble, is that we will sacrifice all the beauty of our lives, will imprison ourselves in totems, taboos, crosses, blood sacrifices, steeples, mosques, races, armies, flags, nations, in order to deny the fact of death, which is the only fact we have.'
THE FIRE NEXT TIME *(1963)*

Baldwin, Stanley, 1st Earl Baldwin of Bewdley (1867–1947)
ENGLISH CONSERVATIVE POLITICIAN, PRIME MINISTER, 1923, 1924–1929 and 1935–1937

4 'There will never in this country be a Communist government, and for this reason, that no gospel founded on hate will ever seize the hearts of our people ... it is no good trying to cure the world by spreading out oceans of bloodshed. It is no good trying to cure the world by repeating that pentasyllabic French derivative, "proletariat".'
House of Commons, 16 February, 1923

5 'I know I have been criticised, and criticised widely, for being too gentle in my handling of the Labour Party, but I have done it deliberately, because I

believe it has been a good thing for this country that that party, comprising as it does so many citizens of this country, should learn by experience what a great responsibility administering an Empire such as ours really is.'
1924. Quoted in R T McKenzie, BRITISH POLITICAL PARTIES, *Chapter 3*

6 'Democracy has arrived at a gallop in England and I feel all the time that it is a race of life; can we educate them before the crash comes?'
Letter to Edward Wood, 1928

7 'Mr Lloyd George has made a statement that the Liberal party is the party of promise. I accept that, and I am not a competitor.'
Speech at London, 18 April, 1929

8 'Most parties when they are beaten go through a fit of cold feet.'
Speech at Sheffield, 1930

9 'The papers conducted by Lord Rothermere and Lord Beaverbrook are not newspapers in the ordinary acceptance of the term. They are engines of propaganda, for the constantly changing policies, desires, personal wishes, personal likes and dislikes of two men ...What the proprietorship of these papers is aiming at is power, and power without responsibility – the prerogative of the harlot throughout the ages.'
Speech in London, 18 March 1931

10 'When you think about the defence of England, you no longer think of the chalk cliffs of Dover. You think of the Rhine. That is where out frontier lies today.'
House of Commons, 30 July 1934

11 'There is a wind of nationalism and freedom blowing round the world, and blowing as strongly in Asia as elsewhere.'
Speech in London, 4 December 1934

12 'When I was a little boy in Worcestershire reading history books I never thought I should have to interfere between a King and his mistress.'
In conversation with Thomas Jones, 20 January 1936. On the abdication crisis

13 'I put before the whole House my own views with appalling frankness ... supposing that I had gone to the country and ... said that we must re-arm, does anybody think that this pacific

democracy would have rallied to the cry?
I cannot think of anything that would
have made the loss of the election from
my point of view more certain.'
House of Commons, 12 November 1936.
On the government's defence policy

1 'Don't lecture them. Dont' joke. Don't
try and be an orator. Don't be sarcastic.
Just talk naturally . . . One thing the
House will NEVER forgive and that is if
a Minister misleads it. If you find you
have given an answer that isn't true,
acknowledge it at once and express your
regret. The blame is always on you and
not on the Civil Service.'
Letter to Sir John Reith, 31 January, 1940.
On Reith's entering the House of
Commons as a minister

2 'You will find in politics that you are
much exposed to the attribution of false
motives. Never complain and never
explain.'
In conversation with Harold Nicolson 21
July, 1943, quoted in Harold Nicolson,
DIARIES AND LETTERS

3 'Socialism and *laisser faire* are like the
north and south poles. They don't really
exist.'
Quoted in K Middlemas and J Barnes,
BALDWIN, *Chapter 9*

4 'If there are those who want to fight the
class war, we will beat them by the
hardness of our heads and the largeness
of our hearts.'
IBID.

5 'When you have lived longer in this
world and outlived the enthusiastic and
pleasing illusions of youth, you will find
your love and pity for the race increased
tenfold, your admiration and attachment
to any particular party or opinion fall
away altogether . . . this is the most
important lesson that a man can learn,
that opinions are nothing but the mere
result of chance and temperament; that
no party is on the whole better than
another.'
IBID., *Chapter 11*

6 'I dont think that anyone who has not
been a Prime Minister can realise the
essential and ultimate loneliness of that
position; there is no veil between him
and the human heart (or rather no veil
through which he cannot see) and in his
less happy moments he may feel himself

to be the repository of the sins and follies
of the whole world.'
IBID., *Chapter 18*

7 'Your instruments by which you work
are dumb – pencils and paints. Ours are
neither dumb nor inert. I often think
that we rather resemble Alice in
Wonderland, who tried to play croquet
with a flamingo instead of a mallet.'
IBID. *On leading a political party, in a*
speech to the Royal Academy

8 'Do not run up your nose dead against
the Pope and the NUM [National Union
of Mineworkers].'
Quoted in R A Butler, THE ART OF MEMORY.
Often-repeated maxim on the method of
governing successfully

9 'A government is *not* in power; it is in
office, put there by the will of the
people.'
Quoted by his daughter, Lorna Howard,
in a letter to THE TIMES, *23 January 1982*

Balfour, Arthur, 1st Earl of
(1848–1930)
ENGLISH CONSERVATIVE POLITICIAN,
PRIME MINISTER, 1902–1905

10 'This is of all others the moment, the
crisis of fate, when it is the bounden
duty of each one of you . . . to do his best
to see that the great Unionist party shall
still control, whether in power or
whether in opposition, the destinies of
this great Empire.'
Speech at Nottingham, 15 January, 1906.
On the defeat of the Conservative
government at the 1906 general election

11 'What is going on here is the faint echo
of the same movement which has
produced massacres in St Petersburg, riots
in Vienna, and Socialist processions in
Berlin. We always catch Continental
diseases, though we usually take them
mildly.'
Letter to Lady Salisbury, 17 January 1906.
On the Liberal landslide at the 1906
general election
SEE ALSO *Metternich*

12 'His Majesty's Government view with
favour the establishment in Palestine of a
national home for the Jewish people, and
will use their best endeavours to facilitate
the achievement of this object, it being
clearly understood that nothing shall be
done which may prejudice the existing

civil and religious rights of existing non-Jewish communities in Palestine, or the rights and political status of Jews in other countries.'
Letter to Lord Rothschild, 2 November 1917. The so-called 'Balfour Declaration'

1 'It is unfortunate, considering that enthusiasm moves the world, that so few enthusiasts can be trusted to speak the truth.'
Letter to Mrs Drew, 1918

2 'It is evident that our whole political machinery pre-supposes a people so fundamentally at one that they can safely afford to bicker; and so sure of their own moderation that they are not dangerously disturbed by the never-ending din of political conflict. May it always be so.'
Introduction to new edition of Bagehot's ENGLISH CONSTITUTION, *November 1927*

Barère de Vieuzac, Bertrand
(1755–1841)
FRENCH REVOLUTIONARY LEADER

3 'The tree of liberty will not grow except it be watered by the blood of tyrants.'
Speech to the National Convention, 1792
SEE ALSO *Jefferson*

4 'Let us make terror the order of the day.'
Speech to the National Convention, 1793

Baruch, Bernard (1870–1965)
AMERICAN FINANCIER AND GOVERNMENT ADVISER

5 'Let us not be deceived – we are today in the midst of a cold war.'
Speech at Columbia, South Carolina, 16 April 1947

Beauvoir, Abbé de (1731–1790)
FRENCH ECCLESIASTIC

6 'The people's silence is the king's lesson.'
Sermon, 27 July 1774. Preached at the funeral of Louis XV of France

Beaverbrook, 1st Baron (William Maxwell Aitken)
(1879–1964)
CANADIAN-BORN ENGLISH PRESS MAGNATE AND CONSERVATIVE POLITICIAN

7 'You are a great man now. You must talk like a great man, behave like a great man.'

In conversation with Bonar Law, 13 November 1911. On Law's becoming leader of the Conservative party.
SEE ALSO *Law*

Bebel, August (1840–1913)
GERMAN SOCIALIST POLITICIAN, CO-FOUNDER OF THE GERMAN SOCIAL DEMOCRATIC PARTY

8 'In time of war the loudest patriots are the greatest profiteers.'
Speech to the Reichstag, November 1870

9 'Anti-semitism is the socialism of fools.'
ANTI-SEMITISM AND SOCIAL DEMOCRACY *(1893)*

10 'The field of politics always presents the same struggle. There are the Right and the Left, and in the middle is the Swamp.'
Speech to the annual congress of the Social Democratic Party, 1906

11 'I am and always will be the mortal enemy of existing society.'
Quoted in J P Nettl, ROSA LUXEMBURG, *Volume I, Chapter 4*

Bee, Barnard (1823–1861)
AMERICAN SOLDIER, CONFEDERATE GENERAL IN THE CIVIL WAR

12 'Let us determine to die here, and we will conquer. See, there is Jackson standing like a stone wall; rally on Virginians.'
Remark made during the first battle of Bull Run, 21 July 1861

Beecher, Henry Ward
(1813–1887)
AMERICAN PREACHER

13 'When a nation's young men are conservative, its funeral bell is already rung.'
PROVERBS FROM PLYMOUTH PULPIT *(1887)*

Begin, Menachem (1913–   )
ISRAELI HERUT POLITICIAN, PRIME MINISTER, 1977–83

14 'I feel as a Prime Minister empowered to instruct a valiant army facing "Berlin", where, amongst innocent civilians, Hitler and his henchmen hide in a bunker deep beneath the surface.'
Letter to President Reagan, 4 August 1982. Of the Palestine Liberation Organisation, during Israel's assault on Beirut

Bellamy, Edward (1850–1898)
AMERICAN WRITER

1 'In the radicalness of the opinions I have expressed I may seem to out-socialize the Socialists, yet the word Socialist is one I could never well stomach. In the first place it is a foreign word itself and equally foreign in all its suggestions. It smells to the average American of petroleum, suggests the red flag with all manner of sexual novelties, and an abusive tone about God and religion, which in this country we at least treat with decent respect.'
Quoted in D Aaron, MEN OF GOOD HOPE, *Chapter 4*

Belloc, Hilaire (Joseph Hilary Belloc) (1870–1953)
FRENCH-BORN ENGLISH MAN OF LETTERS AND LIBERAL POLITICIAN, MEMBER OF PARLIAMENT, 1906–1910

2 'The accursèd power which stands on Privilege
(And goes with Women, and Champagne and Bridge)
Broke – and Democracy resumed her reign:
(Which goes with Bridge, and Women and Champagne).'
'*On a General Election*', COMPLETE POEMS *(1970)*

3 'Sir! you have disappointed us!
We had intended you to be
The next Prime Minister but three:
The stocks were sold; the Press was squared;
The Middle Class was quite prepared.
But as it is! . . . My language fails!
Go out and govern New South Wales!'
Loud Lundy (Second Canto)', IBID.

Beneš, Eduard (1884–1948)
CZECHOSLOVAK NATIONAL SOCIALIST POLITICIAN, PRESIDENT, 1935–1938 and 1946–1948

4 'If ever I have trouble with the Communists in my country, I pick up that telephone and get on to my friend Stalin.'
In conversation with Stephen Spender, 1947. In reply to Spender's question, whether he were not apprehensive about a Communist coup

Bengough, John (1851–1923)
CANADIAN CARTOONIST AND POET

5 'You cannot influence a Political Party to do Right, if you stick to it when it does Wrong.'
THE PROHIBITION AESOP *(c. 1896)*

Benn, Anthony Wedgwood (1925–   )
ENGLISH LABOUR POLITICIAN, MEMBER OF PARLIAMENT, 1950–1960, 1963–83 and 1984–

6 'The House of Lords is the British Outer Mongolia for retired politicians.'
Quoted in the NEW YORK TIMES, *11 February 1962. On his forthcoming renunciation of his hereditary peerage*

7 'The flag of racialism which has been hoisted in Wolverhampton is beginning to look like the one that fluttered twenty-five years ago over Dachau and Belsen.'
Election speech, 3 June 1970. On Enoch Powell's parliamentary election campaign at Wolverhampton

8 'No medieval monarch in the whole of British history ever had such power as every modern British Prime Minister has in his or her hands. Nor does any American President have power approaching this.'
ARGUMENTS FOR SOCIALISM *(1979), Chapter 5. On the prime minister's patronage*

9 'There is no need to feel pessimistic about this country. It is only the upper echelons who are licked.'
IBID., *Chapter 8*

10 'Virtually the whole British establishment has been, at least until recently, educated without any real knowledge of Marxism, and is determined to see that these ideas do not reach the public . . . Anyone today who speaks of class in the context of politics runs the risk of excommunication and outlawry.'
Marx Memorial Lecture, London, 1982

11 'It would be as unthinkable to try to construct the Labour Party without Marx as it would be to establish university faculties of astronomy, anthropology or psychology without permitting the study of Copernicus, Darwin or Freud, and still expect such faculties to be taken seriously.'
IBID.

Benson, Arthur Christopher
(1862–1925)
ENGLISH WRITER

1 'Land of Hope and Glory, Mother of the Free,
How shall we extol thee, who are born of thee?
Wider still and wider shall thy bounds be set;
God, who made thee mighty, make thee mightier yet.'
LAND OF HOPE AND GLORY *(1902): Chorus. Lines written to be sung as finale of Elgar's Coronation Ode with music from first* POMP AND CIRCUMSTANCE MARCH

Bentham, Jeremy (1748–1832)
ENGLISH PHILOSOPHER, POLITICAL THEORIST AND JURIST

2 'Nature has placed mankind under the governance of two sovereign masters, *pain* and *pleasure*. It is for them alone to point out what we ought to do, as well as to determine what we shall do.'
INTRODUCTION TO THE PRINCIPLES OF MORALS AND LEGISLATION *(1789), Chapter 1*

3 'And here we have one *partial*, one *separate*, one *sinister* interest, the *monarchical* – the interest of the ruling *one* – with which the *universal*, the *democratic* interest has to antagonise, and to which that all-comprehensive interest has all along been, – and unless the only possible remedy – even parliamentary reform, and that a radical one, should be applied – is destined to be for ever made a sacrifice ... And here we have another partial, separate, and sinister interest – the *aristocratical* interest.'
PLAN OF PARLIAMENTARY REFORM *(1817), Introduction, Section III*

4 'Talk of *balance;* never will it do: leave that to Mother Goose and Mother Blackstone. Balance! balance! Politicians upon roses ... what mean ye by this your *balance?* Know ye not, that in a machine of any kind, when forces *balance* each other, the machine is at a stand? Well, and in the machine of government, immobility – the perpetual absence of all motion – is that the thing which is wanted? Know ye not that – since an emblem you must

have – since you can neither talk, nor attempt to think, but in hieroglyphics – know you not that, as in the case of the body *natural,* so in the case of the body *politic,* when motion ceases, the body dies?'
IBID., *Introduction, Section IV*

5 'Among the several cloudy appellatives which have been commonly employed as cloaks for misgovernment, there is none more conspicuous in this atmosphere of illusion than the word *Order.* The word *Order* is in a peculiar degree adapted to the purpose of a cloak for tyranny; – the word Order is more extensive than law, or even than government.'
THE BOOK OF FALLACIES *(1824)*

6 'I was ... a great reformist; but never suspected that the people in power were against reform. I supposed they only wanted to know what was good in order to embrace it.'
Inserendum in Memoir of Lind and Forster, 2 February 1827

7 'The greatest happiness of the greatest number is the foundation of morals and legislation.'
THE COMMONPLACE BOOK
SEE ALSO *Francis Hutcheson and Joseph Priestley*

8 '*Natural rights* is simple nonsense: natural and imprescriptible rights, rhetorical nonsense – nonsense upon stilts.'
ANARCHICAL FALLACIES, **undated**

9 'He argues against oppression less because he loves the oppressed many, than because he hates the oppressing few. He fights for the people – not that he cares for the suffering people, but that he cannot tolerate the suffering-creating rulers.'
Fragment, undated. Printed in J Bowring, MEMOIRS OF JEREMY BENTHAM, *Chapter 19. Of James Mill*

Bentley, Edward Clerihew
(1875–1956)
ENGLISH WRITER

10 'George the Third
Ought never to have occurred.
One can only wonder
At so grotesque a blunder.'
MORE BIOGRAPHY FOR BEGINNERS *(1929)*

Benton, Thomas Hart
(1782–1858)
AMERICAN POLITICIAN, SENATOR,
1821–1851

1 'If I was going to establish a working
man's party, it should be on the basis of
hard money: a hard money party against
a paper party.'
Quoted in R Kelley, THE TRANSATLANTIC
PERSUASION, *Chapter 7. Speaking against
the United States Bank*

Berlin, Sir Isaiah (1909–)
ENGLISH PHILOSOPHER AND POLITICAL
THEORIST

2 'We are often told that the present age is
an age of cynicism and despair, of
crumbling values and the dissolution of
the fixed standards and landmarks of
Western civilisation. But this is neither
true nor even plausible. So far from
showing the loose texture of a collapsing
order, the world is today stiff with rigid
rules and codes and ardent, irrational
religions. So far from evincing the
toleration which springs from cynical
disregard of the ancient sanctions, it
treats heterodoxy as the supreme danger.
　Whether in the East or West, the
danger has not been greater since the ages
of faith. Conformities are called for much
more eagerly today than yesterday;
loyalties are tested far more severely;
sceptics, liberals, individuals with a taste
for private life and their own inner
standards of behaviour, are objects of fear
or derision and targets of persecution for
either side, execrated or despised by all
the embattled parties in the great
ideological wars of our time . . . In the
world today individual stupidity and
wickedness are forgiven more easily than
failure to be identified with a recognised
party or attitude, to achieve an approved
political or economic or intellectual
status.'
POLITICAL IDEAS IN THE TWENTIETH CENTURY,
(1950)

Bernstein, Eduard (1850–1932)
GERMAN SOCIALIST POLITICIAN AND
WRITER

3 'One avoids anxiously every concern
with the future organisation of society,
but one substitutes for it a sudden leap
forward *[einem Jähen Sprung]*, from
capitalism into socialism.'
UTOPIANISM AND ECLECTICISM, *(1896)*

Bethmann-Hollweg, Theobald von (1856–1921)
GERMAN POLITICIAN, CHANCELLOR,
1909–1917

4 'Just for a word – "neutrality", a word
which in wartime has so often been
disregarded – just for a scrap of paper,
Great Britain is going to make war on a
kindred nation which desires nothing
better than to be friends with her."
*In conversation with the British
ambassador, Sir Edward Goschen, 4
August 1914. On Great Britain's
declaration of war against Germany after
Germany's invasion of Belgium*

5 'Gentlemen, this is a breach of
international law.'
*Speech to the Reichstag, 4 August 1914.
On Germany's invasion of Belgium*

Bevan, Aneurin (1897–1960)
WELSH LABOUR POLITICIAN, MINISTER
OF HEALTH, 1945–1951

6 'Whereas in Britain we are slaves to the
past, in Russia they are slaves to the
future.'
*Remark, 1930. On returning from a visit
to the Soviet Union*

7 'The Prime Minister wins debate after
debate and loses battle after battle. The
country is beginning to say that he fights
debates like a war and a war like a
debate.'
*House of Commons, 2 July 1942. During
the debate on a censure motion against
Churchill's government*

8 'No amount of cajolery, and no attempts
at ethical and social seduction, can
eradicate from my heart a deep burning
hatred for the Tory party . . . So far as I
am concerned they are lower than
vermin.'
Speech at Manchester, 4 July 1948

9 'You cannot educate a man to be a
trained technician inside a factory and
ask him to accept the status of a political
robot outside . . . a totalitarian state or a
one-party state is a persistent
contradiction with the needs of a thriving
industrial community.'
TRIBUNE, *3 February 1950*

1 'The issue . . . in a capitalist democracy resolves itself into this: either poverty will use democracy to win the struggle against property, or property, in fear of poverty, will destroy democracy.'
IN PLACE OF FEAR *(1952), Chapter 1*

2 'How can wealth persuade poverty to use its political freedom to keep wealth in power? Here lies the whole art of Conservative politics in the twentieth century.'
IBID.

3 'The function of parliamentary democracy, under universal suffrage, historically considered, is to expose wealth-privilege to the attack of the people. It is a sword pointed at the heart of property power.'
IBID.

4 'In one sense the House of Commons is the most unrepresentative assemblies. It is an elaborate conspiracy to prevent the real clash of opinion which exists outside from finding an appropriate echo within its walls. It is a social shock absorber placed between privilege and the pressure of popular discontent.'
IBID.

5 'The first function of a political leader is advocacy. It is he who must make articulate the wants, the frustration, and the aspiration of the masses.'
IBID., *Chapter 2*

6 'The Socialist dare not invoke the authority of Parliament in meeting economic difficulties unless he is prepared to exhaust its possibilities. If he does not, if he acts nervelessly, without vigour, ingenuity and self-confidence, then it is upon him and his that the consequences will alight. He will have played his last card and lost, and, in the loss, parliamentary institutions themselves may be engulfed.'
IBID.

7 'I know that the right kind of political leader for the Labour party is a desiccated calculating machine.'
Said ironically in a speech to a Tribune group meeting at the Labour party annual conference, 29 September 1954. Taken as referring to Hugh Gaitskell, an interpretation denied by Bevan

8 'If the Labour Party is not going to be a Socialist Party, I don't want to lead it . . .

When you join a team in the expectation that you are going to play rugger, you can't be expected to be enthusiastic if you are asked to play tiddly-winks.'
Speech at Manchester, 26 January 1956. Two days after being defeated by James Griffiths in the election of the party's deputy leader

9 'If you carry this resolution and follow out all its implications . . . you will send a Foreign Minister, whoever he may be, naked into the conference chamber.'
Speech to the Labour party annual conference, 2 October, 1957. Opposing a resolution in favour of unilateral nuclear disarmament.

10 'The purpose of getting power is to be able to give it away.'
Quoted in M Foot, ANEURIN BEVAN, *1945-1960, Chapter 1*

11 'A society in which the people's wants do not exceed their possessions is not a Socialist society.'
IBID., *Chapter 2*

Bevin, Ernest (1881-1951)
ENGLISH LABOUR POLITICIAN, FOREIGN SECRETARY, 1945-1951

12 'Do not worry about what it costs . . . You can easily rebuild wealth, but you cannot create liberty when it has gone. Once a nation is put under another, it takes years and generations of struggle to get liberty back.'
Speech to business men at Cardiff, November 1940. On the need for industry to reach maximum production quickly

13 'Civilisation cannot survive if it rests upon a propertyless proletariat.'
Speech at the annual conference of the Transport and General Workers' Union, 18 August 1941

14 'Lansbury has been going about dressed in saint's clothes for years waiting for martyrdom. I set fire to the faggots.'
Quoted in R T McKenzie, BRITISH POLITICAL PARTIES, *Chapter 6. Referring to his speech at the Labour party annual conference of 1935, in which he attacked George Lansbury for 'taking your conscience round from body to body asking to be told what you ought to do with it'*

1 'My [foreign] policy is to be able to take a ticket at Victoria Station and go anywhere I damn well please'
SPECTATOR, *20 April 1951*

Beza, Theodore de (1519–1605)
FRENCH CALVINIST THEOLOGIAN

2 'Since the chief and ultimate end of human society is not that men should live together in peace, but that, living in peace, they should serve God, it is the function of the Magistrate to risk even this outward peace (if no otherwise may it be done) in order to secure and maintain in his land the true service of God in its purity.'
DE HAERETICIS *(1554)*

The Bible

3 'Rebellion is as the sin of witchcraft.'
I SAMUEL, *XV, 23*

4 'By me kings reign, and princes decree justice.'
PROVERBS, *VIII, 15*

5 'Righteousness exalteth a nation.'
IBID., *XIV, 34*

6 'Wisdom is better than weapons of war.'
ECCLESIASTES, *IX, 18*

7 'And he shall judge among the nations, and shall rebuke many people; and they shall beat their swords into plowshares, and their spears into pruninghooks; nation shall not lift up sword against nation, neither shall they learn war any more.'
ISAIAH, *II, 4*

8 'What shall one then answer the messengers of the nation? That the Lord hath founded Zion, and the poor of his people shall trust in it.'
IBID, *XIV, 32*

9 'Blessed are the peacemakers; for they shall be called the children of God.'
ST MATTHEW, *V, 9*

10 'And I will give unto thee the keys of the kingdom of heaven; and whatsoever thou shalt bind on earth shall be bound in heaven; and whatsoever thou shalt loose on earth shall be loosed in heaven.'
IBID., *XVI, 19. Origin of the medieval Papacy's claim, in its quarrel with the Holy Roman Empire, to supremacy in both the spiritual and the temporal affairs of Christendom.*

11 'Render therefore unto Caesar the things which are Caesar's; and unto God the things that are God's.'
IBID., *XXII, 21*

Bierce, Ambrose (1842–?1914)
AMERICAN JOURNALIST

12 'Allegiance, *n.* The traditional bond of duty between the taxer and the taxee. It is not reversible.'
THE DEVIL'S DICTIONARY *(1906)*

13 'Consul, *n.* In American politics, a person who having failed to secure an office from the people is given one by the Administration on condition that he leave the country.'
IBID.

14 'Demagogue, *n.* A political opponent.'
IBID.

15 'Politics, *n.* . . . The conduct of public affairs for private advantage.'
IBID.

16 'Politics, *n.pl.* A means of livelihood affected by the more degraded portion of our criminal classes.'
IBID.

17 'Revolution, *n.* In politics, an abrupt change in the form of misgovernment.'
IBID.

Biko, Steve (1946–1977)
SOUTH AFRICAN BLACK NATIONALIST LEADER

18 'Both black and white walk into a hastily organised integrated circle carrying with them the seeds of destruction of that circle – their inferiority and superiority complexes. The myth of integration as propounded under the banner of the liberal ideology must be cracked because it makes people believe that something is being achieved when in reality the artificially integrated circles are a soporific to the blacks while salving the consciences of the few guilt-stricken whites.'
Address to the Cape Town conference on inter-racial studies, 1971

19 'The most potent weapon in the hands of the oppressor is the mind of the oppressed.'
IBID.

1 'We are aware that the white man is sitting at our table. We know he has no right to be there; we want to remove him from our table, strip the table of all the trappings put on it by him, decorate it in true African style, settle down and then ask him to join us on our terms if he wishes.'
IBID.

Birrell, Augustine (1850–1933)
ENGLISH LIBERAL POLITICIAN, MEMBER OF PARLIAMENT AND CHIEF SECRETARY FOR IRELAND, 1907–1916

2 'I know no place where the great truth that no man is necessary is brought home to the mind so remorselessly, and yet so refreshingly, as the House of Commons. Over even the greatest reputations it closes with barely a bubble. And yet the vanity of politicians is enormous ... I often wonder why, for I cannot imagine a place where men so habitually disregard each other's feelings, so openly trample on each other's egotisms.'
Lecture at Cowdenbeath, 15 October 1896. Published as 'The House of Commons' in SELECTED ESSAYS *(1909)*

Bismarck, Otto von, Prince (1815–1898)
GERMAN POLITICIAN, CHANCELLOR, 1871–1890

3 'The only healthy foundation for a great state is egoism, not romanticism, and it is unworthy of a great state to dispute over something which does not concern its own interest.'
Speech to the parliament of the Erfurt Union, April 1850

4 'Not by speech-making and the decisions of majorities will the great questions of the day be settled – that was the great mistake of 1848 and 1849 – but by iron and blood.'
Speech to the Prussian House of Delegates, 30 September 1862

5 'In Prussia it is only kings who make revolutions.'
In conversation with Napoleon III, 1862

6 'Gentlemen, let us work speedily! Let us put Germany, so to speak, in the saddle. You will see well enough that she can ride.'

Speech to the Constituent Assembly of the North German Confederation, 11 March 1867

7 'Politics is the art of the possible.'
In conversation with Meyer von Waldeck, 11 August 1867

8 'We shall not go to Canossa.'
Speech to the Reichstag, 14 May 1872. On not yielding, in the Kulturkampf, *to the clerical party*

9 'War is never brought about by newspapers. The majority has usually no inclination for war: war is kindled by the minority, or in absolute states by the ruler or cabinet.'
Speech to the Reichstag, 9 February 1876

10 'If we are to negotiate peace ... I imagine an essentially modest role ... that of an honest broker who means to do business.'
Speech to the Reichstag, 19 February 1878. On the eastern crisis, before the Congress of Berlin

11 'I think the Tunisian pear is now ripe, and the time has come for you to pick it; the insolence of the Bey has acted like the August sun on this African fruit, which may well rot or be stolen by another if you leave it on the tree too long.'
In conversation with Count Saint-Vallier, January 1879. Encouraging the French ambassador to take Tunisia as a French colony from the Ottoman empire

12 'I flatter myself on having been the first, in Europe, to break with that old tradition with which the western powers have inoculated all the cabinets: namely, that Constantinople in the hands of Russia would be a European danger. I consider that a false idea, and I do not see why an English interest must become a European interest.'
In conversation with Peter Subarov, the Russian ambassador at Constantinople, November 1880

13 'When I hear of the sufferings of a Negro in China or in some other remote part of the world, I may mention him in my prayers, but I cannot make him an object of German policy.'
In conversation with Sir Edward Goschen, the British Ambassador, January 1881

1 'Liberalism always prospers more than its supporters desire.'
Speech to the Reichstag, 29 November 1881

2 'When Austria has worn that flannel next to her skin for three years, she will no longer be able to discard it without running the risk of catching cold.'
In conversation with Subarov, April, 1881. On the Treaty of Berlin, 1881, which consolidated the alliance of Germany, Russia and Austria

3 'Is it not rooted in our entire moral relationships that the individual who comes before his fellow citizens and says, "I am physically fit, ready for work, but can find no job", is entitled to say, "Give me a job!", and the state is obliged to find a job for him?'
Speech to the Reichstag, 9 May 1884

4 'The German Liberal I regard neither as German nor as a Liberal.'
Speech to the Reichstag, 26 November 1884

5 'The King regarded me as a kind of egg, out of which he might be able some day to hatch a Minister.'
Quoted in C Lowe, BISMARCK'S TABLE TALK, *Chapter 2*

6 'When I wish to estimate the danger that is likely to accrue to me from any adversary, I first of all subtract the man's vanity from his other qualities.'
IBID., *Chapter 4*

7 'He who has once gazed into the glazed eye of a dying warrior on the field of battle will think twice before beginning a war.'
IBID., *Chapter 6*

8 'To rule with the help of one's enemies is ever the worst kind of policy.'
IBID., *Chapter 9*

9 'Prussia must be absorbed by Germany; but Prussia is rather stout.'
IBID., *Chapter 10*

10 'Bohemia in the hands of Russia would be our enslavement. Bohemia in our hands would be war without mercy or truce with the Empire of the Tsars.'
Quoted in R Seton-Watson, MASARYK IN ENGLAND, *Chapter 1*

Blackstone, Sir William
(1723–1780)
ENGLISH JURIST

11 'That the king can do no wrong is a necessary and fundamental principle of the English constitution.'
COMMENTARIES ON THE LAWS OF ENGLAND *(1765–69)*

Blake, William (1757–1827)
ENGLISH POET AND PAINTER

12 'Are not Religion & Politics the Same Thing? Brotherhood is Religion.'
JERUSALEM *(1804)*

Blanc, Louis (1811–1882)
FRENCH SOCIALIST POLITICIAN AND WRITER

13 'What the proletarian lacks is capital, and the duty of the state is to see that he gets it. Were I to define the state, I should prefer to think of it as the poor man's bank.'
THE ORGANISATION OF WORK *(1840), Chapter 1*

14 'From each according to his abilities, to each according to his needs.'
IBID.

Blok, Alexander (1880–1921)
RUSSIAN POET

15 'I shall never take power into my hands, I shall never join any party, I shall never make a choice, I have nothing to be proud of, I understand nothing.'
Diary, 13/26 July 1917

16 'Don't shrink, comrade. Get your rifle out;
Give Holy Russia a taste of shot,
The wooden land,
Where the poor huts stand,
And her rump so grand!'
THE TWELVE *(1918)*

17 'On they march with sovereign tread,
With a starving dog behind,
With a blood-red flag ahead –
In the storm where none can see,
From the rifle bullets free,
Gently walking on the snow,
Where like pearls the snowflakes glow,
Marches rose-crowned in the van
Jesus Christ, the Son of Man.'
IBID. *On the Bolshevik revolution*

Bodin, Jean (c. 1530–1596)
FRENCH POLITICAL THEORIST

1 'Sovereign power given to a prince charged with conditions is neither properly sovereign nor absolute, unless the conditions of appointment are only such as are inherent in the laws of God and nature ... If we insist, however, that sovereign power means exemption from all law whatsoever, there is no prince who can be regarded as sovereign, since all the princes of the earth are subject to the laws of God and of nature, and even to certain human laws common to all nations.'
SIX BOOKS OF THE COMMONWEALTH (1576)

2 'The principal mark of a commonwealth, that is to say the existence of a sovereign power, can hardly be established except in a monarchy.'
IBID.

Bolingbroke, 1st Viscount (Henry Saint-John) (1678–1751)
ENGLISH TORY POLITICIAN, SECRETARY OF STATE, 1710–1714

3 'You know the nature of that assembly; they grow, like hounds, fond of the man who shews them game, and by whose halloo they are used to be encouraged.'
LETTER TO SIR WILLIAM WYNDHAM (1716). On the House of Commons

4 'I am afraid that we came to court in the same dispositions that all parties have done; that the principal spring of our actions was to have the government of the State in our own hands; that our principal views were the conservation of this power, great employments to ourselves, and great opportunities of rewarding those who had helped to raise us, and of hurting those who stood in opposition to us.'
IBID.

5 'What in truth can be so lovely, what so venerable, as to contemplate a king on whom the eyes of a whole people are fixed, filled with admiration, and glowing with affection?'
THE IDEA OF A PATRIOT KING (1749)

Boniface VIII (1235–1303)
ITALIAN PRELATE, POPE, 1294–1303

6 'The Holy Catholic Church is single and apostolic ... This Church, single and unique, has but one body and one head – not two heads, which would make it a monster; that one head is Christ, and the vicar of Christ, Peter, and his successor ... In this Church there are two swords, the spiritual and the temporal ... And of a surety he who denies that the temporal sword is Peter's to wield forgets the words of our Lord: put up your sword in its sheath. The two swords are thus in the hands of the Church, both the spiritual and the temporal.'
The bull, UNAM SANCTAM, 18 November 1302. Written partly as a reply to the arrest of the bishop of Pamiers by Philip the Fair of France

Booth, John Wilkes (1838–1865)
AMERICAN ACTOR

7 'Sic semper tyrannis! [Thus be the fate of tyrants!]. The South is avenged!'
Cry uttered on breaking into Abraham Lincoln's theatre box and assassinating him, 14 April 1865. The Latin words are the motto of the state of Virginia

Boothby, Robert, Baron (1900–)
SCOTTISH CONSERVATIVE POLITICIAN, MEMBER OF PARLIAMENT, 1924–1958

8 'A statesman is judged by results. If his policy fails he goes. It may be unfair, but there is a kind of rough justice about it. Mr Montagu Norman, on the other hand, is never called upon to explain, justify or defend his policies. And it is his policies which have been carried out for the past ten years. Governments may come and governments may go, but the Governor of the Bank of England goes on for ever. It is a classic example of power without responsibility.'
House of Commons, 25 April 1932

9 'Speak for England, Arthur!'
Shouted in the House of Commons, 2 September 1939. As Arthur Greenwood rose to speak

Borges, Jorge Luis (1899–)
ARGENTINIAN AUTHOR AND POET

10 'Democracy is an abuse of statistics.'
Quoted in J Timerman, PRISONER WITHOUT A NAME, CELL WITHOUT A NUMBER, Chapter 2

Bosquet, Pierre (1810-1861)
FRENCH GENERAL

1 'It is magnificent, but it is not war.'
[*C'est magnifique, mais ce n'est pas la guerre.*]
Remark made of the charge of the Light Brigade, Balaclava, 25 October 1854

Botev, Khristo (1848-1876)
BULGARIAN REVOLUTIONARY NATIONALIST AND POET

2 'He who dies for freedom, dies not for his country alone, but for the whole world.'
Quoted in M MacDermott, THE APOSTLE OF FREEDOM, *Preface*

Bottomley, Horatio (1860-1933)
ENGLISH FINANCIER, JOURNALIST AND LIBERAL POLITICIAN

3 'I call for a Vendetta – a vendetta against every German in Britain, whether "naturalised" or not. As I have said elsewhere, you cannot naturalise an unnatural beast – a human abortion – a hellish freak. But you *can* exterminate him. And now the time has come.'
JOHN BULL, *15 May 1915, 'Now for the Vendetta'*

Bracton, Henry de (d. 1268)
ENGLISH ECCLESIASTIC AND JURIST

4 'The king ought not to be under any man but under God and the law, because the law makes the king. Thus the king attributes to the law what the law attributes to him, namely domination and power. For there is no king where will rules and not law. And that he who is the vicar of God should be beneath the law is evident from the example of Jesus Christ, whose viceregent he is on earth.'
DE LEGIBUS ET CONSUETUDINIBUS ANGLIAE
(undated)

5 'While in almost all regions they use *leges* and a written law, England alone employs within her boundaries an unwritten law and custom. In this at least, without being written what usage has approved becomes law. But it will not be absurd to call the English laws *leges* even when unwritten, since whatever is justly defined and approved, with the counsel and consent of the magnates and the common engagement of the community, the authority of the king or prince preceding, should have the force of law.'
IBID.

Brecht, Bertold (1898-1956)
GERMAN PLAYWRIGHT

6 'At present I am very much against Bolshevism: universal military service, food rationing, controls, conspiracies, economic favouritism. On top of that, at best: equilibrium, transformation, compromise. I say thanks a lot and may I have a car.'
Diaries, 12 September 1920

Brezhnev, Leonid (1906-1982)
SOVIET POLITICIAN, GENERAL SECRETARY OF THE COMMUNIST PARTY, 1964-1982

7 'When internal and external forces which are hostile to Socialism try to turn the development of any Socialist country towards the restoration of a capitalist regime ... it becomes not only a problem of the people concerned, but a common problem and concern of all Socialist countries.'
Speech to the Congress of the Polish Communist party, 12 November 1968. Defending, in the so-called 'Brezhnev doctrine', the Soviet Union's military intervention in Czechoslovakia, August 1968
SEE ALSO *Kovalev*

Briand, Aristide (1862-1932)
FRENCH SOCIALIST POLITICIAN, ELEVEN TIMES PRIME MINISTER

8 'Yes, my ninth, and it's always the same thing. So many portfolios to this section, and so many to those others, but I always reserve one portfolio to my own absolute discretion. That portfolio I allot to Time. He is my most useful colleague.'
In conversation with Austen Chamberlain, after forming his ninth government. Quoted in Chamberlain, DOWN THE YEARS, *Chapter 12*

Bright, John (1811-1889)
ENGLISH RADICAL POLITICIAN, MEMBER OF PARLIAMENT, 1847-1857 and 1858-1889

9 'If this phrase of the "balance of power" is to be always an argument for war, the pretence for war will never be wanting, and peace can never be secure.'
House of Commons, 31 March 1854

1 'The angel of death has been abroad throughout the land; you may almost hear the beating of his wings.'
House of Commons, 23 February 1855

2 'This regard for the liberties of Europe, this care at one time for the Protestant interest, this excessive love for the balance of power, is neither more nor less than a gigantic system of outdoor relief for the aristocracy of Great Britain.'
Speech at Birmingham, 29 October 1858. On the maintenance of large overseas establishments

3 'England is the mother of parliaments.'
Speech at Birmingham, 18 January 1865

4 'The right hon. Gentleman is the first of the new Party who has retired into what may be called his political cave of Adullam – and he has called about him everyone that was in distress and everyone that was discontented.'
House of Commons, 13 March 1866. On the opposition of Robert Lowe and other Liberals to Gladstone's parliamentary reform bill of 1866

5 'Bear in mind that it is not easy to drive six omnibuses abreast through the Temple Bar.'
Speech at Birmingham, 11 January 1870. On whether the government would be able to fulfil its extensive legislative obligations

6 'Force is not a remedy.'
Speech at Birmingham, 16 November 1880

Brougham, Henry, 1st Baron Brougham and Vaux (1778–1868)
SCOTTISH WHIG POLITICIAN, LORD CHANCELLOR, 1830–1834

7 'The schoolmaster is abroad, and I trust to the schoolmaster armed with his primer more than I do to the soldier in full military array for expanding and extending the liberties of the country.'
House of Commons, 29 January 1828

8 'It was the boast of Augustus ... that he found Rome of brick, and left it of marble ... how much nobler will be the Sovereign's boast, when he shall have it to say, that he found law dear, and left it cheap; found it a sealed book – left it a living letter; found it the patrimony of the rich – left it the inheritance of the poor; found it the two-edged sword of craft and oppression – left it the staff of honesty and the shield of innocence.'
House of Commons, 7 February 1828

9 'The Bill, the whole Bill, and nothing but the Bill.'
1831. Slogan used by the Whigs (referring to the Reform Bill) in the 1831 election, coined by Brougham according to Lord John Russell, RECOLLECTIONS AND SUGGESTIONS, Chapter 5

Brown, George (1818–1880)
CANADIAN GRIT POLITICIAN AND JOURNALIST

10 'What has republicanism ever done for freedom?'
Quoted in J S Careless, BROWN OF THE GLOBE, Volume I, Chapter 2. In defence of Canada's imperial tie to the British crown

11 'The subject who is truly loyal to the Chief Magistrate will neither advise nor submit to arbitrary measures.'
Motto of his newspaper, THE GLOBE AND MAIL

12 'Is it not wonderful? French Canadianism entirely extinguished! ... You will say our constitution is dreadfully Tory – and so it is – but we have the power in our hands (if it passes) to change it as we like. Hurrah!'
Letter to his wife. Quoted in R Kelley, THE TRANSATLANTIC PERSUASION, Chapter 9. On the British North America Act of 1867, conferring dominion status on Canada

Brown, George, Baron George-Brown (1914–)
ENGLISH LABOUR POLITICIAN, FOREIGN SECRETARY, 1966–1968

13 'The House of Commons ... is a Palace of Illogicalities.'
IN MY WAY (1971), Chapter 10

Brown, John (1800–1859)
AMERICAN ABOLITIONIST

14 'I, John Brown, am now quite certain that the crimes of this guilty land will never be purged away but with blood.'
Last statement, 2 December 1859

Brown, Rita Mae (1944–)
AMERICAN WRITER AND FEMINIST LEADER

15 'This is a celebration of individual freedom, not of homosexuality. No

government has the right to tell its
citizens when or whom to love. The only
queer people are those who don't love
anybody.'
*Speech at San Francisco, 28 August 1982.
At the opening of the Gay Olympics*

Browne, Sir William (1692–1774)
ENGLISH PHYSICIAN

1 'The King to Oxford sent a troop of
horse,
For Tories own no argument but force;
With equal care to Cambridge books he
sent,
For Whigs allow no force but argument.'
Reply to Trapp's epigram, GEORGE I'S
DONATION, *on the royal gift of Bishop
Moore's library to the University of
Cambridge*

Bryan, William Jennings
(1860–1925)
AMERICAN DEMOCRATIC POLITICIAN,
PRESIDENTIAL CANDIDATE, 1896, 1900
and 1908

2 'You come to us and tell us that the great
cities are in favor of the gold standard;
we reply that the great cities rest upon
our broad and fertile prairies. Burn down
your cities and leave our farms, and your
cities will spring up again as if by magic;
but destroy our farms and the grass will
grow up in the streets of every city in
the country … Having behind us the
producing masses of the nation and the
world, supported by the commercial
interests, the labouring interests and the
toilers everywhere, we will answer their
demand for a gold standard by saying to
them: You shall not press down upon the
brow of labor this crown of thorns; you
shall not crucify mankind upon a cross of
gold.'
*Speech to the Democratic National
Convention, 8 July 1896. Accepting the
party's nomination as its presidential
candidate*

Büchner, Georg (1813–1837)
GERMAN DRAMATIST

3 'Peace to the hut, – war to the palaces.'
THE HESSIAN COUNTRYMAN *(1834)*

4 'The Revolution is like Saturn – it eats its
own children.'
DANTON'S DEATH *(1835). From a remark
attributed to Pierre Vergniaud at his trial,
November 1793.*

Bülow, Bernhard, Fürst von
(1849–1929)
GERMAN POLITICIAN, CHANCELLOR,
1900–1909

5 'We do not desire to put anyone else in
the shade, but we want our place in the
sun.'
*Speech to the Reichstag, 6 December
1897. On German colonial activity in East
Africa*

6 'In the new century, Germany must be
either the hammer or the anvil.'
*Speech to the Reichstag, 11 December
1898*

Buol-Schauenstein, Karl
Ferdinand, Graf von (1797–1865)
AUSTRIAN POLITICIAN, PRIME
MINISTER AND FOREIGN SECRETARY,
1852–1859

7 'France plays the part of protectress of
nationalities – we are, and will remain,
protectors of dynastic rights.'
*Quoted in Lord Loftus' despatch to the
Earl of Malmesbury, 15 January 1859. On
Austria's possessions in Italy*

Burke, Edmund (1729–1797)
IRISH POLITICIAN AND POLITICAL
PHILOSOPHER, WHIG MEMBER OF
PARLIAMENT, 1765–1795

8 'Party is a body of men united, for
promoting by their joint endeavours the
national interest, upon some particular
principle in which they are all agreed.'
THOUGHTS ON THE CAUSE OF THE PRESENT
DISCONTENTS *(1770)*

9 'Of this stamp is the cant of *Not men,
but measures;* a sort of charm by which
many people get loose from every
honourable engagement.'
IBID.

10 'Great men are the guide-posts and
landmarks in the state.'
*House of Commons, 19 April 1774. Speech
on American taxation*

11 'To tax and to please, no more than to
love and to be wise, is not given to men.'
IBID.

12 'Certainly, gentlemen, it ought to be the
happiness and glory of a representative to
live in the strictest union, the closest
correspondence, and the most unreserved
communication with his constituents …'

But his unbiassed opinion, his mature judgment, his enlightened conscience, he ought not to sacrifice to you, to any man, or to any set of men living ... Parliament is not a *congress* of ambassadors from different and hostile interests; which interests each must maintain, as an agent and advocate, against other agents and advocates; but parliament is a *deliberative* assembly of *one* nation, with *one* interest, that of the whole ... You choose a member indeed; but when you have chosen him, he is not member of Bristol, but he is a member of *parliament.*'
Speech to the electors of Bristol, 3 November 1774

1 'I do not know the method of drawing up an indictment against an whole people.'
House of Commons, 22 March 1775.
Speech on conciliation with America

2 'Parties must ever exist in a free country.'
IBID.

3 'Magnanimity in politics is not seldom the truest wisdom; and a great empire and little minds go ill together.'
IBID.

4 'Refined policy ever has been the parent of confusion, and ever will be so long as the world endures. Plain good intention, which is as easily discovered at the first view as fraud is surely detected at last, is, let me say, of no mean force in the government of mankind.'
IBID.

5 'When I contemplate these things, when I know that the colonies in general own little or nothing to any care of ours, and that they are not squeezed into this happy form by the constraints of a watchful and suspicious government, but that, through a wise and salutary neglect, a generous nature has been suffered to take her own way to perfection ... I feel all the pride of power sink, and all presumption in the wisdom of human contrivances melt and die away within me. My rigour relents. I pardon something to the spirit of liberty.'
IBID.

6 'If any ask me what a free government is, I answer, that for any practical purpose, it is what the people think so.'
LETTER TO THE SHERIFFS OF BRISTOL *(1777)*

7 'As wealth is power, so all power will infallibly draw wealth to itself by some means or other.'
House of Commons, 11 February 1780

8 'A state without the means of some change is without the means of its conservation.'
REFLECTIONS ON THE REVOLUTION IN FRANCE *(1790)*

9 'Government is a contrivance of human wisdom to provide for human *wants*. Men have a right that these wants should be provided for by this wisdom. Among these wants is to be reckoned the want, out of civil society, of a sufficient restraint upon their passions.'
IBID.

10 'Kings will be tyrants from policy, when subjects are rebels from principle.'
IBID.

11 'Circumstances (which with some gentlemen pass for nothing) give in reality to every political principle its distinguishing colour and discriminating effect. The circumstances are what render every civil and political scheme beneficial or noxious to mankind.'
IBID.

12 'Society is indeed a contract ... it is not a partnership in things subservient only to the gross animal existence of a temporary and perishable nature. It is a partnership in all science; a partnership in all art; a partnership in every virtue, and in all perfection. As the ends of such a partnership cannot be obtained in many generations, it becomes a partnership not only between those who are living, but between those who are living, those who are dead, and those who are to be born. Each contract of each particular state is but a clause in the great primeval contract of eternal society, linking the lower with the higher natures, connecting the visible and invisible world, according to a fixed compact sanctioned by the inviolable oath which holds all physical and all moral natures, each in their appointed place.'

13 'We have obligations to mankind at large, which are not in consequence of any special voluntary pact. They arise from the relation of man to man, and the relation of man to God, which relations

are not a matter of choice ... out of physical causes, unknown to us, perhaps unknowable, arise moral duties, which, as we are able perfectly to comprehend, we are bound indispensably to perform.'
APPEAL FROM THE NEW TO THE OLD WHIGS *(1791). Against the idea that civil society originated in a contract*

1 'A true natural aristocracy is not a separate interest in the state, or separable from it. It is an essential integrant part of any large body rightly constituted.'
IBID.

2 'It is ordained in the eternal constitution of things that men of intemperate minds cannot be free. Their passions forge their fetters.
LETTER TO MEMBER OF THE FRENCH NATIONAL ASSEMBLY (1791).

Bussy-Rabutin, Roger, Comte de (1618–1693)
FRENCH SOLDIER AND WRITER

3 'God is usually on the side of big squadrons against little ones.'
Letter to the Count of Limoges, 18 October 1677. SEE ALSO *Tacitus and Voltaire*

Butler, Richard Austen, Baron (1902–1982)
ENGLISH CONSERVATIVE POLITICIAN, DEPUTY PRIME MINISTER, 1962–1963, FOREIGN SECRETARY 1963–1964

4 'Land of Hope and Glory,
Mother of the Free,
Keep on voting Tory
Till Eternity.'
Lines composed while an undergraduate at Cambridge, c. 1922

5 'What nonsense it is to accept as inevitable and right the so-called swing of the pendulum. If we accept uncritically the theory of "it's time for a change" – still more if we regard government as a sort of cricket match, when each side must have its innings in turn – then we may be condemned for ever to an alternation between sensible and silly policies. After all, if the sillies can always be sure of re-election if they wait long enough, then there is no compulsion on them to make themselves sensible.'
Speech to the Conservative party annual conference, 12 October 1963

6 'If you're not made Pope in the Roman Catholic Church, you can still be a perfectly good Cardinal Archbishop of Milan.'
Remark on BBC television, October 1963. After failing to become prime minister.

7 'I think the Prime Minister has to be a butcher, and know the joints. That is perhaps where I have been not quite competent in knowing the ways that you cut up a carcass.'
Interview on BBC television. Printed in THE LISTENER, *28 June 1966*

Butler, Samuel (1835–1902)
ENGLISH SATIRICAL AND PHILOSOPHICAL AUTHOR

8 'The healthy stomach is nothing if not conservative. Few radicals have good digestions.'
NOTEBOOKS *(1912), 'Mind and Matter: Indigestion'*

Byrom, John (1692–1763)
ENGLISH POET AND SHORTHAND WRITER

9 'God bless the King – I mean the Faith's Defender;
God bless – no Harm in blessing – the Pretender!
But who Pretender is, or who is King –
God Bless us all! that's quite another Thing.'
Epigram, c. 1745

10 'The Parson leaves the *Christian* in the Lurch,
Whene'er he brings his *politics* to Church.'
'On Clergyman Preaching Politics'. undated

11 ' "Balbus, methinks, the Friends of Liberty
Who preach up Freedom should let *all* be free."
"Aye, so think I; but you mistake the Name:
These are not Friends, but Lovers of that same;
And *Lovers* are, you know, such selfish Elves,
They always keep their *Mistress* to themselves." '
Fragment, undated

Byron, George, 6th Baron
(1788–1824)
ENGLISH POET

1 'Famed for contemptuous breach of
sacred ties,
By headless Charles see heartless Henry
lies.
Between them stands another sceptred
thing –
It moves, it reigns – in all but name a
king.
Charles to his people, Henry to his wife,
In him the double tyrant starts to life.
Justice and death have mix'd their dust
in vain;
Each royal vampire waked to life again.
Ah, what can tombs avail! since these
disgorge
The blood and dust of both – to mould a
George.'
WINDSOR POETICS *(1814). Of George IV,
then Prince Regent, who in 1813 went to
visit the tomb of Henry VIII at Windsor,
broken open accidentally by workmen
and discovered to contain also the
remains of Charles I*

2 'Cold-blooded, smooth-faced, placid
miscreant!
Dabbling its sleek young hands in Erin's
gore.'
DON JUAN *(1819–1824), Canto I. Of
Castlereagh*

3 'Nought's permanent among the human
race,
Except the Whigs *not* getting into place.'
IBID., *Canto XI*

4 'Called "Saviour of the Nations" – not yet
saved,
And "Europe's Liberator" – still enslaved.'
IBID. *Of the Duke of Wellington*

5 'See these inglorious Cincinatti swarm,
Farmers of war, dictators of the farm;
Their ploughshare was the sword in
hireling hands,
Their fields manured by gore of other
lands;
Safe in their barns these Sabine tillers
sent
Their brethren out to battle – why? for
rent!
Year after year they voted cent. per cent.,
Blood, sweat, and tear-wrung
millions – why? for rent!
They Roar'd, they dined, they drank,
they swore they meant
To die for England – why then live? for
rent!
The peace has made one general
malcontent
Of these high-market patriots; war was
rent!
Their love of country, millions all
misspent,
How reconcile? by reconciling rent!
And will they not repay the treasures
lent?
No: down with everything, and up with
rent!
Their good, ill, health, wealth, joy or
discontent,
Being, end, aim, religion – rent, rent,
rent!'
THE AGE OF BRONZE *(1823), Canto XIV*

C

Caesar, Julius (100BC–44BC)
ROMAN EMPEROR, 49BC–44BC

1   'The die is cast.' *[Iacta alea est.]*
*Remark on crossing the Rubicon, 19
January 49BC*

2   'I came, I saw, I conquered.' *[Veni, vidi,
vici.]*
*Letter to Amantius, 47BC. Announcing
the victory at Zela*

Calhoun, John (1782–1850)
AMERICAN POLITICIAN, VICE-
PRESIDENT, 1825–1833

3   'Protection and patriotism are reciprocal.'
*Speech to the House of Representatives,
12 December 1811. Advocating high
tariffs*

4   'It is harder to preserve than to obtain
liberty.'
Speech to the Senate, January 1848

5   'We are not a Nation, but a Union, a
confederacy of equal and sovereign
states.'
Letter to Oliver Dyer, 1 January 1849

6   'Democracy, as I understand and accept
it, requires me to sacrifice myself *for* the
masses, not *to* them. Who knows not
that if you would save the people, you
must often oppose them?'
Quoted in R Kirk, THE CONSERVATIVE MIND,
Chapter 5

Caligula (Gaius Caesar)
(AD12–41)
ROMAN EMPEROR, AD37–41

7   'Let them hate me, so they but fear me.'
[Oderint, dum metuant.]
Quoted in Accius, TRAGEDIES

Cameron, Simon (1799–1889)
AMERICAN REPUBLICAN POLITICAN,
SECRETARY OF WAR, 1861–1862, AND
REPUBLICAN BOSS OF PENNSYLVANIA

8   'An honest politician is one who, when
he is bought, will stay bought.'
In conversation, c. 1860

**Campbell-Bannerman, Sir
Henry** (1836–1908)
ENGLISH LIBERAL POLITICIAN, PRIME
MINISTER, 1905–1908

9   'A phrase often used is that "war is war",
but when one comes to ask about it one
is told that no war is going on, that it is
not war. When is war not war? When it
is carried on by methods of barbarism in
South Africa.'
*Speech at the National Reform Union, 14
June 1901*

10 'The people of this country are a
straightforward people. They like
honesty and straightforwardness of
purpose. They may laugh at it and they
may be amused by it and they may in a
sense admire it, but they do not like
cleverness. You may be too clever by
half.'
Speech at Plymouth, 7 June 1907

Camus, Albert (1913–1960)
FRENCH NOVELIST, PLAYWRIGHT AND
ESSAYIST

11 'As to the famous Marxist optimism, it
just makes me laugh. Few men have
mistrusted their fellows more completely.
Marxists do not believe in persuasion or
dialogue. A bourgeois cannot be made
into a worker, and in their world
economic conditions represent a more
terrible form of fatality than the whims
of God.'
NOTEBOOKS *(1937–1951), V*

12 'Communism is the logical consequence
of Christianity. It is a Christian kind of
business.'
IBID.

13 'The nineteenth century is the century
of revolt. Why? Because it was born of a
revolution that failed and where the only
thing that was killed was belief in God.'
IBID., *VI*

14 'I am not made for politics because I am
incapable of wishing for or accepting the
death of my adversary.'
IBID.

15 'Terror is the homage that the malignant
recluse finally pays to the brotherhood of
man.'
THE REBEL *(1951)*

1 'Every revolutionary ends by becoming either an oppressor or a heretic.'
IBID.

2 'Although apparently negative because it creates nothing, revolt is positive in a profound way because it reveals those elements in man which must always be defended.'
IBID.

3 'In relation to crime, how can our civilisation be defined? The reply is easy: for thirty years now, state crimes have been far more numerous than individual crimes. I am not even speaking of wars, general or localised, although bloodshed too is an alcohol that eventually intoxicates like the headiest of wines. But the number of individuals killed directly by the state has assumed astronomical proportions and infinitely outnumbers private murders. There are fewer and fewer condemned by common law and more and more condemned for political reasons. The proof is that each of us, however honourable he may be, can foresee the possibility of someday being condemned to death, whereas that eventuality would have seemed ridiculous at the beginning of the century.'
REFLECTIONS ON THE GUILLOTINE *(1957)*.
(With Arthur Koestler)

Canetti, Elias (1905–)
BULGARIAN-BORN ENGLISH WRITER

4 *'Within the crowd there is equality*. This is absolute and indisputable and never questioned by the crowd itself . . . All demands for justice and all theories of equality ultimately derive their energy from the actual experience of equality familar to anyone who has been part of a crowd.'
CROWDS AND POWER *(1960)*, *'The Crowd: The Attributes of the Crowd'*

5 'Militarists who mock the ballot only betray their own bloodthirsty proclivities. A ballot-form, like a treaty, is to them only a scrap of paper; that it has not been dipped in blood renders it contemptible in their eyes; for them the only valid decisions are those reached through blood.'
IBID. *'The Crowd in History: The Nature of the Parliamentary System'*

6 'Secrecy lies at the very core of power.'
IBID., *'Elements of Power: Secrecy'*

7 'A large part of the prestige of dictatorships is due to the fact that they are credited with the concentrated power of secrecy. In democracies a secret is dispersed among many people and its power thus weakened. People say scornfully that everything is talked to pieces; that everyone has his say and can interfere and that nothing ever happens because everything is known about in advance. Superficially these complaints refer to lack of decisiveness, but in reality to lack of secrecy.'
IBID.

Canning, George (1770–1827)
ENGLISH TORY POLITICIAN, PRIME MINISTER, 1827

8 'And O! if again the rude whirlwind should rise,
The dawning of peace should fresh darkness deform,
The regrets of the good and the fears of the wise,
Shall turn to the pilot who weathered the storm.'
Lines recited at a public banquet, London, 28 May 1802. Of the younger Pitt on his forty-third birthday

9 'Away with the cant of "Measures, not men!" – the idle supposition that it is the harness and not the horses that draw the chariot along. No, sir, if the comparison must be made, if the distinction must be taken, men are everything, measures comparatively nothing.'
House of Commons, 9 December 1802
SEE ALSO *Burke*

10 'For "Alliance" read "England"; and you have the clue to my policy.'
Letter to J H Frere, 7 August 1823. On disengaging Great Britain from the Holy Alliance

11 'In matters of commerce the fault of the Dutch
Is offering too little and asking too much.
The French are with equal advantage content,
So we clap on Dutch bottoms just 20 per cent.'
Despatch to the British ambassador at The Hague, 31 January 1826. Announcing the levy of duties on Dutch shipping

1 'I resolved that if France had Spain it should not be Spain with the Indies; I called a New World into existence to redress the balance of the Old.'
House of Commons, 12 December 1826. On his policy of recognising the independence of former Spanish colonies in South America

Canute (*c.* 995–1035)
KING OF ENGLAND, NORWAY AND DENMARK

2 'Know all inhabitants of earth, that vain and trivial is the power of kings nor is anyone worthy of the name of king save Him whose nod heaven and earth and sea obey under laws eternal.'
Quoted in Henry of Huntingdon, HISTORY OF THE ENGLISH. *After the tide ignored his command not to cover the land*

Carlyle, Thomas (1795–1881)
SCOTTISH ESSAYIST AND HISTORIAN

3 'It was [the Germans] that gave to mankind the three great elements of modern civilisation, Gunpowder, Printing, and the Protestant Religion.'
THE STATE OF GERMAN LITERATURE *(1827)*

4 'France was long a despotism tempered by epigrams.'
HISTORY OF THE FRENCH REVOLUTION *(1837), Volume I, Book I, Chapter 1*

5 'Brave Broglie, "with a whiff of grapeshot *(salve de canons)*", if need be, will give quick account of it.'
IBID., *Volume I, Book V, Chapter 3*

6 ' "A Republic?" said the Seagreen ... "What is that?" O seagreen Incorruptible, thou shalt see.'
IBID., *Volume II, Book IV, Chapter 4. Of Robespierre*

7 'In these complicated times, with Cash Payments as the sole nexus between man and man, the toiling Classes of mankind declare, in their confused but most emphatic way, to the Untoiling, that they will be governed ... Cash payment the sole nexus; and there are so many things which cash will not pay!'
CHARTISM *(1839)*

8 'All men may see, whose sight is good for much, that in democracy can lie no finality; that with the completest winning of democracy there is nothing yet won – except emptiness, and the free chance to win. Democracy is, by the nature of it, a self-cancelling business, and gives in the long-run a net result of *zero*.'
IBID.

9 'Find in any country the Ablest Man that exists there; raise *him* to the supreme place, and loyally reverence him: you have a perfect government for that country; no ballot-box, parliamentary eloquence, voting, constitution-building, or other machinery whatever can improve it a whit. It is in the perfect state; an ideal country.'
ON HEROES, HERO-WORSHIP, AND THE HEROIC IN HISTORY *(1841)*

10 'No great man lives in vain. The history of the world is but the biography of great men.'
IBID.

11 'Burke said there were Three Estates in Parliament; but, in the Reporters' Gallery yonder, there sat a *Fourth Estate*, more important far than they all.'
IBID.
SEE ALSO *Hazlitt* and *Macaulay*

12 'Brothers, I am sorry I have got no Morrison's Pill for curing the Maladies of Society.'
PAST AND PRESENT *(1843), Book I, Chapter 4*

13 'The Leaders of Industry, if Industry is ever to be led, are virtually the Captains of the World ... Captains of Industry are the true Fighters, henceforth recognisable as the only true ones.'
IBID., *Book IV, Chapter 4*

14 'Not a "gay science", I should say, like some we have heard of; no, a dreary, desolate, and indeed quite abject and distressing one; what we might call, by way of eminence, the *dismal science*.'
LATTER-DAY PAMPHLETS *'The Nigger Question' (1849). Of political economy*

15 'Democracy is the grand, alarming, imminent and indisputable Reality ... What *is* Democracy; this huge inevitable product of the Destinies, which is everywhere the portion of our Europe in these latter days? There lies the question for us. Whence comes it, this universal big black Democracy; whither tends it; what is the meaning of it? A meaning it must have, or it would not be here.'
IBID., *'The Present Times' (1850)*

Carson, Edward, Baron
(1854-1935)
IRISH CONSERVATIVE AND UNIONIST
POLITICIAN AND LAWYER, MEMBER OF
THE WAR CABINET, 1917-1918

1 'I belong, I believe, to what is called the
Unionist Party. Why it is called the
Unionist Party I fail to understand,
unless it is to remind people in this
country that it was the Party that
betrayed the Unionists.'
House of Lords, 1933

Carteret, John, 1st Earl
Granville (1690-1763)
ENGLISH WHIG POLITICIAN, SECRETARY
OF STATE, 1721-1724 and 1742-1744

2 'I want to instil a noble ambition into
you; to make you knock the heads of the
Kings of Europe together, and jumble
something out of it that may be of
service to this country.'
*In conversation with Henry Fox, 18
October 1756*

3 'What is it to me who is a judge or who
is a bishop? It is my business to make
kings and emperors, and to maintain the
balance of Europe.'
Quoted in J Morley, WALPOLE, Chapter 4
SEE ALSO *Robert Walpole*

Casement, (Sir) Roger
(1864-1916)
IRISH NATIONALIST LEADER

4 'Loyalty is a sentiment, not a law. It rests
on love, not on restraint. The
government of Ireland by England rests
on restraint and not on law; and since it
demands no love, it can evoke no
loyalty.'
*Speech from the dock at his trial for
treason, July 1916*

Castle, Barbara (1911-)
ENGLISH LABOUR CABINET MINISTER,
MEMBER OF PARLIAMENT, 1945-1979

5 'She is so clearly the best man among
them.'
*Castle Diaries, 11 February 1975. On
Margaret Thatcher's election as leader of
the Conservative party.*

6 'Men never feel at ease with a woman
politician who looks as if her hair has
just been permed.'

*Castle Diaries, 4 March 1975. Recording a
remark made by Roy Jenkins in the
House of Commons.*

7 'In politics, guts is all.'
Castle Diaries, 18 April 1975

Castro, Fidel (1927-)
CUBAN REVOLUTIONARY LEADER,
PRESIDENT, 1959-

8 'So there exists an enemy who can be
called universal, and if there ever was in
the history of humanity an enemy who
was truly universal, an enemy whose acts
and moves trouble the entire world,
threaten the entire world, attack the
entire world in one way or another, that
real and really universal enemy is
precisely Yankee imperialism.'
*Speech to the International Cultural
Congress, Havana, 12 January 1968*

9 'The city is the cemetery of
revolutionaries.'
*Quoted in M Lasky, UTOPIA AND
REVOLUTION, Chapter 3*

10 'You Americans keep saying that Cuba is
ninety miles from the United States. I
say that the United States is ninety miles
from Cuba and for us, that is worse.'
*In conversation with Herbert Matthews,
CASTRO, Chapter 6*

11 'The duty of every revolutionary is to
make a revolution.'
IBID., Chapter 9

Cavaignac, Louis (1802-1857)
FRENCH GENERAL AND POLITICIAN

12 'You say that I have fallen from power. I
did come down, but the national will
does not overthrow; it commands, and we
obey.'
*In conversation with a Montagnard
during the June days, 1849. Quoted in A
de Tocqueville, RECOLLECTIONS, Part III,
Chapter 2*

Cavell, Edith (1865-1915)
ENGLISH NURSE

13 'I realise that patriotism is not enough. I
must have no hatred or bitterness
towards anyone.'
*In conversation with the Rev. Stirling
Gahan, 11 October 1915. Last words
before being shot by the German
occupation authorities in Belgium*

Cavour, Camillo, Conte di
(1810–1861)
ITALIAN NATIONALIST LIBERAL
POLITICIAN, PRIME MINISTER OF
SARDINIA, 1852–59 and 1860–61

1 'I am the son of liberty and to her I owe
all that I am. If it is necessary to veil her
statue it is not for me to do it.'
Letter to the Countess of Circourt,
January 1861. On the necessity of
unifying Italy by parliamentary means

2 'Rome, Rome alone, must be the capital
of Italy . . . I am ready to proclaim in
Italy this great principle: a free Church
in a free State.'
Speech to the Sardinian parliament, 27
March 1861

3 'Italy is made, all is safe.'
Words spoken on his deathbed, 6 June
1861

Chamberlain, (Arthur)
Neville (1869–1940)
ENGLISH CONSERVATIVE POLITICIAN,
PRIME MINISTER, 1937–1940

4 'How horrible, fantastic, incredible it is
that we should be digging trenches and
trying on gas-masks here because of a
quarrel in a faraway country between
people of whom we know nothing.'
Broadcast on BBC radio, 27 September
1938. On the crisis in Czechoslovakia

5 'This is the second time that there has
come back from Germany to Downing
Street peace with honour. I believe it is
peace for our time.'
From the window at 10 Downing Street,
30 September 1938. On his return from
his meeting with Hitler at Munich

6 'I have decided that I cannot trust the
Nazi leaders again.'
In conversation with R A Butler and Lord
Halifax, 16 March 1939. (The day after
Germany's occupation of Prague.)

7 'Whatever may be the reason – whether
it was that Hitler thought he might get
away with what he had got without
fighting for it, or whether it was that
after all the preparations were not
sufficiently complete – however, one
thing is certain: he missed the bus.'
Speech at London, 4 April 1940

8 'I have friends in this House.'
House of Commons, 8 May 1940. In the
debate on the Norwegian campaign
which led to his resignation as prime
minister

Chamberlain, Sir (Joseph)
Austen (1863–1937)
ENGLISH CONSERVATIVE CABINET
MINISTER

9 'Do not weaken the hand of the man
whom you choose for your Leader and do
not ask of him or of any of us that we
should remit executive decisions to be
debated in public meetings. That way
confusion and disaster lie. That has been
the practice of the Labour Party and
unless their arrival in power leads to a
direct breach with past traditions, leads to
their giving to their leaders a confidence,
a responsibility and a power that they
have never been entrusted with so far,
they will come to an early and speedy
disaster.'
Speech to a meeting of the Conservative
parliamentary party, 11 February 1924

Chamberlain, Joseph (1836–1914)
ENGLISH RADICAL AND LIBERAL-
UNIONIST POLITICIAN, COLONIAL
SECRETARY, 1895–1903

10 'Macaulay's illustration of the man who
would not go into the water until he had
learned to swim is the type of all the
objections raised to the extension of self-
government amongst the people.'
Minute for the cabinet, 18 October 1882.
On the Conservatives' opposition to
enfranchising the agricultural labourers

11 'Lord Salisbury constitutes himself the
spokesman of a class, of the class to
which he himself belongs, who "toil not,
neither do they spin".'
Speech at Birmingham, 30 March 1883

12 'Popular government is inconsistent with
the reticence which offical etiquette
formerly imposed on speakers, and which
was easily borne as long as the electorate
was a comparatively small and privileged
class . . . Now, the Platform has become
one of the most powerful and
indispensable instruments of
Government, and any Ministry which
neglected the opportunities afforded by it
would speedily lose the confidence of the

People. A new public duty and personal labour has thus come into existence, which devolves to a great extent and as a matter of necessity, on those members of a Government who may be considered specially to represent the majority who are to be appealed to: and this duty cannot be performed at all if the men on whom it falls are to be confined within the narrow limits of a purely official programme.'
Letter to Gladstone, 7 February 1885. Questioning the wisdom of the convention of cabinet solidarity

1 'In politics there is no use looking beyond the next fortnight.'
In conversation with Arthur Balfour, 22 March 1886

2 'There are those who have adopted the well-known saying of Mark Twain, and who still think that as, upon this continent, the lion must lie down with the lamb, it would be better if the lamb consented at once to lie inside the lion.'
Speech at Toronto, 30 December 1887. On Canada's relations with the United States

3 'Commerce is the greatest of all political interests.'
Speech at Birmingham, 13 November 1896

4 'Learn to think imperially.'
Speech at London, 19 January 1904

5 'The day of small nations has long passed away. The day of Empires has come.'
Speech at Birmingham, 12 May 1904

6 'The character of the individual depends upon the greatness of the ideals upon which he rests, and the character of a nation is the same. The moral grandeur of a nation depends upon its being sometimes able to forget itself, sometimes able to think of the future of the race for which it stands. England without an Empire! Can you conceive it? England in that case would not be the England we love . . . It would no longer be a power, if not supreme, at all events of the greatest influence, generally well-exercised, on the civilisation and the peace of the world. It would be a fifth-rate nation, existing on the sufferance of its more powerful neighbours. We will not have it.'
Speech at Birmingham, 9 July 1906

7 'I sometimes think that great men are like great mountains: one cannot realize their greatness till one stands at some distance from them.'
In conversation with his son, Austen. Quoted in A Chamberlain, DOWN THE YEARS, Chapter 13. Speaking of Gladstone

Chambord, Henri Charles, Comte de (1820–1883)
FRENCH COUNT, BOURBON PRETENDER TO THE THRONE

8 'Henry V cannot give up the flag of Henry IV.'
Manifesto of 6 July 1871

Chamfort, Sébastien (1741–1794)
FRENCH WRITER AND WIT

9 'Only the history of free peoples is worth our attention; the history of men under a despotism is merely a collection of anecdotes.'
MAXIMS AND CONSIDERATIONS *(1796)*

10 'The real Turkey in Europe is France.'
IBID.

11 'An Englishman respects the law & rejects or despises authority; a Frenchman respects authority & despises the law.'
IBID.

12 'You do not desire a liberty which will cost much gold and blood. Do you demand, then, that revolutions be made with rose-water?'
Quoted in J F Marmontel, MEMOIRS OF A FATHER *(1804)*

Charlemont, Lady Anne (d. 1852)
ENGLISH NOBLEWOMAN

13 'Since I have been in the world, I have heard it said each year that we are going to have a revolution, and at the end of the year we always found ourselves in the same place.'
In conversation with Alexis de Tocqueville, 1835. Quoted in G Watson, THE ENGLISH IDEOLOGY, *Chapter 3*

Charlemont, 1st Earl of (James Caulfeild) (1728–1779)
IRISH NATIONALIST LEADER

14 'It is easier for a camel to go through the eye of a needle, or for a rich man to enter the kingdom of heaven, than for a politician to lay aside disguise.'
Letter to the Earl of Chatham, January 1767

Charles I (1600–1649)
KING OF GREAT BRITAIN AND IRELAND,
1625–1649

1 'They are of the nature of cats, that ever grow cursed with age.'
Letter to Lord Wentworth, 22 January 1635. Of parliaments

2 'Well, since I see all the birds are flown, I do expect from you that you shall send them unto me as soon as they return hither.'
House of Commons, 4 January 1642. On arriving at the House to arrest five members and finding them not there

3 'For the people, I desire their liberty and freedom as much as anybody whatever. But I must tell you that their liberty and freedom consists in having of government those laws by which their life and their goods may be most their own. It is not having a share in government; that is nothing pertaining to them. A subject and a sovereign are clean different things.'
Speech on the scaffold, 30 January 1649

4 'I am the martyr of the people.'
IBID.

5 'Some kind of zeal counts all merciful moderation lukewarmness; and had rather be cruel than counted cold.'
EIKON BASILIKE *(1649). (The authorship of this 'spiritual autobiography' is disputed.)*

6 'Public reformers had need first act in private and practise that on their hearts which they purpose to try on others; for deformities within will soon betray the pretenders of public reformations to such private designs as must needs hinder the public good.'
IBID.

Charles II (1630–1685)
KING OF GREAT BRITAIN AND IRELAND,
1660–1685

7 'This is very true: for my words are my own, and my actions are my ministers'.'
Remark on reading Rochester's mock epitaph
SEE ALSO *the Earl of Rochester*

Charles V (1500–1558)
KING OF SPAIN, 1516–1556, AND HOLY
ROMAN EMPEROR, 1519–1558

8 'I came, I saw, God Conquered.'
Remark after the victory of the Imperial forces over the Protestant princes at the battle of Mühlberg, 23 April 1547

Chesterfield, 4th Earl of (Philip Stanhope) (1694–1773)
ENGLISH STATESMAN AND MAN OF
LETTERS

9 'The mystery of the State is become, like that of Godliness, ineffable and incomprehensible, and has likewise the same good luck of being thought the finer for not being understood.'
Letter to Bubb Doddington, 20 August 1716

10 'Our constitution is founded upon common sense itself, and every deviation from one is a violation of the other.'
COMMON SENSE, *5 February 1737*

11 'One of the greatest blessings a people, my Lords, can enjoy is liberty; but every good in this life has its alloy of evil. Licentiousness is the alloy of liberty ... There is such a connection between licentiousness and liberty, that it is not easy to correct the one, without dangerously wounding the other; it is extremely hard to distinguish the true limit between them; like a changeable silk, we cannot easily discover where the one ends, or where the other begins.'
House of Lords, 2 June 1737. Speaking against a bill to suppress licentiousness on the stage

12 'Ninety men out of one hundred, when they talk of forming principles, mean no more than embracing parties, and, when they talk of supporting their party, mean serving their friends; and the service of their friends implies no more than consulting self-interest. By this gradation, principles are fitted to party, party degenerates into faction, and faction is reduced to self.'
OLD ENGLAND, OR THE CONSTITUTIONAL
JOURNAL, *5 February 1743*

13 'Make yourself master of ancient and modern history, and languages. To know perfectly the constitution and form of government of every nation, the growth and decline of ancient and modern empires, and to trace out and reflect upon the causes of both; – to know the strength, the riches, and the commerce of every country; – these little things, trifling as they may seem, are yet very

necessary for a politician to know. . .
There are some additional qualifications
necessary . . . such as, an absolute
command of your temper, so as not to be
provoked to passion upon any account;
patience, to hear frivolous, impertinent,
and unreasonable applications; with
address enough to refuse, without
offending; or, by your manner of
granting, to double the
obligation; – dexterity enough to conceal
a truth, without telling a lie; sagacity
enough to read other people's
countenances; and serenity enough not to
let them discover anything by yours – a
seeming frankness, with a real reserve.
These are the rudiments of a politician;
the world must be your grammar.'
Letter to his son, 15 January 1748

1 'In our Parliamentary government,
connections are absolutely necessary; and,
if prudently formed, ably maintained, the
success of them is infallible.'
Letter to his son, 22 October 1750

2 'No man can make a figure in this
country, but by Parliament.'
Letter to his son, 11 February 1751

3 'Very shining Ministers, like the sun, are
apt to scorch, when they shine the
brightest: in our constitution, I prefer the
milder light of a less glaring Minister.'
Letter to his son, 8 March 1754

4 'For my part, I never saw a froward child
mended by whipping; and I would not
have the mother country become a stepmother.'
*Letter to his son, 27 December 1765. On
the Stamp Act for the American colonies*

5 'To withdraw, in the fulness of his
power, and in the utmost gratification of
his ambition, from the House of
Commons . . . and go into that Hospital of
Incurables, the House of Lords, is a
measure so unaccountable, that nothing
but proof positive could have made me
believe it.'
*Letter to his son, 1 August 1766. On the
elder Pitt's elevation to the House of
Lords*

6 'Be neither a servile courtier nor a noisy
patriot; custom, that governs the world
instead of reason, authorises a certain
latitude in political matters not always
consistent with the strictest morality, but

in all events remember *servare modum,
finemque tueri.'*
*Letter to his son, 'To be delivered after
his own Death', undated*

Chesterton, G(ilbert) K(eith)
(1874–1936)
ENGLISH NOVELIST, POET AND CRITIC

7 'The oligarchic character of the modern
English commonwealth does not rest, like
many oligarchies, on the cruelty of the
rich to the poor. It does not even rest on
the kindness of the rich to the poor. It
rests on the perennial and unfailing
kindness of the poor to the rich.'
HERETICS *(1905), Chapter 15*

Christy, David (1820–c. 1868)
AMERICAN WRITER AND ABOLITIONIST

8 'His majesty, King Cotton, is forced to
continue the employment of his slaves;
and, by their toil, is riding on,
conquering and to conquer.'
COTTON IS KING; OR SLAVERY IN THE LIGHT OF
POLITICAL ECONOMY *(1855)*

Churchill, Lord Randolph
(1849–1895)
ENGLISH CONSERVATIVE POLITICIAN,
CHANCELLOR OF THE EXCHEQUER, 1886

9 'I believe there is a great deal in Villa
Toryism which requires organisation.'
Letter to Sir Stafford Northcote, 1882

10 'For the purpose of recreation he has
selected the felling of trees; and we may
usefully remark that his amusements,
like his politics, are essentially
destructive. Every afternoon the whole
world is invited to assist at the crashing
fall of some beech or elm or oak. The
forest laments, in order that Mr
Gladstone may perspire.'
Speech at Blackpool, 24 January 1884

11 'What is the Tory Democracy that the
Whigs should deride it and hold it up to
the execration of the people? It has been
called a contradiction in terms; it has
been described as a nonsensical
appellation. I believe it to be the most
simple and the most easily understood
political denomination ever assumed. The
Tory Democracy is a democracy which
has embraced the principles of the Tory
party.'
Speech at Manchester, 6 November 1885

1 'If political parties and political leaders, not only Parliamentary but local, should be so utterly lost to every feeling and dictate of honour and courage as to hand over coldly, and for the sake of purchasing a short and illusory Parliamentary tranquillity, the lives and liberties of the Loyalists of Ireland to their hereditary and most bitter foes, make no doubt on this point – Ulster will not be a consenting party; Ulster at the proper moment will resort to the supreme arbitrament of force; *Ulster will fight, and Ulster will be right.*'
Public letter to a Liberal Unionist, 7 May 1886

Churchill, Sir Winston
(1874–1965)
ENGLISH LIBERAL AND CONSERVATIVE POLITICIAN, PRIME MINISTER, 1940–1945 AND 1951–1955

2 'I am an English Liberal. I hate the Tory party, their men, their words, and their methods.'
October 1903. Quoted in R Foster, LORD RANDOLPH CHURCHILL: A POLITICAL LIFE.

3 'The maxim of the British people is "Business as usual".'
Speech in London, 9 November 1914

4 'The loss of India would mark and consummate the downfall of the British Empire. That great organism would pass at a stroke out of life into history. From such a catastrophe there could be no recovery.'
Speech at London, 12 December 1930

5 'I remember when I was a child being taken to the celebrated Barnum's Circus ... the exhibit which I most desired to see was the one described as "the Boneless Wonder". My parents judged that the spectacle would be too revolting for my youthful eyes, and I have waited fifty years to see the Boneless Wonder sitting on the Treasury Bench.'
House of Commons, 28 January 1931. Of Ramsay MacDonald

6 'It is ... alarming and also nauseating to see Mr Gandhi, a seditious Middle Temple lawyer, now posing as a fakir of a type well known in the East, striding half-naked up the steps of the Viceregal Palace, while he is still organising and conducting a defiant campaign of civil disobedience, to parley on equal terms with the representative of the King-Emperor.'
Speech to the West Essex Unionist Association, 23 February 1931

7 'Dictators ride to and fro upon tigers which they dare not dismount. And the tigers are getting hungry.'
WHILE ENGLAND SLEPT *(1936)*

8 'England has been offered a choice between war and shame. She has chosen shame and will get war.'
House of Commons, September 1938. On the Munich agreement

9 'All is over. Silent, mournful, abandoned, broken, Czechoslovakia recedes into darkness ... We have sustained a defeat without a war.'
House of Commons, 5 October 1938. On the Munich agreement

10 'I cannot forecast to you the action of Russia. It is a riddle wrapped in a mystery inside an enigma; but perhaps there is a key. That key is Russian national interest.'
Broadcast on BBC radio, 1 October 1939

11 'You ask, what is our policy? I will say: it is to wage war by sea, land, and air, with all our might and with all the strength that God can give us ... You ask, what is our aim? I can answer in one word: Victory – victory at all costs.'
House of Commons, 13 May 1940

12 'I have nothing to offer but blood, toil, tears and sweat.'
IBID.

13 'We shall fight on the beaches, we shall fight on the landing grounds, we shall fight in the fields and in the streets, we shall fight in the hills; we shall never surrender.'
House of Commons, 4 June 1940

14 'Let us therefore brace ourselves to our duty and so bear ourselves that if the British Empire and its Commonwealth last for a thousand years men will still say, "This was their finest hour".'
House of Commons, 18 June 1940

15 'We shall show mercy, but we shall not ask for it.'
House of Commons, 14 July 1940. On the war against the Axis powers

1 'Never in the field of human conflict was so much owed by so many to so few.'
House of Commons, 20 August 1940. On the conduct of the Royal Air Force during the Battle of Britain

2 'We shall not fail or falter; we shall not weaken or tire ... Give us the tools and we will finish the job.'
Broadcast on BBC radio, 9 February 1941. Appealing to President Roosevelt

3 'When I warned them [the French government] that Britain would fight on alone whatever they did, their Generals told their Prime Minister and his divided Cabinet: "In three weeks England will have her neck wrung like a chicken." Some chicken! Some neck!'
Speech to the Canadian parliament, 30 December 1941

4 'I have not become the King's First Minister in order to preside over the liquidation of the British Empire.'
Speech at London, 10 November 1942. On India's demand for independence

5 'This is not the end. It is not even the beginning of the end. But it is, perhaps, the end of the beginning.'
IBID. *Of the battle of Egypt*

6 'What is to happen about Russia? ... An iron curtain is drawn down upon their front. We do not know what is going on behind.'
Telegram to President Truman, 12 May 1945
SEE ALSO *Goebbels* and *Ethel Snowden*

7 'No socialist system can be established without a political police ... They would have to fall back on some form of Gestapo.'
Election broadcast on BBC radio, 4 June 1945. On the consequences of a Labour victory at the 1945 general election

8 'If this is a blessing, it is certainly *very* well disguised.'
Remark in reply to his wife, of the Conservative defeat at the election of June 1945. Quoted in R Nixon, MEMOIRS OF RICHARD NIXON, PART 6

9 'From Stettin in the Baltic to Trieste in the Adriatic an iron curtain has descended across the Continent.'
Speech at Fulton, Missouri, 5 March 1946

10 'The British Empire seems to be running out almost as fast as the American loan.

The steady and remorseless process of divesting ourselves of what has been gained by so many generations of toil, administration, and sacrifice continues ... This haste is appalling. "Scuttle" is the only word that can be applied.'
House of Commons, 20 December 1946. On the negotiations for the independence of Burma

11 'I have never accepted what many people have kindly said, namely that I inspired the nation. It was the nation and the race dwelling all round the globe that had the lion's heart. I had the luck to be called upon to give the roar.'
Speech at Westminster Hall, London, 30 November 1954

12 'I am not sure I should have dared to start; but I am sure I should not have dared to stop.'
In conversation with Anthony Head. Quoted in H Thomas, THE SUEZ AFFAIR, *Chapter 8. On the invasion of Egypt, 1956*

Cicero, Marcus Tullius
(106BC–43BC)
ROMAN ORATOR, STATESMAN AND PHILOSOPHER

13 'More law, less justice.' *(Summum ius summa iniuria.)*
DE OFFICIIS *(44BC), Book I, Part 10*

14 'Freedom suppressed and again regained bites with keener fangs than freedom never endangered.' *(Acriores autem morsus sunt intermissae libertatis quam retentae.)*
IBID., *Book II, Part 7*

15 'For what people have always sought is equality before the law. For rights that were not open to all alike would be no rights.' *(Ius enim semper est quaesitum aequabile; neque enim aliter esset ius.)*
IBID., *Book II, Part 12*

16 'The good of the people is the supreme law.' *(Salus populi suprema est lex.)*
DE LEGIBUS, *Book III, Part 3*

Clarendon, 4th Earl of (George Villiers) (1800–1870)
ENGLISH WHIG POLITICIAN, FOREIGN SECRETARY, 1853–1859

17 'We are drifting towards war.'
House of Lords, 14 February 1854. On the international tension in the Crimea

Clausewitz, Karl von
(1780–1831)
PRUSSIAN GENERAL AND WRITER

1 'We must further expressly and exactly establish the point of view, no less necessary in practice, from which war is regarded as *nothing but the continuation of politics by other means.*'
ON WAR *(1832): Prefatory note*

2 'It is politics which begets war. Politics represents the intelligence, war merely its instrument, not the other way round. The only possible course in war is to subordinate the military viewpoint to the political.'
IBID.

Clay, Henry (1777–1852)
AMERICAN POLITICIAN, SECRETARY OF STATE, 1825–1829

3 'All religions united with government, are more or less inimical to liberty.'
Speech to the House of Representatives, 24 March 1818

4 'I owe allegiance to two sovereignties . . . one is to the sovereignty of this Union, and the other is to the sovereignty of the State of Kentucky.'
Speech to the Senate, 14 February 1850

Cleaver, Leroy Eldridge
(1935–)
AMERICAN BLACK LEADER AND WRITER

5 'During a certain stage in the psychological transformation of a subjected people who have been struggling for their freedom, an impulse to violence develops in the collective unconscious. The oppressed people feel an uncontrollable desire to kill their masters. But the feeling itself gives rise to myriad troubles, for the people, when they first become aware of the desire to strike out against the slavemaster, shrink from this impulse in terror. Violence then turns in upon itself and the oppressed people fight among themselves: they kill each other, and do all the things to each other which they would, in fact, like to do to the master. Intimidated by the superior armed might of the oppressor, the colonial people feel that he is invincible and that it is futile to even dream of confronting him.'
PSYCHOLOGY: THE BLACK BIBLE *(1967). Précis of Frantz Fanon's argument in* THE WRETCHED OF THE EARTH

6 'From the tension showing on the faces of the people before me, I thought the cops were invading the meeting, but there was a deep female gleam leaping out of one of the women's eyes that no cop who ever lived could elicit. I recognized that gleam out of the recesses of my soul, even though I had never seen it before in my life: the total admiration of a black woman for a black man. I spun round in my seat and saw the most beautiful sight I had ever seen: four black men wearing black berets, powder blue shirts, black leather jackets, black trousers, shiny black shoes – and each with a gun!'
THE COURAGE TO KILL: MEETING THE PANTHERS *(1968). On his first attendance at a Black Panther meeting*

7 'For the revolutionary black youth of today, time starts moving with the coming of Malcolm X. Before Malcolm, time stands still, going down in frozen steps into the depths of the stagnation of slavery. Malcolm talked shit, and talking shit is the iron in a young nigger's blood. Malcolm mastered language and used it as a sword to slash his way through the veil that for four hundred years gave the white man the power of the word. Through the breach in the veil, Malcolm saw all the way to national liberation, and he showed us the rainbow and the golden pot at its end. Inside the golden pot, Malcolm told us, was the tool of liberation. Huey P Newton, one of the millions of black people who listened to Malcolm, lifted the golden lid off the pot and blindly, trusting Malcolm, struck his hand inside and grasped the tool. When he withdrew his hand and looked to see what he held, he saw the gun, cold in its metal and implacable in its message: Death-Life, Liberty or Death, mastered by a black hand at last!'
IBID.

Clemenceau, Georges
(1841–1929)
FRENCH RADICAL POLITICIAN, PRIME MINISTER, 1906–1909 and 1917–1920

8 'My home policy? I wage war. My foreign policy? I wage war. Always, everywhere, I wage war.'
Speech to the Chamber of Deputies, 8 March 1918

1 'Austria is the school of oppression.'
Speech to the Senate committee, 19 April 1918

2 'When I am *fou* I usually try to kill someone – a general if possible.' (Said in English.)
Remark at a meeting of the Supreme War Council, 3 July 1918. Arguing against the proposal to give the Versailles war board responsibility for long-term strategic planning

3 'It is far easier to make war than to make peace.'
Speech at Verdun, 14 July 1919

Cleveland, Stephen Grover
(1837–1908)
AMERICAN DEMOCRATIC POLITICIAN, PRESIDENT, 1885–1889 and 1893–1897

4 'The use of power in the extension of American institutions presents an inconsistency whose evil and dangerous tendency ought to be apparent to all who love these institutions and understand their motives and purposes.'
Letter to Bolton Hall, 8 October 1899. Condemning the American war against Spain

Clynes, John (1869–1949)
ENGLISH LABOUR POLITICIAN, MEMBER OF PARLIAMENT, 1906–1931 and 1935–1945, AND HOME SECRETARY 1929–1931

5 'A Communist is no more a left wing member of the Labour Party than an atheist is a left wing member of the Christian Church.'
Quoted in I Gilmour, INSIDE RIGHT, Part III, Chapter 4

Cobbett, William (1762–1835)
ENGLISH JOURNALIST, ESSAYIST AND RADICAL POLITICIAN, MEMBER OF PARLIAMENT, 1832–1835

6 'No man has a right to pry into his neighbour's private concerns; and the opinions of every man are his private concern, while he keeps them so . . . but when he makes those opinions public; when he once attempts to make converts, whether it be in religion, politics, or anything else; when he once comes forward as a candidate for public admiration, esteem or compassion, his opinions, his principles, his motives, every action of his life, public or private, becomes the fair subject of public discussion.'
OBSERVATIONS ON THE EMIGRATION OF DR PRIESTLEY (1794)

7 'Who will say that an Englishman ought not to despise all nations in the world?'
THE ADVENTURES OF PETER PORCUPINE *(1796)*

8 'Nothing is so well calculated to produce a death-like torpor in the country as an extended system of taxation and a great national debt; and, therefore, all Ministers who, like Mr Pitt, have no notion of governing but by means of the baser passions, have regarded "*a public debt as a public blessing*".'
Letter to W Windham, 10 February 1804
SEE ALSO *Alexander Hamilton*

9 'It is neither a monarchy, an aristocracy, nor a democracy; it is a band of great nobles, who by sham election, and by the means of all sorts of bribery and corruption, have obtained an absolute sway in the country, having under them, for the purposes of *show* and execution, a thing they call a *king*, sharp and unprincipled fellows whom they call *Ministers*, a mummery which they call a *Church*, experienced and well-tried and steel-hearted men whom they call *Judges*, a company of false money-makers whom they call a *Bank*, numerous bands of brave and needy persons whom they call *soldiers and sailors*; and a talking, corrupt, and impudent set, whom they call a *House of Commons*.'
POLITICAL REGISTER, *8 June 1816. On the English constitution*

10 'No Alien Acts here. No long-sworded and whiskered Captains. No Judges escorted from town to town and sitting under the guard of dragoons. No packed juries of tenants . . . No Cannings, Liverpools, Castlereaghs, Eldons, Ellenboroughs or Sidmouths. No Bankers. No Squeaking Wynnes. No Wilberforces. Think of *that*! No Wilberforces!'
POLITICAL REGISTER, *3 October 1818. Of America*

11 'Priests have, in all ages, been remarkable for cool and deliberate and unrelenting cruelty; but it seems to be reserved for the Church of England to produce one who has a just claim to the atrocious pre-eminence. No assemblage of words can give an appropriate designation of you;

and, therefore, as being the single word which best suits the character of such a man, I call you *Parson*, which, amongst other meanings, includes that of Boroughmonger Tool.'
POLITICAL REGISTER, *8 May 1819, 'To Parson Malthus, on the rights of the Poor, and on the cruelty recommended by him to be exercised towards the Poor'*

1 'This nation owes everlasting gratitude to the Queen. It was she that raised us from the very dust. The feeling towards the THING now is much more of *contempt* than *dread*. Its *embarrassments* are so great, and it discovers its own apprehensions in so many ways, that our fears of it are dissipated.'
Letter to Dr Taylor, 2 July 1822. On Queen Caroline's successful resistance to George IV's attempt to gain a divorce from her, 1820. The THING was Cobbett's word for what, roughly, we would today call the 'Establishment'

2 'The great enemies of real liberty have always been the Whigs. The Riot Act, the Septennial Act, the infernal Excise, are all the works of the Whigs. The Tories, as they are called, will find at last, that they have no security but by joining with the people. The people have never hated them as they have hated, and do hate, the Whigs, who are false, designing hypocrites, with liberty on their lips, and tyranny in their hearts.'
POLITICAL REGISTER, *9 January 1830*

3 'I would rather that the people should believe in *witchcraft* and have plenty of bread and meat and good Sunday coats, than that they should laugh at witchcraft, and be fed on potatoes and covered with rags.'
RURAL RIDES *(1830). Attacking the educational projects, especially the Mechanics' Institutes, of the 'Malthusian' middle-class reformers*

Cobden, Richard (1804–1865)
ENGLISH RADICAL POLITICIAN, CO-FOUNDER OF THE ANTI-CORN LAW LEAGUE

4 'Commerce is the grand panacea, which, like a beneficent medical discovery, will serve to inoculate with the healthy and saving taste for civilisation all the nations of the world.'
ENGLAND, IRELAND AND AMERICA *(1835)*

5 'I have speculated, and probably dreamt, in the dim future – ay, a thousand years hence – I have speculated on what the effect of the triumph of this principle may be. I believe that the effect will be to change the face of the world . . . I believe that the desire and motive for large and mighty empires, for gigantic armies and great navies – for those materials which are used for the destruction of life and the desolation of the rewards of labour – will die away . . . and I believe that the speculative philosopher of a thousand years hence will date the greatest revolution that ever happened in the world's history from the triumph of the principle which we have met here to advocate.'
Speech at Manchester, 15 January 1846. On the abolition of the Corn Laws and the winning of the principle of free trade

6 'Are we to be the Don Quixotes of Europe, to go about fighting for every cause where we find that someone has been wronged?'
House of Commons, 22 December 1854. In opposition to the Crimean war

Coke, Sir Edward (1552–1634)
ENGLISH JURIST, JUDGE AND POLITICIAN, MEMBER OF PARLIAMENT, 1589–1629

7 'Prerogative is part of the law, but "sovereign power" is no parliamentary word . . .Magna Charta is such a fellow that he will have no sovereign.'
House of Commons, 17 May 1628. Speaking against the House of Lords' insertion into the Petition of Right of a clause saving the king's 'sovereign power'

8 'A man's house is his castle.'
INSTITUTES *(Part I, 1628), 'Commentary upon Littleton'*

Cole, G(eorge) D(ouglas) H(oward) (1889–1959)
ENGLISH ECONOMIST AND HISTORIAN

9 'Poverty is the symptom; slavery the disease.'
SELF-GOVERNMENT IN INDUSTRY *(1917)*

10 'Fascism is *nonsense*; and that is perhaps the gravest indictment of all. It not merely is nonsense; it spews nonsense out of its mouth. It believes in nonsense, believes that ordinary man is moved by nonsense, and *ought to be so moved*. It

not merely deems men fools and irrational, but wants to keep them so.'
THE PEOPLE'S FRONT *(1937)*

1   'Man in Society is not free where there is no law; he is most free where he co-operates best with his equals in the making of laws.'
ESSAYS IN SOCIAL THEORY *(1950)*

2   'Voting is merely a handy device; it is not to be identified with democracy, which is a mental and moral relation of man to man.'
IBID.

Coleridge, Samuel Taylor
(1772–1834)
ENGLISH POET, CRITIC AND POLITICAL THEORIST

3   'We should be bold in the avowal of political truth among those only whose minds are susceptible of reasoning . . . and consequently should plead *for* the oppressed, not *to* them.'
Bristol lectures, 1795

4   'I have . . . snapped my squeaking baby-trumpet of sedition and have hung its fragments in the Chamber of Penitences.'
Letter to Charles Lloyd, 15 October 1796. On renouncing his enthusiasm for the French revolution

5   'A people are free in proportion as they form their own opinions.'
Prospectus for THE WATCHMAN, *1796*

6   'History has taught me that rulers are much the same in all ages, and under all forms of government; that they are as bad as they dare to be. The vanity of ruin and the curse of blindness have clung to them like an hereditary leprosy.'
Letter to George Coleridge, April 1798

7   'Governments are more the *effect* than the cause of that which we are.'
IBID.

8   'Whoever builds a government on personal and natural rights, is so far a Jacobin. Whoever builds on social rights, that is, hereditary rank, property, and long prescription, is an anti-Jacobin, even though he should nevertheless be a republican, or even a democrat.'
MORNING POST, *1802, 'Once a Jacobin, Always a Jacobin'*

9   'The first man on whom the light of an idea dawned did in that same moment receive the spirit and credentials of a law-giver.'
THE STATESMAN'S MANUAL *(1816)*

10   'It is high time, My Lord, that the subjects of Christian Governments should be taught that neither historically or morally, in fact or by right, have men made the State; but that the State, and that alone, makes them men.'
Letter to Lord Liverpool, 1817

11   'Patriotism itself is a necessary link in the golden chains of our affections and virtues.'
THE FRIEND *(revised edition, 1818), 'Political Knowledge'*

12   'A permanent, nationalized, learned order, a national clerisy or church, is an essential element of a rightly constituted nation, without which it wants the best security alike for its permanence and its progression.'
ON THE CONSTITUTION OF THE CHURCH AND STATE *(1830), Chapter 7*

13   'Religion, true or false, is and ever has been the centre of gravity in a realm, to which all other things must and will accommodate themselves.'
IBID.

14   'Rights! There are no rights whatever without corresponding duties . . . you will find nowhere in our parliamentary records the miserable sophism of the Rights of Man.'
TABLE-TALK, *20 November 1831*

15   'A State, in idea, is the opposite of a Church. A State regards classes, and not individuals; and it estimates classes, not by internal merit, but external accidents, as property, birth etc. But a Church does the opposite of this, and disregards all external accidents, and looks at men as individual persons . . . A Church is, therefore, in idea, the only pure democracy.'
TABLE-TALK, *24 July 1832*

Condorcet, Marie Jean Caritat, Marquis de (1743–1794)
FRENCH PHILOSOPHER, MATHEMATICIAN AND REVOLUTIONARY

16   'Societies which are not enlightened by *philosophes* are cheated by charlatans.'
JOURNAL OF SOCIAL INSTRUCTION *(1793)*

Confucius (c. 551BC–c. 479BC)
CHINESE SAGE

1 'When law and order prevail in the land, a man may be bold in speech and bold in action; but when the land lacks law and order, though he may take bold action, he should lay restraint on his speech.'
ANALECTS (A collection of sayings and dialogues gathered posthumously by his disciples.)

2 'Oppressive government is more terrible than tigers.'
Quoted in Bertrand Russell, POWER, Chapter 18

Connell, James (1852–1929)
IRISH SOCIALIST WRITER

3 'The people's flag is deepest red;
It shrouded oft our martyred dead,
And ere their limbs grew stiff and cold
Their heart's blood dyed its every fold.
(Chorus)
Then raise the scarlet standard high!
Within its shade we'll live or die;
Tho' cowards flinch and traitors sneer,
We'll keep the red flag flying here.'
THE RED FLAG (1889)

Connolly, James (1870–1916)
IRISH LABOUR LEADER, FOUNDER OF THE IRISH SOCIALIST REPUBLICAN PARTY

4 'It is not Socialism but capitalism that is opposed to religion . . . Religion, I hope, is not bound up with a system founded on buying human labour in the cheapest market, and selling its product in the dearest; when the organized Socialist working class tramples upon the capitalist class it will not be trampling upon a pillar of God's Church but upon a blasphemous defiler of the Sanctuary, it will be rescuing the Faith from the impious vermin who made it noisome to the really religious men and women.'
THE HARP, January 1909

5 'An agitation to attain a political or economic end must rest upon an implied willingness and ability to use force. Without that it is mere wind and attitudinizing.'
FORWARD, 14 March 1914

6 'Believing that the British Government has no right in Ireland, never had any right in Ireland, and never can have any right in Ireland, the presence, in any one generation of Irishmen, of even a respectable minority, ready to die to affirm that truth, makes that Government for ever an usurpation and a crime against human progress.'
Statement at his court-martial, 9 May 1916. On the Easter Rising at Dublin, 1916

Constant de Rebecque, Henri-Benjamin (1767–1830)
SWISS AUTHOR AND POLITICIAN

7 'The flames of Moscow were the aurora of the world's liberty.'
OF THE SPIRIT OF CONQUEST AND USURPATION (1814), Preface. On the retreat of Napoleon's army from Russia after the burning of Moscow, 1812

8 'We have arrived at the epoch of commerce, an epoch which is necessarily bound to take the place of the epoch of war . . . When a people is naturally warlike, the authority which rules them has no need to deceive them in order to lead them into war . . . But in our day . . . the Government would talk of national independence, of national honour, of the straightening of its frontiers, of commercial interest, of precautions dictated by foresight – of what else? – for it is inexhaustible, the vocabulary of hypocrisy and injustice.'
IBID.

9 'Your party man, however excellent his intentions may be, is always opposed to any limitation of sovereignty. He regards himself as the next in succession, and handles gently the property that is to come to him, even while his opponents are its tenants.'
COURSE OF CONSTITUTIONAL POLITICS (1817–20)

10 'When no limits are set to representative authority, the representatives of the people are not defenders of Liberty but candidates for tyranny.'
IBID.

Cook, Arthur (1885–1931)
ENGLISH TRADE UNIONIST

11 'Not a penny off the pay, not a second on the day.'
Slogan coined in the prelude to the miners' strike of 1926, sometimes also attributed to Herbert Smith

Coolidge, Calvin (1872–1933)
AMERICAN REPUBLICAN POLITICIAN,
PRESIDENT, 1923–1929

1 'There is no right to strike against the
public safety by anybody, anywhere,
anytime.'
*Telegram to the president of the
American Federation of Labor, 14
September 1919*

2 'Civilisation and profits go hand in hand.'
Speech at New York, 20 November 1920

3 'The business of America is business.'
*Speech to the Society of American
Newspaper Editors, Washington, 17
January 1925*

Cooper, James Fenimore
(1789–1851)
AMERICAN NOVELIST AND SOCIAL
CRITIC

4 'In Democracies there is a besetting
disposition to make publick opinion
stronger than the law. This is the
particular form in which tyranny
exhibits itself in a popular government.'
THE AMERICAN DEMOCRAT *(1838)*

Coventry, Thomas, 1st Baron
(1578–1640)
ENGLISH STATESMAN, LORD KEEPER OF
THE PRIVY SEAL, 1625–1640

5 'The dominion of the sea, as it is an
ancient and undoubted right of the
Crown of England, so it is the best
security of the land. The wooden walls
are the best walls of this kingdom.'
*Speech to the Council, 17 June 1635. On
the Royal Navy*

Cowper, William (1731–1810)
ENGLISH POET

6 'Slaves cannot breathe in England; if their
lungs
Receive our air, that moment they are
free;
They touch our country and their
shackles fall.'
THE TASK *(1784), Book II, 'The Timepiece'*

Creyke, Ralph (died 1826)
ENGLISH LANDOWNER

7 'I shall ever revere his memory for
standing between the dead and the
living, and staying the plague which, in

the French Revolution, had infected the
Continent, and might have spread and
desolated this island.'
*Letter to William Wilberforce, 25 January,
1806. Of the younger Pitt. (The phrase,
'standing between the dead and the
living' is sometimes wrongly attributed to
Wilberforce.)*

Croce, Benedetto (1866–1952)
ITALIAN PHILOSOPHER, CRITIC AND
HISTORIAN

8 'In the field of politics, force and consent
are correlative terms, and one does not
exist without the other. The objection
will be raised that this is a "forced"
consent. But every consent is more or less
forced ... in the most liberal State as in
the most oppressive tyranny there is
always a consent, and it is always forced,
conditioned, changeable.'
ELEMENTS OF POLITICS *(1925)*

9 'The theory of equality, for which there
is no logical place in the political
relation, has its true origin within the
framework of mathematics and
mechanics, both of them unable to
comprehend the living world. In fact,
although the theory of equality
represents a mistake found in all ages and
always reappearing, the period of its
greatest glory was the century of
mechanical discoveries (the 18th
century).'
IBID.

Croker, John Wilson (1780–1857)
IRISH WRITER AND TORY POLITICIAN,
MEMBER OF PARLIAMENT, 1807–1832

10 'I never have and never will (I hope) do
anything for the sake of popularity; he
that steers by any other compass than his
own sense of duty may be a popular, but
cannot be an honest, and I think not a
useful public servant.'
Letter to Lord Exmouth, 23 October 1816

11 'Party is in England a stronger passion
than love, avarice, or ambition; it is often
compounded of them, but is stronger
than any of them individually.'
Diary, 22 June 1821

12 'We are now, as we always have been,
decidedly and conscientiously attached to
what is called the Tory, and which

might with more propriety be called the Conservative, party.'
QUARTERLY REVIEW, *January 1830. Believed to be the origin of the name 'Conservative party'. (Croker's authorship of the article in which this sentence appears has been doubted by M F Brightfield,* J W CROKER *(1940), 403n.)*

1 'I am one of those who have always thought that party attachments and consistency are in the *first* class of a statesman's duties, because without them he must be incapable of performing any useful service to the country.'
Letter to a friend (?Peel), 1830

2 'No minister ever stood, or could stand, against public opinion.'
QUARTERLY REVIEW, *February 1835*

3 'There are two great antagonistic principles at the root of all government – stability and experiment. The former is Tory, and the latter Whig: and the human mind divides itself into these classes as naturally and as inconsiderately, as to personal objects, as it does into indolence and activity, obstinacy and indecision, temerity and versatility, or any other of the various different or contradictory moods of the mind.'
Letter to Lord Brougham, 14 March 1839

Cromwell, Oliver (1599–1658)
ENGLISH GENERAL AND POLITICIAN, LORD PROTECTOR, 1653–1658

4 'I had rather have a plain russet-coated captain that knows what he fights for and loves what he knows, than that which you call a "gentleman" and is nothing else.'
Letter to Sir William Spring, September 1643. On the composition of the New Model Army

5 'I am one of those whose heart God hath drawn out to wait for some extraordinary dispensations, according to those promises that he hath held forth of things to be accomplished in the later time, and I cannot but think that God is beginning of them.'
Speech at Putney, 1 November 1647. During the army debates

6 'The providence of God hath cast this upon us.'
House of Commons, December 1648. Of the decision to bring Charles I to trial

7 'It matters not who is our Commander-in-Chief if God be so.'
Speech to the Council of Officers, 23 March 1649

8 'Truly, I think he that prays best will fight best.'
1650. Quoted in C Hill, GOD'S ENGLISHMAN, *Chapter 3*

9 'I had rather that Mahometanism were permitted amongst us than that one of God's children should be persecuted.'
1650. IBID.

10 'You have stayed in this place too long, and there is no health in you. In the name of God, go!'
House of Commons, 20 April 1653. Dismissing the Rump parliament

11 'You are no Parliament. I say you are no Parliament. I will put an end to your sitting.'
IBID.

12 'What shall we do with this bauble? Here, take it away.'
IBID. *To a soldier, of the mace*

13 'A nobleman, a gentleman, a yeoman, that is a good interest of the land and a great one.'
Quoted in C Firth, OLIVER CROMWELL AND THE RULE OF THE PURITANS IN ENGLAND, *Chapter 12. Arguing against the Levellers*

14 'No man rises so high as he knows not whither he goes.'
Quoted in A J P Taylor, ESSAYS IN ENGLISH HISTORY, *'Cromwell and the Historians'*

Crosland, Anthony (1918–1977)
ENGLISH LABOUR POLITICIAN, FOREIGN SECRETARY, 1976–1977

15 'Total abstinence and a good filing-system are not now the right sign-posts to the socialist Utopia; or at least, if they are, some of us will fall by the wayside.'
THE FUTURE OF SOCIALISM *(1956), Chapter 21*

Crossman, Richard (1907–1974)
ENGLISH LABOUR POLITICIAN, CABINET MINISTER AND MEMBER OF PARLIAMENT, 1945–1974

16 'One of the difficulties of politics is that politicians are shocked by those who are really prepared to let their thinking reach

any conclusion. Political thinking consists in deciding on the conclusion first and then finding good arguments for it. An open mind is considered irresponsible – and perhaps it really is.'
Diary, 13 November 1951

1 'When the Tories are in trouble, they bunch together and cogger up. When we [the Labour party] get into trouble, we start blaming each other and rushing to the press to tell them all the terrible things that somebody else has done.'
Diary, 8 May 1956

2 'The two most important emotions of the Labour Party are a doctrinaire faith in nationalization, without knowing what it means, and a doctrinaire faith in pacifism, without facing its consequences.'
Diary, 4 October 1957

3 'Parliament has joined the monarchy as a dignified, not an effective, element in the Constitution.'
Diary, 19 March 1959
SEE ALSO *Bagehot*

4 'The definition of the Left is a group of people who will never be happy unless they can convince themselves that they are about to be betrayed by their leaders.'
Diary, 3 July 1959

5 'Whenever I am lectured on the virtues of moderation in Labour politics I feel as Hermann Goering did about culture and reach for my revolver. Westminster is a place where moderation thrives and vigour is steadily sapped.'
TIMES, *15 November 1972, 'The Curse of Moderation on Labour'*

6 'A revolutionary party is a contradiction in terms.'
THE CHARM OF POLITICS *(1958), 'Mussolini and Coolidge'. (Reprinted from the* NEW STATESMAN AND NATION, *1939.)*

7 'Politicians are ambitious not to *make* important decisions but to *say* important things.'
IBID., *'Amery and Fisher'.* (NEW STATESMAN AND NATION, *1947.)*

8 'In our traditional cricket match the parties are strong and the best team wins; in the strip poker of American politics, the parties are weak and the best man wins.'
IBID., *'Roosevelt – Warts and All'.* (NEW STATESMAN AND NATION, *1957.)*

9 'The distinction between a statesman and a politician is that the former imposes his will and his ideas on his environment while the latter adapts himself to it.'
IBID.

Cummings, E(dward) E(stlim)
(1894–1962)
AMERICAN POET AND ARTIST

10 'Boosevelt (*taking the mike*): We hold these truths to be self-evident; that all men are created people, and all people are created feeble, and all feeble are created minded, and all minded are created equal. And the sequel to equal being opportunity, it is obvious that opportunity knocks but once and that it boosts. Nothing can really be done unless you and me are willing to fearlessly confront one another with each other; believing, with the common man, that as long as people are men America is the land of opportunity.'
AND IT CAME TO PASS *(1932). (A dramatic sketch of the 1932 American presidential election.)*

Curran, John Philpot
(1750–1817)
IRISH JUDGE

11 'The condition upon which God hath given liberty to men is eternal vigilance.'
Speech at Dublin, 10 July 1790

Curzon of Kedleston, George, 1st Marquess (1859–1925)
ENGLISH CONSERVATIVE POLITICIAN, VICEROY OF INDIA, 1898–1905

12 'There has never been anything so great in the world's history as the British Empire, so great as an instrument for the good of humanity. We must devote all out energies and our lives to maintaining it.'
Remark while an undergraduate at Oxford. Quoted in | Rennell Rodd, SOCIAL AND DIPLOMATIC MEMORIES, *Third Series, 'Epilogue'*

13 'I am afraid it is an idle schoolboy's dream to suppose that Tories can legislate – as I did stupidly. They can govern and make war and increase taxation and expenditure *à merveille*, but legislation is not their province in a democratic constitution.'
Letter to Lord Salisbury, November 1886. On the government's failure to enact the 'Dartford programme'

D

Daladier, Edouard (1884–1970)
FRENCH RADICAL SOCIALIST
POLITICIAN, PRIME MINISTER, 1933 and
1934

1 'It is a phoney war [*une drôle de guerre*].'
*Speech to the Chamber of Deputies, 22
December 1939*

Dalton, Hugh, Baron (1887–1962)
ENGLISH LABOUR POLITICIAN,
CHANCELLOR OF THE EXCHEQUER,
1945–1947

2 'Though politics is, of necessity, a highly
competitive profession, not least in the
Labour Party, we have a strong sense of
social security near the top. To do a man
out of his job, at that eminence, is against
good fellowship.'
CALL BACK YESTERDAY *(1953)*

Danton, Georges (1759–1794)
FRENCH REVOLUTIONARY, MEMBER OF
THE COMMITTEE OF PUBLIC SAFETY

3 'Everything belongs to the fatherland
when the fatherland is in danger.'
*Speech to the National Convention, 28
August 1792*

4 'Boldness, once more boldness, and
boldness for ever [*De l'audace, encore de
l'audace, et toujours de l'audace*] and
France is saved!'
*Speech to the National Convention, 2
September 1792*

5 'A nation in revolution is like boiling
bronze regenerating itself in the crucible.
The Statue of Liberty is not yet moulded.
The metal is bubbling over. Watch the
furnace, or you will all be burned.'
*Speech to the National Convention, 24
March 1793*

6 'Paris wealth and Paris luxury must also
pay. It is a sponge which must be
squeezed.'
*Speech to the National Convention, 27
April 1793. On financing the foreign wars*

7 'Twenty times I offered the Girondins
peace. They would have none of it ... It
is they who have driven us [the Jacobins]
into the arms of sans-culottism, which
has devoured them, will devour us all,
and end by devouring itself.'
October 1793. Quoted in A H Beesly, LIFE
OF DANTON, *Chapter 24*

8 'I hoped soon to have got you all out of
this, but here I am myself, and how it
will end no one can foresee.'
*Remark to the crowd, 1 April 1794. On
being led, after his arrest, into the
Luxembourg prison, Paris*

9 'My abode will soon be nothingness; as
for my name, you will find it in the
Pantheon of History.'
*Remark at his trial, 2 April 1794. On
being asked his name and address*

10 'Men of my stamp have no price. On
their foreheads are stamped in
ineffaceable characters the seal of liberty,
the genius of republicanism.'
IBID.

Davis, Thomas Osborne (1814–1845)
IRISH POET

11 'In Bodenstown churchyard there is a
green grave,
And freely around it let winter winds
rave:
Far better they suit him – the ruin and
gloom –
Till Ireland, a nation, can build him a
tomb.'
TONE'S GRAVE *(1843). Of Wolfe Tone.*

Debray, (Jules) Régis (1941–)
FRENCH JOURNALIST, MARXIST
THEORIST AND GUERRILLA FIGHTER

12 'Guerrilla warfare is to peasant uprisings
what Marx is to Sorel.'
REVOLUTION IN THE REVOLUTION? *(1967),
Chapter 1*

Debs, Eugene (1855–1926)
AMERICAN TRADE UNIONIST AND CO-
FOUNDER OF THE SOCIALIST PARTY OF
THE UNITED STATES

13 'While there is a lower class, I am in it;
while there is a criminal element, I am
of it; and while there is a soul in prison,
I am not free.'
*Speech from the dock, Canton, Ohio, 16
June 1913*
SEE ALSO *Thoreau*

1 'When great changes occur in history, when great principles are involved, as a rule the majority are wrong.'
Speech from the dock, Cleveland, Ohio, 12 September 1918

Decatur, Stephen (1779–1820)
AMERICAN NAVAL OFFICER

2 'Our country! In her intercourse with foreign nations, may she always be in the right; but our country, right or wrong!'
Toast proposed at a dinner at Norfolk, Virginia, April 1816

de Gaulle, Charles (1890–1970)
FRENCH GENERAL AND POLITICIAN, PRESIDENT, 1959–1969

3 'Such as I am, I cannot fail to be, at a given moment, in the centre of the stage.'
Lecture at the Ecole Supérieure de la Guerre, 1927, 'On Character'

4 'I, General de Gaulle, French soldier and leader, am aware that I speak in the name of France.'
Declaration of his leadership of Free France, London, 19 June 1940

5 'I was France.' [*J'étais la France.*]
Press conference, 7 April 1954

6 'Now I shall return to my village and there will remain at the disposition of the nation.'
Press conference, 19 May 1958

7 'The national task that has been incumbent upon me for eighteen years is hereby confirmed.'
Speech to the nation, 28 December 1958. On his election as president of the Fifth Republic

8 'How can you expect to govern a country [France] that has two hundred and forty-six kinds of cheese?'
Quoted in NEWSWEEK, 1 October, 1962

9 'One does not arrest Voltaire.'
Quoted in ENCOUNTER, June 1975. On the Maoist and Communist activities of Jean-Paul Sartre

Derby, 14th Earl of (Edward Stanley) (1799–1869)
ENGLISH WHIG, THEN CONSERVATIVE POLITICIAN, PRIME MINISTER, 1852, 1858–1859 and 1866–1868

10 'When I first came into parliament, Mr Tierney, a great Whig authority, used always to say that the duty of an Opposition was very simple – it was, to oppose everything, and propose nothing.'
House of Commons, 4 June 1841

11 'You know as much as Mr Canning did. They give you the figures.'
Quoted in a memorandum of Disraeli, February 1852. On Disraeli's reluctance to accept the chancellorship of the exchequer

12 'The foreign policy of the noble Earl ... may be summed up in two short homely but expressive words, "meddle" and "muddle".'
House of Lords, February 1864. Of the foreign policy of Earl Russell

13 'No doubt we are making a great experiment and taking a leap in the dark.'
House of Lords, 6 August 1867. On the reform act of 1867
SEE ALSO *the Marquess of Salisbury*

Desmoulins, Camille (1760–1794)
FRENCH REVOLUTIONARY LEADER

14 'The great appear great to us only because we are on our knees: let us rise.'
Quoted in P B Ellis (ed.), JAMES CONNOLLY: SELECTED WRITINGS, Introduction

De Valera, Eamon (1882–1975)
AMERICAN-BORN IRISH FIANNA FÁIL POLITICIAN, PRIME MINISTER, 1937–1948, 1951–1954 and 1957–1959

15 'No longer shall our children, like our cattle, be brought up for export.'
Speech to the Dáil, 19 December 1934

16 'The Six Counties have, towards the rest of Ireland, a status and a relationship which no Act of Parliament can change. They are part of Ireland. They have always been part of Ireland, and their people, Catholic and Protestant, are our people.'
Message delivered to Churchill, 26 May 1941

Devlin, Patrick, Baron (1905–   )
ENGLISH JUDGE

17 'No society has yet solved the problem of how to teach morality without religion. So the law must base itself on Christian morals and to the limit of its ability enforce them, not simply because they are the morals of most of us, nor simply

because they are the morals which are taught by the Established Church – on these points the law recognizes the right to dissent – but for the compelling reason that without the help of Christian teaching the law will fail.'
THE ENFORCEMENT OF MORALS *(1965)*, *Chapter 1*

1 'What the lawmaker has to ascertain is not the true belief but the common belief.'
IBID., *Chapter 5*

Dickinson, John (1732–1808)
AMERICAN REVOLUTIONARY LEADER

2 'The cause of Liberty is a cause of too much dignity to be sullied by turbulence and tumult. It ought to be maintained in a manner suitable to her nature.'
LETTERS FROM A FARMER IN PENNSYLVANIA *(1768)*

Diderot, Denis (1713–1784)
FRENCH ENCYCLOPEDIST AND PHILOSOPHER

3 'From fanaticism to barbarism is only one step.'
ESSAI SUR LE MÉRITE DE LA VERTU *(1745)*

Dilke, Sir Charles Wentworth (1843–1911)
ENGLISH RADICAL POLITICIAN, MEMBER OF PARLIAMENT, 1868–1886, 1892–1911

4 'Russia is the one power which is a comet of eccentric orbit rather than a planet in the European system.'
THE PRESENT POSITION OF EUROPEAN POLITICS *(1887)*

Disraeli, Benjamin, 1st Earl of Beaconsfield (1804–1881)
ENGLISH CONSERVATIVE POLITICIAN AND NOVELIST, PRIME MINISTER, 1868 and 1874–1880

5 'The Continent will not suffer England to be the workshop of the world.'
House of Commons, 15 March 1838

6 'They have a starving population, an absentee aristocracy, and an alien Church, and, in addition, the weakest executive in the world. That is the Irish question. Well, what then would hon. Gentlemen say if they were reading of a country in that position? They would say at once, "The remedy is revolution". But the Irish cannot have a revolution; and why? Because Ireland is connected with another and more powerful country. Then what is the consequence? The connection with England thus becomes the cause of the present state of Ireland. If the connection with England prevents a revolution and a revolution is the only remedy, England logically is in the odious position of being the cause of all the misery of Ireland. What, then, is the duty of an English Minister? To effect by his policy all those changes which a revolution would effect by force. That is the Irish question in its integrity.'
House of Commons, 16 February 1844

7 'Conservatism discards Prescription, shrinks from Principle, disavows Progress; having rejected all respect for Antiquity, it offers no redress for the Present, and makes no preparation for the Future.'
CONINGSBY *(1844), Book II, Chapter 5. On Peelite Conservatism*

8 ' "A sound Conservative government," said Taper, musingly. "I understand: Tory men and Whig measures." '
IBID., *Book II, Chapter 6*

9 'The right hon. Gentleman caught the Whigs bathing, and walked away with their clothes.'
House of Commons, 28 February 1845. On the policies of Peel's government

10 'A Conservative Government is an organised hypocrisy.'
House of Commons, 17 March 1845. Denouncing the enlarged parliamentary grant to the Roman Catholic college at Maynooth

11 'If you are to have a popular Government – if you are to have a Parliamentary Administration, the conditions antecedent are, that you should have a Government which declares the principles upon which its policy is founded, and then you can have the wholesome check of a constitutional Opposition. What have we got instead? Something has risen up in this country as fatal in the political world as it has been in the landed world of Ireland – we have a great Parliamentary middleman. It is well known what a middleman is; he is a man who bamboozles one party and plunders the other.'
House of Commons, 11 April 1845. Attacking Peel's government

1 'He [Peel] is so vain that he wants to figure in history as the settler of all the great questions; but a Parliamentary constitution is not favourable to such ambitions: things must be done by parties, not by persons using parties as tools.'
Letter to Lord John Manners, 17 December 1845. On Peel's willingness to repeal the Corn Laws

2 'Two nations between whom there is no intercourse and no sympathy; who are as ignorant of each other's habits, thoughts and feelings, as if they were dwellers in different zones or inhabitants of different planets . . . the rich and the poor.'
SYBIL *(1845), Book II, Chapter 5*

3 'I was told that the Privileged and the People formed two nations.'
IBID., *Book IV, Chapter 8*

4 'Above all, maintain the line of demarcation between parties; for it is only by maintaining the independence of party that you can maintain the integrity of public men, and the power and influence of Parliament itself.'
House of Commons, 22 January 1846

5 'His life has been a great appropriation clause. He is a burglar of others' intellect. Search the Index of Beatson from the days of the Conqueror to the termination of the last reign, there is no statesman who has committed political petty larceny on so great a scale.'
House of Commons, 17 May 1846. Of Peel

6 'A precedent embalms a principle.'
House of Commons, 22 February 1848. (Perhaps borrowing from Lord Stowell, to whom the phrase has been attributed.)

7 'These wretched Colonies will all be independent, too, in a few years, and are a millstone round our necks.'
Letter to Lord Malmesbury, 13 August 1852

8 'I know what I have to face. I have to face a coalition. The combination may be successful. A coalition before this has been successful. But coalitions, although successful, have found this, that their triumph has been brief. This, too, I know, that England does not love coalitions.'
House of Commons, 16 December 1852. On the opposition to his budget proposals

9 'In ninety-nine cases out of a hundred, when there is a quarrel between two states, it is generally occasioned by some blunder of a ministry.'
House of Commons, 19 February 1858

10 'Finality is not the language of politics.'
House of Commons, 28 February 1859

11 'It will, generally, be found, that all great political questions end in the tenure of Land. What is the nature of that tenure is the first question a Statesman should ask himself, when forming an opinion on public events.'
Fragment of reminiscence, 1860

12 'Colonies do not cease to be colonies because they are independent.'
House of Commons, 5 February 1863

13 'Party is organised opinion.'
Speech at Oxford, 25 November 1864

14 'I trust that the time may never come when the love of fame shall cease to be the sovereign passion of our public men.'
House of Commons, February 1866

15 'Power and influence we should exercise in Asia; consequently in Eastern Europe, consequently also in Western Europe; but what is the use of these colonial deadweights which *we do not govern* . . . Leave the Canadians to defend themselves; recall the African squadron; give up the settlements on the west coast of Africa; and we shall make a saving which will, at the same time, enable us to build ships and have a good Budget. What is more, we shall have accomplished something definite, tangible, for the good of the country.'
Letter to Lord Derby, 30 September 1866

16 'I had to prepare the mind of the country, and to educate – if it be not arrogant to use such a phrase – to educate our Party. It is a large Party, and requires its attention to be called to questions of this kind with some pressure.'
Speech at a Conservative dinner at Edinburgh, 29 October 1867. On the 1867 reform act

17 'A great scholar and a great wit, 300 years ago, said that, in his opinion, there was a great mistake in the Vulgate, which, as you all know, is the Latin translation of the Holy Scriptures, and that, instead of saying "Vanity of vanities, all is vanity" – *Vanitas*

vanitatum, omnia vanitas – the wise and witty king really said: *Sanitas sanitatum, omnia sanitas.* Gentlemen, it is impossible to overrate the importance of the subject. After all, the first consideration of a Minister should be the health of the people.'
Speech at Manchester, 3 April 1872

1 'As I sat opposite the Treasury Bench, the Ministers reminded me of one of those marine landscapes not very unusual on the coasts of South America. You behold a range of exhausted volcanoes. Not a flame flickers on a single pallid chest. But the situation is still very dangerous. There are occasional earthquakes, and ever and anon the dark rumbling of the sea.'
IBID. *Of Gladstone's government*

2 'The Tory party, unless it is a national party, is nothing.'
Speech to the National Union at the Crystal Palace, Sydenham, 24 June 1872

3 'Permissive legislation is the characteristic of a free people.'
House of Commons, 18 June 1875

4 'I am dead; dead, but in the Elysian fields.'
To a friend, 1876. Quoted in R Blake, DISRAELI, *Chapter 24. On being welcomed into the House of Lords*

5 'Lord Salisbury and myself have brought you back peace – but a peace, I hope, with honour.'
House of Lords, 16 July 1878. After signing the Treaty of Berlin
SEE ALSO *Russell, John, 1st Earl*

6 'What we call public opinion is generally public sentiment.'
House of Lords, 3 August 1880

7 'There are several places which are called the keys of India. There is Merv – then there is a place whose name I forget; there is Ghuzni, there is Balkh, there is Kandahar. But, my Lords, the key of India is not Nerat or Kandahar. The key of India is London.'
House of Lords, 4 March 1881

8 'The British People, being subject to fogs and possessing a powerful Middle Class, require grave statesmen.'
Quoted in R Blake, 'The Rise of Disraeli', ESSAYS IN BRITISH HISTORY PRESENTED TO SIR KEITH FEILING

9 'It is not becoming in any minister to decry party who has risen by party. We should always remember that if we were not partisans we should not be ministers.'
Quoted in W L Guttsmann, THE BRITISH POLITICAL ELITE, *Chapter 8*

10 'I am much misunderstood; my forte is revolution.'
In conversation with William Johnson Fox. Quoted in M Foot, DEBTS OF HONOUR, *Chapter 3*

Djilas, Milovan (1911–)
YUGOSLAV POLITICAL LEADER AND WRITER

11 'The *dominant* streak in Lenin's character and political practice was a ruthless will to coerce, dictate and subjugate. Stalin's terror and Stalin's tyranny are unmistakably foreshadowed by Leninism.'
Interview with George Urban, ENCOUNTER, *December 1979*

12 'The terrible thing is that one cannot be a communist and *not* let oneself in for the shameful act of recantation. One cannot be a Communist and preserve an iota of one's personal integrity.'
IBID.

Donnelly, Ignatius (1831–1901)
AMERICAN WRITER AND POLITICIAN, CO-FOUNDER OF THE POPULIST PARTY

13 'The Democratic Party is like a mule. It has neither pride of ancestry nor hope of posterity.'
Speech to the Minnesota state legislature, 13 September 1860

Dostoevsky, Fyodor (1821–1881)
RUSSIAN NOVELIST

14 'Tyranny is a habit; it may develop, and it does develop at last, into a disease.'
THE HOUSE OF THE DEAD *(1862), Part II, Chapter 3*

15 'All "direct" persons and men of action are active just because they are stupid and limited. How explain that? I will tell you: in consequence of their limitation they take immediate and secondary causes for primary ones, and in that way persuade themselves more quickly and easily than other people do that they

have found an infallible foundation for their activity.'
NOTES FROM THE UNDERGROUND *(1864), Part I, Chapter 5*

1 'The only gain of civilisation for mankind is the greatest capacity for variety of sensations – and absolutely nothing more. And through the development of this many-sidedness man may come to finding enjoyment in bloodshed. In fact, this has already happened to him.'
IBID., *Part I, Chapter 7*

Douglas, Thomas (1904–)
CANADIAN POLITICIAN, LEADER OF THE NEW DEMOCRATIC PARTY, 1961–1971

2 'The Liberals talk about a stable government, but we don't know how bad the stable is going to smell.'
Election speech, October 1965

Douglass, Frederick
(c. 1817–1895)
AMERICAN ABOLITIONIST

3 'He who would be free must strike the first blow.'
MY BONDAGE AND MY FREEDOM *(1855)*

4 'No man can put a chain about the ankle of his fellow man without at last finding the other end fastened about his own neck.'
Speech at Washington, 22 October 1883

Dryden, John (1631–1700)
ENGLISH POET

5 'For Polititians neither love nor hate.'
ABSALOM AND ACHITOPHEL *(1681)*

6 'If not; the People have a Right Supreme
To make their Kings; for Kings are made for them.
All Empire is no more than Pow'r in Trust,
Which when resum'd, can be no longer Just.'
IBID.

7 'Yet, grant our Lords the People, Kings can make,
What Prudent man a settled Throne would shake?
For whatsoe'r their Sufferings were before,
That Change they Covet makes them suffer more.
All other Errors but disturb a State;

But Innovation is the Blow of Fate.
If ancient Fabricks nod, and threat to fall,
To Patch the Flaws, and Buttress up the Wall,
Thus far 'tis Duty; but here fix the Mark.
For all beyond it is to touch our Ark.
To change Foundations, cast the Frame anew,
Is work for Rebels who base Ends pursue:
At once Divine and Humane Laws controul;
And mend the Parts by ruine of the Whole.'
IBID.

8 'Kings are the publick Pillars of the State,
Born to sustain and prop the Nations weight.'
IBID.

9 'Gull'd with a Patriots name, whose Modern sense
Is one that would by Law supplant his Prince:
The Peoples Brave, the Politicians Tool;
Never was Patriot yet, but was a Fool.'
IBID.

10 'What Polititian yet e'er scap't his Fate,
Who saving his own Neck not sav'd the State?'
THE SECOND PART OF ABSALOM AND ACHITOPHEL *(1682)*

11 'When Men will, needlessly, their Freedom barter
For lawless Pow'r, sometimes they catch a Tartar.'
PROLOGUE TO THE KING AND QUEEN *(1683)*

Dubček, Alexander (1921–)
CZECHOSLOVAK POLITICIAN, FIRST SECRETARY OF THE COMMUNIST PARTY, 1968–1969

12 'Give socialism back its human face.'
Slogan used frequently in 1968. (The phrase was first suggested to Dubček, by Radovan Richta in a private conversation.)

13 'We wish to meet people's longing for a society in which they can feel human among human beings. This active, humane, integrating quality of socialism, a society without antagonisms, is what we want to realise systematically and gradually.'
Speech to the central committee of the Czechoslovak Communist party, 1 April 1968

Dulles, John Foster (1888–1959)
AMERICAN REPUBLICAN POLITICIAN,
SECRETARY OF STATE, 1953–1959

1 'I dislike isolation, but I prefer it to
identification with a senseless repetition
of the cyclical struggle between the
dynamic and the static forces of the
world ... Were we to act now, it would
be to reaffirm an international order
which by its very nature is self-
destructive and a breeder of violent revolt
... I hear the same talk about "sanctity
of treaties", "law and order", "resisting
aggression" and "enforcement of
morality". Such phrases have always
been the stock in trade of those who
have vested interests which they want to
preserve against those in revolt against a
rigid system.'
Speech at Detroit, 29 Ocotber 1939.
Opposing American entry into the
Second World War

2 'You see before you the former future
Secretary of State.'
To CBS correspondent, David Schoenbrun,
November 1948. Quoted in L Mosley,
DULLES, *Chapter 13. On failing to become*
secretary of state when Thomas Dewey
lost the 1948 presidential election to
Harry Truman

3 'You have to take chances for peace, just
as you must take chances in war. Some
say that we were brought to the verge of
war. The ability to get to the verge of
war without getting into the war is the
necessary art. If you cannot master it,
you inevitably get into wars. If you try to
run away from it, if you are scared to go
to the brink, you are lost. We've had to
look it square in the face – on the
question of enlarging the Korean War, on
the question of getting into the Indo-
China war, on the question of Formosa.
We walked to the brink and we looked it
in the face.'
Interview in LIFE *magazine, 11 January*
1956

Dunning, John, 1st Baron
Ashburton (1731–1783)
ENGLISH POLITICIAN, MEMBER OF
PARLIAMENT, 1768–1782

4 'The influence of the Crown has
increased, is increasing, and ought to be
diminished.'
House of Commons, 6 April 1780

E

Eden, Anthony, 1st Earl of Avon (1897–1977)
ENGLISH CONSERVATIVE POLITICIAN, PRIME MINISTER, 1955–1957

1 'We have not got democratic government today. We have never had it and I venture to suggest to Honourable Members opposite that we shall never have it. What we have done in all the progress of reform and evolution is to broaden the basis of oligarchy.'
House of Commons, 1928. Quoted in R Crossman, THE CHARM OF POLITICS, *'Two Pictures of Anthony Eden'*

2 'There were two kinds of sanctions, effective and ineffective. To apply the latter was provocative and useless. If we were to apply the former, we ran the risk of war, and it would be dangerous to shut our eyes to the fact.'
FACING THE DICTATORS *(1962), Book II, Chapter 11. Reporting his conversation of 5 November 1937, with Norman Davis, President Roosevelt's envoy, about American policy towards Japan*

Edward I (1239–1307)
KING OF ENGLAND, 1272–1307

3 'What touches all shall be approved by all.' *(Quod omnes tangit ab omnibus approbetur.)*
Statement to the Model Parliament, 1295

Edward VIII (1894–1972)
KING OF GREAT BRITAIN AND NORTHERN IRELAND, 1936

4 'Something ought to be done to find these people employment ... Something will be done.'
Speech on a visit to South Wales, 18 November 1936

Ehrenburg, Ilya (1891–1967)
RUSSIAN WRITER

5 'It would be too much to say that I liked Stalin, but for a long time I believed in him and I feared him. When I talked about him, I, like everybody else, called him "the Boss". In the same way the Jews in the past never pronounced the name of God.'
Quoted by George Urban, ENCOUNTER, *November 1981*

Eisenhower, Dwight (1890–1969)
AMERICAN GENERAL AND REPUBLICAN POLITICIAN, PRESIDENT, 1953–1961

6 'Every gun that is fired, every warship launched, every rocket fired signifies, in the final sense, a theft from those who hunger and are not fed, those who are cold and are not clothed. The world in arms is not spending money alone. It is spending the sweat of its labourers, the genius of its scientists, the hopes of its children.'
Speech to the American Society of Newspaper Editors, Washington, April 1953

7 'You have a row of dominoes set up. You knock over the first one, and what will happen to the last one is a certainty that it will go over very quickly.'
Press conference, 7 April 1954. On the strategic importance of Indochina

8 'In the council of government we must guard against the acquisition of unwanted influence, whether sought or unsought, by the military-industrial complex. The potential for the disastrous rise of misplaced power exists and will persist. We must never let the weight of this combination endanger our liberties or democratic processes. We should take nothing for granted. Only an alert and knowledgeable citizenry can compel the proper meshing of the huge industrial and military machinery of defence with our peaceful methods and goals so that security and liberty may prosper together.'
Farewell address on television, 17 January 1961

Eliot, T(homas) S(tearns), (1888–1965)
AMERICAN-BORN ENGLISH POET AND CRITIC

9 'A democracy in which everybody had an equal responsibility in everything would be oppressive for the conscientious and licentious for the rest.'
NOTES TOWARDS THE DEFINITION OF CULTURE *(1948), Chapter 2*

10 'I do not approve the extermination of the enemy; the policy of exterminating or, as it is barbarously said, liquidating

enemies, is one of the most alarming developments of modern war and peace, from the point of view of those who desire the survival of culture. One needs the enemy.'
IBID., *Chapter 3*

1 'Numerous cross-divisions favour peace within a nation, by dispersing and confusing animosities; they favour peace between nations, by giving every man enough antagonism at home to exercise all his aggressiveness ... A nation which has gradations of class seems to me, other things being equal, likely to be more tolerant and pacific than one which is not so organised.'
IBID.

Elizabeth I (1533–1603)
QUEEN OF ENGLAND, 1558–1603

2 'My loving people, we have been persuaded by some that are careful of our safety, to take heed how we commit ourselves to armed multitudes, for fear of treachery ... Let tyrants fear. I have always so behaved myself that, under God, I have placed my chiefest strength and safeguard in the loyal hearts and good will of my subjects; and therefore I am come amongst you, as you see, at this time, not for my recreation and disport, but being resolved, in the midst and heat of the battle, to live or die amongst you all, to lay down for my God, and for my kingdom, and for my people, my honour and my blood, even in the dust. I know I have the body of a weak and feeble woman, but I have the heart and stomach of a king, and of a king of England too.'
Speech to the army at Tilbury, 8 August 1588

Elliott, Ebenezer (1781–1849)
ENGLISH PAMPHLETEER AND POET

3 'What is a communist? One who hath yearnings
For equal division of unequal earnings.'
'Epigram', POETICAL WORKS *(1840)*

Emerson, Ralph Waldo (1803–1882)
AMERICAN ESSAYIST AND POET

4 'A sect or party is an elegant incognito devised to save a man from the vexation of thinking.'
JOURNALS *(1831)*

5 'People say law, but they mean wealth.'
IBID.

6 'Every reform was once a private opinion, and when it shall be private opinion again, it will solve the problem of the age.'
ESSAYS: FIRST SERIES *(1841)*, *'History'*

7 'Conservatism goes for comfort, reform for truth.'
Lecture at Boston, 9 May 1841, 'The Conservatives'

8 'Men are conservatives when they are least vigorous, or when they are most luxurious. They are conservatives after dinner.'
ESSAYS: SECOND SERIES *(1844)*, *'New England Reformers'*

9 'Every actual State is corrupt. Good men must not obey the laws too well. What satire on government can equal the severity of censure conveyed in the word *politic*, which now for ages has signified cunning, intimating that the State is a trick?'
ESSAYS: SECOND SERIES *(1844)*, *'Politics'*

10 'Democracy becomes a government of bullies tempered by editors.'
JOURNALS *(1846)*
SEE ALSO *Carlyle*

Engels, Friedrich (1820–1895)
GERMAN POLITICAL ECONOMIST

11 'The earth is the first condition of our existence. To make it an object of trade was the last step towards making human beings an object of trade. To buy and sell land is an immorality surpassed only by the immorality of selling oneself into slavery.'
OUTLINES OF A CRITIQUE OF POLITICAL ECONOMY *(1844)*

12 'If trade unionists failed to register their protest by striking, their silence would be regarded as an admission that they acquiesced in the pre-eminence of economic forces over human welfare. Such acquiescence would be a recognition of the right of the middle classes to exploit the workers when business was flourishing and to let the workers go hungry when business was slack.'
THE CONDITION OF THE WORKING CLASS IN ENGLAND IN 1844 *(1845)*, *Chapter 9*

13 ' "The removal of all social and political inequalities" is a very dubious phrase with which to replace "the removal of all

class distinctions". There will always be *certain* inequalities in the standard of life in different countries, provinces and places. They can be reduced to a minimum, but they can never be removed . . . The notion that a socialist society is a society of *equals* is a biased French idea inherited from the old revolutionary slogan: "Liberty, equality, fraternity" . . . the idea of equality should now be regarded as out of date since it leads only to confusion and hampers a precise examination of the problem.'
Letter to August Bebel, 28 March 1875. On a passage in the Gotha programme

1 'The first act in which the state really comes forward as the representative of society as a whole – the taking possession of the means of production in the name of society – is at the same time its last independent act as a state . . . The state is not "abolished", it withers away.'
ANTI-DÜHRING *(1878)*

2 'Force . . . in the words of Marx . . . is the midwife of every old society which is pregnant with the new.'
IBID.

3 'In England a real, democratic party is impossible unless it be a working man's party.'
LABOUR STANDARD, *23 July 1881, 'A Working Man's Party'*

4 'According to the materialist conception of history, the production and reproduction of real life constitutes in the *last instance* the determining factor of history. Neither Marx nor I ever maintained more. Now, when someone comes along and distorts this to mean that the economic factor is the *sole* determining factor he is converting the former proposition into a meaningless, abstract, and absurd phrase. The economic system is the basis, but the various factors of the superstructure, the political forms of the class struggles and their results – constitutions, etc., established by victorious classes after hard-won battles, legal forms, and even the reflexes of all those real struggles in the brain of the participants, political, judicial, philosophical theories, religious conceptions which have been developed into systematic dogmas – all these exercise an influence upon the course of

historical struggles and in many cases determine for the most part their form.'
Letter to J Bloch, 21 September 1890

5 'The state is nothing but an instrument of oppression of one class by another – no less so in a democratic republic than in a monarchy.'
Preface to the 1891 edition of Marx's THE CIVIL WAR IN FRANCE
SEE ALSO *Marx*

6 'Dictatorship of the Proletariat. Well and good, gentlemen, do you want to know what this dictatorship looks like? Look at the Paris Commune. That was the Dictatorship of the Proletariat.'
IBID.

7 'These two great dicoveries, the materialistic conception of history and the revelation of the secret of capitalistic production through surplus-value, we owe to Marx. With these discoveries socialism becomes a science.'
SOCIALISM, UTOPIAN AND SCIENTIFIC *(1892)*

8 'An ounce of action is worth a ton of theory.'
Quoted in R Groves, THE STRANGE CASE OF VICTOR GRAYSON, *Chapter 2*

Erasmus, Desiderius (c. 1466–1536)
DUTCH HUMANIST AND THEOLOGIAN

9 'We must everywhere take care never to speak or act arrogantly or in a party spirit: this I believe is pleasing to the spirit of Christ. Meanwhile we must preserve our minds from being seduced by anger, hatred or ambition; these feelings are apt to lie in wait for us in the midst of our striving after piety.'
Letter to Martin Luther, 30 May 1519

10 'You are a man, as you write, of violent temperament, and you take pleasure in this remarkable argument. Why, then, did you not pour forth this marvellous piece of invective on the Bishop of Rochester or on Cochleus? . . . But it does not matter what happens to us two, least of all to myself who must shortly go hence, even if the whole world were applauding us: it is *this* that distresses me, and all the best spirits with me, that with the arrogant, impudent, seditious temperament of yours you are shattering the whole globe in ruinous discord, exposing good men and lovers of good

learning to certain frenzied Pharisees, arming for revolt the wicked and the revolutionary, and in short so carrying on the cause of the Gospel as to throw all things sacred and profane into chaos . . . I know not whom you have saved from the power of darkness; but you should have drawn the sword of your pen against those ungrateful wretches and not against a temperate disputation. I would have wished you a better mind, were you not so delighted with your own. Wish me what you will, only not your mind, unless God has changed it for you.'
Letter to Luther, 11 April 1526. After Luther, in reply to Erasmus' tract on free will, DE LIBERO ARBITRIO, *had published a defence of determinism,* DE SERVO ARBITRIO

F

Falkland, 2nd Viscount (Lucius Cary) (c. 1610–1643)
ENGLISH POLITICIAN AND POET

1 'When it is not necessary to change, it is necessary not to change.'
House of Commons, 22 November 1641

Fanon, Frantz (1925–1961)
MARTINIQUE-BORN FRENCH WRITER

2 'The native intellectual had learned from his masters that the individual ought to express himself fully. The colonialist bourgeoisie had hammered into the native's mind the idea of a society of individuals where each person shuts himself up in his own subjectivity, and whose only wealth is individual thought. Now the native who has the opportunity to return to the people during the struggle for freedom will discover the falseness of this theory. The very forms of organisation of the struggle will suggest to him a different vocabulary. Brother, sister, friend – these are the words outlawed by the colonialist bourgeoisie, because for them my brother is my purse, my friend is part of my scheme for getting on.'
THE WRETCHED OF THE EARTH *(1961)*, *Chapter 1*

3 'Violence is man re-creating himself.'
IBID.

Farley, James (1888–1976)
AMERICAN DEMOCRATIC POLITICIAN

4 'As Maine goes, so goes Vermont.'
Remark on election day, November 1936. Maine and Vermont were the only two states not won by President Roosevelt

Fawkes, Guy (1570–1606)
ENGLISH CONSPIRATOR

5 'A desperate disease requires a dangerous remedy.'
To James I, in Council, 5 November 1605. (After Hippocrates.) On the gunpowder plot to blow up the houses of parliament

Fayau, Joseph-Pierre (1766–1799)
FRENCH REVOLUTIONARY LEADER

6 'As for me, I think anyone, whoever he may be, who has done nothing for liberty, or has not done all he could, deserves to be counted an enemy to it.'
Speech to the National Convention, 26 November 1793

Feuerbach, Ludwig (1804–1872)
GERMAN PHILOSOPHER

7 'The heart makes a revolution, the head a reformation.'
Quoted in R Seton-Watson, MASARYK IN ENGLAND, *Chapter 1*

Fielding, Henry (1707–1754)
ENGLISH NOVELIST AND POLITICAL JOURNALIST

8 'Patriot – A candidate for place.
Politics – The art of getting one.'
THE COVENT GARDEN JOURNAL, *No. 3. Of the 'patriot' party*

Filmer, Sir Robert (c. 1590–1653)
ENGLISH POLITICAL THEORIST

9 'Men are not born free, and therefore could never have the liberty to choose either Governors, or Forms of Government. Princes have their Power Absolute, and by Divine Right, for Slaves could never have a Right to Compact or Consent. Adam was an absolute Monarch, and so are all Princes ever since.'
PATRIARCHA: OR THE NATURAL POWER OF KINGS ASSERTED *(1680)*

Fisher, H(erbert) A(lbert) L(aurens) (1865–1940)
ENGLISH HISTORIAN AND LIBERAL POLITICIAN, MEMBER OF PARLIAMENT, 1916–1926

10 'Go in now while you are young . . . Whether you succeed or fail does not matter. It is the life which matters.'
In conversation with Richard Crossman. Quoted in Crossman, THE CHARM OF POLITICS, *'Amery and Fisher' (reprinted from the* NEW STATESMAN AND NATION, *1947). Advice given to Crossman on whether he should try to enter parliament*

Fonblanque, Albany (1793–1872)
ENGLISH JOURNALIST

1 'A Prime Minister's position brings meanness to his feet, which he must not mistake for the world's stratum.'
Obituary of Lord Melbourne, 1848

Foot, Michael (1913–)
ENGLISH POLITICIAN, LEADER OF THE LABOUR PARTY, 1980–83

2 'Men of power have no time to read; yet the men who do not read are unfit for power.'
DEBTS OF HONOUR *(1980)*

Forster, E(dward) M(organ) (1879–1970)
ENGLISH NOVELIST

3 'So Two cheers for Democracy: One because it admits variety and two because it permits criticism. Two cheers are quite enough: there is no occasion to give three. Only Love the Beloved Republic deserves that.'
TWO CHEERS FOR DEMOCRACY *(1951)*

Foster, Sir George (1847–1931)
CANADIAN LIBERAL-CONSERVATIVE POLITICIAN

4 'He would read the signs of the times not aright, in these somewhat troublesome days when the great Mother Empire stands splendidly isolated in Europe ... who did not feel ... that the country's weal, the country's progress, the country's stability, all of the country's pride and joy must base itself upon the strong arms and willing loyal hearts of the citizenship of that Empire.'
Speech to the Canadian House of Commons, 16 January 1896

Fox, Charles James (1749–1806)
ENGLISH WHIG POLITICIAN, MEMBER OF PARLIAMENT, 1768–1806

5 'He [Pitt] says he is no party man, and he abhors a systematic opposition. I have always acknowledged myself to be a party man; I have always acted with a party in whose principles I have confidence; and if I had such an opinion of any ministry as the gentleman professes to have of us, I would pursue their overthrow by a systematic opposition. I have done so more than

once; and I think that, in succeeding, I saved my country.'
House of Commons, 1 December 1783

6 'I will not barter English commerce for Irish slavery.'
House of Commons, 30 May 1785. Opposing Pitt's proposals for free trade with Ireland

7 'The worst of revolutions is a restoration.'
House of Commons, 10 December 1785

8 'No human government has a right to enquire into private opinions, to presume that it knows them, or to act on that presumption. Men are the best judges of the consequences of their own opinions, and how far they are likely to influence their actions; and it is most unnatural and tyrannical to say, "As you think, so must you act. I will collect the evidence of your future conduct from what I know to be your opinions".'
House of Commons, 8 May 1789. Speaking in favour of the repeal of the Test and Corporation Acts

9 'How much the greatest event it is that ever happened in the World! & how much the best!'
Letter to Richard Fitzpatrick, 30 July 1789. On the fall of the Bastille

10 'Opinions become dangerous to a state only when persecution makes it necessary for the people to communicate their ideas under the bond of secrecy.'
House of Commons, May 1797. Advocating the repeal of the Treason and Sedition acts

France, Anatole (1844–1924)
FRENCH NOVELIST AND CRITIC

11 'To die for an idea is to place a pretty high price upon conjectures.'
THE REVOLT OF THE ANGELS *(1914)*

12 'The vice most fatal to the statesman is virtue.'
Quoted by Frank Johnson in THE TIMES, *15 May 1981*

Franco, Francisco (1892–1975)
SPANISH GENERAL AND DICTATOR, 1939–1975

13 'We are the spiritual reserve of the western world.'
Interview at the end of the film, ESE HOMBRE *(1964)*

Franklin, Benjamin (1706–1790)
AMERICAN REVOLUTIONARY LEADER, SCIENTIST AND WRITER

1 'They that give up their essential liberty to obtain a little temporary safety deserve neither liberty nor safety.'
HISTORICAL REVIEW OF PENNSYLVANIA *(1759)*

2 'There are some Persons besides the Americans so amazingly stupid, as to distinguish in this Dispute [between the colonies and Great Britain] between *Power* and *Right*, as tho' the former did not always imply the latter.'
The PUBLIC ADVERTISER *(London), 26 January 1766*

3 'You may reduce their Cities to Ashes; but the Flame of Liberty in North America shall not be extinguished . . . A great Country of hardy Peasants is not to be subdued.'
The PUBLIC ADVERTISER, *2 April 1774. On the British government's closing of the port of Boston*

4 'Yes, we must all hang together, or most assuredly we shall all hang separately.'
Remark made at the signing of the Declaration of Independence, 4 July 1776. In reply to John Hancock's remark that the revolutionaries must be unanimous in their action

5 'There never was a good war, or a bad peace.'
Letter to Josiah Quincy, 11 September 1783

6 'Our Constitution is in actual operation; everything appears to promise that it will last; but in this world nothing can be said to be certain, except death and taxes.'
Letter to Jean Baptiste le Roy, 13 November 1789

Frederick II (Frederick the Great) (1712–1786)
KING OF PRUSSIA, 1740–1786

7 'All religions must be tolerated . . . every man must get to heaven in his own way.'
RE THE CATHOLIC SCHOOLS *(1740)*

8 'The possession of battle-ready troops, a well-filled state treasury and a lively disposition: these were the real reasons which moved me to war.'
Draft (1741) A HISTORY OF MY TIMES. *On the seizure, in 1740, of Silesia from Austria*

9 'Diplomacy without armaments is like music without instruments.'
Quoted in G P Gooch, STUDIES IN DIPLOMACY AND STATECRAFT

Frere, John Hookham (1769–1846)
ENGLISH MAN OF LETTERS AND POLITICIAN, MEMBER OF PARLIAMENT, 1796–1802

10 'A Conservative is only a Tory who is ashamed of himself.'
In conversation, c. 1835

Freud, Sigmund (1856–1939)
AUSTRIAN PSYCHOANALYST

11 'Human life in common is only made possible when a majority comes together which is stronger than any separate individual and which remains united against all separate individuals. The power of this community is then set up as "right" in opposition to the power of the individual, which is condemned as "brute force". This replacement of the power of the individual by the power of a community constitutes the decisive step of civilisation . . . A good part of the struggles of mankind centres on the single task of finding an expedient accommodation – one, that is, that will bring happiness – between this claim of the individual and the cultural claims of the group; and one of the problems that touches the fate of humanity is whether such an accommodation can be reached by means of some particular form of civilisation or whether this conflict is irreconcilable.'
CIVILISATION AND ITS DISCONTENTS *(1930), Chapter 3*

Friedman, Milton (1912–   )
AMERICAN ECONOMIST

12 'History suggests that capitalism is a necessary condition for political freedom. Clearly it is not a sufficient condition.'
CAPITALISM AND FREEDOM *(1962), Chapter 1*

13 'The kind of economic organization that provides economic freedom directly, namely, competitive capitalism, also promotes political freedom because it separates economic power from political power and in this way enables the one to offset the other.'
IBID.

1 'Five simple truths embody most of what we know about inflation:
1. Inflation is a monetary phenomenon arising from a more rapid increase in the quantity of money than in output (though, of course, the reasons for the increase in money may be various).
2. In today's world Government determines – or can determine – the quantity of money.
3. There is only one cure for inflation: a slower rate of increase in the quantity of money.
4. It takes time – measured in years, not months – for inflation to develop; it takes time for inflation to be cured.
5. Unpleasant side effects of the cure are unavoidable.'
FREE TO CHOOSE: A PERSONAL STATEMENT *(with Rose Friedman), 1980*

Frost, David (1939–)
ENGLISH TELEVISION INTERVIEWER AND PRESENTER

2 'Vote Labour and you build castles in the air. Vote Conservative and you can live in them.'
On the BBC television programme, 'That Was The Year That Was', 31 December 1962. Suggested slogan for the next general election

Fulbright, (James) William (1905–)
AMERICAN DEMOCRATIC POLITICIAN, SENATOR, 1945-1975

3 'A democracy can recover quickly from physical or economic disaster, but when its moral convictions weaken it becomes easy prey for the demagogue and the charlatan. Tyranny and oppression then become the order of the day.'
Speech to the senate, 27 March 1951

4 'We must dare to think about "unthinkable things", because when things become "unthinkable", thinking stops and action becomes mindless. If we are to disabuse ourselves of old myths and to act wisely and creatively upon the new realities of our time, we must think about our problems with perfect freedom.'
Speech to the senate, 25 March 1964

5 'In a democracy dissent is an act of faith. Like medicine, the test of its value is not in its taste, but its effects.'
Speech to the senate, 21 April 1966

6 'Power tends to confuse itself with virtue and a great nation is peculiarly susceptible to the idea that its power is a sign of God's favor ... Once imbued with the idea of a mission, a great nation easily assumes that it has the means as well as the duty to do God's work.'
IBID.

7 'Past experience provides little basis for confidence that reason can prevail in an atmosphere of mounting war fever. In a contest between a hawk and a dove the hawk has a great advantage, not because it is a better bird, but because it is a bigger bird with lethal talons and a highly developed will to use them.'
IBID.

8 'The citizen who criticizes his country is paying it an implied tribute.'
Speech to the American Newspaper Publishers Association, 28 April 1966

Fuller, Thomas (1654-1734)
ENGLISH PHYSICIAN

9 'Lean liberty is better than fat slavery.'
GNOMOLOGIA *(1732)*

G

Gaitskell, Hugh (1906-1963)
ENGLISH POLITICIAN, LEADER OF THE
LABOUR PARTY, 1955-1963

1 'We, as middle-class socialists, have got to
have a profound humility. Though it's a
funny way of putting it, we've got to
know that we lead them because they
can't do it without us, with our abilities,
and yet we must feel humble to working
people. Now that's all right for us upper
middle class, but Tony [Crosland] and
Roy [Jenkins] are not upper, and I
sometimes feel they don't have proper
humility to working people.'
In conversation with Richard Crossman,
August 1959

2 'It is not in dispute that the vast majority
of Labour Members of Parliament are
utterly opposed to unilateralism and
neutralism. So what do you expect them
to do? Change their minds overnight? ...
There are other people too, not in
Parliament, in the Party, who share our
convictions. What sort of people do you
think they are? What sort of people do
you think we are? Do you think we can
simply accept a decision of this kind? Do
you think that we can become overnight
the pacifists, unilateralists and fellow
travellers that other people are? ... There
are some of us, Mr Chairman, who will
fight and fight again to save the Party we
love.'
Speech to the Labour party annual
conference, 5 October 1960. After the
conference had passed a resolution in
favour of unilateral nuclear disarmament

3 'The "sick man of Europe" today, we
shall become the poor relation tomorrow.'
Speech to the Labour party annual
conference, October 1961

4 'It does mean, if this is the idea, the end
of Britain as an independent European
state ... it means the end of a thousand
years of history.'
Speech to the Labour party annual
conference, 3 October 1962. On the
proposal that Great Britain join the
European Economic Community

Galbraith, J(ohn) K(enneth)
(1908 –   )
CANADIAN – BORN AMERICAN
ECONOMIST

5 'In the usual (though certainly not in
every) public decision on economic
policy, the choice is between courses that
are almost equally good or equally bad. It
is the narrowest decisions that are most
ardently debated. If the world is lucky
enough to enjoy peace, it may even one
day make the discovery, to the horror of
doctrinaire free-enterprisers and
doctrinaire planners alike, that what is
called capitalism and what is called
socialism are both capable of working
quite well.'
'The American Economy: its Substance
and Myth' (1949)

6 'There is nothing fortuitous about the
tendency for power to beget
countervailing power; it is organic.
However it does not work evenly. The
buttressing of weak bargaining positions
has become, as a result, one of the most
important of the functions of
government.'
IBID.

7 'Of all the mysteries of the stock
exchange there is none so impenetrable
as why there should be a buyer for
everyone who seeks to sell.'
THE GREAT CRASH, 1929 *(1955), Chapter 6*

8 'An occasional strike is an indication that
countervailing power is being employed
in a sound context where the costs of any
wage increase cannot readily be passed
along to someone else. It should be an
occasion for mild rejoicing in the
conservative press. The *Daily Worker*,
eagerly contemplating the downfall of
capitalism, should regret this
manifestation of the continued health of
the system.'
AMERICAN CAPITALISM *(1957 edition),*
Chapter 9

9 'In an atmosphere of private opulence
and public squalor, the private goods
have full sway.'
THE AFFLUENT SOCIETY *(1958), Chapter 18*

10 'Clearly the most unfortunate people are
those who must do the same thing over
and over again, every minute, or perhaps
twenty to the minute. They deserve the
shortest hours and the highest pay.'
MADE TO LAST *(1964), Chapter 4*

Galsworthy, John (1867-1933)
ENGLISH NOVELIST AND PLAYWRIGHT

11 'There is just one rule for politicians all
over the world: Don't say in Power what

you say in Opposition; if you do, you only have to carry out what the other fellows have found impossible.'
MAID IN WAITING *(1931), Chapter 7*

Gambetta, Léon (1838–1882)
FRENCH RADICAL POLITICIAN, PRIME MINISTER, 1881–1882

1 'I have never been a subscriber to this vague and deceptive theory of a Republican United States of Europe ... I absolutely reject this theory as fatal for the regeneration of France, false as matter of general history, and dangerous for democracy and the freedom of the world.'
Letter to Gustave Naquet, 1871

2 'Had they not seen the workers of town and country, the working world to whom the future belongs make its entry into politics? Did not their entry give notice that, after having tried many forms of government, the country was turning to another social stratum in order to experiment with the Republican form? Yes, I foresee, I feel, I announce the coming and the presence in politics of a new social stratum.'
Speech at Grenoble, 26 September 1872

3 'One is a politician only if one gets to the bottom of a subject ... politics is a matter for tact, study, observation and precision.'
Speech at Paris, February 1876

Gandhi, Mohandas Karamchand (1869–1948)
INDIAN NATIONALIST LEADER AND SOCIAL REFORMER

4 'So long as a minority conforms to the majority, it is not even a minority. They must throw in their whole weight in the opposite direction.'
INDIAN OPINION, *14 September 1907*

5 'As in law so in war, the longest purse finally wins.'
Paper read to the Bombay Provincial Cooperative Conference, 17 September 1917

6 'Victory attained by violence is tantamout to a defeat, for it is momentary.'
SATYAGRAHA LEAFLET NO. 13, *3 May 1919*

7 'Satyagraha differs from passive resistance as North Pole from South. The latter has been conceived as a weapon of the weak and does not include the use of physical force or violence for the purpose of gaining one's end, whereas the former has been conceived as a weapon of the strongest and excludes the use of violence in any shape or form.
The term satyagraha was coined by me in South Africa ... Its root meaning is holding on to truth, hence truth-force. I discovered in the earliest stages that pursuit of truth did not admit of violence being inflicted on one's opponent, but that he must be weaned from error by patience and sympathy.'
Evidence before the Disorders Inquiry Committee, Sabarmati, 5 January 1920

8 'Non-violence is the law of our species as violence is the law of the brute.'
YOUNG INDIA, *11 August 1920*

9 'I claim that in losing the spinning wheel we lost our left lung. We are, therefore, suffering from galloping consumption. The restoration of the wheel arrests the progress of the fell disease.'
YOUNG INDIA, *13 October 1921*

10 'A policy is a temporary creed liable to be changed, but while it holds good it has got to be pursued with apostolic zeal.'
Letter to the general secretary of the Congress party, 8 March 1922

11 'The willing sacrifice of the innocents is the most powerful retort to insolent tyranny that has yet been conceived by God or man.'
YOUNG INDIA, *12 February 1925*

12 'Passive resistance is an all-sided sword; it can be used anyhow; it blesses him who uses it and him against whom it is used without drawing a drop of blood; it produces far-reaching results. It never rusts and cannot be stolen. Competition between passive resisters does not exhaust them. The sword of passive resistance does not require a scabbard and one cannot be forcibly dispossessed of it.'
'Passive Resistance" (undated). Printed in C F Andrews, SPEECHES AND WRITINGS OF M K GANDHI

13 'I do not like the term "passive resistance". It fails to convey all I mean. It describes a method, but gives no hint of the system of which it is only a part. Real beauty, and that is my aim, is in doing good against evil. Still, I adopt the phrase because it is well-known, and

easily understood, and because, at present, the great majority of my people can only grasp that idea.'
IBID. *In answer to a question from his biographer, Joseph Doke*

Garfield, James (1831–1881)
AMERICAN REPUBLICAN POLITICIAN, PRESIDENT, 1881

1 'All free governments are party governments.'
Speech to the House of Representatives, 18 January 1878

Garibaldi, Giuseppe (1807–1882)
ITALIAN NATIONALIST LEADER AND SOLDIER

2 'How splendid were your Thousand, O Italy!'
Quoted in J Ridley, GARIBALDI, *Chapter 29. Of the volunteer 'Redshirts' who sailed with him from Talamone to Sicily, May, 1860*

Garrison, William Lloyd (1805–1879)
AMERICAN ABOLITIONIST

3 'Tell a man whose house is on fire, to give a moderate alarm; tell him to moderately rescue his wife from the hands of the ravisher; tell the mother to gradually extricate her babe from the fire into which it has fallen; but urge me not to use moderation in a cause like the present. I am in earnest – I will not equivocate – will not excuse – I will not retreat a single inch – AND I WILL BE HEARD.'
THE LIBERATOR, *1 January 1831. Launching his newspaper to fight against slavery*

4 'Truth no more relies for success on ballot boxes than it does on cartridge boxes ... Political action is not moral action, anymore than a box on the ear is an argument.'
IBID., *13 March 1846*

5 'Today, I disown the American flag as the symbol of unequalled hypocrisy and transcendent oppression ... Today, I renew my accusation against the American Constitution, that it is 'a covenant with death and an agreement with Hell'', which ought to be annulled now and forever. Today, I pronounce the American Union a league of despotism,

to perpetuate which is a crime against common humanity, and sin against God.'
IBID., 11 July 1856

Geddes, Sir Eric (1875–1937)
SCOTTISH CONSERVATIVE POLITICIAN, BUSINESSMAN, MEMBER OF THE IMPERIAL WAR CABINET, 1918

6 'We will get everything out of her that you can squeeze out of a lemon and a bit more ... I will squeeze her until you can hear the pips squeak.'
Speech at Cambridge, 9 December 1918. On making peace with Germany.

George II (1683–1760)
KING OF GREAT BRITAIN AND IRELAND, 1727–1760

7 'I shall now have no more peace.'
In conversation, 6 March 1754. On the death of his first minister, Henry Pelham

George V (1865–1936)
KING OF GREAT BRITAIN AND NORTHERN IRELAND, 1910–1936

8 'I went to a football match at which there were 73,000 people; at the end they sang the National Anthem and cheered tremendously. There were no bolsheviks there! At least I never saw any. The country is all right; just a few extremists are doing all the harm.'
Letter to Queen Alexandra, 24 April 1921. When British industry lay under the threat of a strike of miners, railway workers and transport workers

George, Henry (1839–1897)
AMERICAN ECONOMIST

9 'Private ownership of land is the nether millstone. Material progress is the upper millstone. Between them, with increasing pressure, the working classes are being ground.'
PROGRESS AND POVERTY *(1879)*

·10 'We cannot safely leave politics to politicians, or political economy to college professors. The people themselves must think, because the people alone can act.'
SOCIAL PROBLEMS *(1883)*

11 'There are three ways by which an individual can get wealth – by work, by gift, and by theft. And, clearly, the

reason why the workers get so little is that the beggars and thieves get so much.'
IBID.

1 'Labour may be likened to a man who as he carries home his earnings is waylaid by a series of robbers. One demands this much, and another that much, but last of all stands one who demands all that is left, save just enough to enable the victim to maintain life and come forth next day to work ... And the robber that takes all that is left, is private property in land.'
PROTECTION OR FREE TRADE *(1885)*

Gilmour, Sir Ian (1926–)
ENGLISH CONSERVATIVE POLITICIAN, MEMBER OF PARLIAMENT, 1962–, LORD PRIVY SEAL 1979–1981

2 'Politicians trim and tack in their quest for power, but they do so in order to get the wind of votes in their sails. If this wind is lacking ... the party and parliamentary systems become becalmed in the muddy waters of intrigue, corruption and influence.'
THE BODY POLITIC *(1969), Part I, Chapter 1*

3 'The more a regime claims to be the embodiment of liberty the more tyrannical it is likely to be.'
INSIDE RIGHT *(1977), Part III, Chapter 1*

4 'A sharp Right turn ... is likely to be followed by an even sharper Left turn. Hence Conservative moderation brings its own reward. The best way of safeguarding the future is by not trying to return to the past.'
IBID., *Part III, Chapter 2*

5 'Conservatives do not worship democracy. For them majority rule is a device ... And if it is leading to an end that is undesirable or is consistent with itself, then there is a theoretical case for ending it.'
IBID., *Part III, Chapter 5*

Gladstone, William Ewart
(1809–1898)
ENGLISH POLITICIAN, LIBERAL PRIME MINISTER, 1868–1874, 1880–1885, 1886 AND 1892–1894

6 'A war more unjust in its origins, a war more calculated in its progress to cover this country with permanent disgrace, I do not know, and I have not read of.'
House of Commons, 7 April 1840. On the First Opium War with China

7 'Ireland, Ireland! that cloud in the west, that coming storm, the minister of God's retribution upon cruel and inveterate and but half-atoned injustice.'
Letter to his wife, 12 October 1845

8 'Politics would become an utter blank to me were I to make the discovery that we were mistaken in maintaining their association with religion.'
Letter to Cardinal Manning, April 1850

9 'This is the negation of God erected into a system of Government.'
LETTER TO THE EARL OF ABERDEEN ON THE STATE PERSECUTIONS OF THE NEAPOLITAN GOVERNMENT *(1851)*

10 'It is, when strictly judged, an act of public immorality to form and lead an opposition on a certain plea, to succeed, and then in office to abandon it.'
Letter to Lord Aberdeen, 5 August 1852

11 'You have now been Minister of England; you are one of a lofty line.'
Letter to Lord Aberdeen, 1855

12 'I venture to say that every man who is not presumably incapacitated by some consideration of personal unfitness or of political danger, is morally entitled to come within the pale of the constitution.'
House of Commons, 11 May 1864. On the desirability of widening the parliamentary franchise

13 'At last, my friends, I am come among you, and I am come – to use an expression which has become very famous and is not likely to be forgotten – I am come among you unmuzzled.'
Speech at Manchester, 18 July 1865. On offering himself as a parliamentary candidate for the popular constituency of South Lancashire after his defeat at Oxford University, July 1865
SEE ALSO *Palmerston*

14 'My mission is to pacify Ireland.'
Remark on receiving the Queen's commission to form a government, 1 December 1868.

15 'We have been borne down in a torrent of gin and beer.'
Letter to Robertson Gladstone, 6 February 1874. On the defeat of the Liberal party at the 1874 general election

1 'Let the Turks now carry off their abuses in the only possible manner, namely by carrying off themselves. Their Zaptiehs and their Mindirs, their Bimbashis and their Yuzbachis, their Kaimakams and their Pashas, one and all, bag and baggage, shall, I hope, clear out from the province they have desolated and profaned.'
THE BULGARIAN HORRORS AND THE QUESTION OF THE EAST *(1876). On Turkey-in-Europe*

2 'Liberalism is trust of the people tempered by prudence; Conservatism is distrust of the people tempered by fear.'
Speech at Plumstead, 1878

3 'Remember that the rights of the savage, as we may call him, remember that the happiness of his humble home, remember that the sanctity of life in the hill villages of Afghanistan among the winter snows, are as inviolate in the eye of Almighty God as can be your own. Remember that He who has united you together as human beings of the same flesh and blood, has bound you by the law of mutual love; that that mutual love is not limited by the shores of this island, is not limited by the boundaries of Christian civilisation; that it passes over the whole surface of the earth, and embraces the meanest along with the greatest in its unmeasured scope.'
Speech at Dalkeith, 26 November 1879. On the war in Afghanistan

4 'Nothing is so dull as political agitation.'
Speech at Glasgow University, 5 December 1879. During the Midlothian campaign

5 'We cannot reckon upon the aristocracy. We cannot reckon upon what is called the landed interest. We cannot reckon upon the clergy of the Established Church in England or in Scotland ... We cannot reckon on the wealth of the country, nor upon the rank of the country ... We must set them down among our most determined foes. But, gentlemen, above all these, and behind all these, there is the nation itself. This great trial [the general election] is now proceeding before the nation. The nation is a power hard to rouse, but when roused harder still and more hopeless to resist.'
Speech at East Calder, 2 April 1880

6 'The downfall of Beaconsfieldism is like the vanishing of some vast magnificent castle of Italian romance.'
Letter to the Duke of Argyll, 12 April 1880. On the defeat of the Conservative party at the 1880 general election

7 'If it shall appear that there is still to be fought a final conflict in Ireland between law on the one side and sheer lawlessness upon the other, if the law purged from defect and from any taint of injustice is still to be repelled and refused, and the first conditions of a political society to remain unfulfilled, then I say, gentlemen, without hesitation, the resources of civilisation against its enemies are not yet exhausted.'
Speech at Leeds, 8 October 1881. Issuing a warning to the Parnellites

8 'These gentlemen wish to march through rapine to the disintegration and dismemberment of the Empire.'
Speech at Liverpool, 27 October 1881. On Parnell and his supporters

9 'If Germany is to become a colonising power, all I say is "God speed her!". She becomes our ally and partner in the execution of the great purposes of Providence for the advantage of mankind.'
House of Commons, 12 March 1885

10 'This is a considerable event.'
Diary, 8 June 1885. On the defeat of his government in the House of Commons

11 'All the world over, I will back the masses against the classes.'
Speech at Liverpool, 28 June 1886

12 'The history of nations is a melancholy chapter; that is, the history of government is one of the most immoral parts of history.'
Quoted in J Morley, RECOLLECTIONS, *Volume II, Book IV, Chapter 1*

13 'There is no broad political idea which has entered less into the formation of the political system of this country than the love of equality.'
Quoted in Matthew Arnold, MIXED ESSAYS, *'Equality'*

Godwin, William (1756–1836)
ENGLISH POLITICAL THEORIST AND AUTHOR

14 'Government is very limited and its powers of making men either virtuous or

happy; it is only in the infancy of society that it can do anything considerable; in its maturity it can only direct a few of our outward actions.'
AN ACCOUNT OF THE SEMINARY ... AT EPSOM IN SURREY *(1784)*

1 'Government was intended to suppress injustice, but its effect has been to embody and perpetuate it.'
ENQUIRY CONCERNING POLITICAL JUSTICE *(1793), 'Summary of Principles'*

2 'If government be founded in the consent of the people, it can have no power over any individual by whom that consent is refused.'
IBID., *Book III, Chapter 3*

3 'The project of a national education ought uniformly to be discouraged, on account of its obvious alliance with national government. This is an alliance of a more formidable nature than the old and much contested alliance of church and state.'
IBID., *Book VI, Chapter 8*

Goebbels, Joseph (1897–1945)
GERMAN NATIONAL SOCIALIST POLITICIAN, MINISTER OF PROPAGANDA, 1933–1945

4 'Whoever can conquer the street will one day conquer the state, for every form of power politics and any dictatorially-run state has its roots in the street.'
Speech to the National Socialist party congress, Nuremberg, August 1927

5 'We [National Socialist deputies] enter parliament in order to supply ourselves, in the arsenal of democracy, with its own weapons. We become members of the Reichstag in order to paralyse the Weimar sentiment with its own assistance. If democracy is so stupid as to give us free tickets and salaries for this bear's work, that is its affair ... We do not come as friends, nor even as neutrals. We come as enemies. As the wolf bursts into the flock, so we come.'
DER ANGRIFF, *30 April 1928*

6 'Prohibitions can ruin only weak parties. They stimulate and heighten the fighting power of strong ones.'
Diary, 14 April 1932. On the German government's banning of the Sturmabteilung organisation, April 1932.

7 'A National Socialist feels himself only when he is at liberty to make a fight of it. I note this especially during my visits to a few S.A. premises. Our boys are quite beside themselves. One could go horse-stealing with them!'
Diary, 10 July 1932

8 'We can do without butter, but ... not without guns. One cannot shoot with butter, but with guns.'
Speech at Berlin, 17 January 1936

9 'There can be no peace in Europe until every Jew has been eliminated from the continent.'
Diary, 7 March 1942

10 'If I had received these powers when I wanted them so badly, victory would be in our pockets today, and the war would probably be over. But it takes a bomb under his arse to make Hitler see reason.'
In conversation with Rudolf Semmler, 26 July 1944. On his being appointed Reich Trustee for Total War

11 'Should the German people lay down its arms, the agreement between Roosevelt, Churchill and Stalin would allow the Soviets to occupy all of eastern and southeastern Europe together with the major part of the Reich. An iron curtain would at once descend on this territory.'
DAS REICH, *25 February 1945*
SEE ALSO *Ethel Snowden*

12 'Thank God, at last. This is the final round.'
In conversation, 6 June 1944. Quoted in R Manvell and H Fraenkel, DOCTOR GOEBBELS, *Chapter 7. On learning of the Allied landings in Normandy*

13 'Politics ruin the character; they develop the worst and meanest qualities by forcing into the front of men's minds their ambition, their vanity, their competitive spirit and their passion for influence and cheap popularity.'
IBID., *Chapter 8*

14 'Justice must not become the mistress of the state, but must be the servant of state policy.'
IBID.

Goering, Hermann (1893–1946)
GERMAN NATIONAL SOCIALIST POLITICIAN, HEAD OF THE GESTAPO, 1933–1936

15 'I measure with two measures. I would

not be just if I did not send the
Communists to hell at last.'
Speech at Frankfurt, 3 March 1933

1 'The giver of law must not put the
arbitrariness of rational abstraction in the
place of the rights of the people.'
Speech to the Prussian diet, 18 May 1933

2 'When the great white nations cannot
find each other, then they look forward
to their twilight. The white people are
chosen for the leadership of the world,
and the white nations must realise and
respect the mission among themselves.'
*Speech at the Krupp Works, Essen, 4
December 1934*

3 'We have no butter, my countrymen, but
I ask you – would you rather have butter
or guns? Shall we import lard or metal
ores? Let me tell you – preparedness
makes us powerful. Butter merely makes
us fat.'
*Speech at Hamburg, (? February), 1936.
(This is the version given in W
Frischauer, GOERING, Chapter 10. The
better known – 'Guns will make us
powerful; butter will only make us
fat' – was broadcast on radio in the
summer of 1936.)*
SEE ALSO *Goebbels*

4 'I know that even now, again and again,
threats are used against Germany ... To
this ridiculous attempt to make us
nervous I would like to answer for the
whole German people, particularly for
the National Socialist fighters, with the
words of the War Minister, Field Marshal
Roon, and assure them of one thing: We
have always been shooters, but never
shitters [*Wir sind allezeit Schiesser
gewesen, niemals aber Scheisser*].'
*Speech to the German Work Front,
Nuremberg, 10 September 1938*

Goldberg, Isaac (1887–1938)
AMERICAN MAN OF LETTERS

5 'Diplomacy is to do and say
The nastiest thing in the nicest way.'
THE REFLEX *(c. 1930)*

Goldman, Emma (1869–1940)
RUSSIAN-BORN AMERICAN ANARCHIST

6 'Anarchism is the only philosophy which
brings to man the consciousness of
himself; which maintains that God, the
State, and society are non-existent, that

their promises are null and void, since
they can be fulfilled only through man's
subordination.'
ANARCHISM AND OTHER ESSAYS *(1910),
'Anarchism'*

Goldsmith, Oliver (1728–1774)
IRISH POET, PLAYWRIGHT AND
NOVELIST

7 'Should it be alleged in defence of
national prejudice, that it is the natural
and necessary growth of love to our
country, and that therefore the former
cannot be destroyed without hurting the
latter, I answer, that this is a gross fallacy
and delusion. That it is the growth of
love to our country, I will allow; but that
it is the natural and necessary growth of
it, I absolutely deny. Superstition and
enthusiasm too are the growth of
religion; but who ever took it in his head
to affirm that they are the necessary
growth of this noble principle?'
ESSAYS *(1765), 'National Prejudices'*

8 'Laws grind the poor, and rich men rule
the law.'
THE TRAVELLER *(1765)*

9 'Here lies our good Edmund, whose
genius was such
We scarcely can praise it, or blame it, too
much!
Who, born for the Universe, narrow'd
his mind,
And to party gave up what was meant for
mankind.'
RETALIATION *(1774). Of Burke*

Goldwater, Barry (1909–   )
AMERICAN REPUBLICAN POLITICIAN,
SENATOR, 1952–64, 1969–

10 'I would remind you that moderation in
the pursuit of justice is no virtue. And let
me also remind you that extremism in
the defence of liberty is no vice.'
*Speech to the Republican national
convention, San Francisco, 16 July 1964.
Accepting the party's nomination as its
presidential candidate*
SEE ALSO *Lyndon Johnson*

11 'A government that is big enough to give
you all you want is big enough to take it
all away.'
*Speech at West Chester, Pennsylvania, 21
October 1964*

Goncourt, Edmond de
(1822–1896) and **Jules de**
(1830–1870)
FRENCH WRITERS, BROTHERS

1 'David and Robespierre in the
Revolution: two icy geniuses in a
volcano.'
Diary, October, 1858

2 'There are only two great currents in the
history of mankind: the baseness which
makes conservatives and the envy which
makes revolutionaries.'
Diary, 12 July 1867

Gorky, Maxim (1868–1936)
RUSSIAN WRITER AND
REVOLUTIONARY

3 'The working class is for a Lenin what
ore is for a metal-worker.'
Article in his weekly newspaper, NOVAYA
ZHIZN *('New Life'), January 1918*

4 'The proletarian state must bring up
thousands of excellent "mechanics of
culture", "engineers of the soul".'
*Speech to the Writers' Conference, 1934.
(Possibly borrowing from a conversation
with Stalin.)*

Goschen, George, 1st Viscount
(1831–1907)
ENGLISH LIBERAL UNIONIST
POLITICIAN, CHANCELLOR OF THE
EXCHEQUER, 1886–1892

5 'I have the courage of my opinions, but I
have not the temerity to give a political
blank cheque to Lord Salisbury.'
House of Commons, 19 February 1884
SEE ALSO *William Henry Smith*

6 'We have stood alone in that which is
called isolation – our splendid isolation, as
one of our colonial friends was good
enough to call it.'
Speech at Lewes, 26 February 1896
SEE ALSO *George Foster*

Grant, Ulysses Simpson
(1822–1885)
AMERICAN GENERAL AND REPUBLICAN,
PRESIDENT, 1869–1877

7 'No terms except unconditional and
immediate surrender can be accepted.'
*To General Buckner at Fort Donelson, 16
February 1862*

8 'I know no method to secure the repeal
of bad or obnoxious laws so effective as
their stringent execution.'
First inaugural address, 4 March 1869

Grattan, Henry (1746–1820)
IRISH PROTESTANT HOME RULE LEADER

9 'The Irish Protestant can never be free
until the Irish Catholic has ceased to be a
slave.'
Quoted in WHO'S WHO IN HISTORY, *Volume
V: England 1789–1837*

Grayson, Victor (1881–?1920)
ENGLISH SOCIALIST POLITICIAN,
MEMBER OF PARLIAMENT, 1907–1910

10 'If the people have no shrapnel, they
have broken bottles.'
Speech at Huddersfield, August 1907

11 'I am simply a bullet fired by the Colne
Valley workers against the established
order.'
*In conversation, 1907. Quoted in
R Groves,* THE STRANGE CASE OF VICTOR
GRAYSON, *Chapter 1. On his election to
parliament at the Colne Valley by-
election, 1907*

12 'It leaves two courses open to the
thinking animal . . . Schopenhauer and
suicide or socialism and struggle.'
IBID. *On living in the Ancoats slum of
Manchester*

Greer, Germaine (1939–)
AUSTRALIAN WRITER AND FEMINIST

13 'Women's liberation, if it abolishes the
patriarchal family, will abolish a
necessary substructure of the
authoritarian state, and once that withers
away Marx will have come true willy-
nilly, so let's get on with it.'
THE FEMALE EUNUCH *(1970), 'Revolution'*

14 'The surest guide to the correctness of
the path that women take is *joy in the
struggle*. Revolution is the festival of the
oppressed.'
IBID.

Grenville, William
Wyndham, 1st Baron (1759–1834)
ENGLISH WHIG POLITICIAN, FOREIGN
SECRETARY, 1791–1801, PRIME MINISTER
1806–1807

15 'The principle in mechanics is by the
smallest power, and the least

complication, to produce the greatest possible effect. This principle is not less applicable to politics, although it is an axiom which the government of this country has for some time back entirely lost sight of.'
House of Lords, 25 June 1804

Grey of Fallodon, 1st Viscount (Edward Grey) (1862–1933)
ENGLISH LIBERAL POLITICIAN, ORNITHOLOGIST, FOREIGN SECRETARY, 1905–1916

1 'Some time ago the atmosphere between ourselves and France may be said to have been of the glacial epoch. It has happily now changed to a genial epoch.'
House of Commons, 1 June 1904. On the ENTENTE CORDIALE

2 'The lamps are going out all over Europe; we shall not see them lit again in our lifetime.'
In conversation, 3 August 1914. Quoted in Grey, TWENTY-FIVE-YEARS, *Volume II, Chapter 18. On the outbreak of the First World War*

3 'It is the greatest step towards Socialism that could possibly have been made. We shall have Labour Governments in every country after this.'
In conversation with Count Mensdorff, 7 August 1914. On the probable consequences of the First World War

4 'I once heard Lord Cromer describe the impossibility of understanding the Turkish oriental mind. I am not sure that I recall accurately what he said, but it was to this effect. If it is important to you to know what an Oriental is going to do you must ask yourself three questions: (1) What would you yourself do under the same conditions? (2) What do you think the wisest man you know would do? (3) What do you think the Oriental

will do? When you have answered these questions you will know three things that the Oriental certainly will not do.'
TWENTY-FIVE YEARS, *Volume I, Chapter 8*

Grimond, Jo (Joseph), Baron (1913–)
SCOTTISH POLITICIAN, LEADER OF THE LIBERAL PARTY, 1956–1967

5 'And in bygone days, commanders were taught that, when in doubt, they should march their troops towards the sound of gunfire. I intend to march my troops towards the sound of gunfire.'
Speech to the Liberal party annual conference, 15 September 1963

Groener, Karl Wilhelm (1867–1939)
GERMAN GENERAL AND WEIMAR POLITICIAN

6 'The German general staff fought against the English parliament.'
1920. Quoted in A J P Taylor, 'Politics in the First World War' (Raleigh Lecture, 1959)

Guevara, Ernesto 'Che' (1928–1967)
ARGENTINIAN-BORN CUBAN REVOLUTIONARY AND WRITER

7 'A revolution that does not continue to grow deeper is a revolution that is retreating.'
GUERRILLA WARFARE: A METHOD *(1961)*

Guizot, François (1787–1874)
FRENCH HISTORIAN AND POLITICIAN, PRIME MINISTER, 1847–1848

8 'The spirit of revolution, the spirit of insurrection, is a spirit radically opposed to liberty.'
Speech at Paris, 29 December 1830

H

Hailsham of St Marylebone, Baron (Quintin Hogg) (1907–)
ENGLISH CONSERVATIVE POLITICIAN, LORD CHANCELLOR, 1970–1974 AND 1979–

1 'The Labour Party almost admittedly aims at the establishment of a single-party system; and it may be said at once that they are almost within striking distance of their goal ... Never since the days of Cromwell has a single force in this country constituted a more formidable menace to political liberty.'
THE CASE FOR CONSERVATISM *(1947)*

2 'Political liberty is nothing else but the diffusion of power.'
IBID.

3 'The man who puts politics first is not fit to be called a civilised being, let alone a Christian.'
IBID.

4 'The introduction of religious passion into politics is the end of honest politics, and the introduction of politics into religion is the prostitution of true religion.'
THE CONSERVATIVE CASE *(1959)*

5 'If the British public falls for this [the programme of the Labour party], I say it will be stark, raving bonkers.'
Press conference, 12 October 1964. On the 1964 general election

Halifax, 1st Marquess of (George Savile) (1633–1695)
ENGLISH WHIG POLITICIAN

6 'This innocent word *Trimmer* signifieth no more than this, that if Men are together in a Boat, and one part of the Company would weigh it down on one side, another would make it lean as much to the contrary; it happeneth there is a third Opinion of those, who conceive it would do as well, if the Boat went even, without endangering the Passengers; now 'tis hard to imagine by what Figure in language, or by what Rule in Sense, this cometh to be a fault, and it is much more wonder it should be thought a Heresy.'
THE CHARACTER OF A TRIMMER *(1700)*

7 'No prince is so Great, as not to think fit, for his own Credit at least, to give an outward, when he refuseth a real, worship to the laws.'
IBID.

8 '*Parties* in a *State* generally, like *Freebooters*, hand out *False Colours*; the pretence is the *Publick Good*; the real *Business* is, to catch *Prizes*; like the *Tartars*, wherever they succeed, instead of Improving their *Victory*, they presently fall upon the *Baggage*.'
MAXIMS OF STATE *(1700)*

9 '*Power* and *Liberty* are like *Heat* and *Moisture*; where they are well mixt, everything prospers; where they are single, they are destructive.'
IBID.

10 'Changing *Hands* without changing *Measures*, is as if a *Drunkard* in a *Dropsey* should change his *Doctors*, and not his *Dyet*.'
IBID.

11 'The Heat of a Party is like the Burning of a Fever; and not a Natural Warmth, evenly distributed to give Life and Vigour.'
SOME CAUTIONS OFFERED TO THE CONSIDERATION OF THOSE WHO ARE TO CHUSE MEMBERS TO SERVE FOR THE ENSUING PARLIAMENT *(1700)*

12 'The best Party is but a kind of Conspiracy against the rest of the Nation.'
POLITICAL THOUGHTS AND REFLECTIONS *(1750)*

13 'Ignorance maketh most Men go into a Party, and Shame keepeth them from getting out of it.'
IBID.

14 'Men are not hanged for stealing Horses, but that Horses may not be stolen.'
IBID.

15 'Power is so apt to be insolent, and Liberty to be saucy, that they are very seldom upon good Terms.'
IBID.

Hamilton, Alexander (1755–1804)
AMERICAN FEDERALIST POLITICIAN, SECRETARY OF THE TREASURY, 1789–1795

16 'All men have one common original: they participate in one common nature,

and consequently have one common right. No reason can be assigned why one man should exercise any power or pre-eminence over his fellow-creatures more than another; unless they have voluntarily vested him with it.'
'A Full Vindication', 15 December 1774

1 'To render it agreeable to good policy, three things are requisite. First, that the necessity of the times requires it; secondly, that it be not the probable source of greater evils than those it pretends to remedy; and lastly, that it have a probability of success.'
IBID.

2 'A national debt, if it is not excessive, will be to us a national blessing.'
Letter to Robert Morris, 30 April 1781

3 'All communities divide themselves into the few and the many. The first are the rich and well born, the other the mass of the people. The voice of the people has been said to be the voice of God; and however generally this maxim has been quoted and believed, it is not true in fact. The people are turbulent and changing; they seldom judge or determine right. Give therefore to the first class a distinct, permanent share in the government. They will check the unsteadiness of the second, and as they cannot receive any advantage by a change, they therefore will ever maintain good government.'
Speech to the Constitutional Convention, Philadelphia, 18 June 1787

4 'Nothing but a permanent body can check the imprudence of democracy.'
IBID.

5 'An executive is less dangerous to the liberties of the people when in office during life, than for seven years.'
IBID.

6 'America, if she attains to greatness, must *creep* to it . . . Snails are a wise generation.'
Letter to Theodore Sedgwick, 27 February 1800

7 'Great ambition, unchecked by principle or the love of glory, is an unruly tyrant.'
Letter to James Bayard, 16 January 1801

8 'Is it a recommendation to have no theory? Can that man be a systematic or able statesman who has none? I believe not. *No general principles* will hardly work much better than erroneous ones.'
IBID.

9 'The genius of republics is pacific; the spirit of commerce has a tendency to soften the manners of men, and to extinguish those inflammable humors which have so often kindled into wars. Commercial republics, like ours, will never be disposed to waste themselves in ruinous contention with each other.'
THE FEDERALIST, *No. 6*

10 'Let the Thirteen States, bound together in a strict and indissoluble union, concur in erecting one great American system.'
IBID., *No. 11*

11 'Money is, with propriety, considered as the vital principle of the body politic; as that which sustains its life and motion, and enables it to perform its most essential functions.'
IBID., *No. 30*

12 'To model our political system upon speculations of lasting tranquillity is to calculate on the weaker springs of the human character.'
IBID., *No. 34*

13 'The process of election [by the electoral college] affords a moral certainty that the office of President will never fall to the lot of any man who is not in an eminent degree endowed with the requisite qualifications.'
IBID., *No. 68*

Hammarskjöld, Dag (1905–1961)
SWEDISH POLITICIAN AND INTERNATIONAL CIVIL SERVANT, SECRETARY GENERAL OF THE UNITED NATIONS, 1953–1961

14 'Only he deserves power who every day justifies it.'
MARKINGS *(1965)*, '*1951*'

15 'To separate himself from the society of which he was born a member will lead the revolutionary not to life, but to death, unless, in his very revolt, he is driven by a love of what, seemingly, must be rejected, and, therefore, at the profoundest level, remains faithful to that society.'
IBID.

Hand, Learned (1872–1961)
AMERICAN JUDGE

1 'Even though counting heads is not an ideal way to govern, it is at least better than breaking them.'
Speech to the Federal Bar Association, 8 March 1932

Hanna, Mark (1837–1904)
AMERICAN INDUSTRIALIST AND REPUBLICAN POLITICIAN, SENATOR 1897–1904

2 'I told William McKinley it was a mistake to nominate that wild man at Philadelphia [as vice-presidential candidate] . . . Now, look, that damned cowboy is President of the United States.'
In conversation with H Kohlstat, September 1901. On the assassination of President McKinley and the consequent assumption of the Presidency by Theodore Roosevelt.

Harcourt, Sir William
(1827–1904)
ENGLISH LIBERAL POLITICIAN, CHANCELLOR OF THE EXCHEQUER, 1886 AND 1892–1895

3 'Your cabinet was a sort of political Sorbonne, in which each doctor was permitted to stamp with all the authority of Government, any opinion which might suit his fancy or convenience.'
Open letter to Lord Derby, MORNING CHRONICLE, 23 May 1853. (Signed 'Englishman'.) Chastising Derby for allowing his followers to appear as free-traders or as protectionists, as they wished, at the 1852 elections

4 'It is not the métier of a Tory to have a policy, any more than it is that of a king to be a democrat. A Tory government may do very well without a policy, just as a country gentleman may sit at home and live upon his rents.'
SATURDAY REVIEW, *21 March 1857, 'Pot and Kettle'*

5 'This is Socialism pure and simple. It begins with national workshops, and ends with what Mr Carlyle calls "a whiff of grapeshot".'
IBID.
SEE ALSO *Carlyle*

6 'Let us, then, disabuse our minds of the *Civis Romanus* idea. It is historically an anachronism and a blunder; legally it is an injustice and a wrong; politically it is a folly and a crime. The phrase belongs to the vocabulary of the bully and the doctrine is the policy of the oppressor. Let us hope we shall hear no more of it here.'
THE TIMES, *6 February 1868*
SEE ALSO *Palmerston*

7 'Let us give our Republic not the best possible laws but the best which they will bear. This is the essence of *politics*; all the rest is *speculation*.'
Letter to Charles Dilke, 1870

8 'The saying has been attributed to me that every one is a socialist now. I do not know whether I ever said that, but this I will say – there are no economists now . . . a Chancellor of the Exchequer preaching against extravagance is the "voice of one crying in the wilderness".'
House of Commons, 24 April 1893. Introducing the budget

9 'Without you the government would have been ridiculous; with you, it is only impossible.'
In conversation with Lord Rosebery, 16 August 1892. During the formation of Gladstone's last government

10 'The minister exists to tell the Civil Servant what the public will not stand.'
Quoted in I Gilmour, THE BODY POLITIC, *Part II, Chapter 1*

Hardie, (James) Keir (1856–1915)
SCOTTISH POLITICIAN, CO-FOUNDER OF THE INDEPENDENT LABOUR PARTY

11 'The demand of the Labour party is for economic freedom. It is the natural outcome of political enfranchisement.'
Speech to the inaugural conference of the Independent Labour party, Bradford, 13 January 1893

12 'The life of one Welsh miner is of greater commercial and moral value to the British nation than the whole Royal Crowd put together, from the Royal Great Grand-mama down to this puling Royal Great Grand-child.'
LABOUR LEADER, *1894. When the House of Commons congratulated the Duke and Duchess of York on the birth of a son, but refused Hardie's request for a message of sympathy to be sent to the families of 250 miners killed by an explosion in the Merthyr valley*

1 'Defeat is not in the Socialist dictionary.'
Remark to supporters after losing the election at Bradford East, 1896

2 'For twenty-one years the S[ocial D[emocratic] F[ederation] has based its propaganda on the class-war theory, and the result is dismal failure. How could it be otherwise? Mankind in the mass is not moved by hatred, but by love of what is right.'
1901. Quoted in I McLean, KEIR HARDIE, *Chapter 8*

3 'It will take the British working man twenty years to learn to elect his equals to represent him. And then it will take him another twenty years not to elect his equals.'
Quoted by Harold Nicolson in his diary, 27 February 1930

Harding, Warren (1865–1923)
AMERICAN REPUBLICAN POLITICIAN, PRESIDENT, 1921–1923

4 'America's present need is not heroics, but healing; not nostrums, but normalcy; not revolution, but restoration.'
Speech at Boston, June 1920

Harington, Sir John (1561–1612)
ENGLISH MAN OF LETTERS AND COURTIER

5 'Treason doth never prosper: what's the reason?
For if it prosper, none dare call it treason.'
EPIGRAMS *(1618), Book IV, No. 5*

Harlan, John (1833–1911)
AMERICAN JUDGE, JUSTICE OF THE SUPREME COURT, 1877–1911

6 'Our constitution is color-blind.'
Dissenting opinion, PLESSY V. FERGUSON, *1896*

Harriman, William Averell (1891–)
AMERICAN DIPLOMAT AND INDUSTRIALIST

7 'The dictatorship of the proletariat is an historically regressive idea for it makes the individual a servant of the state, robs him of his power of decision, and is thus at odds with the aspirations of mankind.'
Interview in ENCOUNTER, *November 1981*

Harrington, James (1611–1677)
ENGLISH POLITICAL THEORIST

8 'No man can be a politician except he be first a historian or a traveller; for except he can see what must be, or what may be, he is no politician.'
OCEANA *(1656), Chapter 3*

Harrison, Benjamin (1833–1901)
AMERICAN REPUBLICAN POLITICIAN, PRESIDENT, 1889–1893

9 'We Americans have no commission from God to police the world.'
Campaign speech, 1888

Harrison, Frederic (1831–1923)
ENGLISH POSITIVIST PHILOSOPHER AND LAWYER

10 'What makes a man minister? Debating power. And what makes a man Premier? Debating power. And what good is debating power to you? What has it ever done for you or for England? It bears the same relation to governing that tournaments did to fighting.'
ORDER AND PROGRESS *(1875)*

Hastings, Warren (1732–1818)
ENGLISH COLONIAL ADMINISTRATOR, GOVERNOR-GENERAL OF INDIA, 1773–1785

11 'Oft have I wondered that on Irish Ground
No poisonous reptiles ever yet were found;
Revealed the secret stands, of Nature's work,
She saved her venom to create a Burke.'
Fragment, written during his impeachment trial. (Possibly written by his counsel.)

Hayek, Friedrich (1899–)
AUSTRIAN-BORN ENGLISH POLITICAL ECONOMIST

12 'The idea that a completely planned or directed economic system could and would be used to bring about distributive justice presupposes, in fact, the existence of something which does not exist and has never existed: a complete moral code in which the relative values of all human ends, the relative importance of all the needs of all the different people, are assigned a definite place and a definite quantitative significance.'
FREEDOM AND THE ECONOMIC SYSTEM *(1940)*

1 'The increasing discredit into which democratic government has fallen is due to democracy having been burdened with tasks for which it is not suited.'
IBID.

2 'If a democratic people comes under the sway of an anti-capitalistic creed, this means that democracy will inevitably destroy itself.'
IBID.

Hayes, Rutherford Birchard
(1822–1893)
AMERICAN REPUBLICAN POLITICIAN, PRESIDENT, 1877–1881

3 'He serves his party best who serves his country best.'
Inaugural address, 5 March 1877

Haywood, William (1869–1928)
AMERICAN TRADE UNIONIST, CO-FOUNDER OF THE INDUSTRIAL WORKERS OF THE WORLD

4 'No Socialist can be a law-abiding citizen. When we come together and are of a common mind, and the purpose of our minds is to overthrow the capitalist system, we become conspirators then against the United States government.'
1912. Quoted in D Aaron, WRITERS ON THE LEFT, *Chapter 1*

Hazlitt, William (1778–1830)
ENGLISH ESSAYIST

5 'No kingdom can be secure in its independence against a greater power that is not free in its spirit, as well as in its institutions.'
FREE THOUGHTS ON PUBLIC AFFAIRS, OR ADVICE TO A PATRIOT *(1806)*

6 'I know it is a general maxim, that we are not to war with the dead. We ought not, indeed, to trample on their bodies; but with their *minds* we may and must make war, unless we would be governed by them after they are dead.'
IBID.

7 'The love of fame is consistent with the steadiest attachment to principle, and indeed strengthens and supports it; whereas the love of power, where this is the ruling passion, requires the sacrifice of principle at every turn, and is inconsistent even with the shadow of it.'
'Character of Mr Fox' (1807)

8 'Political truth is a libel – religious truth blasphemy.'
THE ROUND TABLE *(1817), 'Commonplaces'*

9 'The love of liberty is the love of others; the love of power is the love of ourselves.'
POLITICAL ESSAYS *(1819) 'The Times Newspaper' (1817)*

10 'If Buonaparte was a conqueror, he conquered the grand conspiracy of kings against the abstract right of the human race to be free.'
POLITICAL ESSAYS *(1819), Preface*

11 'He is a kind of *fourth estate* in the politics of the country.'
TABLE TALK *(1821–22), 'Character of Cobbett'. Of William Cobbett*

12 'Public bodies are so far worse than the individuals composing them, because the *official* takes place of the *moral sense*.'
IBID., *'On Corporate Bodies'*

13 'Public opinion is the mixed result of the intellect of the community acting upon general feeling.'
THE LITERARY EXAMINER *(1823), 'Characteristics'*

14 'It is sometimes made a wonder how men of "no mark or likelihood" frequently rise to court-preferment, and make their way against all competition. That is the very reason. They present no tangible point; they offend no feeling of self-importance. They are a perfect unresisting medium of patronage and favour. They aspire through servility; they repose in insignificance.'
'On Knowledge of the World' (1827)

15 'To use means to ends, to set causes in motion, to wield the machine of society, to subject the wills of others to your own, to manage abler men than yourself by means of that which is stronger in them than their wisdom, viz., their weakness and their folly, to calculate the resistance of ignorance and prejudice to your designs, and by obviating to turn them to your account, to foresee a long, obscure and complicated train of events, of chances and openings of success, to unwind the web of others' policy, and weave your own out of it, to judge the effects of things not in the abstract but with reference to all their bearings, ramifications and impediments, to understand character thoroughly, to see

latent talent and lurking treachery, to know mankind for what they are, and use them as they deserve, to have a purpose steadily in view and to effect it after removing every obstacle, to master others and to be true to yourself, asks power and knowledge, both nerves and brain.'
Quoted in M Foot, DEBTS OF HONOUR, *Chapter 2. On the requirements of political leadership*

Hearst, William Randolph
(1863–1951)
AMERICAN NEWSPAPER PROPRIETOR, DEMOCRATIC CONGRESSMAN, 1903–1907

1 'A politician will do anything to keep his job – even become a patriot.'
Leading article, 28 August 1933

Heath, Edward (1916–)
ENGLISH CONSERVATIVE POLITICIAN, PRIME MINISTER, 1970–1974

2 'No one knows better than a former patronage secretary [chief whip] the limitations of the human mind and the human spirit.'
In conversation, June 1962. Quoted in A Sampson, THE NEW ANATOMY OF BRITAIN, *Chapter 5.*

3 'Nor would it be in the interests of the Community that its enlargement should take place except with the full-hearted consent of the Parliament and people of the new member countries.'
Speech to the Franco-British Chamber of Commerce, Paris, 5 May 1970. On the proposed entry of Great Britain into the European Economic Community

4 'It is the unpleasant and unacceptable face of capitalism.'
House of Commons, 15 May 1973. On the activities of the Lonrho international trading group.

5 'We are . . . the trade union for the nation as a whole.'
Speech at Manchester, 20 February 1974. Of the Conservative party

Hegel, Georg (1770–1831)
GERMAN PHILOSOPHER

6 'Herein lies political genius, in the identification of an individual with a principle.'
THE GERMAN CONSTITUTION *(1802)*

7 'In civilised countries true bravery consists in the readiness to give oneself wholly to the service of the state so that the individual counts but as one among many. No personal valour is significant; the important aspect lies in self-subordination to the universal.'
THE PHILOSOPHY OF RIGHT *(1821)*

8 'The state is the divine idea as it exists on earth . . . We must therefore worship the state as the manifestation of the divine on earth . . . The march of God in the world, that is what the state is.'
IBID.

9 'The state is embodied morality. It is the ethical spirit which has clarified itself and has taken substantial shape as will, a will which is manifest before the world, which is self-conscious and knows its purposes and carries through that which it knows to the extent of its knowledge.'
IBID.

10 'Custom and morality are the outward and visible form of the inner essence of the state.'
THE PHILOSOPHY OF HISTORY *(compiled by students from notes after his death)*

Heine, Heinrich (1797–1856)
GERMAN POET

11 'The future smells of Russian leather, of blood, of godlessness, and of much whipping. I advise our grandchildren to come into the world with very thick skins on their backs.'
LUTETIA; OR, PARIS *(1842)*

12 'A revolution is a misfortune, but an unsuccessful revolution is an even greater misfortune.'
Quoted in K S Pinson, MODERN GERMANY, *Chapter 5*

Hellman, Lillian (1905–1984)
AMERICAN PLAYWRIGHT

13 'I cannot and will not cut my conscience to fit this year's fashions.'
Letter to John Wood, 19 May 1952. Informing the House Committee on Un-American Activities that she would answer questions only about her own activities, not those of other persons

Henry, Patrick (1736–1799)
AMERICAN REVOLUTIONARY LEADER,
GOVERNOR OF VIRGINIA 1776–1779,
1784–1786

1 'Ceasar had his Brutus, Charles the First,
his Cromwell, and George the Third
["'Treason!'' cried the Speaker] may profit
by their example. If this be treason, make
the most of it.'
*Speech to the Virginia House of
Representatives, 1765. Against the Stamp
Act*

2 'I am not a Virginian, but an American.'
*Speech to the Continental Congress,
Philadelphia, 5 September 1774*

3 'I know not what course others may take;
but as for me, give me liberty, or give me
death.'
*Speech to the Virginia Convention, 23
March 1775*

4 'To erect and concentrate and perpetuate
a large monied interest . . . must in the
course of human events produce one or
other of two evils, the prostration of
agriculture at the feet of commerce, or a
change in the present form of federal
government, fatal to the existence of
American liberty.'
*Speech to the Virginia House of
Representatives, 23 December 1790*

Herbert, A P (Sir Alan Patrick)
(1890–1971)
ENGLISH WRITER AND INDEPENDENT
MEMBER OF PARLIAMENT, 1935–1950

5 'If you try to make a big reform you are
told you are doing too much, and if you
make a modest contribution you are told
you are only tinkering with the
problem.'
House of Commons, 3 February 1939

6 'Where there is a deliberate and
persistent abuse of liberty, I would curtail
or suspend it without hesitation in order
that men may learn to value it better.'
House of Commons, 26 March 1942

7 'There is no man, no party, no country
which lusts for power, and governs its
activities by the lust for power, that does
not rue it in the end.'
House of Commons, 15 October 1945

8 'The amount paid by those who drink
and smoke was £715,000,000, very nearly
a pre-war Budget, whereas the taxation
paid by those who did not drink and
smoke, on tea, coffee and so on, was
£25,000,000. Yet those citizens expect
and receive precisely the same
protections from the Fleet, the Army, and
the police.'
House of Commons, 29 November 1945

9 'I am sure that the Party System is right
and necessary. All cannot be fly-halves;
there must be a scrum.'
INDEPENDENT MEMBER *(1950), Chapter 66*

Herzen, Alexander (1812–1870)
RUSSIAN REVOLUTIONARY AND
WRITER

10 'Better to perish with the revolution than
to seek refuge in the almshouse of
reaction.'
FROM THE OTHER SHORE *(1848–49),
Introduction, 'To My Son Alexander'*

11 'The liberty of the individual is the
greatest thing of all; it is *on this and on
this alone* that the true will of the people
can develop.'
IBID.

12 'The world will not know liberty until
everything religious and political is
transformed into something simple,
human, susceptible to criticism and
denial . . . the republic has no mystical
saving-clauses, no Divine Right, it stands
on the same level with us all. It is not
enough to despise the crown, one must
give up respecting the Phrygian cap; it is
not enough to consider *lèse majesté* a
crime, one must look on *salus populi* as
being one.'
IBID., *'After the Storm'*

13 'They found strength enough to break
their heavy iron chains, without noticing
that the walls of the prison remained
standing. They wanted to leave the walls
as they were and to give them a new
function – as though the plan of a prison
could be adapted to a free life. What is
there beyond its walls? Fear grips one. All
is empty, vast, free . . . How can one go
without knowing where: how can one
give up what one has, without any
prospects? If Columbus had argued like
this, he would never have weighed
anchor. It was lunacy to sail the Ocean
without knowing one's course, an Ocean
on which no one had travelled before,
and head for a country whose very
existence was in question. By this lunacy

he discovered a new world. Of course, if nations always moved from one set of furnished rooms to another – and always into a better set – things might be easier, but the trouble is that there is no one to prepare the new rooms. The future is worse than the Ocean – there is nothing there. It will be what men and circumstances make it.'

IBID., *'Year LVII of the Republic'. On the failure of the revolution in France, 1848*

1   'This is the position of *reformers* in general: all they do is to lay down the pontoons across which the peoples whom they have aroused cross from one shore to the other.'
IBID.

2   'The forms of European civil order, its civilisation, its good and evil . . . like everything living, were capable of change – but, like everything living, were changeable *only to a certain degree*; an organism can be trained, can deviate from its original function, can adapt itself to influences, until a point is reached when these deviations destroy its peculiarities, its individuality, that which constitutes its personality. When this happens, a struggle ensues and the organism either wins or perishes . . . The state forms of France and other European countries are in their essence compatible with neither liberty, equality, nor fraternity. If any of these ideas were realised, it would be the repudiation of contemporary European life; it would be its death . . .Do you imagine for one moment that Metternich and Guizot did not see the injustices of the social order that surrounded them? But they saw also that these injustices were so much part of the organism as a whole that it needed only a touch and the whole edifice would come tumbling down. Realising this, they became the guardians of the *status quo*.'
IBID.

3   'Aristocracy is really a more or less civilised form of cannibalism: a savage who eats his prisoner, a landowner who draws an enormous rent from his estate, a manufacturer who grows rich at the expense of his workmen, are mere varieties of this same cannibalism.'
IBID.

4   'It is difficult to impregnate the masses with ideas, because for them ideas are not something frivolous.'
IBID., *'Vixerunt'*

5   'Have you ever considered the meaning of the words: "Man is born free"? I will translate them for you. They mean: "Man is born an animal", no more. Take a herd of wild horses. There you have complete freedom and equal rights, perfect communism. But, on the other hand, development is impossible. Slavery is the first step towards civilisation. In order to develop it is necessary that things should be much better for some and much worse for others; then those who are better off can develop at the expense of others.'
IBID., *'Consolatio'*

6   'If only people wanted to save themselves instead of saving the world, to liberate themselves instead of liberating humanity, how much they would do for the salvation of the world and the liberation of humanity.'
IBID., *'Omnia Mia Mecum Porto'*

7   'The death of the contemporary forms of social order ought to gladden rather than trouble the soul. But what is frightening is that the departing world leaves behind it not an heir, but a pregnant widow.'
IBID.

8   'All religions have based morality on obedience, that is to say, on voluntary slavery. That is why they have always been more pernicious than any political organisation. For the latter makes use of violence, the former – of the corruption of the will.'
IBID.

9   'Socialism and rationalism are to this day the touchstones of humanity, the rocks which lie in the course of revolution and science. Groups of swimmers, driven by reflection of the waves of circumstance against these rocks, break up at once into two camps, which, under different guises, remain the same throughout all history, and may be distinguished either in a great political party or in a group of a dozen young men. One represents logic; the other, history: one stands for dialectics; the other for evolution. Truth is the main object of the former, and feasibility of the latter. There is no question of choice between them:

thought is harder to tame than passion and pulls with irresistible force.'
MY PAST AND THOUGHTS (c. 1855)

1 'There is a certain basis of truth in the fear which the Russian government is beginning to have of communism; for communism is Tsarist autocracy turned upside down.'
IBID.

Hindenburg, Paul von
(1847–1934)
GERMAN FIELD MARSHAL AND POLITICIAN, PRESIDENT, 1925–1934

2 'As an English general has very truly said,"The German army was stabbed in the back".'
Statement to the Reichstag committee of inquiry, 18 November 1919. (The identity of the English general, if any, is not known.)

Hirohito (1901–)
EMPEROR OF JAPAN, 1926–

3 'The enemy has begun to employ a new and most cruel bomb, the power of which to do damage is indeed incalculable, taking the toll of many innocent lives. Should we continue to fight, it would not only result in an ultimate collapse and obliteration of the Japanese nation, but it would also lead to the total extinction of human civilisation.'
Radio broadcast, 15 August 1945. Announcing Japan's surrender to the Allies

Hitler, Adolf (1889–1945)
AUSTRIAN-BORN GERMAN NATIONAL SOCIALIST POLITICIAN, CHANCELLOR, 1933–1945

4 'The art of leadership consists in consolidating the attention of the people against a single adversary and taking care that nothing will split up this attention ... The leader of genius must have the ability to make different opponents appear as if they belonged to one category.'
MEIN KAMPF (1924)

5 'Today I believe that I am acting in accordance with the will of the Almighty Creator: by defending myself against the Jew, I am fighting for the work of the Lord.'
IBID.

6 'The great mass of the people ... will more easily fall victim to a big lie than to a small one.'
IBID.

7 'If today I stand here as a revolutionary, it is as a revolutionary against the revolution. There is no such thing as high treason against the traitors of 1918.'
Opening speech from the dock, Munich, 26 February 1924. At his trial for treason after the November putsch

8 'The man who is born to be a dictator is not compelled; he wills it ... The man who feels called upon to govern a people has no right to say: If you want me or summon me, I will cooperate. No, it is his duty to step forward.'
Closing speech from the dock, Munich, 22 March 1924

9 'Struggle is the father of all things ... It is not by the principles of humanity that man lives or is able to preserve himself above the animal world, but solely by means of the most brutal struggle.'
Speech at Kulmbach, February 1928

10 'There is only one right in the world and that right is one's own strength.'
Speech to party leaders, Munich, September 1928

11 'There are no revolutions except racial revolutions: there cannot be a political, economic, or social revolution – always and only it is the struggle of the lower stratum of inferior race against the dominant higher race, and if this higher race has forgotten the law of its existence, then it loses the day.'
In conversation with Otto Strasser, May 1930

12 'If today our action employs among its different weapons that of parliament, that is not to say that parliamentary parties exist only for parliamentary ends. For us parliament is not an end in itself, but merely a means to an end.'
Speech at Munich, 25 September 1930. Speaking ten days after the National Socialists had won 107 seats in the Reichstag at the national election

1 'I go the way that Providence dictates
with the assurance of a sleepwalker.'
Speech at Munich, 15 March 1936

2 'My pride is that I know no statesman in
the world who with greater right than I
can say that he is the representative of
his people.'
Speech at Hamburg, 20 March 1936

3 'I am convinced that 1941 will be the
crucial year of a great New Order in
Europe. The world will open up for
everyone.'
Speech at Berlin, 30 January 1941

4 'Why need we trouble to socialise banks
and factories? We socialise human
beings.'
*In conversation with Hermann
Rauschning. Quoted in Rauschning,*
HITLER SPEAKS, *Chapter 14*

Hobbes, Thomas (1588–1679)
ENGLISH PHILOSOPHER

5 'In the first place, I put for a generall
inclination of all mankind, a perpetuall
and restlesse desire of Power after Power,
that ceaseth onely in Death.'
LEVIATHAN *(1651), Part I, Chapter 11*

6 'Because every Subject is by this
Institution [of the Commonwealth]
Author of all the Actions, and Judgments
of the Soveraigne Instituted; it followes,
that whatsover he doth, it can be no
injury to any of his Subjects; nor ought
he to be by any of them accused of
Injustice. For he that doth any thing by
authority from another, doth therein no
injury to him by whose authority he
acteth.'
IBID., *Part II, Chapter 18. On the nature of
the contract establishing civil government*

7 'And whereas some have attributed the
Dominion to the Man onely, as being of
the more excellent Sex; they misreckon
in it. For there is not alwayes that
difference of strength, or prudence
between the man and the woman, as that
the right can be determined without
War.'
IBID., *Part II, Chapter 20*

8 '*Liberty*, and *Necessity* are consistent.'
IBID., *Part II, Chapter 21*

9 'As for other Lyberties, they depend on
the Silence of the Law.' (*Marginalium:*

'The Greatest Liberty of Subjects,
dependeth on the Silence of the Law.')
IBID.

10 'The *Papacy* is no other, than the *Ghost*
of the deceased *Roman Empire,* sitting
crowned upon the grave thereof.'
IBID., *Part IV, Chapter 47*

11 'The law is all the right reason we have,
and . . . is the infallible rule of moral
goodness. The reason whereof is this, that
because neither mine nor the Bishop's
reason is right reason fit to be a rule of
our moral actions, we have therefore set
up over ourselves a sovereign governor,
and . . . our morality is all contained in
not disobeying of the laws.'
QUESTIONS CONCERNING LIBERTY, NECESSITY
AND CHANCE *(1656). In reply to Dr
Bramhall, Bishop of Derry*

**Hobhouse, John Cam, Ist
Baron Broughton** (1786–1869)
ENGLISH RADICAL POLITICIAN, MEMBER
OF PARLIAMENT, 1820–1831

12 'It is said to be very hard on His
Majesty's ministers to raise objections to
this proposition. For my own part, I think
it is much more hard on His Majesty's
opposition to compel them to take this
course.'
*House of Commons, 26 April 1826. First
use of the phrase, 'His Majesty's
opposition'*

Hobhouse, Leonard (1864–1929)
ENGLISH PHILOSOPHER AND
JOURNALIST

13 'Liberty without equality is a name of
noble sound and squalid result.'
LIBERALISM *(1911), Chapter 4*

Hölderlin, Friedrich (1770–1843)
GERMAN POET

14 'What has always made the state a hell
on earth has been precisely that man has
tried to make it his heaven.'
Quoted in F Hayek, THE ROAD TO SERFDOM,
Chapter 2

Home of the Hirsel, Baron (Alexander [Alec] Douglas-Home)
SCOTTISH CONSERVATIVE POLITICIAN, PRIME MINISTER, 1963–1964

1 'No, because I do my sums with matchsticks.'
Interview in THE OBSERVER, *1962. Quoted in Home,* THE WAY THE WIND BLOWS *(1976), Chapter 13. In answer to the question, whether he would ever become prime minister*

2 'It is becoming more and more clear that there are few halts between Keynes and Marx.'
THE WAY THE WIND BLOWS, *Chapter 20*

Hone, William (1780–1842)
ENGLISH WRITER AND BOOKSELLER

3 'Our Lord who art in the Treasury, whatsoever be thy name, thy power be prolonged, thy will be done throughout the empire, as it is in each session. Give us our usual sops, and forgive us our occasional absences on divisions; as we promise not to forgive those who divide against thee. Turn us not out of our places; but keep us in the House of Commons, the land of Pensions and Plenty; and deliver us from the People. Amen.'
THE PRAYER OF A PLACEMAN *(1817)*

Hoover, Herbert (1874–1964)
AMERICAN REPUBLICAN POLITICIAN, PRESIDENT, 1929–1933

4 'When the war closed ... we were challenged with a peace-time choice between the American system of rugged individualism and a European philosophy of diametrically opposed doctrines – doctrines of paternalism and state socialism.'
Speech at New York, 22 October 1928

5 'The slogan of progress is changing from the full dinner pail to the full garage.'
IBID.

6 'I hesitate to contemplate the future of our institutions, of our country, if the preoccupation of its officials is to be no longer the promotion of justice and equal opportunity, but is to be devoted to barter in the markets. That is not liberalism; it is degeneration.'
Message to Congress, 1931, Vetoing the Norris bill for the construction of a second dam on the Tennessee river and for government manufacture and sale of fertiliser and power

Horsley, Samuel (1733–1806)
ENGLISH BISHOP

7 'The mass of the people have nothing to do with the laws but to obey them.'
House of Lords, 1795

Howe, Julia Ward (1819–1910)
AMERICAN WRITER AND REFORM AGITATOR

8 'Mine eyes have seen the glory of the coming of the Lord;
He is trampling out the vintage where the grapes of wrath are stored;
He hath loosed the fateful lightning of his terrible swift sword;
His truth is marching on.'
THE BATTLE HYMN OF THE REPUBLIC *(1861)*

9 'As He died to make men holy, let us die to make men free.'
IBID.

Howells, William Dean (1837–1920)
AMERICAN NOVELIST AND CRITIC

10 'The State is still, after individual despots have been largely modified or eliminated, a collective despot, mostly inexorable, almost irresponsible, and entirely inaccessible to those personal appeals which have sometimes moved the obsolete or obsolescent tyrants to pity. In its selfishness and meanness, it is largely the legislated and organized ideal of the lowest and stupidest of its citizens, whose daily life is nearest the level of barbarism.'
Quoted in D Aaron, MEN OF GOOD HOPE, *Chapter 6*

11 'You will hear people more foolish than wicked say, "our country, right or wrong", but that is a false patriotism and bad Americanism. When our country is wrong she is worse than other countries when they are wrong, for she has more

light than other countries, and we ought somehow to make her feel that we are sorry and ashamed for her.'
IBID.

Hsu Ching-hsien (*fl.* 1960)
CHINESE COMMUNIST OFFICIAL, LEADER OF THE SHANGHAI REVOLUTIONARY COMMITTEE

1 'Again and again you must wash your brain. If you forget to do it from time to time, the capitalist spirit will soon return. This brainwashing is painful; you feel the pain of it for a long time. If you did not suffer from it, it would mean it had become useless. Ten or a hundred brainwashings are needed in the life of a man. Ten or a hundred Cultural revolutions are needed in the life of China, if she is to remain Red for a thousand or ten thousand years.'
In conversation with A Peyrefitte. Quoted in Peyrefitte, THE CHINESE, *Chapter 11*

Hughes, William (1864–1952)
WELSH-BORN AUSTRALIAN LABOUR POLITICIAN, PRIME MINISTER, 1915–1923

2 'Well, you may decide to do what is proposed to you; all I can say is that whichever way you decide you will before long wish you had done the opposite.'
Often-repeated remark at cabinet and party discussions. Quoted in R Menzies, AFTERNOON LIGHT, *Chapter 6*

Hume, David (1711–1776)
SCOTTISH PHILOSOPHER AND HISTORIAN

3 'Men are not able radically to cure, either in themselves or others, that narrowness of soul which makes them prefer the present to the remote. They cannot change their natures. All they can do is to change their situation, and render the observance of justice the immediate interest of some particular persons, and its violation the more remote.'
A TREATISE OF HUMAN NATURE *(1739–40), Book III, Part II, Chapter 7. On the origins of civil government*

4 'The three fundamental rules of justice, the stability of possession, its transference by consent, and the performance of promises, are duties of princes as well as of subjects . . . Where possession has no stability, there must be perpetual war. Where property is not transferred by consent, there can be no commerce. Where promises are not observed, there can be no leagues or alliances.'
IBID., *Book III, Part II, Chapter 11*

5 'It is, therefore, a just *political* maxim, *that every man must be supposed a knave.*'
ESSAYS MORAL AND POLITICAL *(1741–42), 'Of the Independency of Parliament'*

6 'Did one generation of men go off the stage at once, and another succeed, as is the case with silkworms and butterflies, the new race, if they had sense enough to choose their government, which surely is never the case with men, might voluntarily, and by general consent, establish their own forms of civil polity, without any regard to the laws or precedents which prevailed among their ancestors. But as human society is in perpetual flux, one man every hour going out of the world, another coming into it, it is necessary, in order to preserve stability in government, that the new brood should conform themselves to the established constitution, and nearly follow the path which their fathers, treading in the footsteps of theirs, had marked out to them.'
IBID., *'Of the Original Contract'*

Humphrey, Hubert (1911–1978)
AMERICAN DEMOCRATIC POLITICIAN, VICE-PRESIDENT, 1965–1969

7 'I say the time has come to walk out of the shadow of states' rights and into the sunlight of human rights.'
Speech to the Democratic national convention, August 1948. Urging the party to include a strong commitment to Black civil rights in its platform

Hunt, G W (*c.* 1829–1904)
ENGLISH RHYMESTER

8 'We don't want to fight, but by jingo if we do,
We've got the ships, we've got the men, we've got the money too.
We've fought the Bear before, and while Britons shall be true,
The Russians shall not have Constantinople.'
Music-hall song, c. 1878

Hunt, Leigh (1784–1859)
ENGLISH MAN OF LETTERS

1 'I now look upon war as one of the fleeting necessities of things in the course of human progress; as an evil (like most other evils) to be regarded in relation to some other evil that would have been worse without it, but always to be considered as an indication of comparative barbarism – as a necessity, the perpetuity of which is not to be assumed – or as a half-reasoning mode of adjustment, whether of disputes or of populations, which mankind, on arriving at years of discretion, and coming to a better understanding with one another, may, and must of necessity, do away. It would be as ridiculous to associate the idea of war with an earth covered with railroads and commerce, as a fight between Holborn and the Strand, or between people met in a drawing-room.'
AUTOBIOGRAPHY *(revised edition, 1860),* *Chapter 9*

Hutcheson, Francis (1694–1746)
IRISH PHILOSOPHER

2 'That action is best which procures the greatest happiness for the greatest numbers.'
AN INQUIRY INTO THE ORIGINAL OF OUR IDEAS OF BEAUTY AND VIRTUE *(1725)*

Huxley, Aldous (1894–1963)
ENGLISH NOVELIST AND ESSAYIST

3 'The more cant there is in politics the better. Cant is nothing in itself; but attached to even the smallest quantity of sincerity, it serves like a nought after a numeral, to multiply whatever of genuine good-will may exist.'
JESTING PILATE *(1926)*

4 'When particular men and women are thought of merely as representatives of a class, which has previously been defined as evil and personified in the shape of a devil, then the reluctance to hurt or murder disappears. Brown, Jones and Robinson are no longer thought of as Brown, Jones and Robinson, but as heretics, gentiles, Yids, niggers, barbarians, Huns, communists, capitalists, fascists, liberals . . . and become for users of this fatally inappropriate language mere vermin or worse, demons, whom it is right and proper to destroy.'
THE OLIVE TREE AND OTHER ESSAYS *(1936),* *'Words and Behaviour'*

5 'Idealism is the noble toga that political gentlemen drape over their will to power.'
NEW YORK HERALD TRIBUNE, *25 November 1962*

I

1 **Ibárruri, Dolores** (1895–1981)
SPANISH COMMUNIST LEADER, KNOWN
AS 'LA PASIONARIA'

'Better to die on one's feet than to live on
one's knees.'
Speech at Valencia, 1936

2 **Ibn Taymiyya** (1263–1328)
EGYPTIAN MUSLIM THEOLOGIAN

'He who forsakes the Law of Islam
should be fought.'
PUBLIC POLICY IN ISLAMIC JURISPRUDENCE

J

Jackson, Andrew (1767–1845)
AMERICAN POLITICIAN, PRESIDENT, 1829–1837

1 'I am one of those who do not believe that a national debt is a national blessing . . . it is calculated to raise around the administration a moneyed aristocracy dangerous to the liberties of the country.'
Letter to L H Colman, 26 April 1824
SEE ALSO *Patrick Henry*

2 'When an honest observance of constitutional compacts cannot be obtained from communities like ours, it need not be anticipated elsewhere, and the cause in which there has been so much martyrdom, and from which so much was expected by the friends of liberty, may be abandoned, and the degrading truth that man is unfit for self-government admitted. And this will be the case if expediency be made a rule of construction in interpreting the Constitution.'
Veto message on the Lexington Turnpike Road bill, 27 May 1830

3 'There are no necessary evils in government. Its evils exist only in its abuses.'
Veto message on the bill to renew the charter of the Bank of the United States, 10 July 1832

4 '*Perpetuity* is stamped upon the constitution by the blood of our Fathers.'
Letter to J R Poinsett, 2 December 1832

5 'The Constitution of the United States, then, forms a **government**, not a league; and whether it be formed by compact between the States or in any other manner, its character is the same . . . secession does not break a league, but destroys the unity of a nation; and any injury to that unity is not only a breach which would result from the contravention of a compact, but it is an offense against the whole Union. To say that any State may at pleasure secede from the Union is to say that the United States are not a nation, because it would be a solecism to contend that any part of a nation might dissolve its connection with the other parts, to their injury or ruin, committing any offense. Secession, like any other revolutionary act, may be morally justified by the extremity of oppression; but to call it a constitutional right is confounding the meaning of the term.'
Anti-nullification proclamation, 10 December 1832

Jackson, George (1942–1971)
AMERICAN BLACK REVOLUTIONARY LEADER

6 'I don't think of life in the same sense that you or most black men of your generation think of it, it is not important to me how long I live, I think only of how I live, how well, how nobly. We think if we are to be men again we must stop working for nothing, competing against each other for the little they allow us to possess, stop selling our women or allowing them to be used and handled against their will, stop letting our children be educated by the barbarian, using their language, dress, and customs, and most assuredly stop turning our cheeks.'
Letter to his father, 30 March 1965. From Soledad prison

7 'You know I have grown very, very tired of talking, and listening to talk. [Martin Luther] King and his kind have betrayed our bosom interests with their demagogic delirium. The poor fool knows nothing of the antagonist's true nature and has not the perception to read and learn by history and past events. In a nonviolent movement there must be a latent threat of eruption, a dormant possibility of sudden and violent action if concessions are to be won, respect gained, and the established order altered. That nonviolent theory is practicable in civilized lands among civilized people, the Asians and Africans, but a look at European history shows that anything of great value that ever changed hands was taken by force of arms.'
Letter to his mother, March 1967. From Soledad prison

8 'I love you, mama, but I must be frank. Why did Papa die alone and hungry? Why did you think me insane for wanting a new bicycle instead of the old one I stole piece by piece and put together? Why did you allow us to

worship at a white altar? Why even now,
following tragedy after tragedy, crisis
after crisis, do you still send Jon to that
school where he is taught to feel inferior,
and why do you continue to send me
Easter cards? This is the height of the
disrespect you show me. You never
wanted me to be a man nor Jon either.
You don't want us to resist and defeat our
enemies. What is wrong with you,
Mama?'
Letter to his mother, 26 March 1967.
From Soledad prison

Jacoby, Johann (1805–1877)
PRUSSIAN ROYALIST POLITICIAN

1   'It is the misfortune of kings that they
will not listen to the truth.'
Letter to Frederick William II, 2
November 1848

James I (1566–1625)
KING OF ENGLAND, 1603–1625 (KING
JAMES VI OF SCOTLAND FROM 1567)

2   'A good King will frame his actions to be
according to the Law, yet he is not bound
thereto but of his Good Will.'
THE TRUE LAW OF FREE MONARCHIES *(1598)*

3   'No Bishop, no King.'
Speech to the Hampton Court
Conference, 14 January 1604

4   'Kings are justly called Gods, for that
they exercise a manner or resemblance of
Divine power upon earth. For if you will
consider the attributes of God, you shall
see how they agree in the person of a
King.'
Speech to parliament, 21 March 1609

5   'I will govern according to the common
weal, but not according to the common
will.'
Answer to the House of Commons, 1621

6   'God has made of you a little god, to sit
on your throne and rule men.'
Instuction to his son, the future Charles I.
Quoted in B Jouvenal, POWER, Chapter 2

Jaurès, Jean (1859–1914)
FRENCH SOCIALIST POLITICIAN AND
WRITER

7   'Capitalism carries within itself war, as
clouds carry rain.'
STUDIES IN SOCIALISM *(1902)*

Jefferson, Thomas (1743–1826)
AMERICAN REPUBLICAN POLITICIAN,
PRESIDENT, 1801–1809

8   'When in the Course of human events, it
becomes necessary for one people to
dissolve the political bonds, which have
connected them with another, and to
assume among the powers of the earth,
the separate and equal station to which
the Laws of Nature and of Nature's God
entitle them, a decent respect to the
opinions of mankind requires that they
should declare the causes which impel
them to the separation. We hold these
truths to be self-evident, that all men are
created equal, that they are endowed by
their Creator with certain inalienable
rights, that among these are Life, Liberty
and the pursuit of Happiness. That to
secure these rights, Governments are
instituted among Men, deriving their just
powers from the consent of the governed.
That whenever any Form of Government
becomes destructive of these ends, it is
the Right of the People to alter or to
abolish it, and to institute new
Government.'
The Declaration of Independence, 1776.
(Amended, with others, from Jefferson's
draft.)

9   'And for the support of this Declaration,
with a firm reliance on the protection of
divine Providence, we mutually pledge to
each other our Lives, our Fortunes and
our sacred Honor.'
IBID.

10 'I tremble for my country when I reflect
that God is just; that his justice cannot
sleep forever.'
NOTES ON THE STATE OF VIRGINIA *(1781). On*
the institution of Black slavery

11 'It is error alone which needs the support
of government. Truth can stand by
itself.'
IBID.

12 'The mobs of great cities add just so
much to the support of pure government,
as sores do to the strength of the human
body.'
IBID.

13 'I hold it, that a little rebellion now and
then, is a good thing, and as necessary in
the political world as storms in the
physical . . . It is a medicine for the
sound health of government.'
Letter to James Madison, 30 January 1787

1 'What signify a few lives lost in a century or two? The tree of liberty must be refreshed from time to time with the blood of patriots and tyrants. It is its natural manure.'
Letter to W S Smith, 13 November 1787. On Shay's rebellion

2 'There is not a single crowned head in Europe whose talents or merit would entitle him to be elected a vestryman by the people of any parish in America.'
Letter to George Washington, 2 May 1788

3 'The republican is the only form of government which is not eternally at open or secret war with the rights of mankind.'
Letter to William Hunter, 11 March 1790

4 'We are not to be expected to be translated from despotism to liberty in a featherbed.'
Letter to Lafayette, 2 April 1790

5 'No man will ever carry out of the Presidency the reputation which carried him into it.'
Letter to Edward Rutledge, 1796

6 'Peace, commerce and honest friendship with all nations; entangling alliances with none.'
First inaugural address, 4 March 1801
SEE ALSO *Washington*

7 'Politics, like religion, hold up the torches of martyrdom to the reformers of error.'
Letter to James Ogilvie, 4 April 1811

8 'An honest man can feel no pleasure in the exercise of power over his fellow citizens.'
Letter to John McLish, 13 January 1813

9 'This momentous question, like a firebell in the night, awakened and filled me with terror. I considered it at once as the knell of the Union.'
Letter to John Adams, 22 April 1820. On the Missouri Compromise over slavery extension

10 'The excessive power in our government is not the only, perhaps not even the principal, object of my solicitude. The tyranny of the legislature is really the danger most to be feared, and will continue to be so for many years to come.'
Quoted in A de Tocqueville, DEMOCRACY IN AMERICA, Part I, Chapter 12

11 'Great innovations should not be forced on slender majorities.'
Quoted in I Gilmour, INSIDE RIGHT, Part III, Chapter 5

Jenkins, Robert (*fl.* 1730–1745)
ENGLISH MERCHANT CAPTAIN

12 'I commended my soul to my God and my cause to my country.'
Statement to the House of Commons, 1739. In answer to the question, what his feelings were when the Spanish tore off his ear

Johnson, Lyndon (1908–1973)
AMERICAN DEMOCRATIC POLITICIAN, PRESIDENT, 1963–1969

13 'No political party can be a friend of the American people which is not a friend of American business.'
Speech to the Houston Chamber of Commerce, 12 August 1963

14 'This administration here and now declares unconditional war on poverty in America.'
State of the Union address to Congress, 8 January 1964

15 'The challenge of the next half-century is whether we have the wisdom to use wealth to enrich and elevate our national life – and to advance the quality of American civilisation – for in your time we have the opportunity to move not only toward the rich society and the powerful society, but upward to the Great Society.'
Speech at Ann Arbor, 22 May 1964

16 'This is not a jungle war, but a struggle for freedom on every front of human activity.'
Speech on television, 4 August 1964. On the war in Vietnam, after the second 'Tonkin incident'

17 'We are not about to send American boys nine or ten thousand miles away from home to do what Asian boys ought to be doing for themselves.'
Speech on television, 21 October 1964

18 'Extremism in the pursuit of the Presidency is an unpardonable vice. Moderation in the affairs of the nation is the highest virtue.'
Speech at New York, 31 October 1964. In reply to Barry Goldwater's famous dictum
SEE ALSO *Goldwater*

1 'Poverty has many roots, but the tap root is ignorance.'
Speech to Congress, 12 January 1965

2 'I do not believe that the Great Society is the ordered, changeless, and sterile battalion of the ants. It is the excitement of becoming, trying, probing, failing, resting, and trying again.'
Inaugural address, 20 January 1965

Johnson, Samuel (1709–1784)
ENGLISH MAN OF LETTERS

3 '*Pension*. An allowance made to anyone without an equivalent. In England it is generally understood to mean pay given to a state hireling for treason to his country.'
DICTIONARY OF THE ENGLISH LANGUAGE *(1755)*

4 '*Whig*. The name of a faction.'
IBID.

5 'I would not give half a guinea to live under one form of government rather than another. It is of no moment to the happiness of an individual.'
In conversation, 31 March 1772.

6 'How is it that we hear the loudest *yelps* for liberty among the drivers of negroes?'
TAXATION NO TYRANNY *(1775). On the American revolutionaries*

7 'All government is ultimately and essentially absolute.'
IBID.

8 'Patriotism is the last refuge of a scoundrel.'
In conversation, 7 April 1775. On the 'patriot' party

9 'Politics are now nothing more than a means of rising in the world.'
In conversation, 18 April 1775

10 'I have always said, the first Whig was the Devil.'
In conversation, 28 April 1778

11 'In every government though terrors reign,
Though tyrant King or tyrant laws restrain,
How small, of all that human hearts endure,
That part which laws or Kings can cause or cure.'
Lines appended to the end of Goldsmith's THE TRAVELLER

Jones, Ernest (1819–1869)
ENGLISH CHARTIST LEADER

12 'The Book of Kings is fast closing in the great Bible of Humanity.'
NORTHERN STAR, *4 March 1848. On the abdication of King Louis-Philippe of France*

Jouvenel, Bertrand de, Baron (1903–)
FRENCH POLITICAL ECONOMIST

13 'Politics is a systematic effort to move other men in the pursuit of some design.'
THE PURE THEORY OF POLITICS *(1963)*

Juvenal (*fl.* 1st to 2nd century AD)
ROMAN POET

14 'Two things only the people anxiously desire, bread and the Circus games.'
(Duas tantem res anxius optat,/Panem et Circenses.)
SATIRES, *X*

K

Kant, Immanuel (1724–1804)
GERMAN PHILOSOPHER

1 'The means which nature employs to bring about the development of innate capacities is that of antagonism within society, in so far as this antagonism becomes in the long run the cause of a law-governed social order. By antagonism, I mean in this context the *unsocial sociability* of men, that it, their tendency to come together in society, coupled, however, with a continual resistance which constantly threatens to break this society up. This propensity is obviously rooted in human nature ... Without these asocial qualities (far from admirable in themselves) which cause the resistance inevitably encountered by each individual as he furthers his self-seeking pretensions, man would live an Arcadian, pastoral existence of perfect concord, self-sufficiency and mutual love. But all human talents would remain hidden for ever in a dormant state ... Nature should thus be thanked for fostering social incompatibility, enviously competitive vanity, and insatiable desires for possession or even power. Without these desires, all men's excellent natural capacities would never be roused to develop.'
IDEA FOR A UNIVERSAL HISTORY WITH A COSMOPOLITAN PURPOSE *(1784)*

2 'The greatest problem for the human species, the solution of which nature compels him to seek, is that of attaining a civil society which can administer justice universally.'
IBID.

3 'The problem of establishing a perfect civil constitution is subordinate to the problem of a law-governed *external relationship* with other states, and cannot be solved unless the latter is also solved.'
IBID.

4 'War is only a regrettable expedient for asserting one's rights by force within a state of nature, where no court of justice is available to judge with legal authority. In such cases, neither party can be declared an unjust enemy, for this would already presuppose a judge's decision; only the outcome of the conflict, as in the case of a so-called "judgement of God", can decide who is in the right.'
PERPETUAL PEACE: A PHILOSOPHICAL SKETCH *(1795)*

5 'Of the three forms of sovereignty – autocracy, aristocracy, democracy – *democracy*, in the truest sense of the word, is necessarily a *despotism*, because it establishes an executive power through which all the citizens may make decisions about (and indeed against) the single individual without his consent, so that decisions are made by all the people and yet not by all the people; and this means that the general will is in contradiction with itself, and thus also with freedom.'
IBID.

6 'The best way of making a nation content with its constitution is to *rule* autocratically and at the same time to *govern* in a republican manner, that is to govern in the spirit of republicanism and by analogy with it.'
THE CONTEST OF FACULTIES *(1798)*

7 'That kings should philosophise or philosophers become kings is not to be expected. Nor is it to be wished, since the possession of power inevitably corrupts the untrammelled judgement of reason.'
Quoted in M Lasky, UTOPIA AND REVOLUTION, *Chapter 16*

Kaunda, Kenneth (1924–   )
ZAMBIAN NATIONALIST LEADER, PRESIDENT, 1964–

8 'Some people draw a comforting distinction between "force" and "violence" ... I refuse to cloud the issue by such word-play ... the power which establishes a state is violence; the power which maintains it is violence; the power which eventually overthrows it is violence ... Call an elephant a rabbit only if it gives you comfort to feel that you are about to be trampled to death by a rabbit.'
KAUNDA ON VIOLENCE *(1980), Part I*

9 'Passsive resistance is a sport for gentlemen (and ladies) – just like the pursuit of war, a heroic enterprise for the

ruling classes but a grievous burden on the rest.'
IBID., *Part II*

1 'The drama can only be brought to its climax in one of two ways – through the selective brutality of terrorism or the impartial horrors of war.'
IBID. *On the state of South Africa*

2 'War is just like bush-clearing – the moment you stop, the jungle comes back even thicker, but for a little while you can plant and grow a crop in the ground you have won at such terrible cost.'
IBID., *Part III*

3 'If a lion lies on its back waving its paws in the air you are not disposed to take its growls too seriously.'
IBID., *Part IV. On Rhodesia's defiance of the British government's sanctions against Ian Smith's rebel regime*

Kennan, George (1904–)
AMERICAN DIPLOMAT AND HISTORIAN

4 'If there is any one lesson to be plainly derived from the experiences we have had with disarmament in the past half-century, it is that armaments are a function and not a cause of political tensions and that no limitation of armaments on a multilateral scale can be effected as long as the political problems are not tackled and regulated in some realistic way.'
MEMOIRS, *1950–1963, Chapter 6*

5 'He was the nation's number one Boy Scout.'
IBID. *Chapter 8. Of President Eisenhower*

6 'Until we stop pushing the Kremlin against a closed door, we shall never learn whether it would be prepared to go through an open one.'
Reith Lectures on BBC radio, 1957

7 'The true end of political action is, after all, to affect the deeper convictions of men; this the atomic bomb cannot do. The suicidal nature of this weapon renders it unsuitable both as a sanction of diplomacy and as the basis of an alliance.'
IBID.

Kennedy, John Fitzgerald
(1917–1963)
AMERICAN DEMOCRATIC POLITICIAN, PRESIDENT, 1961–1963

8 'I just received the following wire from my generous Daddy – "Dear Jack. Don't buy a single vote more than necessary. I'll be damned if I'm going to pay for a landslide".'
Speech to journalist at Washington, 1958

9 'We stand today on the edge of a New Frontier – the frontier of the 1960s – a frontier of unknown opportunities and perils – a frontier of unfulfilled hopes and threats.'
Speech at the Democratic national convention, 15 July 1960. Accepting the party's nomination as its presidential candidate

10 'I want every American free to stand up for his rights, even if he has to sit down for them.'
Campaign speech, 3 August 1960. Referring to the sit-in campaign of the Black civil rights movement

11 'Let the word go forth from this time and place, to friend and foe alike, that the torch has been passed to a new generation of Americans ... Let every nation know, whether it wishes us well or ill, that we shall pay any price, bear any burden, meet any hardship, support any friend, oppose any foe to assure the survival and success of liberty.'
Inaugural address, 20 January 1961

12 'If a free society cannot help the many who are poor, it cannot save the few who are rich.'
IBID.

13 'Let us never negotiate out of fear, but let us never fear to negotiate.'
IBID.

14 'All this will not be finished in the first one hundred days. Nor will it be finished in the first one thousand days.'
IBID.

15 'Ask not what your country can do for you; ask what you can do for your country.'
IBID.

16 'Unconditional war can no longer lead to unconditional victory ... Mankind must put an end to war or war will put an end to mankind.'
Speech to the United Nations' general assembly, 25 September 1961

17 'I think this is the most extraordinary collection of human talent, of human knowledge, that has ever been gathered

at the White House – with the possible exception of when Thomas Jefferson dined alone.'
Speech at a dinner honouring Nobel Prize winners, April 1962

1 'Liberty without learning is always in peril and learning without liberty is always in vain.'
Speech at Vanderbilt University, 18 March 1963

2 'No one has been barred on account of his race from fighting or dying for America – there are no "white" or "colored" signs on the foxholes or graveyards of battle.'
Message to Congress, 19 June 1963. On his proposed civil rights bill

3 'Two thousand years ago the proudest boast was *"Civis Romanus sum"*. Today, in the world of freedom, the proudest boast is *"Ich bin ein Berliner"* . . . All free men, wherever they may live, are citizens of Berlin, and, therefore, as a free man, I take pride in the words, *"Ich bin ein Berliner"*.'
Speech at City Hall, West Berlin, 26 June 1963

Kerensky, Alexander
(1881–1970)
RUSSIAN MENSHEVIK POLITICIAN, PREMIER, 1917

4 'At the end of my long life, which has been entirely passed in the critical years of our present historical turning point, I can clearly see that no one gets away with anything and that one has to pay for everything. No one can get away with Machiavellian policy, which teaches that politics and morality do not mix and that what is regarded as unethical and criminal in the life of an individual is permissible and even essential for the good and power of the state. It has always been so, but it must not be so any longer. But should it continue to be so, then the destructive forces which have accumulated in the depths of the soulless mechanical civilisation of the contemporary world will burst out. Man must learn to live not by hatred and revenge, but by love and forgiveness.'
THE KERENSKY MEMOIRS *(1965), Chapter 28*

Keynes, John Maynard, 1st Baron (1883–1946)
ENGLISH ECONOMIST

5 'There is no subtler, no surer means of overturning the existing basis of society than to debauch the currency. The process engages all the hidden forces of economic law on the side of destruction, and does it in a manner which not one man in a million is able to diagnose.'
THE ECONOMIC CONSEQUENCES OF THE PEACE *(1919). On inflation*

6 'Leninism is a combination of two things which Europeans have kept for some centuries in different compartments of the soul – religion and business.'
ESSAYS IN PERSUASION *(1933), 'A Short View of Russia'*

Khrushchev, Nikita (1894–1971)
SOVIET COMMUNIST POLITICIAN, FIRST SECRETARY OF THE CPSU, 1953–1964

7 'A Communist has no right to be a mere onlooker.'
Report to the Central Committee of the party, 14 February 1956

8 'Comrades! The cult of the individual acquired such monstrous size chiefly because Stalin himself, using all conceivable methods, supported the glorification of his own person.'
Speech to the secret session of the 20th Congress of the Communist party, 25 February 1956

9 'Comrades! We must abolish the cult of the individual decisively, once and for all.'
IBID.

10 'We are not ignorant savages anymore. You cannot frighten us as you would have done thirty years ago.'
In conversation with Harold Stassen, James Callaghan, Richard Crossman and others, 24 April 1956

11 'What is there left for us to do? If we let things take their course the West would say we were either stupid or weak, and that's one and the same thing.'
In conversation, October 1956. Quoted in V Micunovic, MOSCOW DIARY. *On the sending of Soviet troops into Hungary, 1956*

1. 'Whether you like it or not, history is on our side. We will bury you.'
In conversation with Western diplomats in Moscow, 26 November 1956

2. 'The Oder-Neisse frontier is a frontier of peace.'
Speech at the Friendship Meeting of the Polish People's Republic and the Soviet Union, 10 November 1958

3. 'Everything is fluid and everything progresses towards Communism.'
In conversation with American trade union leaders, San Francisco, 20 September 1959

4. 'Politicians are the same all over. They promise to build a bridge even where there is no river.'
In conversation with reporters, New York, October 1960

King, Martin Luther (1929–1968)
AMERICAN CIVIL RIGHTS LEADER

5. 'It is my hope that as the Negro plunges deeper into the quest for freedom and justice he will plunge even deeper into the philosophy of non-violence. The Negro all over the South must come to the point that he can say to his white brother: "We will match your capacity to inflict suffering with our capacity to endure suffering. We will meet your physical force with soul force. We will not hate you, but we will not obey your evil laws. We will soon wear you down by pure capacity to suffer".'
Letter to Chester Bowles, 28 October 1957

6. 'If a man hasn't discovered something that he will die for, he isn't fit to live.'
Speech at Detroit, 23 June 1963

7. 'Judicial decrees may not change the heart, but they can restrain the heartless.'
STRENGTH OF LOVE *(1963). On legislation to promote racial equality*

8. 'I say to you today even though we face the difficulties of today and tomorrow, I still have a dream. It is a dream that is deeply rooted in the American dream. I have a dream that one day this nation will rise up, live out the true meaning of its creed: We hold these truths to be self-evident, that all men are created equal. I have a dream that one day on the red hills of Georgia the sons of former slaves and the sons of former slave-owners will be able to sit down together at the table of brotherhood ... I have a dream that one day every valley shall be exalted, every hill and mountain shall be made low. The rough places will be made plain and the crooked places will be made straight.'
Speech at Washington, 28 August 1963

9. 'I just want to do God's will. And he's allowed me to go up to the mountain. And I've looked over, and I've seen the Promised Land.'
Speech at Memphis, Tennessee, 3 April 1964

Kipling, Rudyard (1865–1936)
ENGLISH AUTHOR

10. 'Take up the White Man's Burden –
Send forth the best ye breed –
Go bind your sons to exile
To serve your captives' need;
To wait in heavy harness
On fluttered folk and wild –
Your new-caught, sullen people,
Half-devil and half-child.'
THE WHITE MAN'S BURDEN *(1899)*

Kissinger, Henry (1923–)
GERMAN-BORN AMERICAN REPUBLICAN POLITICIAN, SECRETARY OF STATE, 1973–1977

11. 'The security of Israel is a moral imperative for all free peoples.'
Speech at the presentation of the Stephen Wise Award to Golda Meir, 13 November 1977

12. 'For other nations, utopia is a blessed past never to be recovered; for Americans it is just beyond the horizon.'
Eulogy at the funeral of Nelson Rockefeller, 2 February 1979

13. 'To have striven so hard, to have moulded a public personality out of so amorphous an identity, to have sustained that superhuman effort only to end with every weakness disclosed and every error compounding the downfall – that was a fate of biblical proportions. Evidently the Deity would not tolerate the presumption that all can be manipulated; an object lesson of the limits of human presumption was necessary.'
THE YEARS OF UPHEAVAL *(1982). On the downfall of Richard Nixon*

Kitchener, Horatio Herbert, 1st Earl (1850–1916)
ENGLISH FIELD MARSHAL, SECRETARY OF STATE FOR WAR, 1914–1916

1 'I do not believe any nation ever entered into a great controversy with a clearer conscience.'
House of Commons, 6 August 1914. Two days after Great Britain had declared war on Germany

Knox, John (c. 1515–1572)
SCOTTISH PRESBYTERIAN LEADER

2 'To promote a Woman to bear rule, superiority, dominion, or empire, above any Realm, Nation, or City, is repugnant to Nature; contumely to God, a thing most contrarious to his revealed will and approved ordinance; and finally it is the subversion of good Order, of all equity and justice.'
FIRST BLAST OF THE TRUMPET AGAINST THE MONSTROUS REGIMENT OF WOMEN *(1558)*

Koestler, Arthur (1905–83)
HUNGARIAN-BORN ENGLISH AUTHOR

3 'Politics can be relatively fair in the breathing spaces of history; at its critical turning points there is no other rule possible than the old one, that the end justifies the means.'
DARKNESS AT NOON *(1940), Book II, Part 1*

4 'We seem to be faced with a pendulum movement in history, swinging from absolutism to democracy, from democracy back to absolute dictatorship . . .
Now, every technical improvement creates a new complication to the economic apparatus, causes the appearance of new factors and combinations, which the masses cannot penetrate for a time. Every jump of technical progress leaves the relative intellectual development of the masses a step behind, and thus causes a fall in the political-maturity thermometer. It takes sometimes tens of years, sometimes generations, for a people's level of understanding gradually to adapt itself to the changed state of affairs, until it has recovered the same capacity for self-government, as it had already possessed at a lower stage of civilization. Hence the political maturity of the masses cannot be measured by an absolute figure, but only relatively, i.e. in proportion to the stage of civilization at that moment.
When the level of mass-consciousness catches up with the objective state of affairs, there follows inevitably the conquest of democracy, either peaceably or by force. Until the next jump of technical civilization – the discovery of the mechanical loom, for example – again sets back the masses in a state of relative immaturity, and renders possible or even necessary the establishment of some form of absolute leadership.'
IBID., *Book III, Part 1*

Kossuth, Louis (1802–1894)
HUNGARIAN REVOLUTIONARY NATIONALIST

5 'The power which is called Austria is not a factor in, but a hindrance to, the equilibrium of power – she is not a barrier but a high road; not a guarantee of peace, but a sword of Damocles suspended over the tranquillity of Europe; she is a cavern from which the European volcano is fed . . . The artificial compound community called Austria is a fictitious power, which possesses only the outward show of a great power; it is a tree which has bark outside, but is empty inside. This is so because the Austrian dynasty cannot rule in the interests of a nation.'
Speech at London, 20 May 1859. Combating the notion that the Austro-Hungarian empire was an essential ingredient in the European balance of power

Kovalev, Sergei (fl. 1965)
SOVIET COMMUNIST OFFICIAL, HEAD OF *PRAVDA'S* PROPAGANDA DEPARTMENT

6 'The peoples of the socialist countries and communist parties . . . have freedom to determine the methods of advance in their respective countries. None of their decisions, however, should damage either socialism in their own country or the fundamental interests of other socialist countries . . . The sovereignty of each socialist country cannot be opposed to the interests of the socialist world . . . the Communists of the fraternal countries

could not allow the socialist states to be inactive in the name of abstractedly understood sovereignty, when they saw that the country stood in peril of anti-socialist degeneration.'
PRAVDA, *25 September 1968. On the Soviet Union's military intervention in Czechoslovakia, August 1968. (The first public statement of the so-called 'Brezhnev doctrine'.)*

Kraus, Karl (1874–1936)
AUSTRIAN POET AND JOURNALIST

1 'Communism is in reality nothing but the antithesis of a particular ideology that is both thoroughly harmful and corrosive. Thank God for the fact that Communism springs from a clean and clear ideal, which preserves its idealistic purpose even though, as an antidote, it is inclined to be somewhat harsh. To hell with its practical import, but may God at least preserve it for us as a never-ending menace to those people who own big estates and who, in order to hang on to them, are prepared to despatch humanity into battle, to abandon it to starvation for the sake of patriotic honour. May God preserve Communism so that the evil brood of its enemies may be prevented from becoming more bare-faced still ... If they must preach morality to their victims and amuse themselves with their suffering, at least let some of their pleasure be spoilt!'
DIE FACKEL, *November 1920*

Kropotkin, Peter, Prince (1842–1921)
RUSSIAN ANARCHIST

2 'The word *state* is identical with the word *war*.'
PAROLES D'UN RÉVOLTÉ *(1885)*

3 'Outside of anarchy, there is no such thing as revolution.'
IBID.

4 'Poland will never lose her national character, it is too strongly developed; she has, and will have, her own literature, her own art and industry. Russia can keep her in servitude only by means of sheer force and oppression – a condition of things which has hitherto favoured, and necessarily will favour, oppression in Russia itself.'
MEMOIRS OF A REVOLUTIONIST *(1899), Part III, Chapter 3*

5 'Freedom remains still the wisest cure for freedom's temporary inconveniences.'
IBID., *Part VI, Chapter 4*

Kurbsky, Andrei, Prince (1528–1583)
RUSSIAN MILITARY COMMANDER AND TSARIST ADVISER

6 'Oh, Satan! ... Why have you planted such a godless seed in the heart of a Christian tsar [Ivan the Terrible], from which such a fire swept over all the Holy Russian land.'
HISTORY OF THE PRINCE OF MOSCOW *(undated). First known printed use of the epithet 'Holy Russia'*

Kutuzov, Michael (1745–1813)
RUSSIAN FIELD MARSHAL

7 'Napoleon is a torrent which as yet we have been unable to stem. Moscow will be the sponge to suck him dry.'
Speech to the Russian army commanders, Fili, 13 September 1812

L

Labouchere, Henry (1831–1912)
ENGLISH JOURNALIST AND RADICAL
POLITICIAN, MEMBER OF PARLIAMENT,
1880–1906

1 'Nothing has more conduced to shake
that decent respect for the living symbol
of the State, which goes by the name of
royalty, than the ever-recurring rattle of
the money-box.'
FORTNIGHTLY REVIEW, *February, 1884. On
the civil list*

2 'Long parliaments are as fatal to sound
business as long credits are to sound
trade.'
IBID. *On the desirability of triennial
parliaments*

La Bruyère, Jean de (1645–1696)
FRENCH MAN OF LETTERS

3 'Party loyalty lowers the greatest men to
the petty level of the masses.'
CARACTÈRES *(1688)*

**Lafayette, Marie Joseph,
Marquis de** (1757–1834)
FRENCH SOLDIER, REFORMER AND
DIPLOMAT

4 'Insurrection is the most sacred of duties.'
*Speech to the National Assembly, 20
February 1790*

Lamartine, Alphonse de
(1790–1869)
FRENCH POET AND POLITICIAN,
FOREIGN MINISTER IN THE
PROVISIONAL GOVERNMENT, 1848

5 'I do not like those men whose official
doctrine is liberty, law, progress, and who
adopt as their symbol a sabre and
despotism. I must own that I cannot
account for it. I do not trust these
contradictions. I am afraid that the key to
this enigma may become only too clear
one day.'
*Speech to the Chamber of Deputies, 1840.
Opposing the proposal to return
Napoleon's ashes to France*

6 'France is revolutionary or she is nothing
at all. The Revolution of 1789 is her
political religion.'
HISTORY OF THE GIRONDINS *(1847)*

7 'A drowning man will catch at a red-hot
poker, and society, threatened by anarchy
and plunder, will clutch the blade of a
sword or a bayonet.'
*In conversation with Nassau Senior, 8
May 1857. On the failure of the
revolution of 1848–1849*

Largo Caballero, Francisco
(1869–1946)
SPANISH SOCIALIST POLITICIAN, PRIME
MINISTER, 1936–1937

8 'It is an aspirin to cure an appendicitis.'
1932. Quoted in H Thomas, THE SPANISH
CIVIL WAR, *Book I, Chapter 6. On the
agrarian law passed by the Cortes in 1932*

9 'To carry out socialist work within a
bourgeois democracy is impossible.'
1933. IBID., *Book I, Chapter 10*

**La Rochefoucauld, François,
duc de** (1613–1680)
FRENCH MAN OF LETTERS

10 'The renown of great men should always
be measured by the means which they
have used to acquire it.'
MAXIMS

Laski, Harold (1893–1950)
ENGLISH POLITICAL THEORIST,
CHAIRMAN OF THE LABOUR PARTY,
1945–1946

11 'I now know why the ultimately great
democrats like Lincoln won their instant
faith. They have a power to recognise the
ultimate thing involved, the big aim, the
large principle, that is closer to reality
than the more sophisticated part of the
population. They are not set aside from
the aim by personal ambition or the fear
of possessions in jeopardy. They have just
made up their minds that something has
to be done, and they go straight for it
without counting the cost to themselves.'
*Letter to Felix Frankfurter, 12 September
1940. After witnessing the bravery of
Londoners during the Battle of Britain*

Lasswell, Harold (1902–   )
AMERICAN POLITICAL ECONOMIST

12 'Politics is who gets what, when, how.'
POLITICS: WHO GETS WHAT, WHEN, HOW *(1936)*

Laud, William (1573–1645)
ENGLISH PRELATE, ARCHBISHOP OF
CANTERBURY, 1633–1645

1 'And for the State indeed, my Lord, I am
for Thorough.'
*Letter to the Earl of Strafford, 9
September 1633*

2 'All that I laboured for . . . was, that the
external worship of God in this Church
might be kept up in uniformity and
decency and some beauty of holiness.'
*House of Commons, February 1641.
Answering Puritan charges against him*

Laurier, Sir Wilfrid (1841–1919)
CANADIAN LIBERAL POLITICIAN, PRIME
MINISTER, 1896–1911

3 'We have long said that when Great
Britain is at war, we are at war; today we
realise that Great Britain is at war and
that Canada is at war also.'
House of Commons, 18 August 1914

4 'Conscription is repugnant to the British
character.'
*Speech to the Montreal Reform Club,
October 1914*

5 'No man on this continent is equipped
for the battle of life unless he has an
English education.'
House of Commons, 9 May 1916

6 'Toryism . . . like the serpent sheds its
skin, but ever remains the same reptile.'
*Letter to Sir Allen Aylesworth, 15 May
1917*

7 'In Canada, badges, titles, honours and
trappings will never take root. We are a
democratic country; we have been made
so by circumstances . . . I am quite
prepared, if we can do it without any
disrespect to the Crown of England, to
bring our titles to the market-place and
make a bonfire of them.'
House of Commons, 1919

Law, (Andrew) Bonar (1858–1923)
CANADIAN-BORN ENGLISH
CONSERVATIVE POLITICIAN, PRIME
MINISTER, 1922–1923

8 'If I am a great man, then a good many
great men must have been frauds.'
*In conversation with Max Aitken, 13
November 1911. On becoming leader of
the Conservative party*
SEE ALSO *Beaverbrook*

9 'Before I occupied the position which I
now fill in the party I said that, in my
belief, if an attempt were made to
deprive these men of their birthright – as
part of a corrupt parliamentary
bargain – they would be justified in
resisting such an attempt by all means in
their power, including force. I said it
then, and I repeat now with a full sense
of the responsibility which attaches to
my position, that, in my opinion, if such
an attempt is made, I can imagine no
length of resistance to which Ulster can
go in which I should not be prepared to
support them, and in which, in my
belief, they would not be supported by
the overwhelming majority of the British
people.'
*Speech at Blenheim Palace, 29 July 1912.
On Ulster's resistance to Home Rule for
the whole of Ireland*

Layton, Irving (1912–   )
CANADIAN POET

10 'In Pierre Elliott Trudeau Canada has at
last produced a political leader worthy of
assassination.'
THE WHOLE BLOODY BIRD *(1969): 'Obo II'*

Lazarus, Emma (1849–1887)
AMERICAN POET

11 ' "Keep, ancient lands, your storied
pomp!" cries she
With silent lips. "Give me your tired,
your poor,
Your huddled masses yearning to breathe
free,
The wretched refuse of your teeming
shore.
Send these, the homeless, tempest-tossed
to me;
I lift my lamp beside the golden door." '
THE NEW COLOSSUS *(1886). Sonnet written
for inscription on the Statue of Liberty,
New York harbour.*

Lee, Robert E(dward) (1807–1870)
AMERICAN SOLDIER, COMMANDER OF
THE CONFEDERATE ARMY IN THE CIVIL
WAR

12 'It has been evident for years that the
country was doomed to run the full
length of democracy.'
Letter to his wife, 27 December 1856

1   'It is well that war is so terrible, or we should grow too fond of it.'
Remark at the battle of Fredericksburg, 13 December 1862

Lenin, Vladimir Ilyich
(1870–1924)
RUSSIAN COMMUNIST LEADER AND THEORIST

2   'The European bourgeoisie has its reasons to be frightened. The proletariat has its reasons to rejoice.'
1895. Quoted in I Deutscher, STALIN, A POLITICAL BIOGRAPHY, *Chapter 13. On Japan's defeat of Russia at Port Arthur*

3   'Class political consciousness can be brought to the workers *only from without*, that is, only from outside the economic struggle, from outside the sphere of relations between workers and employers. The sphere from which alone it is possible to obtain this knowledge is the sphere of relationships of *all* classes and strata to the state and the government, the sphere of the interrelations between *all* classes.'
WHAT IS TO BE DONE? *(1902)*

4   'Plekhanov once said to me about a critic of Marxism: "*First*, let's stick the convict's badge on him, and then after that we'll examine his case". And I think that we must "stick the convict's badge" on anyone and everyone who tries to undermine Marxism, even if we don't go on to examine his case . . . Social Democracy is not a seminar where different ideas are compared. It is the fighting class organisation of the revolutionary proletariat . . . There is only one answer to revisionism: smash its face in!'
In conversation with Nikolay Valentin Volsky, 1904. Quoted in Volsky,
ENCOUNTERS WITH LENIN, *Chapter 8*

5   'Internationalism (kindly note) consists in the workers of all countries shooting at each other in the name of the "Defence of the Fatherland".'
Letter to A G Shlyapnikov, 27 October 1914. On the support of Kautsky and the German SPD for the 'war effort', 1914

6   'The idea of a lawful separation between one nationality and the other . . . is a reactionary idea.'
SOCIALISM AND WAR *(1915)*

7   'Dear comrades, soldiers, sailors and workers! I am happy to hail in you the victorious Russian revolution! . . . The hour is not far off when at the summons of our comrade, Karl Liebknecht, the German people will turn their weapons against their capitalist exploiters. The sun of the world socialist revolution has already risen.'
Speech at the Finland Station, Petrograd, 16 April 1917

8   'By its economic essence imperialism is monopolist capitalism. This fact alone determines the place of imperialism in history.'
IMPERIALISM: THE HIGHEST STAGE OF CAPITALISM *(1917), Chapter 10*

9   'Capitalists are no more capable of self-sacrifice than a man is capable of lifting himself by his bootstraps.'
LETTER FROM AFAR *(1917)*

10 'Comrades, either the louse defeats socialism or socialism defeats the louse.'
Speech to the Congress of Soviets, November 1919. During an outbreak of typhus

11 'In one country it is impossible to accomplish such a work as a socialist revolution.'
Speech on the third anniversary of the October rising, 24 October 1920

12 'Socialism is Soviet power plus the electrification of the whole country.'
Report to the Congress of Soviets, 22 December 1920

13 'This cook will give us nothing but spicy dishes.'
1922. Quoted in L Trotsky, 'Is Stalin Weakening or the Soviets?', POLITICAL QUARTERLY, *July 1932. On Stalin's election as general secretary of the Communist party*

14 'We cannot outline socialism. What socialism will look like when it takes on its final form we do not know and cannot say.'
Quoted in M Lasky, UTOPIA AND REVOLUTION, *Part I, Chapter 2*

15 'I can't listen to music too often. If affects your nerves; you want to say nice, stupid things and stroke the heads of people who could create such beauty while living in this vile hell. And now you must not stroke anyone's head – you might get your hand bitten off. You have

to hit them on the head, without any mercy.'
In conversation with Gorky. Quoted in IBID., *Part I, Chapter 2. While listening to Beethoven's 'Appassionata' Sonata*

Lenthall, William (1591–1662)
ENGLISH POLITICIAN, SPEAKER OF THE HOUSE OF COMMONS, 1640–1653

1 'May it please your Majesty, I have neither eyes to see nor tongue to speak in this place but as this House is pleased to direct me, whose servant I am here; and I humbly beg your Majesty's pardon that I cannot give any other answer than this to what your Majesty is pleased to demand of me.'
House of Commons, 4 January 1642. In answer to the question of Charles I, who had come to the House to arrest five members, whether Lenthall saw any of those members present

Leo XIII (1810–1903)
ITALIAN PRELATE, POPE, 1878–1903

2 'To despise legitimate authority, in whomsoever vested, is unlawful, as a rebellion against the Divine Will; and whoever resists that rushes wilfully to destruction.'
The Encyclical, IMMORTALE DEI *(1885)*

3 'It is a public crime to act as though there is no God.'
IBID.

4 'The great mistake made in regard to the matter now under consideration, is to take up the notion that class is naturally hostile to class, and that the wealthy and the working man are intended by nature to live in mutual conflict. So irrational and so false is this view, that the direct contrary is the truth. Just as the symmetry of the human frame is the result of the suitable arrangement of the different parts of the body, so in a state is it ordained by nature that these two classes should dwell in harmony and agreement, so as to maintain the balance of the body politic.'
The Encyclical, RERUM NOVARUM *(1891)*

Levsky, Vasil (1837–1873)
BULGARIAN NATIONALIST AND REVOLUTIONARY LEADER

5 'What have I to be afraid of? First of all, I sent my soul to God, and then I set out on this path.'
Quoted in M MacDermott, THE APOSTLE OF FREEDOM, *Part III, Chapter 3. On the dangers of his anti-Turkish activities*

6 'If I win, I win for the whole people. If I loose, I lose only myself.'
IBID., *Part IV, Chapter 6*

Lincoln, Abraham (1809–1865)
AMERICAN REPUBLICAN POLITICIAN, PRESIDENT, 1861–1865

7 'As a nation of free men, we must live through all time, or die by suicide.'
Speech at Springfield, Illinois, 27 January 1838. On the United States' freedom from external threat

8 'Slavery is founded on the selfishness of man's nature – opposition to it on his love of justice. These principles are in eternal antagonism; and when brought into collision so fiercely as slavery extension brings them, shocks and throes and convulsions must ceaselessly follow.'
Speech at Peoria, 16 October 1854

9 'The party lash and the fear of ridicule will overawe justice and liberty.'
Speech at Bloomington, 19 May 1856

10 'The ballot is stronger than the bullet.'
IBID.

11 'Be not deceived. Revolutions do not go backward. The founder of the Democratic party declared that *all* men were created equal.'
IBID.

12 'Let us revere the Declaration of Independence; let us continue to obey the Constitution and the laws; let us keep step to the music of the Union. Let us draw a cordon, so to speak, around the slave States, and the hateful institution [slavery], like a reptile poisoning itself, will perish by its own infamy.'
IBID.

13 ' "A house divided against itself cannot stand". I believe this government cannot endure permanently, half slave and half free.

I do not expect the Union to be dissolved – I do not expect the house to fall – but I do expect it will cease to be divided. It will become all one thing, or all the other.

Either the opponents of slavery will arrest the further spread of it, and place it where the public mind shall rest in the

belief that it is in the course of ultimate extinction; or its advocates will push it forward till it shall become alike lawful in all the States, old as well as new, North as well as South.'
Speech to the Illinois Republican convention, 16 June 1858. Accepting the party's nomination as its senatorial candidate

1 'As I would not be a *slave*, so I would not be a *master*. This expresses my idea of democracy.'
Autograph fragment, 1 August 1858

2 'I have no purpose, either directly or indirectly, to interfere with the institution of slavery in the States where it exists. I believe I have no lawful right to do so, and I have no inclination to do so. I have no purpose to introduce political and social equality between the white and black races. There is a physical difference between the two, which, in my judgment, will probably for ever forbid their living together upon the footing of perfect equality; and inasmuch as it becomes a necessity that there must be a difference, I, as well as Judge Douglas, am in favour of the race to which I belong having the superior position.'
Reply to Douglas in the debate at Ottawa, Illinois, 21 August 1858

3 'What is conservatism? Is it not adherence to the old and tried, against the new and untried?'
Speech at New York, 27 February 1860

4 'Perpetuity is implied, if not expressed, in the fundamental law of all national governments.'
First inaugural address, 4 March 1861
SEE ALSO *Andrew Jackson*

5 'Must a government, of necessity, be too strong for the liberties of its own people, or too weak to maintain it own existence?'
First message to Congress, 4 July 1861

6 'In giving freedom to the slave, we assure freedom to the free ... We shall nobly save or meanly lose the last, best hope of earth.'
Message to Congress, 1 December 1862

7 'Fourscore and seven years ago our fathers brought forth upon this continent a new nation, conceived in liberty, and

dedicated to the propositon that all men are created equal.
Now we are engaged in a great civil war, testing whether that nation, or any nation so conceived and so dedicated, can long endure. We are met on a great battle-field of that war. We have come to dedicate a portion of that field as a final resting-place for those who here gave their lives that the nation might live. It is altogether fitting and proper that we should do this.
But, in a larger sense, we cannot dedicate, we cannot consecrate, we cannot hallow this ground. The brave men, living and dead, who struggled here, have consecrated it far above our power to add or detract. The world will little note nor long remember what we say here, but it can never forget what they did here. It is for us, the living, rather to be dedicated here to the unfinished work which they who fought here have thus far so nobly advanced. It is rather for us to be here dedicated to the great task remaining before us – that from these honored dead we take increased devotion to that cause for which they gave the last full measure of devotion; that we here highly resolve that these dead shall not have died in vain; that this nation, under God, shall have a new birth of freedom; and that government of the people, by the people, for the people, shall not perish from the earth.'
Address at Gettysburg, 19 November 1863. At the dedication ceremony of a national cemetery
SEE ALSO *Daniel Webster and Theodore Parker*

8 'If slavery is not wrong, nothing is wrong.'
Letter to A G Hodges, 4 April 1864

9 'The presidential election, occurring in regular course during the rebellion, added not a little to the strain. But the election was a necessity. We cannot have free government without elections; and if the rebellion could force us to forego or postpone a national election, it might fairly claim to have already conquered and ruined us.'
Speech to his supporters, 10 November 1864. After being re-elected as president in the midst of the civil war

1 'With malice toward none; with charity for all; with firmness in the right, as God gives us to see the right – let us strive on to finish the work we are in: to bind up the nation's wounds . . . to do all which may achieve and cherish a just and lasting peace among ourselves, and with all nations.'
Second inaugural address, 4 March 1865

Lindsay, Vachel (1879–1931)
AMERICAN POET

2 'I brag and chant of Bryan, Bryan, Bryan, Bryan,
Candidate for president who sketched a silver zion.'
'Bryan, Bryan, Bryan, Bryan', in COLLECTED POEMS *(1938). Of William Jennings Bryan*

3 'Prairie avenger, mountain lion,
Bryan, Bryan, Bryan, Bryan,
Gigantic troubadour, speaking like a siege gun,
Smashing Plymouth Rock with his boulders from the West.'
IBID.

Lin Piao (1908–1971)
CHINESE GENERAL AND COMMUNIST LEADER

4 'The best weapon is not the aircraft, heavy artillery, tanks, or the atom bomb, it is Mao Tse-tung thought; the greatest fighting force is the man armed with Mao Tse-tung thought.'
1965. Quoted in A Peyrefitte, THE CHINESE, *Chapter 3. In a speech to the army on the eve of the Cultural Revolution*

Litvinov, Maxim (1876–1951)
SOVIET COMMUNIST POLITICIAN, COMMISSAR FOR FOREIGN AFFAIRS, 1930–1939

5 'Peace is indivisible.'
Speech, 22 February 1920

Lloyd, Henry Demarest (1847–1903)
AMERICAN WRITER

6 'Nature is rich; but everywhere man, the heir of nature, is poor.'
WEALTH AGAINST COMMONWEALTH *(1894)*

7 'Liberty and monopoly cannot live together.'
IBID.

8 'Liberty produces wealth and wealth destroys liberty.'
IBID.

9 'Liberty recast the old forms of government into the Republic, and it must remould our institutions of wealth into the Commonwealth.'
IBID.

10 'For as true as that a house divided against itself cannot stand, and that a nation half-slave and half-free cannot permanently endure, it is true that a people who are slaves to market-tyrants will surely come to be their slaves in all else, that all liberty begins to be lost when one liberty is lost, that a people half democratic and half plutocratic cannot permanently endure.'
IBID.
SEE ALSO *Lincoln*

11 'We have given the prize of power to the strong, the cunning, the arithmetical, and we must expect nothing else but that they will use it cunningly and arithmetically. For what else can they suppose we gave it to them?'
IBID.

12 'Discontent has a better right to a hearing than content. Every new civilization began as discontent, and we can afford to tolerate the wildest dissents from everlasting to everlasting in the chance of hearing the voice of a Christ or an Emerson at intervals of a thousand years or so.'
Quoted in D Aaron, MEN OF GOOD HOPE, *Chapter 5*

Lloyd George, David, 1st Earl Lloyd-George (1863–1945)
WELSH LIBERAL POLITICIAN, PRIME MINISTER, 1916–1922

13 'The influence of a war must always be brutalising, at best; but still, if you enter upon it for an unselfish purpose, there is something which almost consecrates the sacrifices, bloodshed, and suffering endured. But when you enter upon a war purely and simply for the purposes of plunder, I know of nothing which is more degrading to the country or more hideous in its effects on the mind and character of the people engaged in it.'
House of Commons, 25 July 1900. Against the Boer War

1 'The day will come when a nation that lifts up the sword against a nation will be put in the same felon category as the man who strikes his brother in anger.'
Speech at Manchester, 21 April 1908

2 'It is Mr Balfour's poodle. It fetches and carries for him. It barks for him. It bites anybody that he sets it on to.'
House of Commons, 21 December 1908. In reply to H Chaplin, who had called the House of Lords the 'watchdog of the constitution'

3 'A fully equipped duke costs as much to keep up as two Dreadnoughts; and they are just as great a terror and they last longer.'
Speech at Newcastle, 9 October 1909. In reply to the Duke of Buccleuch's statement that the heavy taxation proposed in the 'People's budget' of 1909 would prevent his paying his subscription to his local football club

4 'Five hundred men, ordinary men, chosen accidentally from among the unemployed.'
IBID. *Of the House of Lords*

5 'An aristocracy is like cheese; the older it is the higher it becomes.'
Speech at Mile End, London, December, 1910

6 'All down History, nine-tenths of mankind have been grinding the corn for the remaining one-tenth, been paid with the husks – and bidden to thank God they had the husks.'
In conversation with a colleague, 1911. Quoted in M Gilbert, LLOYD GEORGE, *Introduction*

7 'The people in all lands will gain more by this struggle than they comprehend at the present moment. It is true they will be free of the greatest menace to their freedom. That is not all. There is something infinitely greater and more enduring which is emerging already out of this great conflict – a new patriotism, richer, nobler, and more exalted than the old. I see amongst all classes, high and low, shedding themselves of selfishness, a new recognition that the honour of the country does not depend merely on the maintenance of its glory in the stricken field, but also in protecting its homes from distress. The great flood of luxury and sloth which had submerged the land is receding, and a new Britain is appearing. We can see for the first time the fundamental things that matter in life, and that have been obscured from our vision by the tropical growth of prosperity.'
Speech at the Queen's Hall, London, 19 September 1914. Of the Great War

8 'When this terrible conflict is over, a wave of materialism will sweep over the land. Nothing will count but machinery and output. I am all for output, and I have done my best to improve machinery and increase output. But that is not all. There is nothing more fatal to a people than that it should narrow its vision to the material needs of the hour. National ideals without imagination are but as the thistles of the wilderness, fit neither for food nor fuel.'
Speech at the Aberystwyth National Eisteddfod, 17 August 1916

9 'What is a Government for except to dictate? If it does not dictate, then it is not a Government.'
In conversation with Labour leaders, December 1916. Quoted in his WAR MEMOIRS, *Volume I, Chapter 38*

10 'What is our task? To make Britain a fit country for heroes to live in.'
Speech at Wolverhampton, 24 November 1918

11 'Injustice, arrogance, displayed in the hour of triumph will never be forgotten or forgiven.'
Fontainbleau memorandum, 1919. Written during the Paris peace conference

12 'Of all the bigotries that savage the human temper there is none so stupid as the anti-Semitic. It has no basis in reason; it is not rooted in faith; it aspires to no ideal; it is just one of those dank and unwholesome weeds that grow in the morass of racial hatred. How utterly devoid of reason it is may be gathered from the fact that it is almost entirely confined to nations who worship Jewish prophets and apostles, revere the national literature of the Hebrews as the only inspired message delivered by the Deity to mankind, and whose only hope of salvation rests on the precept and promises of the great teachers of Judah.'
'Palestine and the Jews', July 1923

1 'To anyone with politics in his blood, this place is like a pub to a drunkard.'
In conversation with Robert Boothby. Quoted in Boothby, RECOLLECTIONS OF A REBEL: *'Interlude Two'. Of the House of Commons*

Locke, John (1632–1704)
ENGLISH PHILOSOPHER

2 'I confess it cannot be thought, but that men should fly from *oppression*, but *disorder* will give them but an incommodious sanctuary.'
FIRST TRACT ON GOVERNMENT *(1660), Preface. (Not Locke's title)*

3 'Nor do men, as some fondly conceive, enjoy any greater share of this freedom in a pure commonwealth, if anywhere to be found, than in an absolute monarchy, the same arbitrary power being there in the assembly (which acts like one person) as in a monarch.'
IBID., *Text*

4 'A man cannot part with his liberty and have it too, convey it by compact to the magistrate and retain it himself.'
IBID.

5 'The *Natural Liberty* of Man is to be free from any Superior Power on Earth, and not to be under the Will or Legislative Authority of Man, but to have only the Law of Nature for his Rule. The *Liberty of Man, in Society,* is to be under no other Legislative Power, but that established, by consent, in the Commonwealth, nor under the Dominion of any will, or Restraint of any Law, but what the Legislative shall enact, according to the Trust put in it ... *Freedom of Men under Government,* is, to have a standing Rule to live by, common to every one of that Society, and made by the Legislative Power erected in it; A Liberty to follow my own Will in all things, where the Rule prescribes not; and not to be subjected to the inconstant, uncertain, unknown, Arbitrary Will of another Man.'
THE SECOND TREATISE ON GOVERNMENT *(1690), Chapter 4*

6 'Government has no other end but the preservation of Property.'
IBID., *Chapter 7*

7 'Men being ... by Nature, all free, equal and independent, no one can be put out of this Estate, and subjected to the Political Power of another, without his own *Consent*.'
IBID. *Chapter 8*

8 'Every Man, by consenting with others to make one Body Politick under one Government, puts himself under an obligation to every one of that Society, to submit to the determination of the *majority*, and to be concluded by it; or else this *original Compact*, whereby he and others incorporates into *one Society*, would signifie nothing.'
IBID.

9 'Where-ever Law ends, Tyranny begins.'
IBID., *Chapter 18*

10 'Whenever the *Legislators endeavour to take away, and destroy the Property of the People*, or to reduce them to Slavery under Arbitrary Power, they put themselves into a state of War with the People, who are thereupon absolved from any farther Obedience, and are left to the common Refuge, which God hath provided for all Men, against Force and Violence – Resistance'.
IBID., *Chapter 19*

Louis IX (1214–1270)
KING OF FRANCE, 1226–1270

11 'There can be only one King of France.'
Quoted in G de Saint-Pathus, VIE DE SAINT LOUIS

12 'If there is a dispute between a poor man and a rich man, uphold the poor against the rich until such time as you know the truth of the matter – and then do justice.'
Instruction to his son. Quoted in Abbé de Villiers, INSTRUCTIONS DE SAINT LOUIS

Louis XVI (1754–1793)
KING OF FRANCE, 1774–1792

13 'Nothing.' (*Rien*.)
Diary entry for 14 July 1789. On the day of the fall of the Bastille

Louis Philippe (1773–1850)
KING OF THE FRENCH, 1830–1848

14 'The sincere friendship which unites me to the Queen of Great Britain and the cordial understanding [*la cordiale entente*] which exists between my government and hers.'
Speech at the opening of parliament, 27 December 1843

Lovett, William (1800–1877)
ENGLISH CHARTIST LEADER

1 'So long as the people of any country place their hopes of political salvation *in leadership of any description*, so long will disappointment attend them.'
Public letter to Daniel O'Connell, 1843

Lowe, Robert, 1st Viscount Sherbrooke (1811–1892)
ENGLISH LIBERAL POLITICIAN, MEMBER OF PARLIAMENT, 1852–1880, CHANCELLOR OF THE EXCHEQUER 1863–1873

2 'I believe it will be absolutely necessary that you should prevail on our future masters to learn their letters.'
House of Commons, 15 July 1867. On the enfranchising of the urban working man by the reform act of 1867

Lowell, James Russell (1819–1891)
AMERICAN POET AND CRITIC

3 'I have always been of the mind that in a democracy manners are the only effective weapons against the bowie-knife.'
Letter to Miss Norton, 4 March 1873

Luce, Clare Booth (1903–   )
AMERICAN WRITER AND REPUBLICAN POLITICIAN, MEMBER OF THE HOUSE OF REPRESENTATIVES, 1943–1947

4 'Much of what Mr Wallace calls his global thinking is, no matter how you slice it, still globaloney. Mr Wallace's warp of sense and his woof of nonsense is very tricky cloth out of which to cut the pattern of a postwar world.'
Speech to the House of Representatives, February 1943

Luther, Martin (1483–1546)
GERMAN RELIGIOUS REFORMER

5 'I will always side with him, however unjust, who endures rebellion and against him who rebels, however justly.'
TO THE CHRISTIAN NOBILITY OF THE GERMAN NATION *(1520)*

6 'Heresy is a spiritual thing, cut with no iron, burned with no fire, drowned with no water . . . Though we should burn by force every Jew and heretic, yet neither would there, nor will there, be one conquered or converted thereby.'
OF WORLDLY POWER *(1523)*

7 'God has erected two forms of government among men. The one spiritual, through the Word and without the sword, through which men may become godly and righteous, so that by such righteousness they may obtain eternal life. And this righteousness he administers through the Word, which he has entrusted to the preachers. The other is a temporal regiment through the sword, so that those who will not become godly and righteous through the Word for eternal life, may nevertheless be compelled through this temporal regiment to become godly and righteous for the purposes of the world. And such righteousness he administers through the sword. And although he will not reward such righteousness with eternal life, he will nonetheless have it so that peace may be maintained among men, and he rewards it with temporal goods.'
Quoted in W D Thompson, 'Martin Luther and the Two Kingdoms' in D Thomson, POLITICAL IDEAS

8 'No one need think that the world can be ruled without blood. The civil sword shall and must be red and bloody.'
Quoted in B Russell, POWER, *Chapter 7*

Luxemburg, Rosa (1871–1919)
POLISH-BORN GERMAN SOCIALIST REVOLUTIONARY

9 'Tariffs today are no longer a means of safeguarding growing capitalist production against mature competitors, but a weapon in the struggle of one nationalist block against another. They do not assist industry to grow and capture the domestic market, but merely serve the cartelisation of industry, i.e. assist the struggle of capitalist *producers* against *consumers* . . . Thus a policy of tariffs is in fact no more than a means of casting *feudal interests in capitalist form.*'
SOCIAL REFORM OR REVOLUTION *(1899)*

10 'Not a man, not a farthing for this system; instead war to the knife.'
SPARTAKUSBRIEFE, *22 April 1916. (Quoting a slogan perhaps originally from August Bebel.)*

Lyndhurst, 1st Baron (John Singleton Copley) (1772–1863)
AMERICAN-BORN ENGLISH JUDGE AND TORY POLITICIAN, LORD CHANCELLOR, 1827–1830, 1834–1835 AND 1841–1846

1 'Perhaps great talents and an ambitious spirit are not to be wished for in a prime minister of this country. The restlessness of spirit with which they are accompanied is fatal to national repose and national prosperity: for repose and prosperity, in a commercial kingdom, are intimately connected with each other.'
Letter to Mr Greene, 9 August 1802

Lytton, 1st Baron (Edward Bulwer-Lytton) (1803–1873)
ENGLISH MAN OF LETTERS AND POLITICIAN

2 'In other countries poverty is a misfortune, – with us it is a crime.'
ENGLAND AND THE ENGLISH *(1833)*

3 'Co-operation is power; in proportion as people combine, they know their strength; civilization itself is but the effect of combining.'
IBID.

4 'A party to *be* strong, should always *appear* strong; the show often wins the battle; as the sultans of the east, in order to defeat rebellion, have usually found it sufficient merely to levy an army.'
IBID.

5 'Where Intelligence is equalized – and flows harmonious and harmonizing throughout all society – then one man can possess no blinding and dangerous power over the mind of another – then demagogues are harmless and theories safe. It is this equality of knowledge, producing unity of feeling, which, if we look around, characterizes whatever nation seems to us the most safe in the present ferment of the world – no matter what their more material form of constitution – whether absolute Monarchy or unqualified Republicanism. If you see safety, patriotism, and order in the loud democracy of America, you behold it equally in the despotism of Denmark, and in the subordination of Prussia. Denmark had even refused a free constitution, because in the freedom of a common knowledge she hath found consent. It is with the streams that refresh and vivify the Moral World as with those in the Material Earth – *they tend and struggle to their level!* Interrupt or tamper with this great law, and city and cottage, tower and temple, may be swept away. Preserve unchecked its vast but simple operation, and the waters will glide on in fertilizing and majestic serenity, to the illimitable ocean of Human Perfectibility.'
IBID. *Advocating a state-supervised system of national education*

M

MacArthur, Douglas (1880–1964)
AMERICAN GENERAL

1 'It seems strangely difficult for some to realize that here in Asia is where the Communist conspirators have elected to make their play for global conquest, and that we have joined the issue thus raised on the battlefield; that here we fight Europe's war with arms while the diplomats there still fight it with words; that if we lose the war to Communism in Asia the fall of Europe is inevitable, win it and Europe most probably would avoid war and yet preserve freedom. As you point out, we must win. There is no substitute for victory.'
Letter to Joseph Martin, March 1951. On the Korean war. (The letter was read by Martin to the House of Representatives on 5 April, 1951.)

Macaulay, Thomas (1800–1859)
ENGLISH MAN OF LETTERS AND WHIG POLITICIAN, MEMBER OF PARLIAMENT, 1830–1834, 1839–1847 AND 1852–1856

2 'The gallery in which the reporters sit has become a fourth estate of the realm.'
EDINBURGH REVIEW, *September 1828, 'Hallam's Constitutional History'*
SEE ALSO *Hazlitt and Carlyle*

3 'Turn where we may, within, around, the voice of great events is proclaiming to us, Reform, that you may preserve. Now, therefore, while everything at home and abroad forebodes ruin to those who persist in a hopeless struggle against the spirit of the age, now, while the crash of the proudest throne of the Continent is still resounding in our ears, now, while the roof of a British palace affords an ignominious shelter to the exiled heir of forty kings, now, while we see on every side ancient institutions subverted, and great societies dissolved, now, while the heart of England is still sound, now, while old feelings and old associations retain a power and a charm which may too soon pass away, now, in this your accepted time, now, in this your day of salvation, take counsel, not of prejudice, not of party spirit, not of the ignominious pride of a fatal consistency, but of history, of reason, of the ages which are past, of the signs of this most portentous time. Pronounce in a manner worthy of the expectation with which this great debate has been anticipated, and of the long remembrance which it will leave behind. Renew the youth of the State. Save property, divided against itself. Save the multitude, endangered by its own ungovernable passions. Save the aristocracy, endangered by its own unpopular power. Save the greatest, the fairest, the most highly civilised community that ever existed, from calamities which may in a few days sweep away all the rich heritage of so many ages of wisdom and glory. The danger is terrible. The time is short. If this bill should be rejected, I pray to God that none of those who concur in rejecting it may ever remember their votes with unavailing remorse, amidst the wreck of laws, the confusion of ranks, the spoliation of property, and the dissolution of social order.'
House of Commons, 2 March 1831. Peroration of his speech in support of the Great Reform Bill

4 'We know no spectacle so ridiculous as the British public in one of its periodical fits of morality.'
EDINBURGH REVIEW, *June 1831, 'Moore's Life of Lord Byron'*

5 'To request an honest man to vote according to his conscience is superfluous. To request him to vote against his conscience is an insult. The practice of canvassing is quite reasonable under a system in which men are sent to Parliament to serve themselves. It is the height of absurdity under a system in which men are sent to Parliament to serve the public.'
Letter to unnamed correspondent, 3 August 1832

6 'Just as a physician understands medicine better than an ordinary man, just as a shoemaker makes shoes better than an ordinary man, so a person whose life is passed in transacting affairs of State becomes a better statesman than an ordinary man. In politics, as well as every other department of life, the public ought to have the means of checking those who serve it. If a man finds that he derives no benefit from the prescription of his

physician, he calls in another. If his shoes do not fit him, he changes his shoemaker. But when he has called in a physician of whom he hears a good report, and whose general practice he believes to be judicious, it would be absurd in him to tie him down to particular pills and particular draughts. While he continues to be the customer of the shoemaker, it would be absurd in him to sit by and mete every motion of that shoemaker's hand. And in the same manner, it would, I think, be absurd in him to require positive pledges, and to exact daily and hourly obedience, from his representative.'
IBID.

1 'The pendulum swung furiously to the left, because it had been drawn too far to the right.'
EDINBURGH REVIEW, *July 1835, 'Sir James Mackintosh'. On the excesses of the French Revolution*

2 'An acre in Middlesex is better than a principality in Utopia.'
EDINBURGH REVIEW, *July 1837, 'Francis Bacon'*

3 'A man in office, and out of the Cabinet, is a mere slave.'
Diary, 10 November 1838

4 'The author of this volume is . . . the rising hope of those stern and unbending Tories.'
EDINBURGH REVIEW, *April 1839, 'Gladstone on Church and State'. Of Gladstone*

5 'Timid and interested politicians think much more about the security of their seats than about the security of their country.'
House of Commons, May 1842

6 'Your constitution is all sail and no anchor.'
Letter to Henry Randall, 23 May 1857. On American universal male suffrage

McCarthy, Joseph (1908–1957)
AMERICAN REPUBLICAN POLITICIAN, SENATOR, 1947–1957

7 'McCarthyism is Americanism with its sleeves rolled.'
Speech at Wisconsin, 1952. Quoted in R Rovere, SENATOR JOE MCCARTHY, *Chapter 1*

MacDonald, (James) Ramsay
(1866–1937)
SCOTTISH LABOUR POLITICIAN, PRIME MINISTER, 1924 AND 1929–1935

8 'With the discussion of general strikes and Bolshevism and all that kind of thing, I have nothing to do at all. I respect the Constitution as much as Sir Robert Horne.'
House of Commons, 3 May 1926. On the eve of the general strike

9 'If God were to come to me and say, "Ramsay, would you rather be a country gentleman than a Prime Minister?", I should reply, "Please God, a country gentleman".'
In conversation with Harold Nicolson and Vita Sackville-West, October 1930

McGee, Thomas D'Arcy
(1825–1868)
IRISH-BORN CANADIAN JOURNALIST AND POLITICIAN

10 'Never yet did the assassin's knife reach the core of a cause or the heart of a principle.'
Speech at Montreal, 1865. On the assassination of President Lincoln

MacKenzie, Alexander
(1822–1892)
SCOTTISH-BORN CANADIAN LIBERAL POLITICIAN, PRIME MINISTER, 1873–1878

11 'I am anxious as it is possible for any British subject to be that that glory [of the British empire] should be unsullied, that the power should never be abridged, and that the English supremacy shall last till the end of time, because it means universal freedom, universal liberty, emancipation from everything degrading.'
Speech at Dundee, Scotland, 13 July 1875

Mackintosh, Sir James
(1765–1832)
SCOTTISH MAN OF LETTERS, LAWYER AND WHIG POLITICIAN, MEMBER OF PARLIAMENT, 1812–1832

12 'The commons, faithful to their system, remained in a wise and masterly inactivity.'
VINDICIAE GALLICAE *(1791), Part I. On the third estate at the first session of the Estates General summoned in France in 1789*

1 'A titled Nobility is the most undisputed progeny of feudal barbarism. Titles had in all nations denoted *offices*; it was reserved for Gothic Europe to attach them to ranks.'
IBID.

2 'Power vegetates with more vigour after these gentle prunings. A slender reform amuses and lulls the people: the popular enthusiasm subsides; and the moment of effectual reform is irretrievably lost. No important political improvement was ever obtained in a period of tranquillity.'
IBID. *On piece-meal, gradualist reform*

3 'This Gothic transfer of genealogy to truth and justice is peculiar to politics . . . It is not because *we have been free*, but because we *have a right to be free*, that we ought to demand freedom. Justice and liberty have neither birth nor race, youth nor age. It would be the same absurdity to assert, that we have a right to freedom, because the Englishmen of Alfred's reign were free, as that three and three are six, because they were so in the camp of Genghis Khan. Let us hear no more of this ignoble and ignominious pedigree of freedom.'
IBID., *Part V. On Burke's organic view of politics*

MacLennan, Hugh (1907–)
CANADIAN MAN OF LETTERS

4 'Give me the writing of a nation's advertising and propaganda, and I care not who governs its politics.'
MACLEAN'S MAGAZINE, *5 November 1960*

MacLeod, Iain (1913–1970)
ENGLISH CONSERVATIVE POLITICIAN, CABINET MINISTER AND MEMBER OF PARLIAMENT, 1950–1970

5 'It is some measure of the tightness of the magic circle on this occasion that neither the Chancellor of the Exchequer nor the leader of the House of Commons had any inkling of what was happening.'
SPECTATOR, *17 January 1964, 'The Tory Leadership'. On the 'emergence' of Lord Home as party leader and prime minister, October 1963*

Macmillan, Harold, Earl of Stockton (1894–)
ENGLISH CONSERVATIVE POLITICIAN, PRIME MINISTER, 1957–1963

6 'Indeed let us be frank about it: most of our people have never had it so good.'
Speech at Bedford, 20 July 1957

7 'I thought the best thing to do was to settle up these little local difficulties, and then turn to the wider vision of the Commonwealth.'
Statement at Heathrow airport, London, 7 January 1958. On the resignation of Treasury ministers

8 'The trouble about Mr Gaitskell is that he is going through all the motions of being a Government when he isn't a Government. It is bad enough having to behave like a Government when one is a Government.'
Interview in the DAILY MAIL, *January 1959*

9 'The most striking of all the impressions I have formed since I left London a month ago is of the strength of African national consciousness . . . The wind of change is blowing through the continent. Whether we like it or not, the growth of national consciousness is a political fact.'
Speech to the South African parliament, 3 February 1960
SEE ALSO *Stanley Baldwin*

10 'There might be one finger on the trigger, but there will be fifteen fingers on the safety catch.'
House of Commons, 30 May 1960. Arguing that Great Britain ought to retain an independent nuclear deterrent beyond NATO's control

11 'I hope that it will soon be possible for the customary processes of consultation to be carried on within the party about its future leadership.'
Statement announcing his resignation as prime minister to the Conservative party annual conference, 10 October 1963. (The statement was read to the conference by R A Butler.)

12 'If people want a sense of purpose they should get it from their archbishop. They should certainly not get it from their politicians.'
In conversation with Henry Fairlie, 1963. Quoted in Fairlie, THE LIFE OF POLITICS, *Chapter 1*

1 'Power? It's like a dead sea fruit; when you achieve it, there's nothing there.'
Quoted in A Sampson, THE NEW ANATOMY OF BRITAIN, *Chapter 37*

McNamara, Robert (1916–)
AMERICAN INDUSTRIALIST, SECRETARY OF DEFENSE, 1961–1968, PRESIDENT OF THE WORLD BANK, 1968–1981

2 'One cannot fashion a credible deterrent out of an incredible action.'
THE ESSENCE OF SECURITY *(1968). On nuclear weapons*

Machiavelli, Niccolò (1469–1527)
ITALIAN STATESMAN AND POLITICAL PHILOSOPHER

3 'When it is a question of saving the fatherland, one should not stop for a moment to consider whether something is lawful or unlawful, gentle or cruel, laudable or shameful; but, putting aside every other consideration, one ought to follow out to the end whatever resolve will save the life of the state and preserve its freedom.'
THE DISCOURSES *(1531)*

4 'The main foundations of every state, new states as well as ancient or composite ones, are good laws and good arms . . . you cannot have good laws without good arms, and where there are good arms, good laws inevitably follow.'
THE PRINCE *(1532), Chapter 12*

5 'A man who wishes to act virtuously in every way necessarily comes to grief among so many who are not virtuous. Therefore if a prince wishes to maintain his rule he must learn how not to be virtuous, and to make use of this knowledge or not according to his need . . . princes who have achieved great things have been those who have given their word lightly, who have known how to trick men with their cunning, and who, in the end, have overcome those abiding by honest principles.'
IBID., *Chapter 15*

6 'A prince being forced to know how to act like a beast, he should learn from the fox and the lion; because the lion is defenceless against traps and a fox is defenceless against wolves. Therefore one must be a fox in order to recognise traps

and a lion in order to frighten off wolves.'
IBID., *Chapter 18*

Madison, James (1751–1836)
AMERICAN REPUBLICAN POLITICIAN, PRESIDENT, 1809–1817

7 'No free Country has ever been without parties, which are a natural offspring of Freedom.'
Note of c. 1821 on his suffrage speech at the Constitutional Convention of 1787

8 'What is government itself but the greatest of all reflections on human nature?'
THE FEDERALIST, *No. 51*

Maine, Sir Henry (1822–1888)
ENGLISH JURIST

9 'But the closest resemblances are between party discipline and military discipline; and indeed, historically speaking, Party is probably nothing more than a survival and a consequence of the primitive combativeness of mankind. It is war without the city transmuted into war within the city, but mitigated in the process. The best historical justification which can be offered for it is that it has often enabled portions of the nation, who would otherwise be armed enemies, to be only factions. Party strife, like strife in arms, develops many high but imperfect and one-sided virtues; it is fruitful of self-denial and self-sacrifice. But wherever it prevails, a great part of ordinary morality is unquestionably suspended . . . and men do acts which, except as between enemies, and except as between political opponents, would be very generally classed as either immoralities or sins.'
POPULAR GOVERNMENT *(1885)*

10 'The Socialists would drag men back from contract to status.'
Quoted in K Middlemas and J Barnes, BALDWIN, *Chapter 11. On the progress of civilisation from status to contract*

Maistre, Joseph Marie de, Comte (1753–1821)
FRENCH POLITICAL PHILOSOPHER AND DIPLOMAT

11 'Every country has the government it deserves.'
Letter from St Petersburg, 27 August 1811. On the new constitutional laws of Russia

1 'The sword of justice has no scabbard.'
LES SOIRÉES DE SAINT-PÉTERSBOURG *(1821)*

Malcolm X (1924–1965)
AMERICAN BLACK REVOLUTIONARY
LEADER

2 'If violence is wrong in America, violence is wrong abroad. If it is wrong to be violent defending black women and black children and black babies and black men, then it is wrong for America to draft us, and make us violent abroad in defense of her. And if it is right for America to draft us, and teach us how to be violent in defense of her, then it is right for you and me to do whatever is necessary to defend our own people right here in this country.'
Speech at New York, November 1963

3 'The Negro revolution is controlled by foxy white liberals, by the Government itself. But the Black Revolution is controlled only by God.'
Speech at New York, 1 December 1963

4 'Revolutions are never waged singing "We Shall Overcome". Revolutions are based upon bloodshed.'
Speech at New York, April 1964

5 'It is the hinge that squeaks that gets the grease.'
In conversation with Alex Haley.
AUTOBIOGRAPHY OF MALCOLM X *(1965)*,
Haley's introduction

6 'You show me a black man who isn't an extremist and I'll show you one who needs psychiatric attention.'
IBID.

7 'For the white man to ask the black man if he hates him is just like the rapist asking the *raped*, or the wolf asking the *sheep*, "Do you hate me?" The white man is in no moral *position* to accuse anyone else of hate!'
IBID., *Chapter 14*

8 'A man who tosses worms in the river isn't necessarily a friend to the fish. All the fish who take him for a friend, who think that worm's got no hooks in it, usually end up in the frying pan.'
Quoted in J H Clarke (ed.), MALCOLM X.
THE MAN AND HIS TIMES, *'Leadership:
Triumph in Leadership Tragedy'. On the
white liberal 'friends' of the Blacks*

Mandela, Nelson (1918–)
SOUTH AFRICAN BLACK LIBERATION
LEADER

9 'The communist bogey is an American stunt to distract the attention of the people of Africa from the real issue facing them, namely, American imperialism.'
LIBERATION, *March, 1958, 'On American
Imperialism'*

Mandeville, Bernard (1670–1733)
DUTCH-BORN ENGLISH PHYSICIAN AND
SATIRIST

10 'A spacious hive well stockt with bees,
That liv'd in luxury and ease,
And yet as fam'd for laws and arms,
As yielding large and early swarms,
Was counted the great nursery
Of sciences and industry.
No bees had better government,
More fickleness, or less content:
They were not slaves to tyranny,
Nor rul'd by wild democracy,
But kings, that could not wrong, because
Their power was circumscribed by laws.'
THE GRUMBLING HIVE; OR, KNAVES TURNED
HONEST *(1705)*

11 'Thus every part was full of vice,
Yet the whole mass a paradise;
Flatter'd in peace, and fear'd in wars,
They were th' esteem of foreigners,
And lavish of their wealth and lives,
The balance of all other hives.
Such were the blessings of that state;
Their crimes conspir'd to make them great:
And virtue, who from politics
Has learn'd a thousand cunning tricks,
Was, by their happy influence,
Made friends with vice; and ever since,
The worst of all the multitude
Did something for the common good.'
IBID.

12 'Then leave complaints: fools only strive
To make a great and honest hive.
T' enjoy the world's conveniences,
Be fam'd in war, yet live in ease
Without great vices, is a vain
Eutopia seated in the brain.'
IBID.

13 'So vice is beneficial found,
When it's by justice lopt and bound;
Nay where the people would be great,
As necessary to the state,

As hunger is to make 'em eat.
Bare virtue can't make nations live
In splendour; they that would revive
A golden age must be as free
For acorns as for honesty.'
IBID.

Mansfield, 1st Earl of (William Murray) (1705–1793)
SCOTTISH JUDGE, LORD CHIEF JUSTICE, 1756–1788

1 'We must not regard political consequences, however formidable they may be; if rebellion was the certain consequence, we are bound to say, "*Justitia fiat, ruat coelum*" ["Let justice be done, though the sky falls"].'
On hearing John Wilkes' appeal against outlawry, 1768

2 'The exercise of the power of a master over his slave, must be supported by the laws of particular countries; but no foreigner can in England claim a right over a man: such a claim is not known to the laws of England.'
Judgment in the James Somersett case, 1772

3 'Whatever is *contra bonos mores et decorum* the principles of our laws prohibit and the King's Court as the general censor and guardian of the public morals is bound to restrain and punish.'
Judgment in Jones v. Randall, 1774

Mann, Thomas (1875–1955)
GERMAN NOVELIST

4 'Let music play her loftiest role, she will thereby but kindle the emotions, whereas what concerns us is to awaken the reason. Music is to all appearance movement itself – yet, for all that, I suspect her of quietism. Let me state my point by the method of exaggeration: my aversion from music rests on political grounds ... Art has moral value in so far as it quickens. But what if it does the opposite? What if it dulls, sends us to sleep, works against action and progress? Music can do that too; she is an old hand at using opiates ... There is something suspicious about music, gentlemen. I insist that she is, by her nature, equivocal. I shall not be going too far in saying at once that she is politically suspect.'
THE MAGIC MOUNTAIN *(1924), Chapter 4. (The words of Herr Settembrini.)*

Mao Tse-tung (1893–1976)
CHINESE COMMUNIST LEADER, CHAIRMAN OF THE SUPREME COUNCIL, 1949–1976

5 'Every communist must grasp the truth, "Political power grows out of the barrel of a gun".'
'Problems of War and Strategy' (1938)

6 'War can be abolished only through war, and in order to get rid of the gun it is necessary to take up the gun.'
IBID.

7 'We should support whatever the enemy opposes and oppose whatever the enemy supports.'
Newspaper interview, 16 September 1939. In SELECTED WORKS, *Volume II*

8 'Letting a hundred flowers blossom and a hundred schools of thought contend is the policy for promoting the progress of the arts and the sciences and a flourishing socialist culture in our land.'
Speech at Peking, 27 February 1957, 'On the Correct Handling of Contradictions Among the People'

9 'All the so-called powerful reactionaries are no more than paper tigers, for they are cut off from their people. Think of Hitler: was he not a paper tiger and was he not overthrown? I have said that the Tsar of Russia, the Emperor of China and the imperialism of Japan were all paper tigers. As we know, they were all overthrown. U.S. imperialism has not yet been overthrown, and it has atomic bombs. But I believe it, too, will be overthrown. It, too, is a paper tiger.'
Speech to the International Communist Congress, Moscow, 18 November 1957

10 'In history it is always those with little learning who overthrow those with much learning ... When young people grasp a truth they are invincible and old people cannot compete with them.'
Address to the Chengtu conference, 22 March 1958

11 'Let other people speak out. The heavens will not fall and you will not be thrown out. If you do not let others speak, then the day will surely come when you will be thrown out.'
Speech to a Central Work Conference, 30 January 1962

1 'Freedom is the understanding of necessity *and* the transformation of necessity.'
Talk on questions of philosophy, 18 August 1964
SEE ALSO *Hobbes and Spinoza*

2 'There may be thousands of principles of Marxism, but in the final analysis they can be summed up in one sentence: Rebellion is justified.'
Quoted in the TIMES, *31 October 1966, 'Thoughts on Mao Tse-tung'*

3 'Politics is war without bloodshed; war is politics with bloodshed.'
QUOTATIONS FROM CHAIRMAN MAO *(1966)*

4 'We Communists are like seeds and the people are like the soil. Wherever we go, we must unite with the people, take root, and blossom among them.'
IBID.

Marcuse, Herbert (1898–1979)
GERMAN-BORN AMERICAN
PHILOSOPHER

5 'In terms of historical function, there is a difference between revolutionary and reactionary violence, between violence practised by the oppressed and by the oppressors. In terms of ethics, both forms of violence are inhuman, and evil – but since when is history made in accordance with ethical standards? To start applying them at the point where the oppressed rebel against the oppressors, the have-nots against the haves, is serving the cause of actual violence by weakening the protest against it.'
A CRITIQUE OF PURE TOLERANCE *(1966)*

Marighela, Carlos (*d.* 1969)
BRAZILIAN GUERRILLA LEADER

6 'It is necessary to turn political crisis into armed crisis by performing violent actions that will force those in power to transform the military situation into a political situation. That will alienate the masses, who, from then on, will revolt against the army and the police and blame them for this state of things.'
MINIMANUAL OF THE URBAN GUERRILLA *(1969)*

Martí y Pérez, José (1853–1895)
CUBAN NATIONALIST REVOLUTIONARY
AND WRITER

7 'The dagger plunged in the name of Freedom is plunged into the breast of Freedom.'
GRANOS DE OROS *(1942). (Collection of his writings.)*

Marvell, Andrew (1621–1678)
ENGLISH POET AND POLITICIAN,
MEMBER OF PARLIAMENT, 1659–1678

8 '*He* nothing common did or mean
Upon that memorable Scene:
But with his keener eye
The Axes edge did try:
Nor call'd the *Gods* with vulgar spight
To vindicate his helpless Right,
But bow'd his comely Head,
Down as upon a Bed.'
AN HORATIAN ODE UPON CROMWELL'S RETURN FROM IRELAND *(c. 1650). On Charles I at the scaffold*

9 'And he whom Nature all for Peace had made,
But angry Heaven unto War had sway'd,
And so less useful where he most desire'd,
For what he least affected was admir'd.'
A POEM UPON THE DEATH OF O.C. *(c. 1658). Of Oliver Cromwell*

Marx, Karl (1818–1883)
GERMAN POLITICAL THEORIST

10 'Communism as a complete naturalism is humanism, and as a complete humanism is naturalism. It is the *definitive* resolution of the antagonism between man and nature, and between man and man. It is the true solution of the conflict between existence and essence, between objectification and self-affirmation, between freedom and necessity, between individual and species. It is the solution of the riddle of history and knows itself to be the solution.'
ECONOMIC AND PHILOSOPHICAL MANUSCRIPTS *(1844)*

11 'Religion is the sigh of the oppressed creatures, the heart of a heartless world, just as it is the soul of soulless conditions. It is the opium of the people.'
A CONTRIBUTION TO THE CRITIQUE OF HEGEL'S PHILOSOPHY OF RIGHT *(1844), Introduction*

1 'The philosophers have only *interpreted* the world differently, the point is to *change* it.'
THE GERMAN IDEOLOGY *(1846)*

2 'A spectre is haunting Europe – the spectre of Communism.'
MANIFESTO OF THE COMMUNIST PARTY *(1848)*. *(With Engels.)*

3 'The history of all hitherto existing society is the history of class struggles.'
IBID.

4 'The proletariat alone is a really revolutionary class. The other classes decay and finally disappear in the face of modern industry; the proletariat is its special essential product.'
IBID.

5 'The essential condition for the existence and the sway of the bourgeois class is the formation and augmentation of capital; the condition for capital is wage labour. Wage labour rests exclusively on competition between labourers. The advance of industry, whose involuntary promoter is the bourgeoisie, replaces the isolation of the labourers, due to competition, by their revolutionary combination, due to association. The development of modern industry, therefore, cuts from under its feet the very foundation on which the bourgeoisie produces and appropriates products. What the bourgeoisie, therefore, produces, above all, is its own grave-diggers. Its fall and the victory of the proletariat are equally inevitable.'
IBID.

6 'Political power, properly so called, is merely the organised power of one class for oppressing another.'
IBID.

7 'Christian socialism is but the holy water with which the priest consecrates the heart-burnings of the aristocrat.'
IBID.

8 'Let the ruling classes tremble at a Communistic revolution. The proletarians have nothing to lose but their chains. They have a world to win. WORKING MEN OF ALL COUNTRIES, UNITE!'
IBID.

9 'What I did that was new was to demonstrate: (1) that the *existence of classes* is merely linked to *particular phases in the development of production*; (2) that class struggle necessarily leads to the *dictatorship of the proletariat*; (3) that this dictatorship itself constitutes the transition to the *abolition of all classes* and to a *classless society.*'
Letter to J Weydemeyer, 1852

10 'It is not the consciousness of men that determines their existence, but on the contrary their social existence which determines their consciousness.'
CRITIQUE OF POLITICAL ECONOMY *(1858)*

11 'Capital is dead labour that, vampire-like, lives only by sucking living labour, and lives the more, the more labour it sucks.'
CAPITAL *(1867–1894)*

12 'If money, according to Augier, "comes into the world with a congenital blood-stain on one cheek", capital comes dripping from head to foot, from every pore, with blood and dirt.'
IBID.

13 'Labour in a white skin cannot be free so long as labour in a black skin is branded.'
IBID.

14 'The English have all the material requisites for the revolution. What they lack is the spirit of generalisation and revolutionary ardour.'
Private circular aginst the Bakuninists, January 1870

15 'The working men's Paris, in the act of its heroic self-holocaust, involved in its flames buildings and monuments. While tearing to pieces the living body of the proletariat, its rulers must no longer expect to return triumphantly into the intact architecture of their abodes . . . The bourgeoisie of the whole world, which looks complacently upon the wholesale massacre after the battle, is convulsed by horror at the desecration of brick and mortar.'
THE CIVIL WAR IN FRANCE *(1871)*

16 'Between capitalist and communist society lies the period of the revolutionary transformation of the one into the other. Corresponding to this is also a political transition period in which the state can be nothing but the revolutionary dictatorship of the proletariat.'
CRITIQUE OF THE GOTHA PROGRAMME *(1875)*

1   'All the houses, in our time, are marked
with a mysterious red cross. The judge is
history, the executioner is the
proletariat.'
Quoted in A Camus, THE REBEL, *'State
Terrorism and Rational Terror'*

Masaryk, Thomas (1850–1937)
CZECH NATIONALIST LEADER,
PRESIDENT OF CZECHOSLOVAKIA,
1918–1935

2   'Revolution or dictatorship can sometimes
abolish bad things, but they can never
create good and lasting ones. Impatience
is fatal in politics.'
THE FOUNDATIONS OF MARXIST THEORY *(1899)*

3   'The way in which, amid the political
and social unrest of his time, Christ
keeps aloof from politics, is truly
sublime.'
THE SPIRIT OF RUSSIA *(1913)*

4   'Jesus, not Caesar, is the meaning of
history.'
IBID.

5   'Austria is degenerated; she is the
Catholic Turkey; she has lost her *raison
d'être*.'
*Confidential memorandum, April 1915,
'Independent Bohemia'*

6   'In politics habits, and not only good
ones, but bad ones just as well, rule
humanity.'
IBID.

7   'Great political and social changes begin
to be possible as soon as men are not
afraid to risk their lives.'
Letter to R Seton-Watson, 16 March 1917

8   'All the small nations in the East of
Europe (Finns, Poles, Esthonians, Letts,
Lithuanians, Czechs, Slovaks and
Roumanians) need a strong Russia, lest
they be left at the mercy of the Germans
and Austrians. The Allies must support
Russia at all costs and by all possible
means.'
Memorandum, 10 April 1918

9   'The efforts and plans of the most gifted
political leaders, of the men who make
history, reveal themselves as *vaticinatio
ex eventu*.'
THE MAKING OF A STATE *(1925)*

Mazzini, Giuseppe (1805–1872)
ITALIAN NATIONALIST
REVOLUTIONARY

10   'Blood calls for blood, and the dagger of
the conspirator is never so terrible as
when sharpened upon the tombstone of a
martyr.'
*Open letter to Charles Albert, King of
Piedmont, December 1831*

11   'Great revolutions are the work rather of
principles than of bayonets, and are
achieved first in the moral, and
afterwards in the material sphere.'
MANIFESTO OF YOUNG ITALY *(1831)*

12   'Insurrection – by means of guerrilla
bands – is the true method of warfare for
all nations desirous of emancipating
themselves from a foreign yoke. This
method of warfare supplies the
want – inevitable at the commencement
of the insurrection – of a regular army; it
calls the greatest number of elements
into the field, and yet may be sustained
by the smallest number. It forms the
military education of the people, and
consecrates every foot of the native soil
by the memory of some warlike deed.
   Guerrilla warfare opens a field of
activity for every local capacity; forces
the enemy into an unaccustomed method
of battle; avoids the evil consequences of
a great defeat; secures the national war
from the risk of treason, and has the
advantage of not confining it within any
defined and determinate basis of
operations. It is invincible,
indestructible.'
GENERAL INSTRUCTIONS FOR THE MEMBERS OF
YOUNG ITALY *(1831), Section 4*

13   'God has given you your country as
cradle, and humanity as mother; you
cannot rightly love your brethren of the
cradle if you love not the common
mother.'
Speech at Milan, 25 July 1848

14   'You should have no joy or repose so long
as a portion of the territory upon which
your language is spoken is separated from
the Nation.'
THE DUTIES OF MAN *(1860)*

15   'Liberty, misunderstood by materialists as
*the right to do or not to do anything not
directly injurious to others*, we
understand as the faculty of choosing,
among the various modes of fulfilling

duty, those most in harmony with our own tendencies.'
ON THE UNITY OF ITALY *(enlarged edition, 1861)*

1 'Without a country, and without liberty, we might, perhaps, produce some prophets of art, but no vital art.'
LIFE AND WRITINGS *(1864–70), Volume I*

2. 'On the day when democracy shall elevate itself to the position of a religious party, it will carry away the victory: not before.'
IBID., *Volume VI*

3 'Liberty, by itself, is Protestantism in religion. Liberty, by itself, is Romanticism in literature. Liberty is a negation – of itself it constructs nothing.'
Quoted in E Hales, MAZZINI AND THE SECRET SOCIETIES, *Chapter 6*

4 'Every revolution is the work of a *principle* which has been accepted as a basis of faith ... without this purpose there may be riots, and at times victorious insurrections, but no revolutions.'
IBID., *Chapter 9*

Mboya, Tom (Thomas) (1930–1969)
KENYAN NATIONALIST LEADER

5 'Whereas seventy-two years ago the scramble for Africa started, from Accra we announce that these same powers must be told in a clear, firm and definite voice: "Scram from Africa".'
Speech to the All-African People's Conference, 13 December 1958

6 'Let us, therefore, join together and match the internationalism of communism, item by item, with the internationalism of democracy. Let us co-operate in the effort to eliminate disease, poverty and ignorance from the face of the earth, and we shall have dealt a death-blow to the root causes of most of the "isms" that currently bedevil the world.'
Speech at New York on the First African Freedom Day, 15 April 1959

Medvedev, Roy (1925–)
SOVIET WRITER AND EXPELLED COMMUNIST PARTY MEMBER

7 'It's a fact that the Russian people have moved forward, not by way of religious uplift, but through revolution; and despite all the disappointments they've encountered on the way, they'll leave our descendants not a religious heritage but socialism and democracy.'
Interview with Piero Ostellino, CORRIERE DELLA SERA, *1977*

8 'Everyone in Russia would feel it as a personal tragedy if any war or accident led to the destruction of Paris, London, Rome, Amsterdam, or Madrid. (Do people in Britain or Italy feel the same about Moscow or Leningrad?)'
NEW LEFT REVIEW, *November/December, 1981, 'The USSR and the Arms Race'. (Written with his brother, Zhores Medvedev.)*

Meiji Mutsuhito (1852–1912)
EMPEROR OF JAPAN, 1868–1912

9 'Knowledge shall be sought for all over the world and thus shall be strengthened the foundation of the imperial polity.'
'The Charter Oath', April 1868. Giving formal statement to the ending of Japan's long period of closure to the West

Melanchthon, Philip (1497–1560)
GERMAN SCHOLAR AND HUMANIST

10 'The highest and ultimate instrument of political power is capital punishment.'
(Nervus potestatis politicae praecipuus et summus est supplicium capitale.)
PHILOSOPHIAE MORALIS EPITOMES

Melbourne, 2nd Viscount (William Lamb) (1779–1848)
ENGLISH WHIG POLITICIAN, PRIME MINISTER, 1834 AND 1835–1841

11 'I am afraid that for the first time the Crown would have an Opposition returned smack against it.'
Queen Victoria's journal, 15 May 1841. Advising against a dissolution of parliament

12 'Mr Pulteney, afterwards Earl of Bath, is reported to have said that political parties were like snakes, guided not by their heads, but by their tails. Lord Melbourne does not know whether this is true of the snake, but it is certainly so of the party.'
Letter to Queen Victoria, 6 April 1842

13 'The whole duty of government is to prevent crime and to preserve contracts.'
Quoted in Lord David Cecil, LORD M., *Chapter 3*

1 'If it was not absolutely necessary, it was the foolishest thing ever done.'
IBID., *Chapter 4. Of the Reform Act of 1832*

2 'My esoteric doctrine is that if you entertain any doubt, it is safest to take the unpopular side in the first instance. Transit from the unpopular, is easy . . . but from the popular to the unpopular the ascent is so steep and so rugged that it is impossible to maintain it.'
IBID.

Menzies, Sir Robert (1894–1978)
AUSTRALIAN LIBERAL POLITICIAN, PRIME MINISTER, 1939–1941 AND 1949–1966

3 'Well, until recently, I did not know that you had one. But I now observe that you are all for sanctions imposed by the League of Nations; that you will most fully support them; and that if this leads to hostilities you will wage war with bows and arrows.'
AFTERNOON LIGHT *(1967), Chapter 5. In answer to Stafford Cripps' question, what he thought of Labour's defence policy, 1936*

4 'Men of genius are not be analyzed by common-place rules. The rest of us who have been or are leaders, more common-place in our quality, will do well to remember two things. One is *never to forget posterity when devising a policy.* The other is *never to think of posterity when making a speech.'*
THE MEASURE OF THE YEARS *(1970), Chapter 1*

5 'Until this surrender by the British Government, threats of riotous assembly were not lawful. Malicious injury to property was not lawful. The threat to inflict it was not lawful . . . The decision is an incitement to lawlessness. The long-established and noble rule of Law, one of the greatest products of the character and tradition of British history, has suffered a deadly blow. Blackmail has become respectable.'
IBID., *Chapter 24. Of the British government's successful appeal to the cricket authorities to cancel the South African tour of England, 1970, in the wake of public protest*

Metternich, Clemens, Fürst von (1773–1859)
AUSTRIAN POLITICIAN, FOREIGN MINISTER OF THE HAPSBURG EMPIRE, 1809–1848

6 'My life has coincided with a wretched epoch. I came into the world too soon or too late; today I know I can do nothing . . . I spend my life in propping up buildings mouldering in decay. I ought to have been born in 1900 and to have had the twentieth century before me.'
Letter to Princess Lieven, 6 October 1820

7 'You have only to mention a social contract and the revolution is made!'
Memorandum for Alexander I of Russia, 1820

8 'Any plan conceived in moderation must fail when the circumstances are set in extremes.'
Letter to General de Vincent, 2 December 1822

9 'People look on me as a kind of lantern to which they draw near in order to see their way through the almost complete darkness.'
Letter to Friedrich von Gentz, 11 April 1825

10 'I consider myself stronger than most of my contemporaries, because I have an invincible hatred of words and empty phrases and my instinct is always towards action.'
Letter to Gentz, 5 August 1825

11 'In an age that is so full of dangers for the very foundations and safeguards of social order, the only good policy is to pursue no policy.'
Letter to Comte d'Apponyi, 27 January 1826

12 'Men like Canning fall twenty times and recover themselves as often; men like me have no need of recovery because they are not subject to falls. The first play to the gallery; the second usually bore it.'
Letter to Neumann, 23 June 1826

13 'Invasion is second nature to the Russian Empire.'
Letter to Prince Esterhazy, 3 December 1827

14 'The world has need of me still if only because my place in it could not be filled by anyone else. To be what I am needs an accumulation of experience, and one

could as easily replace an old tree as an old minister.'
Letter to his son, Viktor, 15 May 1828

1 'If England does not want something to happen, Russia will not do it.'
Letter to Esterhazy, 18 December 1828

2 'When the ground shakes under governments it is no good their trying to sit still; nature will not allow it!'
Letter to Apponyi, 28 October 1829

3 'When Paris sneezes, Europe catches cold.'
In conversation, 1830

4 'In revolutions those who want everything always get the better of those who want only a certain amount.'
Letter to Esterhazy, 17 March 1831

5 'Moderation is fatal to factions, just as it is the vital principle of established power. To ask malcontents to be moderate is like asking them to destroy the foundations of their existence.'
Letter to Apponyi, 6 February 1834

6 'Democracy is in every case a principle of dissolution, of decomposition. It tends to separate men, it loosens society. I am opposed to this because I am by nature and by habit constructive. That is why monarchy is the only government that suits my way of thinking ... Monarchy alone tends to bring men together, to unite them in compact, efficient masses, and to make them capable by their combined efforts of the highest degree of culture and civilisation.'
In conversation with George Ticknor, 1835

7 'Democracy is a truth in America; in Europe it is a falsehood.'
IBID.

8 'Gratitude is not an active sentiment in politics. It is a mistake to take account of it.'
Letter to Esterhazy, 18 March 1841

9 'One must, if one can, kill one's opponent, but never rouse him by contempt and the whiplash.'
Letter to Apponyi, 10 September 1842

10 'Italy is a geographical expression.'
Letter to Lord Palmerston, 6 August 1847

11 'I have always considered politics in the presence of social dangers to be a luxury.'
Letter to the Archduchess Sophie, 31 March 1848

12 'The sovereignty of the people can only be a fictitious idea because, since the meaning of sovereignty is unquestionably that of supreme power, and since that power is incapable of being exercised by the people, it must be delegated by them to an authority *other than the sovereign*. What is there left for the sovereign except a name, whereas *the thing* passes into other hands! Pure invention!'
Letter to Sir Travers Twiss, 11 August 1849

13 'I made a point of never colliding with the impossible.'
Letter to L Veuillot, January 1850

14 'This maxim, "to preserve is to act", has always served me as a line of conduct, while those who should have backed me up were confusing the duty of preservation with inactivity.'
MEMOIRS *(1880-1884), Volume VIII*

Miaja Menant, José (1878–1958)
SPANISH GENERAL

15 'The socialists talk first, then act. If the communists talk, they do so after acting.'
*In conversation with Pietro Nenni.
Quoted in H Thomas,* THE SPANISH CIVIL WAR, *Book III, Chapter 30*

Mill, James (1773–1836)
SCOTTISH POLITICAL ECONOMIST AND PHILOSOPHER

16 'The population in this country with regard to some important improvement in their government may be compared to a vessel of water exposed to a temperature of 32°. Leave it perfectly still, and the water will remain uncongealed; shake it a little, and it shoots into ice immediately. All great changes are easily effected, when the time is come. Was it not an individual, without fortune, without name, and in fact without talents, who produced the reformation?'
Letter to Ricardo, 23 September 1818

17 'The benefits of the Representative system are lost, in all cases in which the interests of the choosing body are not the same with those of the community.'
ESSAY ON GOVERNMENT *(1821)*

Mill, John Stuart (1806–1873)
ENGLISH PHILOSOPHER AND POLITICAL
ECONOMIST, LIBERAL MEMBER OF
PARLIAMENT, 1865–1868

1 'No society in which eccentricity is a
matter of reproach, can be in a
wholesome state.'
PRINCIPLES OF POLITICAL ECONOMY *(1848),*
Book II, Chapter 1

2 'The only security against political
slavery, is the check maintained over
governors, by the diffusion of
intelligence, activity, and public spirit
among the governed ... A democratic
constitution, not supported by democratic
institutions in detail, but confined to the
central government, not only is not
political freedom, but often creates a
spirit precisely the reverse, carrying
down to the lowest grade in society the
desire and ambition of political
domination. In some countries the desire
of the people is for not being tyrannised
over, but in others it is merely for an
equal chance to everybody of
tyrannising.'
IBID., *Book V, Chapter 11*

3 'The object of this essay is to assert one
very simple principle ... That principle
is that the sole end for which mankind
are warranted, individually or
collectively, in interfering with the
liberty of action of any of their number
is self-protection. That the only purpose
for which power can be rightfully
exercised over any member of a civilised
community, against his will, is to prevent
harm to others. His own good, either
physical or moral, is not a sufficient
warrant.'
ON LIBERTY *(1859), Chapter 1*

4 'If all mankind minus one were of one
opinion, and only one person were of the
contrary opinion, mankind would be no
more justified in silencing that one
person, than he, if he had the power,
would be justified in silencing mankind
... If the opinion is right, they are
deprived of the opportunity of
exchanging error for truth; if wrong,
they lose, what is almost as great a
benefit, the clearer perception and
liveliness of truth, produced by its
collision with error.'
IBID., *Chapter 2*

5 'One person with a belief is a social
power equal to ninety-nine who have
only interests.'
CONSIDERATIONS ON REPRESENTATIVE
GOVERNMENT *(1861), Chapter 1*

6 'Well would it be for England if
Conservatives voted consistently for
everything conservative, and Liberals for
everything liberal ... The Conservatives,
as being by the law of their existence the
stupidest party, have much the greatest
sins of this description to answer for.'
IBID., *Chapter 7*

7 'Was there ever any domination which
did not appear natural to those who
possessed it?'
THE SUBJECTION OF WOMEN *(1869)*

Miller, Ray (d. 1966)
AMERICAN DEMOCRATIC POLITICIAN

8 'The 45,000,000 immigrants who came to
the United States between the adoption
of the Constitution and 1921 did so
because the Democratic party supported
God. Canada and Australia have as much
opportunity, as many natural resources
and as much land, but your mothers and
mine came here because this country
supports God, and because of the
Democratic party, which has always
supported God.'
Quoted in H G Nicholas, THE NATURE OF
AMERICAN POLITICS, *Chapter 4. While
campaigning in the primary for the
Democratic nomination for governor of
Ohio, 1948*

Milner, Alfred, 1st Viscount
(1854–1925)
ENGLISH POLITICIAN, MEMBER OF THE
WAR CABINET, 1916–1918

9 'If we believe a thing to be bad, and if
we have a right to prevent it, it is our
duty to try to prevent it, and to damn the
consequences.'
*Speech at Glasgow, 26 November 1909.
Justifying the House of Lords' opposition
to Lloyd George's budget of 1909*

Milton, John (1608–1674)
ENGLISH POET

10 'I deny not, but that it is of greatest
concernment in the Church and
Commonwealth, to have a vigilant eye
how Bookes demeane themselves, as well
as men; and thereafter to confine,

imprison, and do sharpest justice on them as malefactors. For Books are not absolutely dead things, but do contain a potencie of life in them to be as active as that soule whose progeny they are.'
AREOPAGITICA *(1644)*

1 'To overcome in Battle, and subdue Nations, and bring spoils with infinite Man-slaughter, shall be held the highest pitch
Of human Glorie, and for Glorie done
Of triumph, to be styl'd great Conquerors,
Patrons of Mankind, Gods, and Sons of Gods,
Destroyers rightlier call'd and Plagues of men.'
PARADISE LOST *(1667): XI*

Mirabeau, Honoré Gabriel, Comte de (1749–1791)
FRENCH REVOLUTIONARY LEADER

2 'Should Prussia perish, the art of government would return to its infancy.'
THE PRUSSIAN MONARCHY *(1788)*

3 'A silent and mournful reception is due to the monarch; in the moment of sorrow, the silence of the people is a lesson for kings.'
Speech to the National Assembly, 15 July 1789. On the appearance there, the day after the storming of the Bastille, of Louis XVI
SEE ALSO *Beauvoir*

4 'To administer is to govern: to govern is to reign. That is the essence of the problem.'
MEMORANDUM, *3 July 1790*

5 'Nobility, say the aristocracy, is the intermedium between the king and the people – true; just as a sporting dog is the intermedium between the sportsman and the hare.'
MIRABEAU'S LETTERS DURING HIS RESIDENCE IN ENGLAND *(1832)*, '*Apophthegms*'

6 'Patriots rise up like mushrooms ... we have always the patriot of the day, like the favourite player ... a pretence to the famed virtue is the road to corruption, and marks a man as the one who wants only a bidder that will rise to his price.'
IBID.
SEE ALSO *Robert Walpole*

7 'Society is composed of two great classes: they who have more dinners than

appetite, and they who have more appetite than dinners.'
IBID.

8 'The body politic is like a tree; as it proceeds upwards, it stands as much in need of heaven as of earth.'
IBID.

Mola, Emilio (1887–1937)
SPANISH NATIONALIST GENERAL

9 'The Fifth Column.'
In conversation with a reporter, October 1937. When asked which of his four army columns would capture Madrid from the Republicans

Moltke, Helmuth Graf von (1800–1891)
PRUSSIAN ARMY OFFICER

10 'War is a factor in God's plan of the world ... Without war the world would sink into materialism.'
Letter to Dr Bluntschli, 11 December 1880

Monck, George, 1st Duke of Albemarle (1608–1670)
ENGLISH GENERAL

11 'I am engaged in conscience and honour to see my country freed from that intolerable slavery of a sword government, and I know England cannot, nay, will not endure it.'
1659. Quoted in C Firth, CROMWELL'S ARMY, *Chapter 14. Of his decision to support the restoration of Charles II*

Montesquieu, Charles Louis, Baron de (1689–1755)
FRENCH PHILOSOPHER AND JURIST

12 'Ever since the invention of gunpowder ... I continually tremble lest men should, in the end, uncover some secret which would provide a short way of abolishing mankind, of annihilating peoples and nations in their entirety.'
THE PERSIAN LETTERS *(1721)*

13 'The state owes to every citizen an assured subsistence, proper nourishment, suitable clothing, and a mode of life not incompatible with health.'
THE SPIRIT OF LAWS *(1748)*

14 'A new disease is spreading over Europe; it has seized upon our princes and

induces them to maintain an inordinate number of soldiers. The disease is attended by complications and it inevitably becomes contagious; for, as soon as one state increases what it calls its forces, the others immediately increase theirs; so that nothing is gained except mutual ruination. Each sovereign keeps mobilised all the divisions he would need if his subjects were threatened with extermination. And the name of "peace" is given to this condition in which all compete against all ... The result of such a state of affairs is the perpetual increase of taxation. And what prevents the finding of any remedy is that the state no longer relies on its income but wages war with its capital. It is no unheard-of thing for a government to mortgage its securities even in time of peace and to employ for bringing about its own ruin – what are called extraordinary measures – measures indeed so extraordinary that they could hardly have entered the dreams of the wildest young spendthrift.'
IBID.

Morley of Blackburn, John, 1st Viscount (1838–1923)
ENGLISH MAN OF LETTERS AND LIBERAL POLITICIAN, MEMBER OF PARLIAMENT, 1883–1895 AND 1896–1908, SECRETARY OF STATE FOR INDIA 1905–1910

1 'Of all societies since the Roman Republic, and not even excepting the Roman Republic, England has been the most emphatically and essentially political. She has passed through military phases and through religious phases, but they have been transitory, and the great central stream of national life has flowed in political channels.'
ON COMPROMISE (1874), Chapter 3

2 'The political spirit is the great force in throwing love of truth and accurate reasoning into a secondary place.'
IBID.

3 'It is an old saying that, after all, the great end and aim of the British Constitution is to get twelve honest men into a box. That is really a very sensible way of putting the theory, that the first end of government is to give security to life and property, and to make people keep their contracts.'

Presidential address to the Midland Institute, Birmingham, 5 October 1876. Published as 'On Popular Culture' in CRITICAL MISCELLANIES *(1886), Volume I*

4 'Most mistakes in politics arise from flat and invincible disregard of the plain maxim that is is possible for the same thing to be and not to be.'
RECOLLECTIONS (1917), Volume I, Book II, Chapter 3

5 '*Prima facie* is not meant for serious politics.'
IBID., *Volume I, Book III, Chapter 3*

Morris, William (1834–1896)
ENGLISH WRITER, CRAFTSMAN AND SOCIAL REFORMER

6 'So long as the system of competition in the production and exchange of the means of life goes on, the degradation of the arts will go on; and if that system is to last for ever, then art is doomed, and will surely die; that is to say, civilization will die.'
ART UNDER PLUTOCRACY (1883)

7 'The chief accusation I have to bring against the modern state of society is that it is founded on the art-lacking or unhappy labour of the greater part of men.'
IBID.

8 'The very essence of competitive commerce is waste; the waste that comes of the anarchy of war.'
IBID.

9 'The most grinding poverty is a trifling evil compared with the inequality of classes.'
Letter to Andreas Scheu, 5 September 1883

10 'It has become an article of the creed of modern morality that all labour is good in itself – a convenient belief to those who live on the labour of others.'
USEFUL WORK VERSUS USELESS TOIL (1884)

11 'Social morality, the responsibility of man towards the life of man, will, in the new order of things, take the place of theological morality, the responsibility of man to some abstract idea.'
IBID.

12 'It is not revenge we want for poor people, but happiness; indeed, what revenge can be taken for all the

thousands of years of the sufferings of the poor?'
HOW WE LIVE AND HOW WE MIGHT LIVE *(1884)*

1 'When our opponents say, as they sometimes do, How should we be able to procure the luxuries of life in a Socialist society? answer boldly, We could not do so and we don't care, for we don't want them and won't have them; and indeed, I feel sure that we cannot if we are all free men together.'
THE SOCIETY OF THE FUTURE *(1887)*

2 'Not one, not one, nor thousands must they slay
But one and all if they would dusk the day.'
A DEATH SONG *(1887). On the killing of Alfred Linnel at the Trafalgar Square demonstration of 26 November 1887*

3 'I call myself a Communist . . . All genuine Socialists admit that Communism is the necessary development of Socialism.'
SOCIALISM AND ANARCHISM *(1889)*

4 'Truth to say, my friends, I do not know what Marx's Theory of Value is, and I'm damned if I want to know. Truth to say, my friends, I have tried to understand Marx's theory, but political economy is not in my line, and much of it appears to me to be dreary rubbish. But I am, I hope, a Socialist none the less. It is enough political economy for me to know that the idle rich class is rich and the working class is poor, and that the rich are rich because they rob the poor.'
In conversation, in answer to a question from a follower of Hyndman. Quoted in J B Glasier, WILLIAM MORRIS AND THE EARLY DAYS OF THE SOCIALIST MOVEMENT, *Chapter 4*

Mosley, Sir Oswald (1896–1980)
ENGLISH POLITICIAN, FOUNDER OF THE BRITISH UNION OF FASCISTS

5 '[Its object was] to make working-class bees without a sting, who were to gather honey for the rich, but be deprived of the right to defend themselves.'
THE STAR, *15 December 1926. On Baldwin's anti-trade union object in 1926*

6 'When not realities but words are to be discussed Parliament wakes up. Then we are back in the comfortable pre-war world of make-believe. Politics are safe again; hairs are to be split, not facts to be

faced. Hush! Do not awaken the dreamers. Facts will waken them in time with a vengeance.'
BIRMINGHAM TOWN CRIER, *23 December 1929*

7 'We have to get away from the belief that the only criterion of British prosperity is how many goods we can send abroad for foreigners to consume.'
House of Commons, 28 May 1930. On his resignation from the Labour government

8 'The only methods we shall employ will be English ones. We shall rely on the good old English fist.'
MANCHESTER GUARDIAN, *16 May 1931. On the recruiting of a youth movement for his New Party*

9 'Faced with the alternative of saying good-bye to the gold standard, and therefore to his own employment, and good-bye to other people's employment, Mr Churchill characteristically selected the latter course.'
Quoted in R Skidelsky, OSWALD MOSLEY, *Chapter 7. On Churchill's decision to return Great Britain to the gold standard, 1925*

10 'Statesmen must learn to live with scientists as the Medici once lived with artists.'
IBID., *Chapter 10*

11 'What would you think of a Salvation Army which took to its heels on the day of judgment?'
Quoted in M Foot, ANEURIN BEVAN, *Volume I, Chapter 4. Of Ramsay MacDonald's coalition with the Conservatives in 1931*

12 'War is to man what childbirth is to woman.'
Quoted in R Skidelsky, OSWALD MOSLEY, *Chapter 18*

Muggeridge, Malcolm (1903–)
ENGLISH JOURNALIST

13 'To succeed pre-eminently in English public life it is necessary to conform either to the popular image of a bookie or of a clergyman; Churchill being a perfect example of the former, Halifax of the latter.'
In conversation with Lord Linlithgow, 1934

Murray, Sir George (1849–1936)
ENGLISH CIVIL SERVANT

1 'This may be safely turned down. No sane enemy, acquainted with our institutions, would destroy the War Office.'
Minute on memorandum laid before Asquith. Quoted in A Chamberlain, DOWN THE YEARS, *Chapter 23. On a proposal to construct an underground passage from the War Office to the Horse Guards, with cellars for storing papers in the event of an air attack*

Mussolini, Benito (1883–1945)
ITALIAN FASCIST POLITICIAN, PRIME MINISTER AND DICTATOR, 1922–1943

2 'Italy has need of a blood bath.'
Letter to Bruno Buozzi, 1913

3 'The perfecting of instruments of war is no hindrance to warlike instincts. It might have the opposite effect.'
Speech at Parma, 13 December 1914

4 'It is human, civilised, socialistic, to stop quietly at the window while blood is flowing in torrents . . . It is necessary to act, to move, to fight and, if necessary, to die. Neutrals have never dominated events. They have always gone under. It is blood which moves the wheels of history.'
IBID. *Calling for Italian entry into the First World War*

5 'I am not displeased, gentlemen, to make my speech from the benches of the Extreme Right, where formerly no one dared to sit. I may say at once, with the supreme contempt I have for all nominalism, that I shall adopt a reactionary line throughout my speech, which will be, I do not know how Parliamentary in form, but anti-Socialist and anti-Democratic in substance.'
Speech to the Chamber of Deputies, 21 June 1921. (The opening statement of his first major speech as a member of the Italian parliament.)

6 'We deny your internationalism [i.e. of the Socialists], because it is a luxury which only the upper classes can afford; the working people are hopelessly bound to their native shores.'
IBID.

7 'Our programme is simple: we wish to govern Italy.'
Speech at Udine, 20 September 1922. On the Fascist programme

8 'The Liberal State is a mask behind which there is no face; it is a scaffolding behind which there is no building.'
Speech at Milan, 6 October 1922

9 'Fascism, the more it considers and observes the future and the development of humanity, quite apart from political considerations of the moment, believes neither in the possibility nor the utility of perpetual peace.'
THE POLITICAL AND SOCIAL DOCTRINE OF FASCISM *(1932)*

10 'If the nineteenth century was a century of individualism . . . it may be expected that this will be the century of collectivism, and hence the century of the State.'
IBID.

11 'When the war in Spain is over, I shall have to find something else: the Italian character has to be formed through fighting.'
1936. Quoted in P Monelli, MUSSOLINI, *Chapter 12*

12 'This Berlin-Rome connection is not so much a diaphragm as an axis, around which can revolve all those states of Europe with a will towards collaboration and peace.'
Speech at Milan, 1 November 1936

13 'It is a law of history that when there are two contrary currents of opinion in a nation, one wanting war and the other peace, the latter party is invariably defeated even when, as always happens, it represents, numerically speaking, the majority.'
MEMOIRS, *1942–1943, Chapter 12*

N

Napoleon I (1769–1821)
FRENCH GENERAL AND POLITICIAN,
EMPEROR, 1804–1814

1 'The outcome of the greatest events is
always determined by a trifle.'
*Letter to the foreign secretary, 7 October
1797*

2 'Let us be masters of the Straits [of
Dover] for six hours, and we shall be
masters of the world.'
*Letter to Vice-Admiral Latouche-Tréville,
2 July 1804*

3 'If they want peace nations should avoid
the pin-pricks which precede cannon-
shots.'
*In conversation with Alexander I at
Tilsit, 22 June 1807*

4 'Remember that the sun never set on the
immense heritage of Charles V, and that
I shall have the Empire of the two
Worlds.'
In conversation with J Fouché, 1808

5 'In war one sees one's own difficulties,
and does not take into account those of
the enemy; one must have confidence in
oneself.'
*Letter to Eugène Beauharnais, 30 April
1809*

6 'The love of country is the first virtue in
a civilised man.'
*Speech to the Polish deputies, 14 July
1812*

7 'Anarchy is always the stepping-stone to
absolute power.'
Imperial séance, 7 June 1813

8 'Men are powerless to secure the future;
institutions alone fix the destinies of
nations.'
IBID.

9 'I did not come back from Elba in order
to drench Paris in blood.'
*In conversation with Benjamin Constant,
21 June 1815. On his failure to exploit the
support of the Paris crowds during the
'Hundred Days'*

10 'I am not being deposed by Liberty; it is
Waterloo which has deposed me.'
IBID.

11 'Who saves his country violates no law.'
MAXIMS. *(This and the following maxims*

*are taken from the numerous collections
of Napoleon's maxims.)*

12 'The true policy of a government is to
make use of aristocracy, but under the
forms and in the spirit of democracy.'
IBID.

13 'A democracy may be furious, but it has
a heart and can be moved; an aristocracy
is always cold and never pardons.'
IBID.

14 'Republican despotism is more fertile in
acts of tyranny, because everyone has a
hand in it.'
IBID.

15 'A revolution is an opinion backed by
bayonets.'
IBID.

16 'Revolutions are like the most noxious
dunghills which bring into life the
noblest vegetables.'
IBID.

17 'The art of governing consists in not
allowing men to grow old in their jobs.'
IBID.

18 'Men are more easily governed through
their vices than their virtues.'
IBID.

19 'Men must be led by an iron hand in a
velvet glove.'
IBID.

20 'The heart of a statesman should be in
his head.'
IBID.

21 'A people which is able to say everything
becomes able to do everything.'
IBID.

22 'Hunger, the stomach, governs the
world.'
Quoted in Comte de Las Cases, MEMORIAL
OF SAINT-HELÈNE

23 'If you wish to get mixed up in
government, you must be ready to pay
with your life, you must be ready to be
assassinated.'
Quoted in Comte Thibaudeau, MEMOIRS OF
THE CONSULATE

24 'The people is a tiger when it is loosed
from its chains.'
Quoted in Thibaudeau, THE CONSULATE
AND THE EMPIRE

1 'Give me a button and I will make
people live or die for it.'
Quoted in I Silone, THE SCHOOL FOR
DICTATORS, *Chapter 8*

Narayan, Jayaprakash
(1902–1979)
INDIAN POLITICIAN, FOUNDER OF THE
CONGRESS SOCIALIST PARTY

2 'What the masses vote or do not vote for
is not important – their opinion depends
wholly on the extent to which they have
been made conscious of their rights and
potentialities. All the problems of society
would have disappeared immediately if
the masses really knew what was good
for them.'
WHY SOCIALISM? *(1936), Chapter 3*

3 'We must remember, that whatever we
do, however we try, we can never
prevent British statesmen, whether Tory
or Labour, from telling lies; for lies are
one of the central pillars of the Empire.'
TO ALL FIGHTERS FOR FREEDOM, II *(1943)*

4 'Labour throughout the western world
has become the camp-follower of the
capitalist class and has thus sold its
conscience and forfeited its leadership of
society and of the new world. In these
circumstances India alone actively
represents the aspirations and promptings
of the disinherited and dispossessed of the
earth.'
IBID.

5 'All democratic parties should, by
definition, be prepared, nay anxious, to
hand over power to the people as soon as
possible, in the same manner as every
good father is anxious to hand over to his
sons when they are of age.'
FROM SOCIALISM TO SARVODAYA *(1957)*

Nasser, Gamal Abdul
(1918–1970)
EGYPTIAN POLITICIAN, PRESIDENT,
1956–1970

6 'Israel itself was nothing more than one
of the consequences of imperialism.'
EGYPTIAN LIBERATION. THE PHILOSOPHY OF THE
REVOLUTION *(1958)*

Nehru, Jawaharlal (1889–1964)
INDIAN CONGRESS POLITICIAN, PRIME
MINISTER, 1947–1964

7 'The conflict between capitalism and
democracy is inherent and continuous; it
is often hidden by misleading propaganda
and by the outward forms of democracy,
such as parliaments, and the sops that the
owning classes throw to the other classes
to keep them more or less contented.'
GLIMPSES OF WORLD HISTORY *(1933)*

8 'The British Government in India is like
a tooth that is decaying but is still
strongly imbedded. It is painful, but it
cannot be easily pulled out.'
TOWARDS FREEDOM *(1935)*

9 'Adventurist tactics in politics or warfare
seldom succeed. Daring does succeed and
risks may be taken, but adventurism is
infantile.'
Letter to J Narayan, 20 November 1950

10 'A dictator or a dumb politician, who is
insensitive, who can stand all the din and
noise in the world, and yet remain
standing on his two feet . . . gets elected
while his rival collapses because he
cannot stand all this din.'
*Speech at a UNESCO symposium, New
Delhi, 20 December 1951*

Newman, John Henry, Cardinal (1801–1890)
ENGLISH ANGLICAN, SUBSEQUENTLY
ROMAN CATHOLIC THEOLOGIAN

11 'People say to me, that it is but a dream
to suppose that Christianity should regain
the organic power in human society
which once it possessed. I cannot help
that; I never said it could. I am not a
politician; I am proposing no measures,
but exposing a fallacy, and resisting a
pretence. Let Benthamism reign in men
who have no aspirations; but do not tell
them to be romantic, and then solace
them with glory; do not attempt by
philosophy what once was done by
religion. The ascendancy of faith may be
impracticable, but the reign of knowledge
is impossible. The problem for statesmen
of this age is how to educate the masses,
and literature and science cannot give the
solution.'
TAMWORTH READING ROOM *(1841)*

Newton, Huey (1942–)
AMERICAN BLACK REVOLUTIONARY
LEADER, CO-FOUNDER OF THE BLACK
PANTHER PARTY

12 'By having no family,
I inherited the family of humanity.
By having no possessions,

I have possessed all.
By rejecting the love of one,
I received the love of all.
By surrendering my life to the
    revolution,
I found eternal life.
Revolutionary Suicide.'
REVOLUTIONARY SUICIDE *(1973), Frontispiece*

1 'Reactionary suicide ... is a spiritual
death that has been the experience of
millions of Black people in the United
States.'
IBID., *'Manifesto'*

2 'I suggested that we use the panther as
our symbol and call our political vehicle
the Black Panther Party. The panther is a
fierce animal, but he will not attack until
he is backed into a corner; then he will
strike out.'
IBID., *Chapter 16*

3 'One day, while working on the paper,
Eldridge [Cleaver] showed us a postcard
from Beverly Axelrod. On the front was
the slogan "Support Your Local Police";
there was a sherriff's star above the
phrase, and in the center of the star a
grinning, slobbering pig. It was just what
we were looking for. We began to show
policemen as pigs in our cartoons, and
from time to time used the word. "Pig"
caught on; it entered the language.'
IBID., *Chapter 22*

Nicholas I (1796–1855)
TSAR OF RUSSIA, 1825–1855

4 'We have on our hands a sick man, a
very sick man; it will be, I tell you,
frankly, a great misfortune if one of these
days he should slip away from us,
especially before all necessary
arrangements can be made.'
*Letter to Sir George Seymour 1853. Of
Turkey-in-Europe.*
SEE ALSO *Palmerston*

5 'We must have the key of our house.'
Quoted in J Y Simpson (ed.), THE SABUROV
MEMOIRS, *Chapter 3. On the importance of
Constantinople to Russia*

Nicolson, Sir Harold (1886–1968)
ENGLISH DIPLOMAT AND AUTHOR

6 'We shall have to walk and live a
Woolworth life hereafter.'
*Diary, 4 June 1941. On the effects of the
Second World War*

7 'A preventive war is always evil. Let us
rather die.'
Diary, 29 November 1948

Niebuhr, Reinhold (1892–1971)
AMERICAN RELIGIOUS AND SOCIAL
WRITER

8 'Man's capacity for justice makes
democracy possible, but man's inclination
to injustice makes democracy necessary.'
THE CHILDREN OF LIGHT AND THE CHILDREN OF
DARKNESS *(1944), Foreword*

Nietzsche, Friedrich (1844–1900)
GERMAN PHILOSOPHER

9 'If we wish a change to be as radical as
possible, we have to apply the remedy in
small doses, but unremittingly, for long
periods. Can a great action be
accomplished all at once?'
THE DAWN *(1881), Aphorism 534*

10 'You say it is the good cause which
hallows even war. I tell you, it is the
good war that hallows every cause!'
THUS SPAKE ZARATHUSTRA *(1883–85): 'Of
War and Warriors'*

11 'The state lies in all languages of good
and evil; and whatever it says, it
lies – and whatever it has, it has stolen
... Confusion of the language of good
and evil; I offer you this sign as the sign
of the state.'
IBID., *'Of the New Idol'*

12 'Where the state *ceases* – look there, my
brothers. Do you not see it: the rainbow
and the bridges to the Superman?'
IBID.

13 'Every high degree of power always
involves a corresponding degree of
freedom from good and evil.'
THE WILL TO POWER *(1888)*

14 'People demand freedom only when they
have no power.'
IBID.

15 'Culture and State – one should not
deceive oneself about this – are
antagonists: "Culture-State" [*Kultur-Staat*]
is merely a modern idea. One lives off
the other, one thrives at the expense of
the other. All great ages of culture are
ages of political decline: what is great
culturally has always been unpolitical,
even anti-political. Goethe's heart opened
up at the phenomenon of Napoleon – it
closed up at the "wars of liberation". At

the same moment when Germany comes up as a great power, France gains a new importance as a *cultural power*.'
THE TWILIGHT OF THE GODS *(1889)*

Nixon, Richard (1913–)
AMERICAN REPUBLICAN POLITICIAN, PRESIDENT, 1969-1974

1 'As I leave you I want you to know – just think how much you're going to be missing. You won't have Nixon to kick around anymore, because, gentlemen, this is my last press conference.'
Press conference, 7 November 1962. After losing the California gubernatorial election

2 'And so tonight – to you, the great silent majority of my fellow Americans – I ask for your support.'
Speech to the nation on television, 3 November 1969

3 'North Vietnam cannot defeat or humiliate the United States. Only Americans can do that.'
IBID.

4 'I was faced with having to fire my friends for things that I myself was a part of, things that I could not accept as morally or legally wrong, no matter how much that opened me to charges of cynicism and amorality. There had been no thievery or venality. We had all simply wandered into a situation unthinkingly, trying to protect ourselves from what we saw as a political problem. Now, suddenly, it was like a Rorschach ink blot: others, looking at our actions,

pointed out a pattern that we ourselves had not seen.'
MEMOIRS OF RICHARD NIXON, *Part VII. On asking for the resignations of Robert Haldeman and John Erlichman in the wake of the Watergate scandal, 1974*

Nkrumah, Kwame (1909-1972)
GHANAIAN NATIONALIST LEADER, PRESIDENT, 1960-1966

5 'To say that a Union Government of Africa is premature is to sacrifice Africa on the altar of neo-colonialism.'
Speech at the meeting of the Organisation of African Unity, Cairo, July 1964

North, Frederick, 8th Baron (1732–1792)
ENGLISH TORY POLITICIAN, PRIME MINISTER, 1770-1782

6 'Men may be popular without being ambitious; but there is rarely an ambitious man who does not try to be popular.'
House of Commons, March 1769

7 'I was the creature of Parliament in my rise; when I fell I was its victim. I came among you without connexion. It was here I was first known; you raised me up; you pulled me down. I have been the creature of your opinion and your power, and the history of my political life is one proof which will stand up against and overturn a thousand wild assertions, that there is a corrupt influence in the Crown which destroys the influence of the House.'
House of Commons, 7 May 1783

O

O'Connell, Daniel (1775–1847)
IRISH NATIONALIST LEADER, MEMBER
OF PARLIAMENT, 1828–1847

1 'Ireland is in your hands, in your power.
If you do not save her, she cannot save
herself.'
House of Commons, 8 February 1847

Ortega y Gasset, José (1883–1955)
SPANISH PHILOSOPHER AND CRITIC

2 'The characteristic of the hour is that the
commonplace mind, knowing itself to be
commonplace, has the assurance to
proclaim the rights of the commonplace
and to impose them wherever it will.'
THE REVOLT OF THE MASSES *(1930), Chapter 1*

3 'This leads us to note down in our
psychological chart of the mass-man of
today two fundamental traits: the free
expansion of his vital desires, and,
therefore, of his personality; and his
radical ingratitude towards all that has
made possible the ease of his existence.
These traits together make up the well-
known psychology of the spoilt child.'
IBID, *Chapter 6*

4 'Under the species of Syndicalism and
Fascism there appears for the first time in
Europe a type of man who does not want
to give reasons or to be right, but simply
shows himself resolved to impose his
opinions.'
IBID., *Chapter 8*

Orwell, George (1903–1950)
ENGLISH NOVELIST AND ESSAYIST

5 'The "Communism" of the English
intellectual is something explicable
enough. It is the patriotism of the
deracinated.'
INSIDE THE WHALE *(1940). Of the English
intelligentsia in the 1930s*

6 'Probably the battle of Waterloo *was* won
on the playing fields of Eton, but the
opening battles of all subsequent wars
have been lost there.'
THE LION AND THE UNICORN *(1941), Part I,
Chapter 4*

7 'An army of unemployed led by
millionaires quoting the Sermon on the
Mount – that is our danger . . . The lady
in the Rolls-Royce car is more damaging

to morale than a fleet of Goering's
bombing planes.'
IBID., *Part II, Chapter 3*

8 'All animals are equal, but some animals
are more equal than others.'
ANIMAL FARM *(1945), Chapter 10*

9 'Political language – and with variations
this is true of all political parties, from
Conservatives to Anarchists – is designed
to make lies sound truthful and murder
respectable.'
*'Politics and the English Language' (1946).
Included in* SHOOTING AN ELEPHANT *(1950)*

10 'Big brother is watching you.'
NINETEEN EIGHTY-FOUR *(1949), Part I,
Chapter 1*

11 'The Ministry of Truth – Minitrue, in
Newspeak – was startlingly different from
any other in sight.'
IBID.

12 'There are certain people like vegetarians
and communists whom one cannot
answer. You just have to go on saying
your say regardless of them, and then the
extraordinary thing is that they may start
listening.'
*In conversation with Stephen Spender, 11
January 1950*

O'Sullivan, John (1813–1895)
AMERICAN JOURNALIST

13 'Why, were other reasons wanting in
favor of now elevating this question of
the reception of Texas into the Union,
out of the lower region of our past party
dissensions, up to its proper level of a
high and broad nationality, it surely is to
be found abundantly in the manner in
which the other nations have undertaken
to intrude themselves into it between us
and the proper parties to the case, in a
spirit of hostile interference against us,
for the avowed object of thwarting our
policy and hampering our power,
limiting our greatness and checking the
fulfilment of our manifest destiny to
overspread the continent allotted by
Providence for the free development of
our yearly multiplying millions.'
THE U.S. MAGAZINE AND DEMOCRATIC REVIEW,
*July 1845. First known use of the phrase,
'manifest destiny'*

Otis, James (1725–1783)
AMERICAN REVOLUTIONARY LEADER

1 'Taxation without representation is tyranny.'
Speech to the Superior Court of Massachusetts, February 1761. Arguing against writs of assistance. (From notes made by John Adams.)

Owen, Robert (1771–1858)
WELSH MILLOWNER, SOCIAL REFORMER, PIONEER OF CO-OPERATIVE MOVEMENT

2 'Courts of law, and all the paraphernalia and folly of law . . . cannot be found in a rational state of society.'
Speech to the National Equitable Labour Exchange, 1 May 1833

3 'If we cannot yet reconcile all opinions, let us endeavour to unite all hearts.'
Motto of his newspaper, THE CRISIS

Owen, Wilfred (1893–1918)
ENGLISH POET

4 'If in some smothering dream, you too
  could pace
Behind the wagon that we flung him in,
And watch the white eyes writhing in
  his face,
His hanging face, like a devil's sick of
  sin;
If you could hear, at every jolt, the blood
Come gargling from the froth-corrupted
  lungs,
Bitter as the cud
Of vile, incurable sores on innocent
  tongues, –
My friend, you would not tell with such
  high zest
To children ardent for some desperate
  glory,
The old Lie: *Dulce et decorum est
Pro patria mori.*'
DULCE ET DECORUM EST *(c. 1916)*

P

Paine, Tom (Thomas)
(1737–1809)
ENGLISH RADICAL POLITICAL
PHILOSOPHER

1 'Society is produced by our wants, and government by our wickedness; the former promotes our happiness positively by uniting our affections, the latter negatively by restraining our vices.'
COMMON SENSE *(1776)*

2 'Government, even in its best state, is but a necessary evil; in its worst state an intolerable one ... Government, like dress, is the badge of lost innocence; the palaces of kings are built upon the ruins of the bowers of paradise.'
IBID.

3 'Though the flame of liberty may sometimes cease to shine, the coal can never expire.'
AMERICAN CRISIS, *23 December 1776*

4 'Those who expect to reap the blessing of freedom must, like men, undergo the fatigue of supporting it.'
IBID.

5 'These are the times that try men's souls. The summer soldier and the sunshine patriot will, in this crisis, shrink from the service of his country; but he that stands it NOW deserves the love and thanks of man and woman.'
IBID., *12 September 1777*

6 'Britain, as a nation, is, in my inmost belief, the greatest and most ungrateful offender against God on the face of the whole earth ... Like Alexander, she has made war her sport, and inflicted misery for prodigality's sake. The blood of India is not yet repaid, nor the wretchedness of Africa yet requited. These are serious things, and whatever a foolish tyrant, a debauched court, a trafficking legislature, or a blinded people may think, the national account with Heaven must some day or other be settled: all countries have sooner or later to be called to their reckoning; the proudest empires have sunk when the balance was struck; and Britain, like an individual penitent, must undergo her day of sorrow, and the sooner it happens to her the better.'
LETTER TO LORD HOWE *(1777)*

7 'The circumstances of the world are continually changing, and the opinions of men change also; and as Government is for the living, and not for the dead, it is the living only that have any right in it.'
THE RIGHTS OF MAN *(1792). Arguing against political justification by the appeal to historical precedent*

8 'Every civil right grows out of a natural right; or, in other words, is a natural right exchanged ... civil power properly considered as such is made up of the aggregate of that class of the natural rights of man, which becomes defective in the individual in point of power, and answers not his purpose, but when collected to a focus becomes competent to the purpose of every one.'
IBID.

9 'War is the faro table of government, and nations the dupes of the games.'
IBID.

10 'To make war upon those who trade with us is like setting a bulldog upon a customer at the shop-door.'
THE AGE OF REASON *(1794)*

11 'The crown signifies a nominal office of a million sterling a year, the business of which consists in receiving the money.'
Quoted in H W C Davis, THE AGE OF GREY AND PEEL, *Chapter 13*

Palacký, František (1798–1876)
CZECH NATIONALIST LEADER AND HISTORIAN

12 'If the Austrian empire had not long been in existence, in the interest of Europe – indeed, in the interest of humanity – one would make haste to create it.'
Letter to the Frankfurt parliament, 11 April, 1848 Arguing against Bohemia's being absorbed in a 'Greater Germany'

13 'Before Austria was, we [Bohemia] were, and when Austria no longer is, we still shall be.'
Quoted in R Seton-Watson, MASARYK IN ENGLAND, *Chapter 1*

Palmerston, 3rd Viscount (Henry Temple) (1784–1865)

ENGLISH POLITICIAN, PRIME MINISTER, 1855–1858 and 1859–1865

1 'To maintain that the legislature of a country has not the right to impose such political disabilities upon any class of the community, as it may deem necessary for the safety and welfare of the whole, would be to strike at once at the fundamental principles on which a civilised government is founded.'
House of Commons, 1 March 1813. On the civil disabilities of the Roman Catholics

2 'Under a pure despotism, a people may be contented, because all are slaves alike; but those who, under a free government, are refused equal participation, must be discontented.'
House of Commons, 18 March 1829. On the wisdom of granting Roman Catholic emancipation

3 'I confess I should not be sorry some day or other to see the Turk kicked out of Europe and compelled to go and sit cup-legged, smoke his pipe, chew his opium and cut off heads on the Adriatic side of the Bosphorus. We want civilisation, activity, trade and business in Europe, and your Mustaphas have no idea of any traffic beyond rhubarbs, figs and red slippers; what energy can be expected from a nation who have no heels to their shoes and pass their whole lives slip shod?'
Letter to E Littleton, 16 September 1829

4 'A quarter of a century of peace does not pass over a nation in vain.'
Letter to Lord Granville, 10 June 1839. Of France

5 'Half the wrong conclusions at which mankind arrive are reached by the abuse of metaphors. . . . All that we hear every day of the week about the decay of the Turkish empire, and its being a dead body or a sapless trunk, and so forth, is pure and unadulterated nonsense.'
Letter to Henry Bulwer, 1 September 1839

6 'The sun never sets upon the interests of this country.'
House of Commons, 1 March 1843
SEE ALSO *John Wilson*

7 'We have no eternal allies, and we have no perpetual enemies. Our interests are eternal, and those interests it is our duty to follow.'
House of Commons, 1 March 1848

8 'As the Roman in days of old held himself free from indiginity when he could say *Civis Romanus sum*, so also a British subject, in whatever land he may be, shall feel confident that the watchful eye and the strong arm of England will protect him against injustice and wrong.'
House of Commons, 25 June 1850. Defending the use of English naval strength to support Don Pacifico's claims for damages against the Greek government

9 'The Time is fast coming when we shall be obliged to strike another Blow in China. . . These half-civilized Governments such as those in China, Portugal, Spanish America all require a Dressing every eight or ten years to keep them in order. Their Minds are too shallow to receive an Impression that will last longer than some such Period and warning is of little use. They care little for words and they must not only see the Stick but actually feel it on their Shoulders before they yield.'
Autograph note, 29 September 1850

10 'The House of Commons allows itself to be led, but does not like to be driven, and is apt to turn upon those who attempt to drive it.'
Letter to Gladstone, 16 May 1861

11 'He is a dangerous man; keep him in Oxford and he is partially muzzled; but send him elsewhere, and he will run wild.'
Remark by Palmerston about Gladstone quoted by Lord Shaftesbury in his diary, 25 October 1865

Pankhurst, Christabel, Dame (1880–1958)

ENGLISH SUFFRAGETTE

12 'We are here to claim our rights as women, not only to be free, but to fight for freedom.'
Speech at London, 23 March 1911

Pankhurst, Emmeline (1858–1928)

ENGLISH SUFFRAGETTE

13 'We are here, not because we are law-breakers; we are here in our efforts to become law-makers.'
Speech from the dock, London, 21 October 1908

1 'I am what you call a hooligan.'
Speech at New York, 25 October 1909

2 'The militancy of men, through all the centuries, has drenched the world with blood, and for these deeds of horror and destruction men have been rewarded with monuments, with great songs and epics. The militancy of women has harmed no human life save the lives of those who fought the battle of righteousness.'
MY OWN STORY *(1914), Foreword*

3 'If we women are wrong in destroying private property in order that human values may be restored, then I say, in all reverence, that it was wrong for the Founder of Christianity to destroy private property, as He did when He lashed the money changers out of the Temple and when He drove the Gadarene swine into the Sea.'
IBID., *Book III, Chapter 4. Of the suffragettes' campaign*

Parker, Horace (1837–1921)
AMERICAN JOURNALIST

4 'A mugwump is a person educated beyond his intellect.'
Slogan adopted by Grover Cleveland in the 1884 election campaign

Parker, Theodore (1810–1860)
AMERICAN THEOLOGIAN AND SOCIAL REFORMER

5 'The American idea. . . is a democracy, that is a government of all the people, by all the people, and for all the people.'
Speech at Boston, 29 May 1850

6 'If you do not say what you think, soon you will dare to say what you do not think.'
COMMONPLACE BOOK

7 'Democracy is not possible except in a nation where there is so much property, and that so widely distributed, that the whole people can have considerable education – intellectual, moral, affectional, and religious.'
Quoted in D Aaron, MEN OF GOOD HOPE, *Chapter 2*

8 'If powerful men will not write justice with black ink, on white paper, ignorant and violent men will write it on the soil, in letters of blood.'
IBID.

Parkes, Joseph (1796–1865)
ENGLISH RADICAL AGITATOR

9 'Tories are burked, no resurrection for them. Whigs will, of course, raise their bidding with the People's growing power and demand. They are an unnatural party standing between the People and the Tory aristocracy chiefly for the pecuniary value of offices and vanity of power. Their hearse is ordered.'
Letter to Francis Place, 1836

Parnell, Charles Stewart (1846–1891)
IRISH NATIONALIST POLITICIAN, MEMBER OF PARLIAMENT, 1875–1891

10 'No man has the right to fix the boundary of the march of a nation. No man has a right to say to his country, "Thus far shalt thou go and no further", and we have never attempted to fix the *ne plus ultra* to the progress of Ireland's nationhood, and we never shall.'
Speech at Cork, 21 January 1885. (The first sentence is engraved on Parnell's statue in Dublin.)

11 'I rely on Dublin. Dublin is true. What Dublin says today Ireland will say tomorrow.'
Speech at Dublin, 10 December 1890

Pearse, Patrick (1879–1916)
IRISH NATIONALIST REVOLUTIONARY AND AUTHOR

12 'The Gael is not like other men; the spade, and the loom, and the sword are not for him. But a destiny more glorious than that of Rome, more glorious than that of Britain, awaits him: to become the saviour of idealism in modern intellectual and social life.'
Presidential address to the New Ireland Society, 1897

13 'A thing that stands demonstrable is that nationhood is not achieved otherwise than in arms. . . We may make mistakes in the beginning and shoot the wrong people; but bloodshed is a cleansing and a sanctifying thing, and the nation which regards it as the final horror has lost its manhood. There are many things more horrible than bloodshed; and slavery is one of them.'
THE COMING REVOLUTION *(1913)*

Pearson, Lester (1897–1972)
CANADIAN DIPLOMAT, LIBERAL
POLITICIAN, PRIME MINISTER, 1963–1968

1   'Diplomacy is letting someone else have
    your way.'
    Quoted in the Vancouver SUN, *18 March
    1965*

Peel, Sir Robert (1788–1850)
ENGLISH CONSERVATIVE POLITICIAN,
PRIME MINISTER, 1834–1835 AND
1841–1846

2   'Do you not think that the tone of
    England, – of that great compound of
    folly, weakness, prejudice, wrong feeling,
    right feeling, obstinacy and newspaper
    paragraphs, which is called public
    opinion, – is more liberal, to use an
    odious and intelligible phrase, than the
    policy of the government?'
    Letter to J W Croker, March 1820

3   'What is right must unavoidably be
    politic.'
    *Letter to Henry Goulburn, 23 September
    1822*

4   'What I propose is to break this sleep of a
    century.'
    *House of Commons, 9 March 1826.
    Introducing a liberalisation of the
    criminal law*

5   'I do not think it was an unnatural or
    unreasonable struggle. I resign it, in
    consequence of the conviction that it can
    be no longer advantageously maintained;
    from believing that there are not
    adequate materials or sufficient
    instruments for its effectual and
    permanent continuance. I yield,
    therefore, to a moral necessity which I
    cannot control, unwilling to push
    resistance to a point which might
    endanger the Establishments that I wish
    to defend.'
    *House of Commons, 4 March 1829.
    Announcing his yielding to the necessity
    of Roman Catholic emancipation*

6   'All my experience in public life is in
    favour of the employment of what the
    world would call young men instead of
    old ones.'
    Letter to the Duke of Wellington, 1829

7   'I feel a want of many essential
    qualifications which are requisite in party
    leaders, among the rest personal
    gratification in the game of politics, and
    patience to listen to the sentiments of
    individuals whom it is equally imprudent
    to neglect and an intolerable bore to
    consult.'
    *Letter to Henry Goulburn, November,
    1830*

8   'We are here to consult the interests and
    not to obey the will of the people.'
    House of Commons, 1831

9   'Of all vulgar arts of government, that of
    solving every difficulty which might
    arise by thrusting the hand into the
    public purse is the most delusory and
    contemptible.'
    House of Commons, 1834

10 'The advice which I give to the
    Conservatives is this – "register, register,
    register".'
    Speech at Tamworth, 7 August 1837

11 'Can there be a more lamentable picture
    than that of a Chancellor of the
    Exchequer, seated on an empty chest, by
    the pool of bottomless deficiency, fishing
    for a budget.'
    *House of Commons, 18 May 1841.
    Attacking the Whig government's
    financial measures*

12 'No considerations of mere political
    support should induce me to hold such
    an office as that which I fill by a servile
    tenure, which would compel me to be
    the instrument of carrying other men's
    opinions into effect.'
    *House of Commons, 17 September 1841.
    On taking office as prime minister*

13 'When a country is tolerably quiet, it is
    better for a Government to be **hard of
    hearing** in respect of seditious language
    than to be very agile in prosecuting.'
    *Letter to Sir James Graham, December
    1841*

14 'Priests are not above sublunary
    considerations. Priests have nephews.'
    *Letter to Graham, 13 August 1845. On
    the burden of meting out a prime
    minister's patronage*

15 'I have thought it consistent with true
    Conservative policy to promote so much
    of happiness and contentment among the
    people that the voice of disaffection
    should be no longer heard, and that
    thought of the dissolution of our

institutions should be forgotten in the midst of physical enjoyment.'
House of Commons, 22 January 1846. On his decision to repeal the Corn Laws

1 'In relinquishing power I shall leave a name severely censured I fear by many who on public grounds deeply regret the severance of party ties, deeply regret that severance, not from interested or personal motives, but from the firm conviction that fidelity to party engagements – the existence and maintenance of a great party – constitutes a powerful instrument of government. I shall surrender power severely censured also by others, who from no interested motives, adhere to the principle of protection, considering the maintenance of it to be essential to the welfare and interests of the country. I shall leave a name execrated by every monopolist who, from less honourable motives, clamours for protection because it conduces to his own individual benefit; but it may be that I shall leave a name sometimes remembered with expressions of good will in the abodes of those whose lot it is to labour, and to earn their daily bread by the sweat of their brow, when they shall recruit their exhausted strength with abundant and untaxed food, the sweeter because it is no longer leavened by a sense of injustice.'
House of Commons, 29 June 1846. Announcing the resignation of his government

2 'I will take care too not again to burn my fingers by organising a party. There is too much truth in the saying "The head of a party must be directed by the tail"... As heads see and tails are blind, I think heads are the best judges as to the course to be taken.'
Letter to Henry Hardinge, 24 September 1846
SEE ALSO *Melbourne*

3 'There seem to me very few facts, at least ascertainable facts, in politics.'
Letter to Lord Brougham, 1846

4 'Great public measures cannot be carried by the influence of mere reason.'
Letter to Lord Radnor, 1846

5 'The modern history of France is the substitution of one crisis for another.'
Letter to Lord Aberdeen, 1849

Penn, William (1644–1718)
ENGLISH QUAKER COLONIST, FOUNDER OF PENNSYLVANIA

6 'Let the people think they govern and they will be governed.'
SOME FRUITS OF SOLITUDE *(1693)*

Perón, Juan Domingo (1895–1974)
ARGENTINIAN POLITICIAN, PRESIDENT, 1946–1955 AND 1973–1974

7 'The order of the day for every Peronist... is to answer a violent action with another action still more violent.'
Speech at Buenos Aires, September 1958

Phillips, Wendell (1811–1884)
AMERICAN ABOLITIONIST AND ORATOR

8 'Every step of progress the world has made has been from scaffold to scaffold, and from stake to stake.'
Speech at Worcester, Massachusetts, 15 October 1851

9 'The manna of popular liberty must be gathered each day or it is rotten.'
Speech at Boston, 28 June 1852

10 'Eternal vigilance is the price of liberty.'
Speech, 1852
SEE ALSO *John Curran*

11 'Whether in chains or in laurels, liberty knows nothing but victories.'
Speech at Harper's Ferry, 1 November 1859

12 'All that is valuable in the United States constitution is one thousand years old.'
Speech at Boston, 17 February 1861

13 'Politicians are like the bones of a horse's fore-shoulder – not a straight one in it.'
Speech, July 1864

Pitt, Thomas (1653–1726)
EAST INDIA MERCHANT AND POLITICIAN, MEMBER OF PARLIAMENT, 1695–1698 AND 1710–1726

14 'Avoid faction, and never enter the House pre-possessed; but attend diligently to the end whatever. I had rather see any child of mine want than he get his bread by voting in the House of Commons.'
Advice to his son, William 1702. Quoted in P Brown, WILLIAM PITT, EARL OF CHATHAM, *Chapter 1*

Pitt, William, 1st Earl of Chatham (1708–1778)
ENGLISH WHIG POLITICIAN, PRIME MINISTER, 1766–1768

1 'I know that I can save this country and that no one else can.'
To the Duke of Devonshire, October 1775. Quoted in P Brown, WILLIAM PITT, EARL OF CHATHAM, *Chapter 6*

2 'I borrowed the Duke of Newcastle's majority to carry on the public business.'
Remark, 1757. Quoted in J Morley, WALPOLE, *Chapter 6. On becoming secretary of state*

3 'The press is, like the air, a chartered libertine.'
Letter to Lord Grenville, 1757

4 'I was called by my Sovereign and by the Voice of the People to assist the state when others had abdicated the service of it. That being so no one can be surprised that I will go on no longer since my advice is not taken. Being responsible I *will* direct, and will be responsible for nothing that I do not direct.'
Statement to the cabinet, 2 October 1761. On his resignation as secretary of state

5 'I rejoice that America has resisted. Three millions of people, so dead to all the feelings of liberty, as voluntarily to submit to be slaves, would have been fit instruments to make slaves of the rest.'
House of Commons, 14 January 1766. Of the colonies' resistance to the Stamp act

6 'Where laws end, there tyranny begins.'
House of Lords, 9 January, 1770. On the John Wilkes affair.
SEE ALSO *Locke*

7 'Unlimited power is apt to corrupt the minds of those who possess it.'
IBID.

8 'The little I know of it has not served to raise my opinion of what is vulgarly called the "Monied Interest"; I mean, that blood-sucker, that muckworm, that calls itself "the friend of government".'
House of Lords, 22 November 1770

9 'The spirit which now resists your taxation in America is the same which formerly opposed loans, benevolences and ship-money in England; the same spirit which called all England on its legs, and by the Bill of Rights vindicated the English constitution; the same spirit which established the great, fundamental, essential maxim of your liberties – that no subject of England shall be taxed but by his own consent. This glorious spirit of Whiggism animates three millions in America, who prefer poverty with liberty to gilded chains and sordid affluence.'
House of Lords, 20 January 1775

10 'If I were an American, as I am an Englishman, while a foreign troop was landed in my country, I never would lay down my arms – never, never, never!'
House of Lords, 18 November 1777

Pitt, William (1759–1806)
ENGLISH POLITICIAN, PRIME MINISTER, 1783–1801 AND 1804–1806

11 'Necessity is the plea for every infringement of human freedom. It is the argument of tyrants; it is the creed of slaves.'
House of Commons, 18 November 1783

12 'There never was a time in the history of this country when from the situation of Europe we might not more reasonably expect fifteen years of peace than at the present moment.'
House of Commons, 17 February 1792

13 'On every principle by which men of justice and honour are actuated, it is the foulest and most atrocious deed which the history of the world has yet had occasion to attest.'
House of Commons, 1 February 1793. On the execution of Louis XVI of France

14 'There is no principle of the law of nations clearer than this, that, when in the course of war any nation acquires new possessions, such nation has only temporary right to them, and they do not become property till the end of the war.'
House of Commons, 30 December 1796

15 'We are not in arms against the opinions of the closet, nor the speculations of the school. We are at war with armed opinions; we are at war with those opinions which the sword of audacious, unprincipled, and impious innovation seeks to propagate amidst the ruin of empires, the demolition of the altars of all religion, the destruction of every venerable, and good, and liberal institution, under whatever form of polity they have been raised... We will not leave the monster to prowl the world

unopposed. He must cease to annoy the abode of peaceful men. If he retire into the cell, whether of solitude or repentance, thither we will not pursue him; but we cannot leave him on the throne of power.'
House of Commons, 7 June 1799. On the war against France

1 'We have gained everything that we would have lost if we had not fought this war.'
House of Commons, 1805. In reply to the question, what England had gained by the war against France

2 'England has saved herself by her exertions, and will, as I trust, save Europe by her example.'
Speech at London, 9 November 1805

3 'Roll up that map [of Europe]; it will not be wanted these ten years.'
Remark, January 1806. After Napoleon's victory at Austerlitz

Pius IX (1792–1878)
ITALIAN PRELATE, POPE, 1846–1878

4 'It is an error to believe that the Roman Pontiff can and ought to reconcile himself to, and agree with, progress, liberalism, and contemporary civilisation.'
SYLLABUS OF ERRORS *(1876)*

Pius XI (1857–1939)
ITALIAN PRELATE, POPE, 1922–1939

5 'Whether considered as a doctrine, or as an historical fact, or as a movement, socialism, if it really remains socialism, cannot be brought into harmony with the dogmas of the Catholic Church... Religious socialism, Christian socialism, are expressions implying a contradiction in terms.'
The encyclical, QUADRAGESIMO ANNO *(1931)*

Place, Francis (1771–1854)
ENGLISH TAILOR AND RADICAL LEADER

6 'To stop the Duke, go for gold.'
Autobiographical manuscript, 12 May 1832. Slogan adopted in May 1832, to try to prevent the formation of a Tory government under the Duke of Wellington

Plato (*c.* 427 BC–347 BC)
GREEK PHILOSOPHER

7 'The rulers of the state are the only ones who should have the privilege of lying, either at home or abroad; they may be allowed to lie for the good of the state.'
THE REPUBLIC, *Book II.*

8 'Any musical innovation is full of danger to the whole state, and ought to be prohibited... when modes of music change, the fundamental laws of the state always change with them.'
IBID., *Book IV*

9 'There is no occupation concerned with the management of social affairs which belongs either to women or to men, as such... and every occupation is open to both.'
IBID., *Book V*

10 'Unless either philosophers become kings in their countries or those who are now called kings and rulers come to be sufficiently inspired with a genuine desire for wisdom, unless, that is to say, political power and philosophy meet together.... there can be no rest from troubles.'
IBID.

11 'Is it not a simple fact that in any form of government revolution always starts from the outbreak of internal dissension in the ruling class? The constitution cannot be upset so long as that class is of one mind, however small it may be.'
IBID., *Book VIII*

12 'A society cannot hold wealth in honour and at the same time establish a proper self-control in its citizens. One or the other must be sacrificed.'
IBID.

Podmore, Frank (1856–1910)
ENGLISH WRITER ON PSYCHICAL RESEARCH, A FOUNDER OF THE FABIAN SOCIETY

13 'For the right moment you must wait, as Fabius did most patiently when warring against Hannibal, though many censured his delays; but when the time comes you must strike hard, as Fabius did, or your waiting will be in vain and fruitless.'
Quoted in E Pease, HISTORY OF THE FABIAN SOCIETY, *Chapter 2. On the strategy of 'Fabianism', thus giving the Fabian Society its name*

Pombal, Sebastião José de Carvalho e Melo, Marquês de (1699–1782)
PORTUGUESE POLITICIAN, CHIEF MINISTER TO KING JOSEPH, 1765–1777

1 'As a maxim of government it is certainly true that the worst of all policy is to remain unalterably determined on peace when all the other Powers of Europe are at war.'
Quoted in Conde da Carnota, THE MARQUIS OF POMBAL, *Chapter 5*

2 'The cultivation of literary pursuits forms the basis of all sciences, and in their perfection consist the reputation and prosperity of kingdoms.'
IBID., *Chapter 11*

Pompadour, Jeanne Antoinette, Marquise de (1721–1764)
FRENCH COURTESAN, MISTRESS OF LOUIS XV

3 'After us the deluge!' [*Après nous le déluge.*]
In conversation with Louis XV, 1757. After the battle of Rossbach, quoting an old French proverb

Pope, Alexander (1688–1744)
ENGLISH POET

4 'I find myself... hoping a total end of all the unhappy divisions of mankind by party-spirit, which at best is but the madness of many for the gain of a few.'
Letter to E Blount, 27 August 1714

5 'Statesman, yet Friend to Truth! of Soul sincere,
In Action faithful, and in Honour clear!
Who broke no promise, serv'd no private end,
Who gain'd no Title, and who lost no Friend.'
VERSES OCCASION'D BY MR ADDISON'S TREATISE OF MEDALS *(1720). Of Joseph Addison*

6 'For forms of government let fools contest;
Whate'er is best administer'd is best.'
ESSAY ON MAN *(1733), Epistle III*

7 'Seen him I have; but in his happier hour
Of Social Pleasure, ill-exchanged for Power;
Seen him, uncumber'd with the Venal tribe,
Smile without Art and win without a Bribe.'
PROLOGUE TO THE SATIRES *(1738). Of Robert Walpole*

8 'A Patriot is a Fool in ev'ry age.'
IBID.
SEE ALSO *Dryden*

9 ' "Oh" (cried the Goddess) "for some pedant Reign!
Some gentle James, to bless the land again;
To stick the Doctor's Chair into the Throne,
Give law to Words, or war with Words alone,
Senates and Courts with Greek and Latin rule,
And turn the Council to a Grammar School!
For sure, if Dulness sees a grateful Day,
'Tis in the shade of Arbitrary Sway.
O! if my sons may learn one earthly thing,
Teach but that one, sufficient for a King;
That which my Priests, and mine alone maintain,
Which as it dies, or lives, we fall, or reign:
May you, may Cam and Isis, preach it long!
'The RIGHT DIVINE of Kings to govern wrong".'
THE DUNCIAD *(1742), Book IV*

Popper, Sir Karl (1902–)
AUSTRIAN-BORN ENGLISH PHILOSOPHER AND BIOCHEMIST

10 'Work for the elimination of concrete evils rather than for the realisation of abstract goods. Do not aim at establishing happiness by political means. Rather, aim at the elimination of poverty by direct means.'
CONJECTURES AND REFUTATIONS *(1962), 'Utopia and Violence'*

Pottier, Eugène (1816–1887)
FRENCH WRITER

11 'Arise, ye prisoners of starvation!
Arise, ye wretched of the earth,
For Justice thunders condemnation,
A better world's in birth.
No more tradition's chains shall bind us,
Arise, ye slaves! No more in thrall!
The earth shall rise on new foundations,
We have been naught, but shall be all.

(*Refrain*)

'Tis the final conflict,
Let each stand in his place.
The International Party,
Shall be the human race.'

[*'Debout! les damnés de la terre!*
Debout! les forçats de la faim!
La raison tonne en son cratère,
C'est l'éruption de la fin.
Du passé faisons table rase,
Foule esclave, debout, debout!
Le monde va changer de base,
Nous ne sommes rien, soyons tout!

C'est la lutte finale
Groupons-nous, et, demain,
L'Internationale
Sera le genre humain.']
L'INTERNATIONALE *(1871)*

Powell, Enoch (1912–)
ENGLISH CONSERVATIVE,
SUBSEQUENTLY ULSTER UNIONIST
POLITICIAN, MEMBER OF PARLIAMENT,
1950–

1 'We on our day ought well to guard, as highly to honour, the parent stem of England, and its royal talisman; for we know not what branches yet that wonderful tree will have the power to put forth. The danger is not always violence and force; them we have withstood before and can withstand again. The peril can also be indifference and humbug, which might squander the accumulated wealth of tradition and devalue our sacred symbolism to achieve some cheap compromise or some evanescent purpose.'
Speech to the Royal Society of St George,
22 April 1964

2 'Those whom the gods wish to destroy, they first make mad. We must be mad, literally mad, as a nation to be permitting the annual inflow of some 50,000 dependants, who are for the most part the material of the future growth of the immigrant-descended population. It is like watching a nation busily engaged in heaping up its own funeral pyre... As I look ahead, I am filled with foreboding. Like the Roman, I seem to see "the river Tiber foaming with much blood".'
Speech at Birmingham, 20 April 1968

3 'I was born a Tory, am a Tory and shall die a Tory... I never yet heard that it was any part of the faith of a Tory to take the institutions and liberties, the laws and customs which his country has evolved over centuries and merge them with those of eight other nations into a new-made artificial state, and, what is more, to do so without the willing approbation and consent of the nation.'
Speech at Shipley, 25 February 1974.
Advising Conservatives opposed to British membership of the European Economic Community to vote for Labour party candidates at the general election
SEE ALSO *Daniel Webster*

4 'When a separate and strange population establishes numerical ascendancy in an area, then the very nature of its separateness and self-identification promotes the exploitation of the violent and criminal impulses which are common to humanity; and there is nothing strange in this. It is not Powell who says this. You can observe it anywhere. And of course, colour is part of this, because colour is the uniform.'
Interview in DER SPIEGEL, *1978*

5 'To me the nation is the ultimate political reality. There is no political reality beyond it. But what it is cannot be determined scientifically; you cannot pick it up; you cannot measure it.'
Interview in THE LISTENER, *28 May 1981*

6 'A populist politician is a politician who says things because he believes them to be popular. At least that is my understanding of the term. I have never been that. My worst enemies couldn't say that.'
IBID.

7 'There is one thing you can be sure of with the Conservative Party, before anything else – they have a grand sense for where the votes are.'
IBID.

8 'We find ourselves using the vocabulary deployed over the last thirty-five years to deny nationhood, sovereignty, and the rest; we are obliged to use a vocabulary which doesn't fit... We say it is in defence of liberty, or for the benefit of all nations which might find themselves aggressed. Well, quite plainly, nothing we do in the Falklands makes it more or less easy for any other nation, in other circumstances, to resist an aggressor.'
Interview in the GUARDIAN, *15 June 1982.*
On the battle for the Falkland Islands being called a 'conflict', not a 'war'

1 'It is the very capital and new Jerusalem of humbug.'
IBID. *Of the United Nations*

2 'I slightly bridle. . . when the word "democracy" is applied to the United Kingdom. Instead of that I say: "We are a Parliamentary nation".'
IBID.

3 'A politician crystallises what most people mean, even if they don't know it.'
Quoted in A Sampson, THE NEW ANATOMY OF BRITAIN, *Chapter 6*

Pretyman, Ernest (1860–1931)
ENGLISH CONSERVATIVE POLITICIAN

4 'Great leaders of parties are not elected, they are evolved. . . I think it will be a bad day for this or any party to have solemnly to meet to elect a leader. The leader is there, and we all know it when he is there.'
Speech to a meeting of the Conservative parliamentary party, 21 March 1921

Price, Richard (1723–1791)
WELSH NONCONFORMIST MINISTER, AND MORAL AND POLITICAL PHILOSOPHER

5 'What an eventful period is this! I am thankful that I have lived to it; and I could almost say, *Lord, now lettest thou thy servant depart in peace, for mine eyes have seen thy salvation.*'
Sermon, 4 November 1789, published as A DISCOURSE ON THE LOVE OF OUR COUNTRY. *On the revolution in France. (It was this sermon that provoked Burke to write his* REFLECTIONS ON THE REVOLUTION IN FRANCE.)

Priestley, Joseph (1733–1804)
ENGLISH SCIENTIST, THEOLOGIAN AND POLITICAL THEORIST

6 'The good and happiness of the members, that is the majority of the members of any state, is the great standard by which every thing relating to that state must finally be determined.'
ESSAY ON GOVERNMENT *(1768)*
SEE ALSO *Francis Hutcheson*

7 'It is an universal maxim, that the more liberty is given to everything which is in a state of growth, the more perfect it will become.'
IBID.

8 'Governments will never be awed by the voice of the people, so long as it is a mere voice, without overt acts.'
THE FIRST PRINCIPLES OF GOVERNMENT *(1771)*

9 'Men of wealth and influence, who act upon the principle of virtue and religion, and conscientiously make their power subservient to the good of their country, are the men who are the greatest honour to human nature, and the greatest blessing to human societies.'
LECTURES ON HISTORY *(1788)*

10 'Every successful revolt is termed a revolution, and every unsuccessful one a rebellion.'
Letter to Edmund Burke, 1791

Primo de Rivera, José Antonio (1903–1936)
SPANISH POLITICIAN, FOUNDER OF THE FALANGE

11 'No other dialectic is admissible save the dialectic of fists and pistols when justice or the *Patria* is offended.'
Speech at Madrid, 29 October 1933

12 'Paradise is not rest. Paradise is against rest. In Paradise one cannot lie down; one must hold oneself up, like the angels. Very well: we, who have already borne on the road to Paradise the lives of the best among us, want a difficult, erect, implacable Paradise; a Paradise where one can never rest and which has, beside the threshold of the gates, angels with swords.'
Quoted in S Payne, FALANGE, *Chapter 7*

13 'Fascism is a European inquietude. It is a way of knowing everything – history, the state, the achievement of the proletarianisation of public life, a new way of knowing the phenomena of our epoch.'
Quoted in H Thomas, THE SPANISH CIVIL WAR, *Book 1, Chapter 8*

Proudhon, Pierre Joseph (1809–1865)
FRENCH POLITICAL THEORIST

14 'Property is theft.'
WHAT IS PROPERTY? *(1840)*

15 'At the moment that man inquires into the motives which govern the will of his sovereign – at that moment man revolts. If he obeys, no longer because the king

commands, but because the king demonstrates the wisdom of his commands, it may be said that henceforth he will recognise no authority, and that he has become his own king.'
IBID.

1   'Communism is inequality, but not as property is. Property is exploitation of the weak by the strong. Communism is exploitation of the strong by the weak.'
IBID.

2   'As man seeks justice in equality, so society seeks order in anarchy.'
IBID.

3   'Whoever puts his hand on me to govern me is an usurper and a tyrant; I declare him my enemy.'
CONFESSIONS OF A REVOLUTIONARY *(1849)*

4   'All parties, without exception, in so far as they seek power, are varieties of absolutism.'
IBID.

5   'Universal suffrage is counter-revolution.'
THE GENERAL IDEA OF THE REVOLUTION IN THE NINETEENTH CENTURY *(1851)*

6   'There is no middle way between Reaction and Revolution. But Reaction is mathematically impossible: we are not free to remain unrevolutionised; our only choice is how fast it will occur. For myself, I prefer the locomotive.'
IBID.

Pyrrhus *(c.* 318BC–272BC)
MOLOSSIAN KING OF EPIRUS

7   'One more such victory over the Romans and we are utterly undone.'
Remark, 279BC. Quoted in Plutarch, LIVES. *After victory over the Romans at Asculum. (Hence the phrase, 'pyrrhic victory'.)*

Q

Qadhafi, Muammar al (1938–)
LIBYAN SOLDIER AND NATIONALIST
POLITICIAN, HEAD OF STATE, 1969–

1 'By socialism we mean above all an
Islamic socialism. We are a Muslim
nation. We shall therefore respect, as
bidden in the Quran, the principle of
private property, even of hereditary
property.'
*First Proclamation of the Revolutionary
Command Council, 1 September 1969*

2 'The works of Lenin, Marx and Engels
are meaningless now; history has passed
them by.'
*Speech to the law faculty at Benghazi, 28
April 1973*

3 'We need to read again the teachings of
Christ, and to find in them the voice
which says to us: 'Give up Palestine,
South-East Asia, Ireland, Germany, and
the African colonies''. The world needs
Christ again.'
*New Year's message to the heads of world
governments, 1 January 1975*

4 'Representation is fraud.'
THE GREEN BOOK *(1976–79), Part I:
'Parliaments'*

5 'Party is the contemporary dictatorship. It
is the modern dictatorial instrument of
governing.'
IBID., *'Party'*

6 'The natural law of any society is either
tradition (custom) or religion. Any other
attempt to draft law for any society,
outside these two sources, is invalid and
illogical.'
IBID., *'The Law of Society'*

7 'In need freedom is latent.'
IBID., *Part II: 'Need'*

8 'The purpose of the socialist society is the
happiness of man, which can be realised
only through material and spiritual
freedom. Attainment of such freedom
depends on the extent of man's
ownership of his needs, ownership that is
personal and sacredly guaranteed.'
IBID., *'Conclusion'*

9 'Nations whose nationalism is destroyed
are subject to ruin.'
IBID., *Part III: 'The Social Basis of the
Third Universal Theory'*

10 'Discrimination between man and
woman is a flagrant act of oppression
without any justification.'
IBID., *'Woman'*

11 'The woman who rejects pregnancy,
marriage, make-up and femininity for
reasons of health, abandons her natural
role in life under these coercive
conditions of health. The woman who
rejects marriage, pregnancy or
motherhood etc., because of work,
abandons her natural role under the same
coercive conditions. The woman who
rejects marriage, pregnancy or maternity
etc., without any concrete cause,
abandons her natural role as a result of a
coercive condition which is a moral
deviation from the norm. . .
Consequently, there must be a world
revolution which puts an end to all
materialistic conditions hindering woman
from performing her natural role in life
and driving her to carry out man's duties
in order to be equal in rights.'
IBID.

12 'We do not veto popular initiatives,
neither in Libya nor in Tunisia. I have
no objection should the masses in Libya
today stage an uprising, pronounce
themselves as one with the Tunisian
masses, and declare the two countries as
one.'
*Speech to the joint meeting of the Libyan
General People's Committee and the
Tunisian cabinet, 19 July 1983*

13 'The Third Theory is founded upon
socialism. . . With the Communist system
on one side and the capitalist system on
the other, we must try to find a "Third
System" which would be equally
different from either. For while
capitalism, by handing over the reins to
the individual without any restraints, has
transformed society into a sort of circus,
communism's claim to solve economic
problems by the total and final abolishing
of private property has ended by turning
individual human beings into sheep.'
Quoted in M Bianco (trans. M Lyle),
GADAFI. VOICE FROM THE DESERT, *Part III,
Chapter 2*

14 'In the Quran, the Arab nation is
expressly recognised as such by God, as
appears in the text:

Cling one and all to the faith of Allah
and let nothing divide you.

And again:

Let there become of you a nation that
shall speak for righteousness, enjoin
justice, and forbid evil. Such men shall
surely triumph.

I believe that this injunction to the Arab
nation constitutes in itself a recognition
of the Arab entity; of the existence of a
national link between Arabs, through
whom the Islamic message has been
disseminated. . . It is this Arab nation,
and not the great company of those who
have come to embrace Islam, which
should rise and advance, and proclaim
the call to Islam. Thus we shall be the
heralds of the sublime message, not only
among our own peoples but also in the
Third World, and in the entire universe.
Looked at from this point of view, the
call to Arab nationalism is identified with
the call to Islamic power.'

In conversation with Mirella Bianco. IBID.,
Part III, Chapter 3

Quesnay, François (1694–1774)
FRENCH PHYSIOCRAT POLITICAL
ECONOMIST

1 *'Laissez faire.'* (Leave things to take their
course.)
LE DROIT NATUREL *(1765). (Borrowing, for
use in political economy, the old cry of
'laissez faire, laissez passer' from
mediaeval tournaments.)*

The Quran

2 'O Believers! take not the Jews or
Christians as friends. They are but one
another's friends. If any one of you
taketh them for his friends, he surely is
one of them! God will not guide the evil
doers.'
Sura V, 'The Table', Verse 56

R

Raineborough, Thomas (*d.* 1648)
ENGLISH PURITAN SOLDIER AND
POLITICIAN, MEMBER OF PARLIAMENT,
1647–1648

1 'I think that the poorest He that is in
England hath a life to live as the greatest
He, and therefore truly, sirs, I think that
every man that is to live under a
government ought first by his own
consent to put himself under that
government.'
*Speech at Putney, 29 October 1647.
During the army debates.*

Rakowski, Mieczyslaw (1926–)
POLISH JOURNALIST AND COMMUNIST
POLITICIAN

2 'It was a very vast operation; it's quite
possible that something regrettable
happened. But even if you mention case
by case, I answer: of course that case is
important for that human being, but on
the whole it does not count. In politics
the individual does not count.'
In conversation with Oriana Fallaci, THE
TIMES, *22 February 1982. On the
treatment of persons under the martial
law imposed in Poland in December 1981*

3 'Freedom, freedom, freedom! For two
hundred years the Poles sold nothing but
freedom, Chopin, the *Polonaise*. What
freedom is a freedom which doesn't
provide anything in the stomach? The
hotheads of Solidarity supplied those poor
workers with the most unrealistic ideas
about freedom, and look where we are!'
IBID. *On the trade union, 'Solidarity'*

4 'Solidarity was needed in Poland, and not
only as a trade union, but as a control on
the authorities. You know, even an angel
becomes a whore if he is not controlled
when he enters the church of power.'
IBID., *23 February 1982*

Randolph, John (1773–1833)
AMERICAN POLITICIAN, SENATOR,
1825–1827

5 'With all the fanatical and preposterous
theories about the rights of man (the
theories, not the rights themselves, I
speak of) there is nothing but power that
can restrain power.'
Speech, April 1824. Quoted in the
RICHMOND ENQUIRER, *4 June 1824*

6 'You cannot divorce property from
power. You can only make them change
hands.'
Speech to the Senate, 1826

7 'If any man raises against me that hue
and cry of being an enemy to
republicanism, I cannot help that; for, if
my life will not speak for me, my tongue
cannot.'
RICHMOND ENQUIRER, *18 June 1833,
'Randolphiana'*

Reith, John, 1st Baron
(1889–1971)
ENGLISH PUBLIC SERVANT, ENGINEER
AND DIRECTOR-GENERAL OF THE BBC,
1927–1938

8 'Assuming the B.B.C. is for the people
and that the Government is for the
people, it follows that the B.B.C. must be
for the Government in this crisis too.'
*Memorandum to Stanley Baldwin, May
1926. Protesting against the desire of a
section of the government to
commandeer the B.B.C. during the general
strike of 1926*

Ricardo, David (1772–1823)
ENGLISH ECONOMIST

9 'Labour, like all other things which are
purchased and sold, and which may be
increased or diminished in quantity, has
its natural and its market price. The
natural price of labour is that price
which is necessary to enable the
labourers, one with another, to subsist
and perpetuate their race, without either
increase or diminution.'
ON THE PRINCIPLES OF POLITICAL ECONOMY AND
TAXATION *(1817), Chapter 1. The so-called
'iron law of wages'*

Robespierre, Maximilien
(1758–1794)
FRENCH REVOLUTIONARY LEADER,
MEMBER OF THE COMMITTEE OF PUBLIC
SAFETY

10 'In politics nothing is just save what is
honest; nothing is useful except what is
just.'
*Speech to the National Assembly, May
1791*

1 'I prefer the individual whom chance, birth, and circumstances have given us for a King to all those kings whom the people wish to give us.'
Speech to the Jacobin society, March 1792

2 'Citizens, do you want a revolution without revolution?'
Speech to the National Convention, 5 November 1792

3 'Louis must die that the country may live.'
Speech to the National Convention, 3 December 1792

4 'To honour God and to wage war on kings is one and the same thing.'
Speech in answer to the manifesto of the allied monarchs of December 1793

5 'The government of the Revolution is the despotism of liberty against tyranny.'
Speech to the National Convention, 5 February 1794

6 'Terror is nothing other than justice, prompt, secure and inflexible.'
IBID.

7 'Pity is treason.'
Speech to the National Convention, 26 February 1794

8 'Liberty cannot be established unless the heads of scoundrels fall.'
In conversation with Danton, 22 March 1794

Rochester, 2nd Earl of (John Wilmot) (1647–1680)
ENGLISH COURTIER AND POET

9 'Here lies our sovereign lord the King,
Whose promise none relies on;
He never said a foolish thing,
Nor ever did a wise one.'
Lines written on the door of Charles II's bedchamber
SEE ALSO *Charles II*

Roosevelt, Eleanor (1884–1962)
AMERICAN PUBLIC SERVANT, WRITER, 'FIRST LADY', 1933–1945

10 'The Democrats today trust in the people, the plain, ordinary, everyday citizen, neither superlatively rich nor distressingly poor, not one of the "best minds" but the average mind. The Socialists believe in making the Government the people's master; the Republicans believe that the moneyed "aristocracy", the few great financial minds, should rule the Government; the Democrats believe that the whole people should govern.'
CURRENT HISTORY, *June 1928, 'Jeffersonian Principles the Issue in 1928'*

Roosevelt, Franklin Delano (1882–1945)

AMERICAN DEMOCRATIC POLITICIAN, PRESIDENT, 1933–1945

11 'I pledge you, I pledge myself, to a new deal for the American people.'
Speech to the Democratic national convention, 2 July 1932. Accepting the party's nomination as its presidential candidate

12 'First of all, let me assert my firm belief that the only thing we have to fear is fear itself – nameless, unreasoning, unjustified terror.'
Inaugural address, 4 March 1933

13 'In the field of foreign policy I would dedicate this nation to the policy of the good neighbour.'
IBID.

14 'I should like to have it said of my first Administration that in it the forces of selfishness and of lust for power met their match. . . I should like to have it said of my second Administration that in it these forces met their master.'
Speech at New York, 31 October 1936

15 'A conservative is a man with two perfectly good legs who, however, has never learned to walk forwards. . . A reactionary is a somnambulist walking backwards. . . A radical is a man with both feet firmly planted – in the air.'
'Fireside chat' on radio, 26 October 1939

16 'We must be the great arsenal of democracy.'
'Fireside chat' on radio, 29 December 1940

17 'We look forward to a world founded upon four essential human freedoms. The first is freedom of speech and expression – everywhere in the world. The second is the freedom of every person to worship God in his own way – everywhere in the world. The third is freedom from want . . . everywhere in the world. The fourth is freedom from fear . . . anywhere in the world.'
Address to Congress, 6 January 1941

1 'I don't know a good Russian from a bad Russian. I can tell a good Frenchman from a bad Frenchman. I can tell a good Italian from a bad Italian. I know a good Greek when I see one. But I don't understand the Russians.'
In conversation with Francis Perkins. Quoted in Perkins, THE ROOSEVELT I KNEW, *Chapter 7*

Roosevelt, Theodore (1858–1919)
AMERICAN REPUBLICAN AND SUBSEQUENTLY PROGRESSIVE POLITICIAN, PRESIDENT, 1901–1909

2 'I wish to preach, not the doctrine of ignoble ease, but the doctrine of the strenuous life.'
Speech at Chicago, 10 April 1899

3 'In every instance the expansion has taken place because the race was a great race. It was a sign and proof of greatness in the expanding nation, and moreover bear in mind that in each instance it was of incalculable benefit to mankind. . . When great nations fear to expand, shrink from expansion, it is because their greatness is coming to an end. Are we still in the prime of our lusty youth, still at the beginning of our glorious manhood, to sit down among the outworn people, to take our place with the weak and the craven? A thousand times no!'
Speech at Akron, September 1899. Justifying the United States' war against Spain

4 'I am as strong as a bull moose, and you can use me to the limit.'
Letter to Mark Hanna, 27 June 1900

5 'There is a homely adage which runs: "Speak softly and carry a big stick; you will go far".'
Speech at the Minnesota state fair, 2 September 1901

6 'The government is us; we are the government, you and I.'
Speech at Asheville, North Carolina, 9 September 1902

7 'A man who is good enough to shed his blood for his country is good enough to be given a square deal afterwards.'
Speech at Springfield, Illinois, 4 June 1903

8 'There are a large number of well-meaning ambassadors . . . who belong to what I call the pink-tea type.'
Letter to R H Davis, 3 January 1905

9 'The men with the muck-rakes are often indispensable to the well-being of society; but only if they know when to stop raking the muck.'
Speech at Washington, 14 April 1906. Of crusading journalists

10 'The American people are right in demanding that New Nationalism. . . The New Nationalism puts the national need before sectional or personal advantage. . . This New Nationalism regards the executive power as the steward of the public welfare. It demands of the judiciary that it shall be interested primarily in human welfare rather than in property, just as it demands that the representative body shall represent all the people rather than any one class or section of the people. The man who wrongly holds that every human right is secondary to his profit must now give way to the advocate of human welfare, who rightly maintains that every man holds his property subject to the general right of the community to regulate its use to whatever degree the public welfare may require it.'
Speech at Osawatomie, Kansas, 31 August 1910

11 'My hat's in the ring. The fight is on and I'm stripped to the buff.'
Announcement of his presidential candidacy, 1912

12 'Every reform movement has a lunatic fringe.'
Speech, 1913

Rosebery, 5th Earl of (Archibald Primrose) (1847–1929)
ENGLISH LIBERAL POLITICIAN, PRIME MINISTER, 1894–1895

13 'I believe that the labour of those who would ameliorate the conditions of the working classes is slower and more imperceptible than that of the insect which raises the coral reef from the bed of the ocean.'
Speech to the Working Men's Club and Insitute Union, 17 July 1875

14 'There is no word so prostituted as patriotism. It is part of the base coinage of controversy. Every government fails in it, and every opposition glows with it. . . It smiles impartially on the acceptance and resignation of office; it impels people

to enter and to quit public life with equal reason and equal precipitation. . . It patronises almost every crime and every virtue in history.'
Rectorial address, University of Edinburgh, 4 November 1882

1 'There is no need for any nation, however great, leaving the Empire, because the Empire is *a Commonwealth of Nations.'*
Speech at Adelaide, Australia, 18 January 1884

2 'Imperialism, sane Imperialism, as distinguished from what I might call "wild cat" Imperialism, is nothing but this – a larger patriotism.'
Speech, autumn of 1885. Quoted in R Rhodes James, ROSEBERY, *Chapter 5*

3 'There are two supreme pleasures in life. One is ideal, the other real. The ideal is when a man receives the seals of office from his Sovereign. The real pleasure comes when he hands them back.'
SIR ROBERT PEEL *(1899)*

4 'For the present, at any rate, I must proceed alone. I must plough my own furrow alone, but before I get to the end of that furrow it is possible that I may not find myself alone.'
Speech to the City of London Liberal Club, 19 July 1901. On his remaining outside the councils of the Liberal party

5 'A gentleman will blithely do in politics what he would kick a man downstairs for doing in ordinary life.'
1914. Quoted in R Rhodes James, ROSEBERY, *Chapter 13*

Rosenberg, Ethel (1916–1953)
AMERICAN HOUSEWIFE

6 'Ethel wants it made known that we are the first victims of American Fascism.'
Letter, with her husband, Julius, to Emanuel Bloch, 19 June 1953. Written on the day that she and Julius were executed after being convicted of passing atomic secrets to the Soviet Union

Rousseau, Jean Jacques
(1712–1778)
SWISS-BORN FRENCH POLITICAL PHILOSOPHER, EDUCATIONIST AND ESSAYIST

7 'The first man who, having enclosed a piece of ground, thought to himself to say, *This is mine,* and found people simple enough to believe him, was the true founder of civil society.'
DISCOURSE ON THE ORIGIN OF INEQUALITY AMONG MEN *(1755)*

8 'Man is born free, and everywhere he is in chains.'
THE SOCIAL CONTRACT *(1762), Book I, Chapter 1*

9 'To find a form of association which defends and protects with all its common force the person and goods of each of its associates, and by which each, uniting himself with all, nevertheless obeys only himself and remains as free as before! Such is the fundamental problem to which the Social Contract gives the solution.'
IBID., *Book I, Chapter 6*

10 'If we discard from the social compact what is not of its essence, we find that it reduces itself to the following terms: "Each of us places his person and all his power in common under the supreme direction of the general will, and in our corporate capacity we receive each member as an indivisible part of the whole." '
IBID.

11 'Sovereignty, being nothing more than the exercise of the general will, can never alienate itself, and the sovereign, which is simply a collective being, cannot be represented except by itself: power it may well transfer, but not the will.'
IBID., *Book II, Chapter 1*

12 'The general will, to be really such, must be general in its object as well as its essence; it must both come from all and apply to all; and it loses its natural rectitude when it is directed to some particular and determinate object, because in such a case we are judging of something foreign to us, and have no true principle of equity to guide us . . . what makes the general will general is less the number of voters than the common interest uniting them.'
IBID., *Book II, Chapter 4*

13 'Those people who treat politics and morality separately will never understand either of them.'
EMILE *(1762)*

1 'Women have, or ought to have, but little liberty; they are apt to indulge themselves excessively in what is allowed them.'
IBID.

2 'It is in order not to become victims of an assassin that we consent to die if we become assassins.'
Quoted in A Camus, THE REBEL, *'The Regicides'*

Royden, Agnes Maude
(1876–1956)
ENGLISH SOCIAL REFORMER AND PREACHER

3 'The Church should no longer be satisfied to represent only the Conservative Party at prayer.'
Address at the City Temple, London 1917

Rupert, Prince (1619–1682)
COUNT PALATINE OF THE RHINE AND ROYALIST COMMANDER IN THE ENGLISH CIVIL WAR

4 'Banquets are not for soldiers.'
Letter to the burgesses of Preston, June 1644. Declining an invitation to a banquet

Ruskin, John (1819–1900)
ENGLISH MAN OF LETTERS AND ART CRITIC

5 'This is what she [England] must do, or perish: she must found colonies as fast and as far as she is able, formed of her most energetic and worthiest men; seizing every piece of fruitful waste ground she can set foot on, and there teaching these her colonists that their chief virtue is to be fidelity to their country, and that their first aim is to be to advance the power of England by land and sea.'
Inaugural lecture as professor of art, Oxford 1870

Russell, Bertrand, 3rd Earl
(1872–1970)
ENGLISH PHILOSOPHER, MATHEMATICIAN AND LOGICIAN

6 'I believe there are still some people who think that a democratic State is scarcely distinguishable from the people. This, however, is a delusion. The State is a collection of officials, different for different purposes, drawing comfortable incomes so long as the *status quo* is preserved. The only alteration they are likely to desire in the *status quo* is an increase of bureaucracy and of the power of bureaucrats.'
Maurice Conway lecture, 1922

7 'Our education teaches us to admire the qualities that were biologically useful in the Homeric age, regardless of the fact that they are now harmful and ridiculous. The instinctive appeal of every successful political movement is to envy, rivalry or hate, never to the need for co-operation. This is inherent in our present political methods, and in conformity with pre-industrial habits.'
Presidential address to the Students' Union, London School of Economics, 10 October 1923.

8 'Marx's *Capital* is in essence, like the Bryce Report, a collection of atrocity stories designed to stimulate martial ardour against the enemy. Very naturally, it also stimulates the martial ardour of the enemy. It thus brings about the class-war which it prophesies.'
IBID.

9 'The conception of an "honest" politician is not altogether a simple one. The most tolerant definition is: one whose political actions are not dictated by a desire to increase his own income. In this sense, Mr Lloyd George is honest. The next stage would be the man whose political actions are not dictated by desire to secure or preserve his own power any more than by pecuniary motives. In this sense, Lord Grey is an honest politician. The last and most stringent sense is: one who, in his public actions, is not only disinterested, but does not fall very far below the standard of veracity and honour which is taken for granted between acquaintances. In this sense the late Lord Morley was an honest politician; at least, he was honest always, and a politician until his honesty drove him out of politics. But even a politician who is honest in the highest sense may be very harmful; one may take George III as an illustration. Stupidity and unconscious bias often work more damage than venality. Moreover, an honest politician will not be tolerated by a democracy unless he is very stupid, like the late Duke of Devonshire; because only a very stupid man can honestly

share the prejudices of more than half the nation. Therefore any man who is both able and public-spirited must be a hypocrite if he is to succeed in politics; but the hypocrisy will in time destroy his public spirit.'
IBID.

1 'Next to enjoying ourselves, the next greatest pleasure consists in preventing others from enjoying themselves, or, more generally, in the acquisition of power.'
SCEPTICAL ESSAYS *(1928), 'The Recrudescence of Puritanism'*

2 'Advocates of capitalism are very apt to appeal to the sacred principles of liberty, which are embodied in one maxim: *The fortunate must not be restrained in the exercise of tyranny over the unfortunate.'*
IBID. *'Freedom in Society'*

3 'Politicians, who have not time to become acquainted with human nature, are peculiarly ignorant of the desires that move ordinary men and women. Any political party whose leaders knew a little psychology could sweep the country.'
IBID.

4 'To prevent resentment, governments attribute misfortunes to natural causes; to create resentment, oppositions attribute them to human causes.'
IBID.

5 'Those who in principle oppose birth control are either incapable of arithmetic or else in favour of war, pestilence and famine as permanent features of human life.'
IBID. *'Some Prospects: Cheerful and Otherwise'*

6 'In a social system in which power is open to all, the posts which confer power will, as a rule, be occupied by men who differ from the average in being exceptionally power-loving.'
POWER*(1938), Chapter 1*

7 'Mankind need government, but in regions where anarchy has prevailed they will, at first, submit only to despotism. We must therefore seek first to secure government, even though despotic, and only when government has become habitual can we hope successfully to make it democratic.'
IBID. *Chapter 2*

8 'If law-abiding citizens are to be protected against unjust persecution by the police, there must be two police forces and two Scotland Yards, one designed, as at present, to prove guilt, the other to prove innocence; and in addition to the public prosecutor there must be a public defender, of equal legal eminence.'
IBID. *Chapter 18*

9 'To acquire immunity to eloquence is of the utmost importance to the citizens of a democracy.'
IBID.

Russell, George William Erskine (1853–1919)
ENGLISH MAN OF LETTERS AND LIBERAL POLITICIAN, MEMBER OF PARLIAMENT, 1880–1885 AND 1892–1895

10 'When the Government of the day and the Opposition of the day take the same side, one can be almost sure that some great wrong is at hand.'
ONE LOOK BACK *(1912), Chapter 11. Quoting an unnamed contemporary*

11 'The perfection of Parliamentary style is to utter cruel platitudes with a grave and informing air; and, if a little pomposity be superadded, the House will instinctively recognize the speaker as a Statesman.'
IBID., *Chapter 12*

Russell, John, 1st Earl (1792–1878)
ENGLISH WHIG POLITICIAN, PRIME MINISTER, 1846–1852 AND 1865–1866

12 'It is impossible that the whisper of a faction shall prevail against the voice of a nation.'
House of Commons, 12 October 1831. On the Lords' rejection of the great reform bill

13 'I rely with confidence on the people of England; and I will not bate a jot of heart or hope, so long as the glorious principles and the immortal martyrs of the Reformation shall be held in reverence by the great mass of a nation which looks with contempt on the mummeries of superstition, and with scorn at the laborious endeavours which are now being made to confine the intellect and enslave the soul.'
Open letter to the Bishop of Durham, 4 November 1850. On the so-called 'papal aggression' exhibited by the Vatican in

dividing England into twelve sees and making Nicholas Wiseman archbishop of Westminster

1 'If peace cannot be maintained with honour, it is no longer peace.'
Speech at Greenock, 19 September 1853. On the growing crisis in the Crimea

2 'There is one thing worse than the cant of patriotism, and that is the recant of patriotism.'
Quoted in D MacCarthy and A Russell, LADY JOHN RUSSELL, A MEMOIR, *Chapter 3. In*

reply to Sir Francis Burdett's speech on the 'cant of patriotism' in the House of Commons

Russell, Sir William Howard
(1820–1907)
ENGLISH WAR CORRESPONDENT

3 'The Russians dashed on towards this thin red streak tipped with a line of steel.'
Despatch to THE TIMES, *25 October 1854. Of the British infantry at Balaclava*

S

Saint-Just, Louis de (1767–1794)
FRENCH REVOLUTIONARY LEADER,
MEMBER OF THE COMMITTEE OF PUBLIC
SAFETY

1 'Happiness is a new idea in Europe.'
THE SPIRIT OF THE REVOLUTION AND OF THE
FRENCH CONSTITUTION *(1791)*

2 'No one can rule guiltlessly.'
*Speech to the National Convention, 13
November 1792. Arguing that Louis XVI
should be brought to trial*

3 'There are no political virtues without
pride; there is no pride where there is
distress.'
*Speech to the National Convention, 29
November 1792*

4 'You have no right to be merciful or
compassionate where traitors are
concerned. You are working not on your
own account, but on behalf of the
people.'
*Report on Parisian prisoners to the
National Convention, 26 February 1794*

5 'The world has been empty since the
days of Rome. Today it is filled with the
memory of Rome, still prophesying
liberty.'
*Speech to the National Convention, 31
March 1794*

6 'Jealous mediocrity will ever wish to
bring genius to the scaffold.'
*Speech to the National Convention, 27
July 1794. On the occasion of the arrest
of Robespierre, himself, and others*

7 'He who makes jokes as the head of a
government has a tendency to tyranny.'
Quoted in A Camus, THE REBEL, *'The
Regicides'*

8 'A revolution such as ours is not a trial,
but a clap of thunder for the wicked.'
IBID.

Saint-Simon, Claude Henri, Comte de (1760–1825)
FRENCH POLITICAL ECONOMIST

9 'A state may prosper under any form of
government, provided it is well
administered. . . If political freedom is
more advantageous for the development
of wealth, it is indirectly because it is
more favourable to learning.'
INDUSTRY *(1817), Volume I, Part 2*

10 'It is in the interests of *those who govern*
and *those who are governed* to extend the
political importance of the *industrialists,*
since, on the one hand, they are always
inclined to support the existing
government and, on the other, they work
ceaselessly to limit *power* and to decrease
taxation.'
IBID., *Volume II, Part 1*

11 'The greatest, the most important power
entrusted to the government is the right
to tax the citizens; it is from this right
that all the others flow. Today, therefore,
political science consists essentially in
being able to draw up a good budget.
Now, the ability to do this is an
administrative ability, from which it
follows that administrative ability is the
principal ability needed in politics.'
POLITICS *(1819)*

Salazar, António de Oliviera (1889–1970)
PORTUGUESE CHRISTIAN DEMOCRATIC
POLITICIAN, PRIME MINISTER, 1932-1968

12 'We have arrived at a stage of political
and social evolution in which a political
party founded upon the individual
interests of citizens or electors has no
longer the right to exist. Isolated man is
an abstraction – a fiction created chiefly
under the dominating influence of
erroneous principles current in the last
century.'
*Speech to the Academic Centre of
Christian Democracy, April 1922*

Salisbury, 3rd Marquess of (Robert Gascoyne-Cecil) (1830–1903)
ENGLISH CONSERVATIVE POLITICIAN,
PRIME MINISTER, 1885-1886; 1886-1892
and 1895-1902

13 'The best form of Government (setting
aside the question of morality) is one
where the masses have little power, and
seem to have a great deal.'
OXFORD ESSAYS *(1858), 'The Theories of
Parliamentary Reform'*

14 'A gram of experience is worth a ton of
theory.'
SATURDAY REVIEW, *25 June 1859, 'Fiat
Experimentum in Corpore Viti'*

1 'The leap which the House of Commons is taking with such philosophic calmness is a leap absolutely in the dark.'
QUARTERLY REVIEW, *April 1860, 'The Budget and the Reform Bill'*

2 'Once admitted that a direct tax may be laid on for the purpose of taking off an indirect tax which presses hard, or which is much complained of, and there is no reason that the process should not be repeated *ad infinitum.* Inasmuch as all classes alike pay indirect taxation, while only those who do not receive weekly wages pay the income-tax, this change is a direct and simple transfer of taxes from one class of the community to another. . . This question of the incidence of taxation is in truth the vital question of modern politics. It is the field upon which the contending classes of this generation will do battle. . . The mists of mere political theory are clearing away, and the true character of the battle-ground, and the real nature of the prize at stake are standing out more and more distinctly every year. . . The struggle between the English constitution on the one hand, and the democratic forces that are labouring to subvert it on the other, is now, in reality . . . a struggle between those who have, to keep what they have got, and those who have not, to get it.'
IBID. *On the substitution of a penny on the income tax for the paper duty in Gladstone's budget of 1860*

3 'It is the multiplication table which furnishes in the last resort the essential test that distinguishes right from wrong in the government of a nation. If one man imprisons you, that is tyranny; if two men, or a number of men imprison you, that is freedom.'
QUARTERLY REVIEW, *July 1865, 'Parliamentary Reform'*

4 'It is one of the misfortunes of our political system that parties are formed, more with reference to controversies that are gone by, than to the controversies which these parties have actually to decide.'
QUARTERLY REVIEW, *January 1866, 'The Coming Session'*

5 'The first object of a treaty of peace should be to make future war improbable.'
QUARTERLY REVIEW, *October 1870, 'The Terms of Peace'*

6 'So long as we have government by party, the very notion of repose must be foreign to English politics. Agitation is, so to speak, endowed in this country.'
QUARTERLY REVIEW, *October 1871, 'The Commune and the Internationale'*

7 'The optimist view of politics assumes that there must be some remedy for every political ill, and rather than not find it, it will make two hardships to cure one. . . Is it not just conceivable that there is no remedy that we can apply for the Irish hatred of ourselves? that other loves or hates may possibly some day elbow it out of the Irish peasant's mind, that nothing we can do by any contrivance will hasten the advent of that period? . . . there is no precedent in our history or in any other, to teach us that political measures can conjure away hereditary antipathies which are fed by constant agitation. The free institutions which sustain the life of a free and united people sustain also the hatred of a divided people.'
QUARTERLY REVIEW, *October 1872, 'The Position of Parties'*

8 'In descriptions of this kind a great deal of misapprehension arises from the popular use of maps on a small scale. As with such maps you are able to put a thumb on India and a finger on Russia, some persons at once think that the political situation is alarming, and that India must be looked to. If the noble lord would use a larger map – say one on the scale of the ordnance map of England – he would find that the distance between Russia and British India is not to be measured by the finger and thumb, but by a rule.'
House of Lords, 11 June 1877. Replying to Lord de Mauley's alarming description of Russian penetration into central Asia

9 'The commonest error in politics is sticking to the carcass of dead policies.'
Letter to Bulwer Lytton, 1878. On the preservation of Turkish integrity as a permanent element in British foreign policy

10 'You may roughly divide the nations of the world as the living and the dying. . . The weak states are becoming weaker and the strong states are becoming stronger . . . the living nations will gradually encroach on the territory of the

dying, and the seeds and causes of
conflict among civilised nations will
speedily appear.'
Speech at London, 4 May 1898

1   'I rank myself no higher in the scheme
of things than a policeman – whose
utility would disappear if there were no
criminals.'
Quoted in Lady Gwendolen Cecil,
BIOGRAPHICAL STUDIES . . . OF ROBERT, THIRD
MARQUESS OF SALISBURY, *'Home Policy'. Of
the Liberals' existence being the necessary
condition for Conservative success*

Santayana, George (1863–1952)
SPANISH-BORN AMERICAN PHILOSOPHER

2   'Progress, far from consisting in change,
depends on retentiveness. . . Those who
cannot remember the past are condemned
to fulfil it.'
LIFE OF REASON *(1905–06), Volume I,
Chapter 12*

Sartre, Jean-Paul (1905–1980)
FRENCH PHILOSOPHER, PLAYWRIGHT
AND NOVELIST

3   'The revolutionary wants to change the
world; he transcends it and moves
towards the future, towards an order of
values which he himself invents. The
rebel is careful to preserve the abuses
from which he suffers so that he can go
on rebelling against them.'
BAUDELAIRE *(1947)*

4   'Fascism is not defined by the number of
its victims, but by the way it kills them.'
LIBÉRATION, *22 June 1953. On the
execution of Julius and Ethel Rosenberg*

Schumpeter, Joseph (1883–1950)
AUSTRIAN-BORN AMERICAN
ECONOMIST

5   'Economic progress, in capitalist society,
means turmoil.'
CAPITALISM, SOCIALISM AND DEMOCRACY
(1942)

6   'Democracy is a political *method*, that is
to say, a certain type of institutional
arrangement for arriving at
political – legal and
administrative – decisions and hence
incapable of being an end in itself.'
IBID.

Scott, Sir Walter (1771–1832)
SCOTTISH POET AND NOVELIST

7   'Now is the stately column broke,
The beacon-light is quench'd in smoke,
The trumpet's silver sound is still,
The warder silent on the hill!'
MARMION: A TALE OF FLODDEN FIELD *(1808),
Canto 8. Of the death of the younger Pitt*

Seeckt, Hans von (1866–1936)
GERMAN GENERAL

8   'Whenever our policy in the West has
run aground, it has always been wise to
try something in the East.'
1921. Quoted in E Eyck, A HISTORY OF THE
WEIMAR REPUBLIC, *Volume I, Chapter 7*

9   'Poland is the nub of our Eastern
problem. Poland's existence is intolerable;
it is incompatible with the conditions of
Germany's existence. . . *Poland must
disappear* and it will disappear thanks to
its own internal weakness and *to
Russia – with our help.* For Poland is even
more intolerable to Russia than to us; no
Russian regime can abide a Polish state.'
Memorandum, autumn, 1922

10 'War is not the continuation of policy. It
is the breakdown of policy.'
THOUGHTS OF A SOLDIER *(1929)*
SEE ALSO *Clausewitz*

Seely, Sir John (1834–1895)
ENGLISH CLASSICIST AND HISTORIAN

11 'Politics are vulgar when they are not
liberalised by history, and history fades
into mere literature when it loses sight of
its relation to practical politics.'
THE EXPANSION OF ENGLAND *(1883), Second
Course, Chapter 1. (Published lectures
delivered at Cambridge, 1881–82.)*

Shakespeare, William
(1564–1616)
ENGLISH DRAMATIST AND POET

12 'Not all the water in the rough rude sea
Can wash the balm from an anointed
   king.'
KING RICHARD II *(c. 1595), III, ii*

13 'Therefore doth heaven divide
The state of man in divers functions,
Setting endeavour in continual motion;
To which is fixed as an aim or butt
Obedience; 'for so work the honey-bees,

Creatures that by a rule in nature teach
The act of order to a peopled kingdom.
They have a king, and officers of sorts;
Where some, like magistrates, correct at
home,
Others, like merchants, venture trade
abroad,
Others, like soldiers, armed in their
stings,
Make boot upon the summer's velvet
buds;
Which pillage they with merry march
bring home
To the tent-royal of their emperor:
Who, busied in his majesty, surveys
The singing masons building roofs of
gold,
The civil citizens kneading up the
honey,
The poor mechanic porters crowding in
Their heavy burdens at his narrow gate,
The sad-ey'd justice, with his surly hum,
Delivering o'er to executors pale
The lazy yawning drone.'
KING HENRY V *(c. 1599) Act I, scene 2*

1   'There's such divinity doth hedge a king,
    That treason can but peep to what it
    would.'
    HAMLET *(1600-1601), IV, v, 123*

2   'The heavens themselves, the planets,
    and this centre,
    Observe degree, priority, and place,
    Insisture, course, proportion, season,
    form,
    Office and custom, in all line of order...
    O, when degree is shak'd,
    Which is the ladder of all high designs,
    The enterprise is sick! How could
    communities,
    Degrees in schools, and brotherhoods in
    cities,
    Peaceful commerce from dividable shores,
    The primogenity and due of birth,
    Prerogative of age, crowns, sceptres,
    laurels,
    But by degree, stand in authentic place?
    Take but degree away, untune that
    string,
    And hark what discord follows! Each
    thing melts
    In mere oppugnancy: the bounded waters
    Should lift their bosoms higher than the
    shores
    And make a sop of all this sordid globe;
    Strength should be lord of imbecility,
    And the rude son should strike his father
    dead;

Force should be right; or, rather, right
and wrong –
Between whose endless jar justice
resides –
Should lose their names, and so should
justice too.
Then everything includes itself in power,
Power into will, will into appetite;
And appetite, an universal wolf,
So doubly seconded with will and power,
Must make perforce an universal prey,
And last eat up himself.'
TROILUS AND CRESSIDA *(1609), I, iii, 85, 101*

Shaw, George Bernard
(1856–1950)
IRISH DRAMATIST CRITIC, ESSAYIST
AND FABIAN SOCIALIST

3   'There is nothing so bad or so good that
    you will not find Englishmen doing it;
    but you will never find an Englishman in
    the wrong. He does everything on
    principle. He fights you on patriotic
    principles; he robs you on business
    principles; he enslaves you on imperial
    principles.'
    THE MAN OF DESTINY *(1897)*

4   'Any person under the age of thirty,
    who, having knowledge of the existing
    social order, is not a revolutionist, is an
    inferior. And yet Revolutions have never
    lightened the burden of tyranny: they
    have only shifted it to another shoulder.'
    MAN AND SUPERMAN *(1903)*

5   'Give women the vote, and in five years
    there will be a crushing tax on
    bachelors.'
    IBID., *Preface*

6   'Assassination is the extreme form of
    censorship.'
    THE REJECTED STATEMENT *(1916)*

7   'A Bolshevik as far as I can tell is nothing
    but a socialist who wants to do something
    about it. To the best of my knowledge I
    am a Bolshevik myself.'
    Interview in THE LIBERATOR, *1919. Quoted
    in D Caute,* THE FELLOW TRAVELLERS,
    Chapter 2

8   ''The more Communism, the more
    civilization.'
    THE INTELLIGENT WOMAN'S GUIDE TO
    SOCIALISM, CAPITALISM, SOVIETISM AND FASCISM
    (1937), Chapter 6

9   'Under fully developed Capitalism
    civilization is always on the verge of

revolution. We live as in a villa on Vesuvius.'
IBID., *Chapter 66*

1 'If you rebel against high-heeled shoes, take care to do it in a very smart hat.'
IBID., *Chapter 79*

2 'How great, of all that human hearts endure,
That part that Factory Acts alone can cure!'
IBID., *Chapter 85*
SEE ALSO *Samuel Johnson*

3 'Socialism means equality of income or nothing.'
IBID., *Appendix*

4 'Unimaginative people disparage Socialism because it will, they fear, reduce life to a dead level. Never was an apprehension less plausible. Millions of well-fed bumptious citizens with plenty of leisure for argument will provide all the excitement the most restless spirits can desire.'
EVERYBODY'S POLITICAL WHAT'S WHAT? *(1944)*, *Chapter 7*

5 'The great corruption of Socialism which threatens us at present . . . calls itself Fascism in Italy, National Socialism (Nazi for short) in Germany, New Deal in the United States, and is clever enough to remain nameless in England; but everywhere it means the same thing: Socialist production and Unsocialist distribution.'
IBID., *Chapter 30. On state capitalism*

Shawcross, Hartley, Baron
(1902–)
ENGLISH LABOUR POLITICIAN, MEMBER OF PARLIAMENT, 1945–1958, ATTORNEY-GENERAL 1945–1951

6 'We are the masters at the moment – and not only for the moment, but for a very long time to come.'
House of Commons, 2 April 1946. On the third reading of the Trade Disputes and Trade Union bill

Shelley, Percy Bysshe
(1792–1822)
ENGLISH POET

7 'I met Murder on the way –
He had a mask like Castlereagh –
Very smooth he looked, yet grim;
Seven blood-hounds followed him:
All were fat; and well they might

Be in admirable plight,
For one by one, and two by two,
He tossed them human hearts to chew
Which from his wide cloak he drew.
Next came Fraud, and he had on,
Like Eldon, an ermined gown;
His big tears, for he wept full well,
Turned to mill-stones as they fell.'
THE MASK OF ANARCHY *(1819). Written on the occasion of the 'Peterloo' massacre at Manchester*

8 'Clothed with the Bible, as with light,
And the shadows of the night,
Like Sidmouth, next, Hypocrisy
On a crocodile rode by.'
IBID.

9 'Rise like Lions after slumber
In unvanquishable number,
Shake your chains to earth like dew
Which in sleep had fallen on you –
Ye are many – they are few.'
IBID.

10 'Poets and philosophers are the unacknowledged legislators of the world.'
A PHILOSOPHICAL VIEW OF REFORM *(1819–20)*, *Chapter 1*

11 'Monarchy is only the string which ties the robbers' bundle.'
IBID., *Chapter 2*

Sheridan, Philip (1831–1888)
AMERICAN GENERAL

12 'The only good Indian I ever saw is a dead Indian.'
Remark at Fort Cobb, January 1869. On being told that he was to meet a good Indian chief

Sheridan, Richard Brinsley
(1751–1816)
IRISH DRAMATIST AND WHIG POLITICIAN, MEMBER OF PARLIAMENT, 1780–1812

13 'Conscience has no more to do with gallantry than it has with politics.'
THE DUENNA *(1775)*

14 'The serpent may as well abandon the characteristic obliquity of his motion for the direct flight of an arrow, as he can excuse his purposes with honesty and fairness.'
House of Commons, 7 February 1787. Attacking Warren Hastings for his treatment of the Begums of Oude

1 'His crimes are the only great things about him, and these are contrasted by the littleness of his motives.'
IBID.

Sherman, William (1820–1891)
AMERICAN GENERAL

2 'Vox populi, vox humbug.'
Letter to his wife, 2 June 1853

3 'There is many a boy here to-day who looks on war as all glory, but boys, it is all hell.'
Speech at Columbus, Ohio, 11 August, 1880

4 'I will not accept if nominated and will not serve if elected.'
Telegram to General Henderson, 5 June, 1884. On being pressed to stand for the Republican presidential nomination

Shinwell, Emanuel, Baron (1884–)
ENGLISH LABOUR POLITICIAN, MEMBER OF PARLIAMENT, 1922–1924, 1928–1931 AND 1935–1970

5 'We know that you, the organised workers of the country, are our friends. . . As for the rest, they do not matter a tinker's cuss.'
Speech to the Electrical Trades Union conference at Margate, 7 May 1947

Sieyès, Emmanuel (1748–1836)
FRENCH *ABBÉ* AND POLITICIAN

6 'What is the Third Estate? – Everything. What has it hitherto been in the political order? – Nothing. What does it ask? – To be something.'
QU'EST-CE QUE LE TIERS ETAT? *(1789)*

Silone, Ignazio (1900–1978)
ITALIAN WRITER AND SOCIALIST POLITICIAN

7 'A dictatorship is a regime in which people quote instead of thinking.'
THE SCHOOL FOR DICTATORS *(1939)*, *Chapter 2*

8 'Fascism was a counter-revolution against a revolution that never took place.'
IBID., *Chapter 4*

9 'It is true that every ruling class has at its disposal, up to the very day the regime falls, all the necessary material means with which to defend itself. But it lacks the will, the ability, the courage to use them, and these are the essential attributes of men who would rule.'
IBID.

10 'For democrats in troubled countries, the height of the art of governing seems to consist in accepting slaps so as to avoid kicks. . . The enemies of democracy take advantage of this and grow daily more insolent.'
IBID.

11 'A declining political class has all the infirmities of old age, including deafness.'
IBID.

12 'The king presupposes subjects; the leader, followers.'
IBID., *Chapter 6*

13 'The behaviour of the priests might surprise us, if the pagans had not already advised us that a winning cause has always pleased the gods.'
IBID., *Chapter 7*

Sinclair, Upton (1878–1968)
AMERICAN WRITER AND SOCIALIST POLITICIAN

14 'Fascism is Capitalism plus Murder.'
SINGING JAILBIRDS *(1924)*

Smith, Adam (1723–1790)
SCOTTISH POLITICAL ECONOMIST AND MORAL PHILOSOPHER

15 'The rich only select from the heap what is most precious and agreeable. They consume little more than the poor, and in spite of their natural selfishness and rapacity, though they mean only their own conveniency, though the sole end which they propose from the labours of all the thousands whom they employ, be the gratification of their own vain and insatiable desires, they divide with the poor the produce of all their improvements. They are led by an invisible hand to make nearly the same distribution of the necessaries of life, which would have been made, had the earth been divided into equal portions among all its inhabitants; and thus, without intending it, without knowing it, advance the interest of the society, and afford means to the multiplication of the species.'
THE THEORY OF MORAL SENTIMENTS *(1759)*

16 'Labour, therefore, it appears evidently, is the only universal, as well as the only

accurate, measure of value, or the only standard by which we can compare the values of different commodities, at all times, and at all places.'
AN INQUIRY INTO THE NATURE AND CAUSES OF THE WEALTH OF NATIONS *(1776)*

1 'To found a great empire for the sole purpose of raising up a people of customers, may at first sight appear a project fit only for a nation of shopkeepers. It is, however, a project altogether unfit for a nation of shopkeepers; but extremely fit for a nation that is governed by shopkeepers.'
IBID.

Smith, Alfred (1873–1944)
AMERICAN DEMOCRATIC POLITICIAN, GOVERNOR OF NEW YORK, 1919–1920 AND 1923–1928

2 'All the ills of democracy can be cured by more democracy.'
Speech at Albany, 27 June 1933

Smith, Ian (1919–)
RHODESIAN POLITICIAN, PRIME MINISTER, 1964–1980

3 'We have struck a blow for the preservation of justice, civilisation, and Christianity; and in the spirit of this belief we have this day assumed our sovereign independence.'
Broadcast on Rhodesian radio, 11 November 1965. Proclaiming Rhodesia's unilateral declaration of independence from Great Britain

Smith, Sydney (1771–1845)
ENGLISH CLERGYMAN AND JOURNALIST

4 'Gentlemen, be at your ease – be quiet and steady. You will beat Mrs Partington.'
Speech at Taunton, 11 October 1831. On the Lords' rejection of the great reform bill

5 'Tory and Whig in turn shall be my host,
I taste no politics in boiled and roast.'
Letter to John Murray, [August, 1834]

6 'The plough is not a political machine; the loom and the steam-engine are furiously political, but the plough is not.'
COLLECTED WORKS *(1839), Volume II, 'Ballot'*

7 'There is only one principle of public conduct. *Do what you think right, and take place and power as an accident.* Upon every other plan, office is shabbiness, labour, and sorrow.'
IBID, *Note appended to 'Speech at the Taunton Reform Meeting'*

8 'Ministers have a great deal of patience, but no resignation.'
Remark, June 1841. Quoted in E Longford, VICTORIA R.I., *Chapter 12. On Lord Melbourne's decision to dissolve, not resign, after his government was defeated in the House of Commons*

Smith, William Henry (1825–1891)
ENGLISH BOOKSELLER AND CONSERVATIVE POLITICIAN, MEMBER OF PARLIAMENT, 1868–1891

9 'Mr Gladstone is willing to give the great support of his name in favour of the expression of our views in the Congress [of Berlin], but he thinks it right to say that he refuses . . . to give the six millions. It appears that the right hon. Gentleman refuses to give the Government a cheque for six millions, but he will give us a blank cheque, without money expressed, to be filled up by ourselves at the right time.'
House of Commons, February 1878

Snow, C(harles) P(ercy), Baron (1905–1980)
ENGLISH NOVELIST AND PHYSICIST

10 'If you use words for political purposes, they soon lose whatever meaning they may have had. If you are tempted to brandish the word "free", remember that over the gates of Auschwitz there stretched – and still stretches – the inscription *Arbeit Macht Frei.*'
Speech at Loyola University, Chicago, 1970

Snowden, Ethel, Viscountess (1881–1951)
ENGLISH SUFFRAGETTE AND SOCIALIST

11 'We were behind the "iron curtain" at last!'
THROUGH BOLSHEVIK RUSSIA *(1920). On her arrival, with a Labour party delegation, at Petrograd*

Snowden, Philip, 1st Viscount
(1864–1937)
ENGLISH LABOUR POLITICIAN,
CHANCELLOR OF THE EXCHEQUER, 1924
AND 1929–1931

1   'I hope you have read the election
programme of the Labour Party. It is the
most fantastic and impracticable
programme ever put before the electors
. . . This is not socialism. It is Bolshevism
run mad.'
*Election broadcast on BBC radio, 17
October 1931 (after joining the National
Government)*

Solzhenitsyn, Alexander
(1918–)
SOVIET WRITER AND DISSIDENT

2   'These days, as we observe the Chinese
Cultural Revolution at the same stage [as
the Russian revolution] – in the
seventeenth year after its final
victory – we can begin to consider it very
likely that there exists a fundamental
law of historical development. And even
Stalin himself begins to seem only a
blind and perfunctory executive agent.'
THE GULAG ARCHIPELAGO *(1973),* Volume I,
Part I, *Chapter 2*

3   'The confrontation between a man – any
man – and Communism is always over in
two rounds. Communism nearly always
wins the first round, like a wild beast
that leaps at its adversary and bowls him
over. But, if there *is* a second round,
Communism nearly always loses. The
man's eyes open and he sees that he
admired a bundle of cast-offs, a
semblance, an optical illusion. Then he's
immunised, and for ever.'
Interview with Georges Suffert,
ENCOUNTER, *April 1976*

Sontag, Susan (1933–)
AMERICAN WRITER

4   'The truth is that Mozart, Pascal, Boolean
algebra, Shakespeare, parliamentary
government, baroque churches, Newton,
the emancipation of women, Kant, Marx,
and Balanchine ballets don't redeem what
this particular civilization has wrought
upon the world. The white race *is* the
cancer of human history.'
'What's Happening in America' (1966)

5   'Communism is successful fascism.'
Speech at New York, February 1982

Sorel, Georges (1847–1922)
FRENCH POLITICAL PHILOSOPHER

6   'I do not hesitate to assert that Socialism
could not continue to exist without an
apology for violence . . . War, carried on
in broad daylight, without hypocritical
attenuation, for the purpose of ruining an
irreconcilable enemy, excludes all the
abominations which dishonoured the
middle-class revolution of the eighteenth
century.'
REFLECTIONS ON VIOLENCE *(1908)*

Southey, Robert (1774–1843)
ENGLISH POET AND MAN OF LETTERS,
POET LAUREATE, 1813–1843

7   'The ablest physician can do little in the
great lazar house of society.'
*Letter to J May, 26 June 1797. On his
abandoning the cause of the French
revolution in the face of the English
Church-and-King reaction of the 1790s*

Spender, Sir Stephen (1909–)
ENGLISH POET AND ESSAYIST

8   'By comparison with the greatest subjects
of art . . . all politics seem like provincial
struggles for booty between dusky tribes.'
HORIZON, *September 1940, 'A Look at the
Worst'*

9   'What we call the freedom of the
individual is not just the luxury of one
intellectual to write what he likes to
write, but his being a voice which can
speak for those who are silent. And if he
permits his freedom of expression to be
abolished, then he has abolished their
freedom to find in his voice a voice for
their wrongs.'
THE THIRTIES AND AFTER *(1978), Part III*

10 'Politics without ideology, and with a
strong tendency towards autobiography,
equals Liberalism.'
IBID., *Postscript*

Spinoza, Benedict (1632–1677)
DUTCH PHILOSOPHER AND POLITICAL
THEORIST

11 'Action done by order, i.e. obedience,
does destroy freedom in a sense, but it
does not of itself make a man a slave;
what makes a man a slave is the object of
his action. If its object is not the benefit
of the agent himself, but of the man who
gives the order, then the agent is a slave,

and useless to himself. But in a state where the welfare of the whole people, and not of the ruler, is the highest law, he who obeys the sovereign in everything must not be called a slave, useless to himself, but a subject.'
TRACTATUS THEOLOGICO-POLITICUS *(1670)*, *Chapter 16*

1 'The order maintained by any state is called political.'
TRACTATUS POLITICUS *(1677)*, *Chapter 3*

2 'Rebellions, wars, and contemptuous disregard for law must certainly be attributed to the corrupt condition of the commonwealth rather than to the wickedness of its subjects . . . if wickedness is more dominant and crime more prevalent in one commonwealth than another, this is certainly due to the fact that the first has not done enough to promote harmony, has not framed its laws with sufficient foresight, and so has failed to acquire its absolute right as a commonwealth.'
IBID., *Chapter 5*

3 'Freedom is the recognition of necessity.'
THE ETHICS *(1677)*, *Part I*

4 'The man, who is guided by reason, is more free in a State, where he lives under a general system of law, than in solitude, where he is independent.'
IBID., *Part IV*

Stalin, Joseph (1879–1953)
SOVIET COMMUNIST POLITICIAN, GENERAL SECRETARY OF THE PARTY, 1922–1953

5 'Only on the bones of the oppressors can the people's freedom be founded – only the blood of the oppressors can fertilise the soil for the people's self-rule.'
Appeal written on behalf of the Tiflis Social Democratic committee, 1905

6 'The revolution is incapable either of regretting or of burying its dead.'
Article attacking Gorky, 1917. Quoted in I Deutscher, STALIN, A POLITICAL BIOGRAPHY, *Chapter 5*

7 'The principal task of socialism – the organisation of socialist production – has still to be fulfilled. Can this task be fulfilled, can the final victory of socialism be achieved in one country, without the joint efforts of the

proletarians in several advanced countries? No, it cannot.'
THE FOUNDATIONS OF LENINISM *(1924)*

8 'What do we mean by the possibility of the victory of socialism in one country? We mean the possibility of solving the contradictions between the proletariat and the peasantry with the aid of the internal forces of our country, the possibility of the proletariat's assuming power, and using that power to build a complete socialist society in one country . . . without the preliminary victory of the proletarian revolution in other countries.'
PROBLEMS OF LENINISM *(1924). Recanting his position in the earlier 1924 pamphlet on Leninism*

9 'Objectively, Social Democracy is the moderate wing of fascism.'
1924. Quoted in I Deutscher, STALIN, *Chapter 10*

10 'The Pope! How many divisions has *he* got?'
In conversation with Pierre Laval, 13 May 1935. In reply to the suggestion that the Soviet Union should propitiate the Pope

11 'We are under no illusion that they [the Russian people] are fighting for us [the Communist party]. They are fighting for Mother Russia.'
In conversation with Averell Harriman, September, 1941. On the Russian war effort

12 'In the Soviet Army it takes more courage to retreat than to advance.'
IBID.

13 'Communism fits Germany as a saddle fits a cow.'
In conversation with Mikolajczyk, August 1944

14 'There is really nothing more delightful than carefully plotting a trap into which your enemy in the party is bound to fall, and then going to bed.'
In conversation with L Kamenev. Quoted in I Silone, THE SCHOOL FOR DICTATORS, *Chapter 6*

Steffens, Lincoln (1866–1936)
AMERICAN WRITER AND EDITOR

15 'The business man has failed in politics as he has in citizenship. Why? Because politics is business. That's what's the

matter with everything – art, literature, religion, journalism, law, medicine – they're all businesses, and all – as you see them. Make politics a sport, as they do in England, or a profession, as they do in Germany, and we'll have – well, something else than we have now – if we want it, which is another question.'
THE SHAME OF THE CITIES *(1904)*, *Introduction*

1 'I have been over into the future, and it works.'
In conversation with Bernard Baruch, 1919. After visiting the Soviet Union as a member of the Bullitt mission

Stephen, Sir James Fitzjames (1829–1894)
ENGLISH JURIST AND MAN OF LETTERS

2 'Was Pilate right in crucifying Christ? I reply, Pilate's paramount duty was to preserve the peace in Palestine, to form the best judgment he could as to the means required for that purpose, and to act upon it when it was formed. Therefore, if and in so far as he believed, in good faith and on reasonable grounds, that what he did was necessary for the preservation of the peace of Palestine, he was right. It was his duty to run the risk of being mistaken, notwithstanding Mr Mill's principle as to liberty, and particularly as to liberty in the expression of opinion.'
LIBERTY, EQUALITY, FRATERNITY *(1873)*, *Chapter 2*

3 'In a pure democracy the ruling men will be the wirepullers and their friends.'
IBID., *Chapter 5*

4 'Equality, like Liberty, appears to me to be a big name for a small thing.'
IBID.

5 'Humanity is only I writ large, and love for Humanity generally means zeal for MY notions as to what men should be and how they should live.'
IBID., *Chapter 6*

Stevenson, Adlai (1900–1965)
AMERICAN DEMOCRATIC POLITICIAN, PRESIDENTIAL CANDIDATE, 1952 AND 1956

6 'To strike freedom of the mind with the fist of patriotism is an old and ugly subtlety.'
Speech at New York, 27 August 1952

7 'My definition of a free society is a society where it is safe to be unpopular.'
Speech at Detroit, October 1952

8 'I will make a bargain with the Republicans. If they will stop telling lies about the Democrats, we will stop telling the truth about them.'
Campaign Speech, 1952. Quoted in L Harris, THE FINE ART OF POLITICAL WIT

9 'Eggheads of the the world, arise – I was even going to add that you have nothing to lose but your yolks.'
Speech at Oakland, 1 February 1956

Stewart, (Robert) Michael, Baron (1906–)
ENGLISH LABOUR POLITICIAN, FOREIGN SECRETARY 1965-1966 AND 1968-1970

10 'It was . . . a Foreign Office joke that I could never make a speech of any length without using the word "mankind": it seems to me a good word for a Foreign Secretary to have firmly fixed in his head.'
LIFE AND LABOUR *(1980)*, *Chapter 1*

11 'The politician who will refuse the Foreign Office is not yet born.'
IBID., *Chapter 6*

Stimson, Henry (1867–1950)
AMERICAN REPUBLICAN POLITICIAN, SECRETARY OF WAR, 1940-1945

12 'If you are going to try to go to war, or to prepare for war, in a capitalist country, you have got to let business make money out of the process or business won't work.'
Diary, 26 August 1940

Stirner, Max (1806–1856)
GERMAN POLITICAL THEORIST

13 'The revolution commands one to make arrangements; rebellion demands that one *rise or exalt oneself.*'
THE EGO AND HIS OWN *(1843)*

Stone, Isidor Feinstein (1907–1982)
AMERICAN JOURNALIST

14 'We Smiths want peace so bad we're prepared to kill every one of the Joneses to get it.'
Leading article, 24 January 1949. Reprinted in I F Stone, THE TRUMAN ERA. *On the Truman administration and the Cold war*

Strafford, 1st Earl of (Thomas Wentworth) (1593–1641)
ENGLISH POLITICIAN, LORD DEPUTY OF IRELAND, 1632–1640

1 'Never came man to so lost a business.'
Remark to Charles I, 13 September 1640. When receiving the Order of the Garter

2 'These gentlemen tell me they speak in defence of the Commonweal against my arbitrary laws. Give me leave to say that I speak in defence of the Commonweal against their arbitrary treason.'
House of Lords, 13 April 1641. Defending himself against a bill of attainder, condemning him to death

Sukarno, Achmed (1901–1970)
INDONESIAN POLITICIAN, PRESIDENT, 1945–1967

3 'We must be on guard lest our Revolution die out. Therefore . . . give it romanticism. Give it dynamism. Give it dialecticalism. Never allow it to stagnate. Let it march on ever forward! Let it keep being a Revolution! Let it continue to be progressive. Progressiveness is an absolute condition for a Modern Revolution in the twentieth century.'
Independence Day message, Djakarta, 17 August 1964

Sumner, William (1840–1910)
AMERICAN POLITICAL ECONOMIST AND SOCIOLOGIST

4 'The yearning after equality is the offspring of covetousness, and there is no possible plan for satisfying that yearning which can do aught else than rob A to give to B; consequently all such plans nourish some of the meanest vices of human nature, waste capital, and overthrow civilization.'
WHAT SOCIAL CLASSES OWE TO EACH OTHER *(1883), Conclusion*

Sun Yat-sen (1866–1925)
CHINESE REVOLUTIONARY LEADER

5 'The civilisation of Europe and America is completely materialistic. There is nothing more vulgar, more brutal, more evil. We Chinese call that barbarism. Our inferiority as a power derives from the fact that we have always scorned and avoided it. The Chinese Way is the way of mankind and morals. Our ancient books call this system the royal Way.'
1925. Quoted in A Peyrefitte, THE CHINESE, *Chapter 1*

Surkov, Alexei (1899–)
SOVIET WRITER, FIRST SECRETARY OF THE WRITERS' UNION, 1953–1960

6 'Many people thought we had changed cars at the 20th Congress. Quite wrong. We threw out some luggage, but we are still travelling in the same car.'
In conversation with Richard Crossman, 25 August 1958. On the 20th Congress of the Soviet Communist party, 1956, at which Khrushchev announced the policy of de-Stalinisation

7 'We would not have published Nietzsche and that would have prevented the rise of Hitlerism.'
IBID. *In defence of Soviet literary censorship*

Swift, Jonathan (1667–1745)
IRISH SATIRIST AND MAN OF LETTERS

8 'Ambition often puts Men upon doing the meanest offices; so climbing is performed in the same position with creeping.'
THOUGHTS ON VARIOUS SUBJECTS *(1706)*

Swinburne, Algernon (1837–1909)
ENGLISH POET AND CRITIC

9 'Men, born of the land that for ages
Has been honoured where freedom was dear,
Till your labour wax fat on its wages
You shall never be peers of a peer.
Where might is, the right is:
Long purses make strong swords.
Let weakness learn meekness:
God save the House of Lords.'
A WORD FOR THE COUNTRY *(1884)*

10 'You are equal in right to obey:
You are brothers in bonds, and the nation
Is your mother – whose sons are her prey.'
IBID.

Szasz, Thomas (1920–   )
HUNGARIAN-BORN AMERICAN
PSYCHIATRIST

1   'Institutional psychiatry is a continuation
of the Inquisition. All that has really
changed is the vocabulary and the social
style. The vocabulary conforms to the
intellectual expectations of our age: it is a
pseudomedical jargon that parodies the
concepts of science. The social style
conforms to the political expectations of
our age: it is a pseudoliberal social
movement that parodies the ideals of
freedom and rationality.'
MANUFACTURE OF MADNESS *(1971)*,
Chapter 1

2   'The fundamental conflicts in human life
are not between competing ideas, one
"true" and the other "false" – but rather
between those who hold power and use it
to oppress others, and those who are
oppressed by power and seek to free
themselves of it.'
IBID., *Chapter 4*

T

Tacitus (*c.* 55–*c.* 117)
ROMAN HISTORIAN

1   'They make a wilderness and call it peace.' [*Ubi solitudinem faciunt, pacem appellant.*]
Tacitus's account of the speech delivered by Celgacus before the advance to Mons Grampius, AD 84

2   'It was to the stronger that the gods gave their aid.' [*Deos fortioribus adesse.*]
HISTORIES, *Book IV*, 17

Taft, William (1857–1930)
AMERICAN REPUBLICAN POLITICIAN, PRESIDENT, 1909–1913

3   'Next to the right of liberty, the right of property is the most important individual right guaranteed by the Constitution and the one which, united with that of personal liberty, has contributed more to the growth of civilization than any other institution established by the human race . . . Socialism proposes no adequate substitute for the motive of enlightened selfishness that to-day is at the basis of all human labor and effort, enterprise and new activity.'
POPULAR GOVERNMENT *(1913), Chapter 3*

Taine, Hippolyte (1828–1893)
FRENCH HISTORIAN AND CRITIC

4   'The doctrine of popular sovereignty, interpreted by the masses, will produce perfect anarchy until the moment when, interpreted by the rulers, it produces perfect despotism.'
THE ORIGINS OF CONTEMPORARY FRANCE *(1876–93), Volume I*

Talleyrand, Charles Maurice de (1754–1838)
FRENCH STATESMAN AND DIPLOMAT

5   'No money, no patriotism.'
Letter to a friend, 6 June 1793. Of the English 'friends of liberty'

Tawney, Richard (1880–1962)
ENGLISH ECONOMIC HISTORIAN

6   'Inequality . . . leads to the misdirection of production. For, since the demand of one income of £50,000 is as powerful a magnet as the demand of 500 incomes of £100, it diverts energy from the creation of wealth to the multiplication of luxuries.'
THE ACQUISITIVE SOCIETY *(1921)*

7   'An organised money market has many advantages. But it is not a school of social ethics or of political responsibility.'
RELIGION AND THE RISE OF CAPITALISM *(1926)*

8   'Those who dread a dead-level of income or wealth . . . do not dread, it seems, a dead-level of law and order, and of security of life and property. They do not complain that persons endowed by nature with unusual qualities of strength, audacity or cunning are prevented from reaping the full fruits of these powers.'
EQUALITY *(1931)*

9   'Political principles resemble military tactics; they are usually designed for a war which is over.'
IBID.

10 'Cruel boys tie tin cans to the tails of dogs; but even a mad dog does not tie a can to its own tail.'
POLITICAL QUARTERLY, *July-September 1932, 'The Choice Before the Labour Party'. On peerages*

11 'Thank you for your letter. What harm have I ever done to the Labour Party?'
Letter to Ramsay MacDonald, 1933. Quoted in the EVENING STANDARD, *18 January 1962. Declining the offer of a peerage*

12 'Talk is nauseous without practice. Who will believe that the Labour Party means business so long as some of its stalwarts sit up and beg for sugar-plums, like poodles in a drawing-room . . . To kick over an idol, you must first get off your knees.'
1934. Quoted in the GUARDIAN, *29 March 1982. Attacking the Honours system*

13 'In the transition to political democracy, this country . . . underwent . . . no inner conversion. She accepted it as a convenience, like an improved system of telephones . . . She changed her political garments, but not her heart. She carried into the democratic era, not only the institutions, but the social habits and mentality of the oldest and toughest

plutocracy in the world ... She went to the ballot-box touching her hat.'
THE HIGHWAY, *January 1937, 'The Realities of Democracy'*

Taylor, A J P (Alan John Percivale) (1906–)
ENGLISH HISTORIAN

1 'Trotsky tells how, when he first visited England, Lenin took him round London and, pointing out the sights, exclaimed: "That's *their* Westminster Abbey! That's *their* Houses of Parliament!" Lenin was making a class, not a national, emphasis. By *them* he meant not the English, but the governing classes, the Establishment. And indeed in no other European country is the Establishment so clearly defined and so complacently secure.'
'William Cobbett', in ESSAYS IN ENGLISH HISTORY (*originally a review in the* NEW STATESMAN, 1953). *The first use, in its contemporary meaning, of the phrase, 'the Establishment'.*

2 'There is nothing more agreeable in life than to make peace with the Establishment – and nothing more corrupting.'
IBID.

Tennyson, Alfred, 1st Baron (1809–1892)
ENGLISH POET, POET LAUREATE, 1850–1892

3 'It is the land that freemen till,
That sober-suited Freedom chose;
The land, where, girt with friends or foes,
A man may speak the thing he will;
A land of settled government,
A land of just and old renown,
Where Freedom slowly broadens down,
From precedent to precedent.'
YOU ASK ME, WHY (1833)

4 'For the peace, that I deem'd no peace, is over and done,
And now by the side of the Black and the Baltic deep,
The deathful-grinning mouths of the fortress, flames
The blood-red blossom of war with a heart of fire.'
MAUD (1855), *Part III. On the Crimean war*

Thatcher, Margaret (1925–)
ENGLISH CONSERVATIVE POLITICIAN, PRIME MINISTER, 1979–

5 'One of the things being in politics has taught me is that men are not a reasoned or reasonable sex.'
In conversation with Anthony King, BBC radio, 14 January 1972

6 'I don't think it will come for many, many years. I don't think it will come in my lifetime.'
IBID. *On the probability of there being a woman prime minister*

7 'I stand before you tonight in my green chiffon evening gown, my face softly made up, my fair hair gently waved ... the Iron Lady of the Western World. Me? A cold war warrior? Well, yes – if that is how they wish to interpret my defence of values and freedoms fundamental to our way of life.'
Speech at London, 31 January 1976. On the description of her by the Soviet press

8 'To those waiting with bated breath for that favourite media catch-phrase, the U-turn, I have only one thing to say: you turn if you want to. The lady's not for turning.'
Speech to the Conservative party annual conference, October 1980. On the government's economic policy

9 'When you stop a dictator there are always risks. But there are greater risks in not stopping a dictator.'
Interview on BBC television, 5 April 1982. On the Argentinian occupation of the Falkland Islands

Thiers, (Louis) Adolphe (1797–1877)
FRENCH HISTORIAN AND LIBERAL POLITICIAN, PRESIDENT OF THE REPUBLIC, 1871–1873

10 'A statesman should be possessed of good sense, a primary political quality; and its fortunate possessor needs a second quality – the courage to show that he has it.'
Speech to the Chamber of Deputies, 6 May 1834

11 'The cornerstone of my policy has always been the English alliance.'
In conversation with Nassau Senior, 8 March 1852

1 'Constitutional monarchy is the form that suits us best. We are unfit for a republic; we cannot breathe under a despotism.'
In conversation with Nassau Senior, 27 March 1852

2 'The king reigns and does not govern.'
IBID. *Explaining that he was the first to use the phrase, in 1830*
SEE ALSO *Zamojski*

3 'The error of the political economists [meaning free-traders] is that they think only of the consumer; a real statesman thinks more of the producer. Nothing is so easy as to make consumers, nothing so difficult as to make producers.'
In conversation with Nassau Senior, 19 May 1860

4 'I would never advise any party, even the opposition, to hunt for popularity, and yet it would be natural enough in an opposition. But governments have nothing to do with seeking popularity. Governments have a great and infallible judge against whom there is no appeal. Do you know what that judge is? The issue. Their policy must be endorsed by the issue. When the issue does not endorse it no applause can replace the approval of the supreme judge.'
Speech to the Chamber of Deputies, 14 March 1867

5 'I have no fear for my memory. It is not before a party tribunal that I would consent to appear, for I might fail there. I shall not fail before the bar of history, and it is there that I claim to be heard.'
Speech to the Chamber of Deputies, 24 May 1873. In the debate on the confidence motion which led to his resignation as president

6 'In politics one must take nothing tragically and everything seriously.'
IBID.

7 'We must cross the Channel, but not the Atlantic.'
Often-repeated maxim. Quoted in A J Grant and D Gunnell, THREE SPEECHES OF ADOLPHE THIERS, *Introduction. On the need for France to look to Great Britain, not to the United States, for a constitutional model*

8 'A free nation is a being that thinks before it acts.'
Quoted in P de Rémusat, A THIERS, *Chapter 5*

Thomson, James (1700–1748)
SCOTTISH POET

9 'When Britain first, at Heaven's command,
Arose from out the azure main,
This was the charter of the land,
And guardian angels sang this strain,
Rule Britannia, rule the waves,
Britons never will be slaves.'
Part of the libretto for the masque, ALFRED *(1740)*

Thoreau, Henry David (1817–1862)
AMERICAN ESSAYIST, POET AND NATURALIST

10 'The objections which have been brought against a standing army, and they are many and weighty, and deserve to prevail, may also at last be brought against a standing government.'
ON THE DUTY OF CIVIL DISOBEDIENCE *(1849)*

11 'Trade and commerce, if they were not made of Indian rubber, would never manage to bounce over the obstacles which legislators are continually putting in their way.'
IBID.

12 'All voting is a sort of gaming, like chequers or backgammon, with a slight moral tinge to it.'
IBID.

13 'Under a government which imprisons any unjustly, the true place for a just man is also in prison.'
IBID.

Thorpe, Jeremy (1929–)
ENGLISH POLITICIAN, LEADER OF THE LIBERAL PARTY, 1967–1976

14 'Greater love hath no man than this, that he lay down his friends for his life.'
Remark on Harold Macmillan's sacking of one-third of his cabinet, July 1962

15 'Looking around the House, one realises that we are all minorities now – indeed, some more than others.'
House of Commons, 6 March 1974. On the failure of any party to gain an overall majority at the elections of February 1974

Tilden, Samuel (1814–1886)
AMERICAN DEMOCRATIC POLITICIAN,
DEFEATED PRESIDENTIAL CANDIDATE,
1876

1 'In our body politic, as in the human
system, what can be digested and
assimilated is nutrition; it is the source of
health and life. What remains incapable
of being digested and assimilated can be
only an element of disease and death.
The question in respect to it is always
this – whether the vital forces are strong
enough to prevail over it and excrete it
from the system.'
*Speech to the New York Democratic state
convention, 11 March 1868. Of the Black
population in the United States*

Timerman, Jacobo (1923–)
ARGENTINIAN JOURNALIST AND
NEWSPAPER PUBLISHER

2 'The political defeat of subversion is as
important as its military defeat. Applying
legal methods to repression eliminates
one of the major elements exploited by
subversion: the illegal nature of
repression.'
PRISONER WITHOUT A NAME, CELL WITHOUT A
NUMBER *(1981), Chapter 5*

3 'The person who wants to fight senses his
solitude and is frightened. Whereupon
the silence reverts to patriotism. Fear
finds its great moral revelation in
patriotism.'
IBID. *On political quietism in the face of
totalitarianism*

4 'One point has already been proved.
Everything that happened once can
happen again.'
IBID., *Chapter 6. On the anti-Semitic
persecution in Argentina in the 1970s*

Tocqueville, Alexis de
(1805–1859)
FRENCH HISTORIAN AND POLITICIAN,
MINISTER OF FOREIGN AFFAIRS, 1849

5 'It is evident to all alike that a great
democratic revolution is taking place
amongst us; but all do not look at it in
the same light. To some it appears to be
novel, but accidental, and, as such, they
hope it may still be checked; to others it
seems irresistible, because it is the most
uniform, the most ancient, and the most
permanent tendency which is to be
found in history.'
DEMOCRACY IN AMERICA *(1835),
Introduction*

6 'The gradual development of the
principle of equality is . . . a Providential
fact. It has all the chief characteristics of
such a fact: it is universal, it is durable, it
constantly eludes all human interference,
and all events as well as all men
contribute to its progress.'
IBID.

7 'Men are not corrupted by the exercise of
power, or debased by the habit of
obedience; but by the exercise of a power
which they believe to be illegitimate, and
by obedience to a rule which they
consider to be usurped and oppressive.'
IBID.

8 'Small nations have . . . ever been the
cradle of political liberty; and the fact
that many of them have lost their liberty
by becoming larger, shows that their
freedom was more a consequence of their
small size than of the character of the
people.'
IBID., *Chapter 7*

9 'A long war almost always reduces
nations to the wretched alternative of
being abandoned to ruin by defeat, or to
despotism by success.'
IBID.

10 'If you do not succeed in connecting the
notion of right with that of private
interest, which is the only immutable
point in the human heart, what means
will you have of governing the world
except by fear?'
IBID., *Chapter 11*

11 'The tyranny of the majority.'
IBID., *Chapter 12, Sub-heading*

12 '*Individualism* is a novel expression, to
which a novel idea has given birth. Our
fathers were acquainted only with *egoism*
. . . Invidualism is a mature and calm
feeling, which disposes each member of
the community to sever himself from the
mass of his fellows . . . Selfishness blights
the germ of all virtue; individualism, at
first, only saps the virtues of public life;
but in the long run, it attacks and
destroys all others, and is at length
absorbed in downright selfishness.
Selfishness is a vice as old as the world,
which does not belong to one form of
society more than to another:

individualism is of democratic origin, and it threatens to spread in the same ratio as the equality of condition.'
IBID., *Part II, Chapter 27*

1 'The French Revolution, which abolished all privileges and destroyed all exclusive rights, did leave one, that of property ... When the right to property was merely the basis of many other rights, it could be easily defended, or rather, it was not attacked: it was like the encircling wall of a society whose other rights were the advance defence posts; the shots did not reach it; there was not even a serious intention to reach it. But now that the right to property is the last remnant of a destroyed aristocratic world, and it alone still stands, an isolated privilege in a levelled society; when it no longer has the cover of other more doubtful and more hated rights, it is in great danger; it alone now has to face the direct and incessant impact of democratic opinions.'
RECOLLECTIONS *(1893), Part I, Chapter 1. Fragment of 1847*

2 'I have always noticed in politics how often men are ruined by having too good a memory.'
IBID., *Chapter 4*

3 'In France there is only one thing that we cannot make: a free government; and only one thing that we cannot destroy: centralisation.'
IBID., *Part II, Chapter 10*

Togliatti, Palmiro (1893–1964)
ITALIAN COMMUNIST POLITICIAN, CO-FOUNDER OF THE ITALIAN COMMUNIST PARTY

4 'In judging a regime it is very important to know what it finds amusing.'
In conversation with Ignazio Silone, c. *1924. Quoted in Silone,* THE SCHOOL FOR DICTATORS

Tolstoy, Leo, Count (1828–1910)
RUSSIAN NOVELIST

5 'The error at the root of all the political doctrines (the most conservative, as well as the most advanced) which have brought men to their present wretched condition, is always one and the same. It is, that people considered, and still consider, it possible so to unite men by force that they should all unresistingly submit to one and the same scheme of

life, and to the guidance for conduct flowing therefrom.'
THE LAW OF VIOLENCE AND THE LAW OF LOVE *(1908), Chapter 3*

6 'People already understand the pitiful degradation of the spy or the executioner, and are beginning to understand the same about a gendarme, a policeman, or even to some extent about an army man; but they do not yet understand it about a Judge, a Senator, a Minister, a Monarch, or the Leader or participator in a Revolution. Yet the business of Senator, Minister, Monarch, or Party Leader, is as mean, unnatural to human nature, and horrid; it is even worse than the business of an executioner or spy, because while similar to the business of the executioner or spy, it is shrouded in hypocrisy. Everyone, and especially the young, should understand that to devote your lives, or even to occupy yourselves, with arranging by violence the lives of others according to your own ideas, is not only a crude superstition, but an evil, criminal business, pernicious to the soul.'
IBID., *Chapter 18*

Treitschke, Heinrich von
(1834–1896)
GERMAN HISTORIAN AND POLITICAL ECONOMIST

7 'No state can pledge its future to another.'
POLITICS *(1897–1901), Chapter 1. On the making of treaties between nations*

8 'The masses must for ever remain the masses. There would be no culture without kitchen maids.'
IBID.

9 'Without war no state could exist. All those we know of arose through war ... War, therefore, will endure to the end of history, as long as there is a multiplicity of states.'
IBID., *Chapter 2*

10 'The great strides which civilisation makes against barbarism and unreason are only made actual by the sword.'
IBID.

11 'If the state has the power to send the flower of its manhood to die in thousands for the sake of the lives of the whole community, it would be absurd to deny

it the right to put criminals to death if they are a danger to the public weal.'
IBID., *Chapter 5*

1 'Fair-minded Jews must themselves admit that after a nation has become conscious of its own personality there is no place left for the cosmopolitanism of the Semites ... Whenever he finds his life sullied by the filth of Judaism the German must turn from it, and learn to speak the truth boldly about it.'
IBID., *Chapter 8*

Trollope, Anthony (1815–1882)
ENGLISH NOVELIST

2 'I have always thought that to sit in the British Parliament should be the highest object of ambition to every educated Englishman ... that to serve one's country without pay is the grandest work that a man can do, – that of all studies the study of politics is the one in which a man may make himself useful to his fellow-creatures, – and that of all lives, public political life is capable of the greatest efforts.'
AN AUTOBIOGRAPHY *(1883), Chapter 16*

3 'I think I am guilty of no absurdity in calling myself an advanced conservative liberal.'
IBID.

Trotsky, Leon (1879–1940)
SOVIET REVOLUTIONARY, COMMISSAR FOR FOREIGN AFFAIRS, 1917–1925

4 'Even a successful solution of the elementary problem of food, clothing, shelter and even of literacy, would in no way signify a complete victory of the new historic principle, that is, of Socialism. Only a movement of scientific thought on a national scale and the development of a new art would signify that the historic seed had not only grown into a plant, but had even flowered. In this sense, the development of art is the highest test of the vitality and significance of each epoch.'
LITERATURE AND REVOLUTION *(1924), Introduction*

5 'It is fundamentally incorrect to contrast bourgeois culture and bourgeois art with proletarian culture and proletarian art. The latter will never exist, because the proletarian regime is temporary and transient. The historic significance and the moral grandeur of the proletarian revolution consist in the fact that it is laying the foundations of a culture which is above classes and which will be the first culture that is truly human.'
IBID.

6 'A proletarian church is impossible.'
IBID., *Chapter 1*

7 'They have no revolutionary past whatever and if they broke away from anything at all it was from bagatelles. In general their literary and spiritual front has been made by the Revolution, by that angle of it which caught them, and they have all accepted the Revolution, each one in his own way. But in these individual acceptances, there is one common trait which sharply divides them from Communism, and always threatens to put them in opposition to it. They do not grasp the Revolution as a whole and the Communist ideal is foreign to them ... They are not the artists of the proletarian Revolution, but her artist 'fellow-travellers' [*paputchiki*], in the sense in which this word was used by the old Socialists.'
IBID., *Chapter 2*

8 'The Revolution is, above all, a city one; without the city there could have been no abolition of the nobles' estates.'
IBID.

9 'If the Revolution has the right to destroy bridges and art monuments whenever necessary, it will stop still less from laying its hand on any tendency in art which, no matter how great its achievement in form, threatens to disintegrate the revolutionary environment or to arouse the internal forces of the Revolution, that is, the proletariat, the peasantry and the intelligentsia, to a hostile opposition to one another. Our standard is, clearly, political, imperative and intolerant.'
IBID., *Chapter 7*

10 'The party in the last instance is always right, because it is the single historic instrument which the working class possesses for the solution of its fundamental problems ... I know that one must not be right against the party. One can be right only with the party, and through the party, because history

has created no other road for the realisation of what is right.'
Speech to the Communist party congress, May 1924

1 'British pigeon-fanciers, by means of artificial selection, achieve special varieties, with a continually shortening beak. But there comes a moment when the beak of a new stock is so short that the poor creature is unequal to breaking the egg shell and the young pigeon perishes ... one can say that the political art of the British bourgeois consists in shortening the revolutionary beak of the proletariat, thereby not enabling him to pierce the shell of the capitalist state.'
WHERE IS BRITAIN GOING? *(1925)*

2 'Revolutions are as a rule not made arbitrarily. If it were possible to map out the revolutionary road beforehand and in a rational way, then it would probably also be possible to avoid the revolution altogether. Revolution is an expression of the impossibility of reconstructing class society by rational methods.'
WHERE IS BRITAIN GOING? *(1926). (This book, a reply to his British critics, has the same title as the preceding one, but is a separate publication.)*

3 'It is impossible to build a socialist paradise as an oasis amid the inferno of world capitalism.'
CRITIQUE OF THE PROGRAMME OF THE THIRD INTERNATIONAL *(1928)*

4 'The dictatorship of the proletariat which has risen to power as the leader of the democratic revolution is inevitably and very quickly confronted with tasks, the fulfilment of which is bound up with deep inroads into the rights of bourgeois property. The democratic revolution grows directly into the socialist revolution and thereby becomes a *permanent* revolution ... The completion of the socialist revolution within national limits is unthinkable ... The socialist revolution begins in the national arena, it unfolds in the international arena, and is completed in the world arena.'
THE PERMANENT REVOLUTION *(1930)*

5 'England is nothing but the last ward of the European madhouse, and quite possibly it will prove to be the ward for particularly violent cases.'
DIARY IN EXILE, *11 April 1935*

Truman, Harry S (1884–1972)
AMERICAN DEMOCRATIC POLITICIAN, PRESIDENT, 1945–1953

6 'This is the greatest thing in history.'
Remark on hearing that the atomic bomb had been dropped on Hiroshima, 6 August 1945. Quoted in A J P Taylor, ENGLISH HISTORY, 1914–1945, *Chapter 16*

7 'Every segment of our population, and every individual, has a right to expect from his government a Fair Deal.'
Speech to Congress, 6 September 1945

8 'I never did give anybody hell. I just told the truth and they thought it was hell.'
Interview on CBS television, February 1958

9 'The atom bomb was no "great decision" ... It was merely another powerful weapon in the arsenal of righteousness.'
Seminar at Columbia University, 28 April 1959. On the dropping of atomic bombs on Hiroshima and Nagasaki in 1945

10 'Wherever you have an efficient government you have a dictatorship.'
IBID.

11 'There is nothing new in the world except the history you do not know.'
In conversation with William Hillman. Quoted in Hillman, MR. PRESIDENT, *Part II, Chapter 1*

12 'A man who is not interested in politics is not doing his patriotic duty towards maintaining the constitution of the United States.'
IBID., *Part V, Chapter 1*

13 'When you get to be President, there are all those things, the honors, the twenty-one gun salutes, all those things. You have to remember it isn't for you. It's for the Presidency.'
In conversation with Merle Miller. Quoted in Miller, PLAIN SPEAKING: CONVERSATIONS WITH HARRY S TRUMAN, *Chapter 10*

U

Urban II (*c.* 1042–1099)
FRENCH PRELATE, POPE, 1088–1099

1   'Rid the sanctuary of God of the unbelievers, expel the thieves and lead back the faithful. Let no loyalty to kinsfolk hold you back; man's loyalty lies in the first place to God. No love of native heath should delay you, for in one sense the whole world is exile for a Christian, and in another the whole world is his country: so exile is our fatherland, our fatherland exile.'

Speech to the Council of Clermont, 1095. Exhorting the faithful to set forth on what turned out to be the first Crusade

Uvarov, Serge, Count (1786–1855)
RUSSIAN POLITICIAN, MINISTER OF EDUCATION TO NICHOLAS I

2   'Autocracy is the main condition of Russia's political existence.'
Quoted in M Cherniavsky, TSAR AND PEOPLE, *Chapter 5*

165

V

Valéry, Paul (1871–1945)
FRENCH POET

1 'If the state is strong, it crushes us. If it is
weak, we perish.'
Quoted in F Mauriac, DE GAULLE,
Chapter 2

Vanderbilt, William (1821–1885)
AMERICAN RAILROAD INDUSTRIALIST

2 'When I want to buy up any politician I
always find the anti-monopolists the most
purchasable – they don't come so high.'
Interview in the CHICAGO DAILY NEWS, *9
October 1882*

Vansittart, Robert, 1st Baron
(1881–1957)
ENGLISH DIPLOMAT AND CIVIL
SERVANT, PERMANENT
UNDERSECRETARY AT THE FOREIGN
OFFICE, 1930–1937

3 'Time is the very material commodity
which the Foreign Office is expected to
provide in the same way as other
departments provide *other* war material.'
Minute, 31 December 1936

Veblen, Thorstein (1857–1929)
AMERICAN SOCIAL SCIENTIST

4 'The leisure class stands at the head of
the social structure in point of
reputability; and its manner of life and
its standards of worth therefore afford the
norm of reputability for the community
... The basis on which good repute in
any highly organized industrial
community ultimately rests is pecuniary
strength; and the means of showing
pecuniary strength, and so of gaining or
retaining a good name, are leisure and a
conspicuous consumption of goods.'
THE THEORY OF THE LEISURE CLASS *(1899),
Chapter 4*

Vegetius (*fl*. 385)
ROMAN MILITARY STRATEGIST

5 'Let him who desires peace prepare for
war.' (*Qui desiderat pacem, praeparet
bellum.*)
Quoted in PLANUS V RENATUS *(1375)*
SEE ALSO *George Washington*

Vergniaud, Pierre (1753–1793)
FRENCH REVOLUTIONARY LEADER

6 'When justice has spoken, humanity
must have its turn.'
*Speech to the National Assembly, 17
January 1793. Arguing in favour of
executing King Louis XVI*

Verwoerd, Hendrik (1901–1966)
SOUTH AFRICAN NATIONAL
POLITICIAN, PRIME MINISTER, 1958–1966

7 'Present-day international politics prove
that the world is sick ... it is not up to
South Africa to allow herself to be
dragged into that sickbed ... The tragedy
of the present time is that in this crucial
stage of present-day history, the white
race is not playing the role which it is
called upon to play and which only the
white race is competent to fulfil ... Is
not our role to stand for the one thing
which means our own salvation here but
with which it will also be possible to
save the world, and with which Europe
will be able to save itself, namely the
preservation of the white man and his
state?'
*1964. Quoted in M Wilson and L
Thompson (ed.),* THE OXFORD HISTORY OF
SOUTH AFRICA, *Volume II, Chapter 10*

8 'It may be regrettable that the United
Nations no longer embodies the hopes of
mankind. Everyone must face the fact,
however, that since young, duck-tailed
nations practically took charge ... the
grand adventure of nations has become a
sordid scramble for the microphone – the
new toy of the exhibitionist and the
agitator.'
IBID.

Victor Emmanuel II (1820–1878)
KING OF ITALY, 1861–1878

9 'My only ambition is to be the first
soldier of Italian independence.'
Proclamation from Turin, 29 April 1859

Victoria (1819–1901)
QUEEN OF GREAT BRITAIN AND
IRELAND, 1837–1901

10 'Obedience to the laws and to the
Sovereign, is obedience to a higher
Power, divinely instituted for the good of

the *people*, not of the Sovereign, who has equally duties & obligations.'
In conversation with Lord John Russell, 6 August 1848

1 'Shake this in the masses & you shake the foundations of everything. An Empire without religion is like a house built upon sand.'
Letter to the Princess Royal, 17 June 1878

2 'He speaks to me as if I was a public meeting.'
Quoted in Lord John Russell, COLLECTIONS AND RECOLLECTIONS, *Chapter 14. Of Gladstone*

Voltaire, François Marie Arouet de (1694–1778)
FRENCH MAN OF LETTERS

3 'This body, which called itself and still calls itself the Holy Roman Empire, was neither Holy, nor Roman, nor an Empire.'
ESSAY ON MORALS AND THE CHARACTER OF NATIONS *(1756)*

4 'In this country [England] it is good to kill an admiral from time to time to encourage the others [*pour encourager les autres*].'
CANDIDE *(1759), Chapter 23. In supposed reference to the execution of Admiral* Byng *after his failure to relieve Minorca in 1756*

5 'Whatever you do, crush the infamous thing [*écrasez l'infâme*].'
Letter to Jean d'Alembert, 28 November 1762

6 'Don't you bless God to see the people of Calvin take the side of Jean-Jacques Rousseau? Let us not consider his person; let us consider his cause.'
Letter to E Damilaville, 23 August 1763. On the political quarrel provoked in Geneva by the publication of Rousseau's EMILE

7 'Whoever has power in his hands wants to be despotic; the craze for domination is an incurable disease.'
Letter to Damilaville, 16 October 1765

8 'Pure despotism is the punishment for men's bad conduct. If a community of men is subdued by an individual or by a few, that is obviously because it has neither the courage nor the ability to govern itself.'
REPUBLICAN IDEAS *(1765)*

9 'The number of wise men will always be small. It is true that it has increased; but that is nothing compared with the fools, and unfortunately it is said that God is always on the side of the big battalions.'
Letter to M le Riche, 6 February 1770
SEE ALSO *Bussy-Rabutin and Tacitus*

W

Wałesa, Lech (1943–)
POLISH TRADE UNION LEADER

1 'It depends on the way you measure the concept of good, bad, better, worse, because, if you choose the example of what we Polish have in our pockets and in our shops, then I answer that Communism has done very little for us. If you choose the example of what is in our souls, instead, I answer that Communism has done very much for us. In fact our souls contain exactly the contrary of what they wanted. They wanted us not to believe in God and our churches are full. They wanted us to be materialistic and incapable of sacrifices: we are anti-materialistic, capable of sacrifice. They wanted us to be afraid of the tanks, of the guns, and instead we don't fear them at all.'
Interview with Oriana Fallaci, THE SUNDAY TIMES, *22 March 1981. In answer to the question whether Communism had failed*

Wallace, George (1919–)
AMERICAN DEMOCRATIC POLITICIAN, GOVERNOR OF ALABAMA 1963-67, 1971-1979, 1983–

2 'Segregation now, segregation tomorrow and segregation forever!'
Inaugural address, January 1963

Wallace, Henry (1888–1965)
AMERICAN DEMOCRATIC POLITICIAN, VICE-PRESIDENT, 1941-1945

3 'The century on which we are entering can be and must be the century of the common man.'
Speech at New York, 8 May 1942

Waller, Sir William
(c. 1597–1668)
ENGLISH GENERAL

4 'Certainly my affections to you are so unchangeable, that hostility itself cannot violate my friendship to your person, but I must be true to the cause wherein I serve; the old limitation *usque ad aras* holds still, and where my conscience is interested, all other obligations are swallowed up ... The great God, which is the searcher of my heart, knows with what a sad sense I go upon this service, and with what a perfect hatred I detest this war without an enemy ... We are both upon the stage and must act these parts that are assigned us in this tragedy; let us do it in a way of honour, and without personal animosities, whatsoever the issue may be.'
Letter to Sir Ralph Hopton, June 1643. Explaining to Hopton, his comrade-in-arms in the German wars twenty years earlier, but now enlisted on the parliamentary side in the English civil war, why he would not meet him and why he would continue in his command in the royalist army

Walpole, Horace, 4th Earl of Orford (1717–1797)
ENGLISH MAN OF LETTERS AND POLITICIAN, MEMBER OF PARLIAMENT, 1741-1768

5 'Our party was more popular than fashionable; and in a very corrupt age fashion is very formidable.'
MEMOIRS OF THE REIGN OF KING GEORGE III, *Volume II, Chapter 1*

6 'A country will never be saved by the best men in it. Ours has been rescued by two of the worst – Lord Temple and Wilkes.'
IBID.

7 'It must not be supposed that I would pass off these trifling anecdotes of myself and others for a history of England. But they contain that most useful part of all history, a picture of human minds. They show how little men are, though riding at what is called *the Top of the World*. These ... were what filled me with disgust, and made me quit that splendid theatre of pitiful passions.'
IBID. *Of his retirement from the House of Commons*

8 'It is the kindest way of ruling men to govern them as they will be governed, not as they ought to be governed ... and to *reconcile* is perhaps a more amiable virtue in a patriot than to reform.'
IBID., *Chapter 3*

9 'Authority never measures liberty downwards.'
IBID., *Volume III, Chapter 2*

Walpole, Sir Robert, 1st Earl of Orford (1676–1745)
ENGLISH WHIG POLITICIAN, FIRST LORD OF THE TREASURY, 1721–1742

1 'They may ring their bells now; before long they will be wringing their hands.'
House of Commons, 19 October 1739. On the public celebration of the outbreak of war against Spain

2 'A patriot, sir! Why, patriots spring up like mushrooms! I could raise fifty of them within the four and twenty hours. I have raised many of them in one night. It is but refusing to grant an unreasonable or an insolent demand, and up starts a patriot.'
House of Commons, 13 February 1741

3 'We were not in honour obliged to take any share in the war which the Emperor brought upon himself in the year 1733, nor were we in interest obliged to take a share in that war as long as neither side attempted to push its conquests farther than was consistent with the balance of power in Europe, which was a case that did not happen.'
House of Commons, 13 February 1741

4 'As long as the old firm was Townshend and Walpole, the utmost harmony prevailed; but it no sooner became Walpole and Townshend than things went wrong.'
Quoted in J Morley, WALPOLE, Chapter 5

5 'I advise my young men never to use *always*.'
IBID., *Chapter 6*

6 'All these men have their price.'
IBID. *Referring to certain members among the 'patriot' opposition*

7 'This dance will no further go.'
IBID., *Chapter 8. On the decision to abandon the excise tax, 1733*

Walwyn, William (b.c. 1600)
ENGLISH LEVELLER PAMPHLETEER

8 'To be short, all the quarrel we have at this day in the Kingdome, is no other than a quarrel of Interests, and Partyes, a pulling down of one Tyrant, to set up another, and, instead of Liberty, heaping upon our selves a greater slavery than that we fought against.'
THE BLOODY PROJECT *(1648)*

9 'They have voted that the Kingdom shall be governed by King, Lords and Commons; which is a riddle that no man understands; for who knoweth what appertains to the King, what to the Lords, or what to the House of Commons? It is all out as uncertain as at first; and if the trumpet gives an uncertain sound, who shall prepare himself for the battel?'
IBID.

10 'You must note that you are a free people, and are not to be pressed or enforced to serve in Wars like horses and bruit beasts, but are to use the understanding God hath given you, in judging of the Cause ... for it is not enough to fight by lawful authority, but you must be sure to fight for what is just.'
IBID.

Waryński, Ludwik (1856–1889)
POLISH SOCIALIST POLITICIAN

11 'There is only one nation more unfortunate than the Polish nation; and that is the nation of proletarians.'
Quoted in J P Nettl, ROSA LUXEMBURG, Volume I, Chapter 2

Washington, George (1732–1799)
AMERICAN GENERAL AND POLITICIAN, PRESIDENT, 1789–1797

12 'The primary cause of all our disorders lies in the different State Governments, and in the tenacity of that power which pervades the whole of their system ... incompatibility in the laws of different States, and disrespect to those of the general government must render the situation of this great Country weak, inefficient and disgraceful.'
Letter to David Stuart, 1 July 1787

13 'To be prepared for war is one of the most effectual means of preserving peace.'
Speech to Congress, 8 January, 1790
SEE ALSO *Vegetius*

14 'There can be no greater error than to expect, or calculate upon, real favors from nation to nation.'
Farewell address to the people of the United States, 17 September 1796

15 'Europe has a set of primary interests, which to us have none, or a very remote relation. Hence she must be engaged in

frequent controversies, the causes of which are essentially foreign to our concerns. Hence, therefore, it must be unwise in us to implicate ourselves, by artificial ties in the ordinary vicissitudes of her politics, or the ordinary combinations and collisions of her friendships or enmities . . . 'Tis our true policy to steer clear of permanent alliances with any portion of the foreign world.'
IBID.

1 'The very idea of the power and the right of the people to establish government presupposes the duty of every individual to obey the established government. All obstructions to the execution of the laws, all combinations and associations, under whatever plausible character, with the real design to direct, control, counteract or awe the regular deliberation and action of the constituted authorities, are destructive of this fundamental principle, and of fatal tendency. They serve to organize faction . . . to put in the place of the delegated will of the nation the will of a party.'
IBID. *Against organised political parties*

Webb, Beatrice (1858–1943)
ENGLISH FABIAN SOCIALIST

2 'The Germans are shockingly bad politicians: they do not understand how to get their own way without raising opposition: they apply to the whole world the bad manners and intolerable insolence which we English show only to little or weak races on the borders of our great Empire, when no one is looking.'
Diary, 28 August 1914

3 'The Trade Union Movement has become, like the hereditary peerage, an avenue to political power through which stupid untrained persons may pass up to the highest office if only they have secured the suffrages of the members of a large union. One wonders when able rascals will discover this open door to remunerative power.'
Diary, 7 June 1917. On the appointment of George Barnes, former general secretary of the Amalgamated Society of Engineers and minister of pensions since 1916, to the war cabinet

4 'Hot-air propaganda in mean streets and industrial slums with chill moderation on the Treasury Bench and courtly phrases at Society functions may be the last word in political efficiency; but it is unsavoury, and leads, among the rank and file, to deep discouragement.'
Diary, 15 March 1924. On the first Labour government

5 'Are all Cabinets congeries of little autocrats with a super-autocrat presiding over them?'
Diary, 7 April 1924. On Ramsay MacDonald's first cabinet

6 'Permeation of one British class or party, by another, still holds the field. *The middle man governs*, however *extreme* may seem to be the men who sit on the Front Bench, in their reactionary or revolutionary opinions.'
Diary, 10 November 1925

Webb, Sidney (Baron Passfield) (1859–1947)
ENGLISH FABIAN SOCIALIST

7 'It is impossible that all persons can be equally moralised: therefore the laws and institutions must be altered so as to prevent the unmoral people any longer preying unwittingly on the world. This is why we work for Socialism.'
Letter to Jane Burdon-Sanderson, 25 November 1887

8 'Elections and parties are quite subordinate – *even trivial* – parts of political action. More is done in England in politics whilst ignoring elections and parties than by or with them.'
Letter to H G Wells, 15 June 1907

9 'First let me insist on what our opponents habitually ignore, and indeed what they seem intellectually incapable of understanding, namely the inevitable gradualness of our scheme of change.'
Presidential address to the Labour party conference, 26 June 1925

Weber, Max (1864–1920)
GERMAN SOCIOLOGIST AND POLITICAL ECONOMIST

10 'Only he has the calling for politics who is sure that he will not crumble when the world from his point of view is too stupid or base for what he wants to offer. Only he who in the face of all this can say "In spite of all!" has the calling for politics.'
POLITICS AS VOCATION *(1918)*

1 'Only those characters are fitted for political leadership who have been selected in the political struggle, since all politics is in its essence "struggle" [*Kampf*]. The much abused "work of the demagogue" provides this training on average better than the administrator's office.'
Quoted in D Beetham, MAX WEBER AND THE THEORY OF MODERN POLITICS, *Chapter 4*

2 'In democracy the people elect a leader in whom they have confidence. Then the elected leader says: "Now shut up and obey me." People and parties may no longer meddle in what he does.'
In conversation with General Ludendorff. IBID., *Chapter 8*

Webster, Daniel (1782-1852)
AMERICAN POLITICIAN, SENATOR, 1827-1841 AND 1845-1850, SECRETARY OF STATE, 1841-1843

3 'While the Union lasts we have high, exciting, gratifying prospects spread out before us, for us and our children. Beyond that I seek not to penetrate the veil. God grant that in my day at least that curtain may not rise! God grant that on my vision never may be opened what lies behind! When my eyes shall be turned to behold for the last time the sun in heaven, may I not see him shining on the broken and dishonoured fragments of a once glorious Union; on States dissevered, discordant, belligerent; on a land rent with civil feuds, or drenched, it may be, in fraternal blood! Let their last feeble and lingering glance rather behold the gorgeous ensign of the republic, now known and honored throughout the earth, still full high advanced, its arms and trophies streaming in their original lustre, not a stripe erased or polluted, not a single star obscured, bearing for its motto no such miserable interrogatory as "What is all this worth?" nor those other words of delusion and folly, "Liberty first and Union afterwards"; but everywhere, spread all over in characters of living light, blazing on its ample folds, as they float over the sea and over the land, and in every wind under the whole heaven, that other sentiment, dear to every true American heart – Liberty *and* Union, now and forever, one and inseparable.'
Speech to the Senate, 26 January 1830

4 'It is, Sir, the people's Constitution, the people's government, made for the people, made by the people, and answerable to the people.'
IBID.

5 'I was born an American; I live an American; I shall die an American.'
Speech to the Senate, 17 July 1850

Weighell, Sidney (1920-   )
ENGLISH TRADE UNIONIST, GENERAL SECRETARY OF THE NATIONAL UNION OF RAILWAYMEN, 1975-1982

6 'If you want it to go out . . . that you now believe in the philosophy of the pig trough – those with the biggest snouts get the largest share – I reject it.'
Speech to the Labour party annual conference, 6 October 1978

7 'I don't see how we can talk with Mrs Thatcher . . . I will say to the lads, come on, get your snouts in the trough.'
Speech at London, 10 April 1979

Wellington, 1st Duke of (Arthur Wellesley) (1769-1852)
BRITISH GENERAL AND TORY POLITICIAN, PRIME MINISTER, 1828-1830

8 'Nothing except a battle lost can be half so melancholy as a battle won.'
Despatch from the field of Waterloo, June 1815

9 'It has been a damned serious business. Blücher and I have lost 30,000 men. It has been a damned nice thing – the nearest run thing you ever saw in your life.'
In conversation with Thomas Creevey, 18 June 1815. On the battle of Waterloo

10 'Oh! he is a very good bridge for the rats to cross over.'
Remark quoted in Lord Holland's diary, 8 March 1828. On bringing William Huskisson into his cabinet

11 'I am fully convinced that the country possesses at the present moment a legislature which answers all the good purposes of legislation, and this to a greater degree than any legislature ever has answered in any country whatever. I will go further and say that the legislature and the system of

representation possess the full and entire confidence of the country.'
House of Lords, 2 November 1830.
Declaring himself and his government opposed to all parliamentary reform

1 'I always had a horror of revolutionising any country for a political object. I always said, if they rise of themselves, well and good, but do not stir them up – it is a fearful responsibility.'
In conversation with Lord Mahon, 2 November 1831

2 'All that I hope for is, that the change in the position of the country may be gradual, that it may be effected without civil war, and may occasion as little sudden destruction of individual interests and property as possible. We may all by degrees take out respective stations in the new order of things, and go on until further changes take place *ad infinitum*.'
Letter to J W Croker, 26 October 1836

3 'I have invariably objected to all violent and extreme measures, which is not exactly the mode of acquiring influence in a political party in England, particularly one in opposition to Government.'
Letter to Lord Stanley, 1846

4 'Say what you have to say, don't quote Latin, and sit down.'
Quoted in Macaulay's diary, 15 May 1851. Advice to Sir George Murray on how to speak in the House of Commons

Wilberforce, William
(1759–1833)
ENGLISH REFORMER, TORY POLITICIAN, MEMBER OF PARLIAMENT, 1780–1825

5 'God Almighty has placed before me two great objects, the suppression of the slave trade, and the reformation of manners.'
Diary, Sunday, 1787

Wilde, Oscar (1856–1900)
IRISH WRITER

6 'As long as war is regarded as wicked, it will always have its fascination. When it is looked upon as vulgar, it will cease to be popular.'
THE CRITIC AS ARTIST *(1891), 'Intentions'*

7 'It is immoral to use private property in order to alleviate the horrible evils that result from the institution of private property. It is both immoral and unfair.'
FORTNIGHTLY REVIEW, *February 1891, 'The Soul of Man Under Socialism'*

8 'If property had simply pleasures, we could stand it; but its duties make it unbearable. In the interest of the rich we must get rid of it.'
IBID.

9 'Misery and poverty are so absolutely degrading, and exercise such a paralysing effect over the nature of men, that no class is ever really conscious of its own suffering. They have to be told of it by other people, and they often entirely disbelieve them. What is said by great employers of labour against agitators is unquestionably true. Agitators are a set of interfering, meddling people, who come down to some perfectly contented class of the community, and sow the seeds of discontent amongst them. That is the reason why agitators are so absolutely necessary.'
IBID.

10 'The recognition of private property has really harmed Individualism, and obscured it, by confusing a man with what he possesses.'
IBID.

11 '*All modes of government are failures* ... High hopes were once formed of democracy; but democracy means simply the bludgeoning of the people by the people for the people.'
IBID.

12 'In old days men had the rack. Now they have the press.'
IBID.

13 'There are three kinds of despots. There is the despot who tyrannizes over the body. There is the despot who tyrannizes over the soul. There is the despot who tyrannizes over soul and body alike. The first is called the Prince. The second is called the Pope. The third is called the People.'
IBID.

Wilhelm II (1859–1941)
GERMAN EMPEROR, 1888–1918

14 'We have fought for our place in the sun and won it. Our future is on the water.'
Speech at Elbe, June 1901

1 'The Tsar is not treacherous, but he is weak. Weakness is not treachery, but it fulfils all its functions.'
Marginal note written on a despatch from the German ambassador to Russia, 16 March 1907

William III (1650-1702)
DUTCH STADTHOLDER AND KING OF GREAT BRITAIN AND IRELAND, 1689-1702

2 'There is one certain means by which I can be sure never to see my country's ruin: I shall die in the last ditch.'
In conversation with the Duke of Buckingham, 1672

Williams, Roger (*c.* 1603-1683)
ENGLISH PURITAN COLONIST, FOUNDER OF RHODE ISLAND

3 'The doctrine of persecution for cause of conscience is most evidently and lamentably contrary to the doctrine of Christ Jesus the Prince of Peace.'
THE BLOUDY TENANT OF PERSECUTION FOR CAUSE OF CONSCIENCE *(1644)*

Wilson, Charles (1890-1961)
AMERICAN MOTOR-CAR INDUSTRIALIST, SECRETARY OF DEFENCE, 1953-1957

4 'What's good for the country is good for General Motors, and what's good for General Motors is good for the country.'
Statement to US congressional committee, 1953

Wilson, Sir (James) Harold (Baron Wilson of Rievaulx) (1916-)
ENGLISH LABOUR POLITICIAN, PRIME MINISTER, 1964-1970 AND 1974-1976

5 'No one should be in a political party unless he believes that party represents his own highest religious and moral ideas.'
DAILY MAIL, *21 June 1948*

6 'And all these financiers, all the little gnomes of Zurich and the other financial centres about whom we keep on hearing, started to make their dispositions in regard to sterling.'
House of Commons, 12 November 1956

7 'You must understand that I am running a Bolshevik Revolution with a Tsarist Shadow Cabinet.'
In conversation with Richard Crossman, Barbara Castle and others, 12 March 1963

8 'We are re-defining and we are re-stating our socialism in terms of the scientific revolution ... The Britain that is going to be forged in the white heat of this revolution will be no place for restrictive practices or out-dated methods on either side of industry.'
Speech to the Labour party annual conference, 1 October 1963

9 'The Labour Party is a moral crusade or it is nothing.'
Speech at Rothesay, 5 September 1964

10 'Smethwick Conservatives can have the satisfaction of having topped the poll, of having sent a Member who, until another election returns him to oblivion, will serve his time here as a Parliamentary leper.'
House of Commons, 4 November 1964. Of Peter Griffiths who, in an allegedly racialist campaign, had defeated Patrick Gordon Walker at Smethwick at the 1964 general election

11 'We are a world power, and a world influence, or we are nothing.'
Speech at the Lord Mayor's Banquet, London, 16 November 1964

12 'I'm not a Kennedy, I'm a Johnson. I fly by the seat of my pants.'
1964. Quoted in D Butler and A King, THE BRITISH GENERAL ELECTION OF 1964, *Chapter 4*

13 'A prime minister governs by curiosity and range of interest.'
OBSERVER *magazine, 24 October 1965*

14 'I hope no one is going to bring sterling into this election ... sterling should be above politics.'
Interview on BBC television, 10 March 1966

15 'Every dog is allowed one bite, but a different view is taken of a dog that goes on biting all the time ... He .nay not get his licence renewed when it falls due.'
Speech to the Labour parliamentary party, 2 March 1967. On backbench revolts, after 42 Labour members of parliament had abstained on the government's defence white paper

1 'From now on the pound abroad is worth fourteen per cent or so less in terms of other currencies. It does not mean, of course, that the pound here in Britain, in your pocket or purse, or in your bank, has been devalued.'
Speech on BBC television, 20 November 1967. On his government's devaluation of the pound

2 'Selsdon Man is designing a system of society for the ruthless and the pushing, the uncaring ... His message to the rest is: you're out on your own.'
Speech at London, 21 February 1970. On the meeting of the Conservative policy-making committee at Selsdon Park, Croydon, 1970

3 'I have no wish to lead a party of political Zombies.'
Speech at the Labour party annual conference, 30 September 1975. On the 'extreme left' section of the party

Wilson, John (1785–1854)
SCOTTISH PROFESSOR OF MORAL PHILOSOPHY AND AUTHOR

4 [There is not] 'a more abstemious man than old Kit North in his Majesty's dominions, on which the sun never sets.'
BLACKWOOD'S EDINBURGH MAGAZINE, *April, 1829, 'Noctes Ambrosianae'. Christopher North was John Wilson's pseudonym.*
SEE ALSO *Napoleon I*

Wilson, (Thomas) Woodrow (1856–1924)
AMERICAN DEMOCRATIC POLITICIAN, PRESIDENT, 1913–1921

5 'Liberty has never come from the government. Liberty has always come from the subjects of the government. The history of liberty is a history of resistance. The history of liberty is a history of the limitation of governmental power, not the increase of it.'
Speech at New York, 9 September 1912

6 'It is harder for a leader to be born in a palace than to be born in a cabin.'
Speech at Denver, 7 October 1912

7 'The world must be made safe for democracy.'
Address to Congress, 2 April 1917. Defending the decision to enter the First World War

8 'Self-determination is not a mere phrase. It is an imperative principle of action, which statesmen will henceforth ignore at their peril.'
Address to Congress, 11 February 1918

9 'There can be but one issue. The settlement must be final. There can be no compromise. No halfway decision is conceivable. These are the ends for which the associated peoples of the world are fighting and which must be conceded by them before there can be peace:
1. The destruction of every arbitrary power anywhere that can separately, secretly, and of its single choice disturb the peace of the world ...
2. The settlement of every question, whether of territory, of sovereignty, or economic arrangement, or of political relationship, upon the basis of the free acceptance of that settlement by the people immediately concerned ...
3. The consent of all nations to be governed in their conduct towards each other by the same principles of honour and of respect for the common law of civilized society that govern the individual citizens of all modern states in their relations with one another ...
4. The establishment of an organization of peace which shall make it certain that the combined power of free nations will check every invasion of right and serve to make peace and justice the more secure by affording a definite tribunal of opinion to which all must submit and by which every international readjustment that cannot be amicably agreed upon by the peoples directly concerned shall be sanctioned.'
The 'Four Ends', 4 July 1918. Of the ends of the First World War

10 'Sometimes people call me an idealist. Well, that is the way I know I am an American. America is the only idealistic nation in the world.'
Speech at Sioux Falls, North Dakota, 8 September 1919. Speaking in favour of the treaty of Versailles, not yet ratified by the Senate

11 'There are a great many hyphens left in America. For my part, I think the most un-American thing in the world is a hyphen.'
Speech at St Paul, Minnesota, 9 September 1919. Of double-barrelled names

1 'Tolerance is an admirable intellectual gift; but it is of little worth in politics. Politics is a war of *causes*; a joust of principles. Government is too serious a matter to admit of meaningless courtesies.'
Quoted in R Hofstadter, THE AMERICAN POLITICAL TRADITION, *'Woodrow Wilson: the Conservative as Liberal'*

Wollstonecraft, Mary
(1759–1797)
ENGLISH FEMINIST

2 'If the abstract rights of man will bear discussion and explanation, those of woman, by a parity of reasoning, will not shrink from the same test: though a different opinion prevails in this country.'
A VINDICATION OF THE RIGHTS OF WOMAN *(1792), 'Dedication'*

3 'When man, governed by reasonable laws, enjoys his natural freedom, let him despise woman, if she do not share it with him.'
IBID., *Chapter 3*

Wordsworth, William
(1770–1850)
ENGLISH POET

4 'Bliss was it in that dawn to be alive, But to be young was very heaven!'
THE PRELUDE, *Book XI. (*THE PRELUDE *was completed in 1805, but was not published until after Wordsworth's death.) Wordsworth is referring to the French Revolution*

Wotton, Sir Henry (1568–1639)
ENGLISH POET AND DIPLOMAT

5 'An ambassador is an honest man sent to lie abroad for the good of his country.'
Epigram entered in Christopher Fleckamore's Album (1604)

Y

Yeats, (W)illiam (B)utler
(1865–1939)
IRISH POET AND PLAYWRIGHT

1 'Moses was little good to his people until
he had killed an Egyptian; and for the
most part a writer or public man of the
upper classes is useless to this country
[Ireland] till he has done something that
separates him from his class.'
SAMHAIN, *October 1901*

2 'MacDonagh and MacBride
And Connolly and Pearse
Now and in time to be,
Wherever green is worn,
Are changed, changed utterly:
A terrible beauty is born.'
EASTER 1916 *(1916)*

3 ' "But where can we draw water,"
Said Pearse to Connolly,
"When all the wells are parched away?
O plain as plain can be
There's nothing but our own red blood
Can make a right Rose Tree." '
THE ROSE TREE *(1921)*

4 'The ghost of Roger Casement
Is beating on the door.'
THE GHOST OF ROGER CASEMENT *(c. 1936)*

Yoffe, Adolf *(d. 1927)*
SOVIET COMMUNIST POLITICIAN AND
DIPLOMAT

5 'All my life I have been convinced that
the revolutionary politician should know
when to make his exit and that he
should make it in time . . .when he
becomes aware that he can no longer be
useful to the cause he has served. It is
more than thirty years since I embraced
the view that human life has sense only
in so far as it is spent in the service of
the infinite – and for us mankind is the
infinite. To work for any finite
purpose – and everything else is finite – is
meaningless. Even if mankind's life were
to come to a close this would in any case
happen at a time so remote that we may
consider humanity as the absolute
infinite. If one believes, as I do, in
progress, one may assume that when the
time comes for our planet to vanish,
mankind will long before that have
found the means to migrate and settle on
other younger planets . . . Thus anything
accomplished in our time for mankind's
benefit will in some way survive into
future ages; and through this our
existence acquires the only significance it
can possess.'
*Suicide note to Trotsky, 16 November
1927*

Z

Zamojski, Jan (1542–1605)
POLISH GENERAL AND STATESMAN

1 'Reign, but do not govern!' (*Rege, sed non impera!*)
Speech to the Polish Diet, 1605. Advice to King Sigismund III
SEE ALSO *Thiers*

Zangwill, Israel (1864–1926)
ENGLISH WRITER

2 'America is God's Crucible, the great Melting-Pot where all the races of Europe are melting and re-forming!'
THE MELTING POT *(1920), Act 1*

Zinoviev, Alexander (1922–)
SOVIET PHILOSOPHER

3 'They were right. The Soviet regime is not the embodiment of evil as you think in the West. They have laws and I broke them. I hate tea and they love tea. Who is wrong?'
Interview in THE SUNDAY TIMES, *3 May 1981. On his forced exile from the Soviet Union*

Guide to the Indexes

The first and largest index is a 'key-word' index, in which readers may look up a quotation under what might be considered its 'key-word' (or 'key-words'). The numerals refer to the page on which a quotation appears and the number of the quotation on that page. Thus 133.6 refers to quotation 6 on page 133.

There are, however, cases in which a quotation may be about some concept, institution or person, but that concept, etc. is not specifically mentioned in the quotation. The supplementary index, which follows the 'key-word' index, covers such cases. A reader looking for quotations about democracy, for example, should first refer to the 'key-word' index where 29 quotations in which the word 'democracy' appears are indexed, and then turn to the supplementary index where a further 25 quotations are indexed in which the idea of democracy is referred to. Similarly, persons who are referred to in a quotation, but not mentioned by name, are indexed in the supplementary index.

Key-word Index

ABSTINENCE
Total a. and a good filing system, 43.15

ACTION
a body in a. must overcome an equal body at rest, 3.10
An ounce of a. is worth a ton of theory, 54.8
men of a. are active just because they are stupid, 49.15
my instinct is always towards a., 113.10
one of the half-dozen great men of a. of this century, 5.10

ACTIONS
my a. are my ministers, 33.6

ADMINISTER
To a. is to govern, 116.4

ADMINISTER'D
Whate'er is best a. is best, 133.6

ADMINISTERED
A state may prosper . . . provided it is well a., 146.9

ADMINISTERS
He who a. governs 4.9

ADMINISTRATION
to have it said of my second A. that in it these forces met their master, 140.14

ADMINISTRATIVE
a. ability is the principal ability needed in politics, 146.11

ADVENTURISM
a. is infantile, 121.9

ADVERTISING
Give me the writing of a nation's a. and propaganda, 105.4

ADVISE
neither a. nor submit to arbitrary measures, 22.11

AFRAID
What have I to be a. of?, 96.5

AFRICA
'Scram from A.', 112.5
to sacrifice A. on the altar of neo-colonialism, 123.5

AGITATION
A. is . . . endowed in this country, 147.6
Nothing is so dull as political a., 64.4

AGITATORS
A. are a set of interfering, meddling people, 172.9

ALICE
we rather resemble A. in Wonderland, 11.7

ALL
What touches a. shall be approved by a., 52.3

ALLIANCE
For 'A.' read 'England', 28.10
The cornerstone of my policy has always been the English a., 159.11

ALLIANCES
our true policy to steer clear of permanent a., 169.15
Peace . . . with all nations, entangling a. with none, 85.6
Where promises are not observed, there can be no a., 80.4

ALWAYS
I advise my young men never to use *a.*, 169.5

AMBASSADOR
An a. is an honest man sent to lie abroad, 175.5

AMBITION
A. often puts Men upon doing the meanest offices, 156.8
Great a., . . . is an unruly tyrant, 70.7

AMERICA
A. if she attains to greatness, must *creep* to it, 70.6
A. is the land of opportunity, 44.10
A. is the only idealistic nation in the world, 174.10
A.'s present need is not heroics, but healing, 72.4
I rejoice that A. has resisted, 131.5
If violence is wrong in A., violence is wrong abroad, 107.2
the Flame of Liberty in North A. shall not be extinguished, 58.3
the loud democracy of A., 102.5
to be elected a vestryman by . . . any parish in A., 85.2

AMERICAN
I am not a Virginian, but an A., 75.2
I want every A. free to stand up for his rights, 88.10
I was born an A.; I live an A.; I shall die an A., 171.5
Let the Thirteen States . . . concur in erecting one great A. system, 70.10
today, I disown the A. flag, 62.5
The communist bogey is an A. stunt, 107.9
the strip poker of A. politics, 44.8
We are not about to send A. boys . . to do what Asian boys ought to be doing, 85.17

AMERICANISM
false patriotism and bad A., 79.11
McCarthyism is A. with its sleeved rolled, 104.7

AMERICANS
for A. it [utopia] is just beyond the horizon, 90.12
the torch has been passed to a new generation of A., 88.11
We A. have no commission from God to police the world, 72.9

AMUSING
it is very important to know what it [a regime] finds a., 162.4

ANARCHISM
A. is the only philosophy which brings to man the consciousness of himself, 66.6

ANARCHY
A. is always the stepping-stone to absolute power, 120.7
Outside of a., there is no such thing as revolution, 92.3
Society seeks order in a., 136.2
society, threatened by a., and plunder, will clutch the blade, 93.7

ANCHOR
your constitution is all sail and no a., 104.6

ANNIHILATING
a short way of . . . a. peoples and nations, 116.12

ANTAGONISM
by a. I mean . . . the *unsocial sociability* of men, 87.1
this a. becomes . . . the cause of a law-governed social order, 87.1

ANTI-CAPITALIST
If a democratic people comes under the sway of an a.-c. creed, 73.2

ANTI-MONOPOLISTS
I always find the a.-m. the most purchasable, 166.2

ANTI-SEMITIC
of all the bigotries . . . there is none so stupid as the a.-s., 99.12

ANTI-SEMITISM
A-s is the socialism of fools, 12.9

ANTI-SOCIALIST
they saw that the country stood in peril of a.-s. degeneration, 91.6

APPETITE
they who have more a. than dinners, 116.7

APPROPRIATION
a great a. clause, 48.5

ARAB
the call to A. nationalism, 137.14

ARBITRARY
I speak in defence of the Commonweal against their a. treason, 156.2

neither advise nor submit to a. measures, 22.11

ARISTOCRACIES
A. . . . consist . . . of barbaric conquerors or their descendants, 2.8

ARISTOCRACY
an a. is always cold, 120.13
An a. is like cheese, 99.5
a. is Consumption, 5.7
A. is really a . . . civilised form of cannibalism, 76.3
A true natural a. is not a separate interest in the state, 25.1
gigantic system of outdoor relief for the a., 22.2
The true policy of a government is to make use of a., 120.12
We cannot reckon upon the a., 64.5
when an a. is not thoroughly corrupted, its strength is incalculable, 5.6

ARISTOCRATICAL
the *a.* interest, 14.3

ARMAMENTS
a. are a function and not a cause of political tensions, 88.4
Diplomacy without a. is like music without instruments, 58.9

ARMS
I never would lay down my a. – never, never, never!, 131.10
where there are good a., good laws inevitably follow, 106.4

ARMY
I expect to hear nothing of politics from the A., 6.3

ARSENAL
We must be the great a. of democracy, 140.6

ART
society is . . . founded on the a.-lacking or unhappy labour, 117.7
the development of a. is the highest test of the vitality of each epoch, 163.4
we might . . . produce some prophets of a., but no vital a., 112.1

ASIA
the natives of A. . . . are wanting in spirit, 4.8

ASPIRIN
an a. to cure an appendicitis, 93.8

ASSASSIN
Never yet did the a.'s knife reach the core of a cause, 104.10

ASSASSINATED
you must be ready to be a., 120.23

ASSASSINATION
A. is the extreme form of censorship, 149.6

ASSASSINS
we consent to die if we become a., 143.2

ASSEMBLY
the same arbitrary power ... in the a. .... as in a monarch, 100.3

ASSIMILATED
incapable of being ... a., 161.1

AUSCHWITZ
over the gates of A. there stretched ... the inscription, 152.10

AUSTRIA
A. is ... the Catholic Turkey, 111.5
A. is the school of oppression, 38.1
Before A. was, we [Bohemia] were, 126.13
the artificial compound community called A. 91.5
when A. has worn that flannel next to her skin, 19.2

AUSTRIAN
If the A. empire had not long been in existence, 126.12
The A. government ... is a system of despotism tempered by casualness, 2.5

AUTHORITY
A. never measures liberty downwards, 168.9
To despise legitimate a. .... is unlawful, 96.2

AXIS
This Berlin-Rome connection is ... an a., 119.12

BBC
the B. must be for the Government in this crisis too, 139.8

BACHELORS
in five years there will be a crushing tax on b., 149.5

BALANCE
b. ....: leave that to Mother Goose, 14.4
'b. of power' ... always an argument for war, 21.9
maintain the b. of Europe, 30.3
push its conquests farther than was consistent with the b. of power in Europe, 169.3

BALLOT
The B. is stronger than the bullet, 96.10

BANNER
the red b. of economic equality, 9.14

BANQUETS
B. are not for soldiers, 143.4

BARBARIANS
B., Philistines, Populace, 4.12

BARBARISM
war ... carried on by methods of b., 27.9

BATTLE
Nothing ... half so melancholy as a b. won, 171.8

BAUBLE
What shall we do with this b.?, 43.12

BEACONSFIELDISM
The downfall of B., 64.6

BEAK
shortening the revolutionary b. of the proletariat, 164.1

BEAUTY
A terrible b. is born, 176.2

BEAVERBROOK
the voice of Churchill, but the mind was the mind of B., 6.13

BEES
for so work the honey-b., 148.13
No b. had better government, 107.10

BELIEF
One person with a b. is a social power, 115.5

BERLINER
I take pride in the words, 'Ich bin ein B.', 89.3

BILL
The B., the whole B., and nothing but the B., 22.9

BIRDS
since I see all the b. are flown, 33.2

BIRTH
Those who ... oppose b. control are ... incapable of arithmetic, 144.5

BISHOP
No B., no King, 84.3

BITE
Every dog is allowed one b., 173.15

BLACK
For the revolutionary b. youth ... time starts moving with ... Malcolm X, 37.7
four b. men ... each with a gun!, 37.6
I don't think of life in the same sense that ... b. men of your generation think of it, 83.6
so long as labour in a b. skin is branded, 110.3
the experience of millions of B. people in the United States, 122.1
You show me a b. man who isn't an extremist, 107.6

BLACKMAIL
B. has become respectable, 113.5

BLESSING
If this is a b., it is certainly *very* well disguised, 36.8

BLISS
B. was it in that dawn to be alive, 175.4

BLOOD
b., toil, tears and sweat, 35.12

crimes of this guilty land will never be purged away but with blood, 22.14

I did not come back ... to drench Paris in b., 120.9

It is b. which moves the wheels of history, 119.4

nothing but our own red b. can make a right Rose Tree, 176.3

BLOODSHED
man may come to finding enjoyment in b., 50.1

There are many things more horrible than b., 128.13

BLOODY
The civil sword shall and must be red and b., 101.8

BOHEMIA
B. in the hands of Russia, 19.10

BOLDNESS
B., once more b., and b. for ever, 45.4

BOLSHEVIK
A B. ... is nothing but a socialist who wants to do something about it, 149.7

BOLSHEVIKS
There were no b. there!, 62.8

BOLSHEVISM
At present I am very much against B., 21.6

BOMB
The atom b. was ... another powerful weapon in the arsenal of righteousness, 164.9

The enemy has begun to employ a new and most cruel b., 77.3

BONELESS
the B. Wonder sitting on the Treasury Bench, 35.5

BONKERS
If the British public falls for this ... it will be stark, raving b., 69.5

BOOKES
have a vigilant eye how B. demeane themselves, 115.10

BOOKIE
the popular image of a b. or a clergyman, 118.13

BOTTOMS
so we clap on Dutch b. just 20 per cent, 28.11

BOUNDARY
No man has the right to fix the b. of the march of a nation, 128.10

BOURGEOIS
A b. cannot be made into a worker, 27.11

socialist work in a b. democracy is impossible, 93.9

BOURGEOISIE
The b. ... is convulsed by horror at the desecration of brick and mortar, 110.15

BOWS
you will wage war with b. and arrows, 113.3

BRAINWASHINGS
Ten or a hundred b. are needed in the life of a man, 80.1

BRIBE
win without a B., 133.7

BRIDGE
goes with B., and Women and Champagne, 13.2

he is a very good b. for the rats to cross over, 171.10

BRINK
We walked to the b. and we looked it in the face, 51.3

BRITAIN
B. ... must undergo her day of sorrow, 126.6

for a scrap of paper, Great B. is going to make war, 15.4

Great B. has lost an Empire, 1.3

It does mean ... the end of B. as an independent European State, 60.4

the great flood of luxury ... is receding, and a new B. is appearing, 99.7

BRITANNIA
Rule B., rule the waves, 160.9

BRITISH
a B. subject ... shall feel confident that the strong arm of England will protect him, 127.8

the ... aim of the B. Constitution is to get twelve honest men into a box, 117.3

the B. ... able to put new wine into old bottles, 7.3

The B. People ... require grave statesmen, 49.8

the B. public in one of its periodical fits of morality, 103.4

BROKER
an honest b. who means to do business, 18.10

BROTHER
Big b. is watching you, 124.10

BROOD
the new b. should conform ... to the established constitution, 80.6

BRYAN
I brag and chant of B., B., B., B., 98.2

Prairie avenger, mountain lion, B., B., B., B., 98.3

BUDGET
political science consists essentially in being able to draw up a good b., 146.11

seated on an empty chest, fishing for a b.,
129.11

BUFF
The fight is on and I'm stripped to the b.,
141.11

BULLET
I am simply a b. fired by the Colne Valley
workers, 67.11

BUONAPARTE
If B. was a conqueror, 73.10

BURGLAR
a b. of others' intellect, 48.5

BURKE
saved her venom to create a B., 72.11

BUS
Hitler . . . missed the b., 31.7

BUSINESS
'B. as usual.', 35.3
No political party . . . which is not a friend of
American B., 85.13
politics is b., 154.13
The b. of America is b., 42.3
you have got to let b. make money out of it
[war], 155.12

BUTTER
B. merely makes us fat, 66.3
One cannot shoot with b., but with guns, 65.8

BUTTON
Give me a b. and I will make people . . . die
for it, 121.1

CABINET
A man in office, and out of the C., is a mere
slave, 104.3
Your c. was a sort of political Sorbonne, 71.3

CABINETS
Are all C. congeries of little autocrats, 170.5

CAESAR
Render therefore unto C., 17.11

CANADA
In C., badges, titles . . . will never take root,
94.7
we realise . . . that C. is at war also, 94.3

CANAL
WE are a c., not a dam, 3.3

CANOSSA
We shall not go to C., 18.8

CANT
The more c. there is in politics the better,
81.3

CANVASSING
the practice of c. . . . is the height of
absurdity, 103.5

CAPITAL
the condition for c. is wage labour, 110.5

c. comes dripping . . . with blood and dirt,
110.12

CAPITALISM
c. and . . . socialism are both capable of
working quite well, 60.5
C. carries within itself war, 84.7
c. . . . has transformed society into a sort of
circus, 137.13
c. is a necessary condition for political
freedom, 58.12
competitive c. . . . separates economic power
from political power, 58.13
impossible to build a socialist paradise . . .
amid the inferno of world c., 164.3
the unpleasant and unacceptable face of c.,
74.4

CAPITALIST
Economic progress, in c. society, means
turmoil, 148.5
great political want . . . is a c. conservatism,
8.9

CAPITALISTS
C. are no more capable of self-sacrifice, 95.9

CAR
We threw out some luggage, but we are still
travelling in the same c., 156.6

CASEMENT
The ghost of Roger C. is beating on the door,
176.4

CASH
C. payment the sole nexus, 29.7

CASTLE
A man's house is his c., 39.8

CASTLEREAGH
I met Murder on the way – He had a mask
like C., 150.7

CATS
c., that ever grow cursed with age, 33.1

CAUSE
Let us not consider his person; let us consider
his c., 167.6

CAVE
his political c. of Adullam, 22.4

CENTRALISATION
In France there is . . . only one thing that we
cannot destroy: c. 162.3

CENTURY
the c. of the common man, 168.3

CHAIN
No man can put a c. about the ankle of his
fellow man, 50.4

CHAINS
Man is born free, and everywhere he is in c.,
142.8
Shake your c. to earth like dew, 150.9

The proletarians have nothing to lose but
their c., 110.8

CHANCELLOR
a C. of the Exchequer ... fishing for a budget,
129.11
a C. of the Exchequer preaching against
extravagance, 71.8

CHANGE
All that I hope for is, that the c. ... may be
gradual, 172.2
as if a *Drunkard* in a *Dropsy* should c. his
Doctors, 69.10
If we wish a c. to be as radical as possible,
122.9
The wind of c. is blowing through the
continent, 105.9
To c. Foundations, cast the Frame anew, 50.7
When it is not necessary to c., 56.1

CHANGED
this country ... c. her political garments, but
not her heart, 158.13

CHANGES
All great c. are easily effected, when the time
is come, 114.16

CHANNEL
We must cross the C., but not the Atlantic,
160.7

CHARLATANS
Societies which are not enlightened by
philosophes are cheated by c., 40.15

CHARLES
By headless C. see heartless Henry lies, 26.1

CHEERS
So Two c. for Democracy, 57.3

CHEESE
a country that has two hundred and forty-six
kinds of c., 46.8

CHEQUE
I have not the temerity to give a political
blank c. to Lord Salisbury, 67.5
the right hon. Gentleman ... will give us a
blank c., 152.9

CHICKEN
Some c.! Some neck!, 36.3

CHILDREN
No longer shall our c. ... be brought up for
export, 46.15

CHILE
C. is going to feel like a football, 3.2

CHINA
we shall be obliged to strike another Blow in
C., 127.9

CHINESE
The C. Way is the way of mankind and
morals, 156.5

CHRIST
The way in which ... C. keeps aloof from
politics, 111.3
The world needs C. again, 137.3

CHRISTIAN
C. socialism ... a contradiction in terms,
132.5
C. socialism is but the holy water, 110.7
without the help of C. teaching the law will
fail, 46.17

CHRISTIANITY
C. ... the most formidable obstacles to the
emancipation of society, 9.7

CHURCH
A C. is ... the only pure democracy, 40.14
a national clerisy or c., is an essential element
of a rightly constituted nation, 40.11
a proletarian c. is impossible, 163.6
In this C. there are two swords, 20.6
that the external workshop of God in this C.
might be kept up in uniformity, 94.2
the route of the wine-shop or the c., 9.18
Whene'er he brings his *politics* to C., 25.10

CHURCHILL
the voice of C., but the mind ... of
Beaverbrook, 6.13

CIRCLE
It is some measure of the tightness of the
magic c., 105.5

CIRCUS
bread and the c. games, 86.14

CITY
The Revolution is ... a c. one, 163.8

CIVIL SERVICE
The blame is ... *not* on the C. S., 11.1

CIVILISATION
c. will die, 117.6
Slavery is the first step towards c., 76.5
the resources of c. against its enemies are not
yet exhausted, 64.7

CIVIS
The *C. Romanus* idea ... is historically an
anachronism, 71.6

CLARISSA
the people is C., 1.11

CLASS
A nation which has gradations of c. seems ...
more tolerant and pacific, 53.1
Anyone ... who speaks of c. in the context of
politics, 13.10
C. political consciousness can be brought ...
only from without, 95.3
Lord Salisbury constitutes ... the spokesman
of a c., 31.11
Marx's *Capital* ... brings about the c.-war
which it prophesies, 143.8

no c. is ever really conscious of its own
suffering, 172.9

Political power ... is ... the organised power
of one c. for oppressing another, 110.6

the history of society ... c. struggles, 110.3

the notion that c. is naturally hostile to c.,
96.4

those who want to fight the c. war, 11.4

useless ... till he has done something that
separates him from his c., 176.1

We, as middle-c. socialists, have got to have a
profound humility, 60.1

CLASSES

a trifling evil compared with the inequality of
c. 117.9

the sops that the owning c. throw to the other
c., 121.7

the three great c. into which our society is
divided [*Barbarians, Philistines, Populace*],
4.12

CLERGY

the c. ... are making themselves individually
guilty, 5.3

CLERISY

a national c., 40.12

CLEVERNESS

The people of this country ... do not like c.,
27.10

COALITION

Nothing is so demoralising ... as the
atmosphere of a c., 6.7

COALITIONS

England does not love c., 48.8

COLD

we are today in the midst of a c. war, 12.5

COLNE

I am simply a bullet fired by the C. Valley
workers, 67.11

COLONIAL

these c. deadweights which *we do not govern*,
48.15

COLONIALIST

Brother, sister, friend – these are the words
outlawed by the c. bourgeoisie, 56.2

COLONIES

C. do not cease to be c. because they are
independent, 48.12

She [England] ... must found c. as fast ... as
she is able, 143.5

the c. in general own little or nothing to any
care of ours, 24.5

These wretched c. ... a millstone round our
necks, 48.7

COLOR

Our constitution is c.-blind, 72.6

COLOUR

c. is the uniform, 134.4

COLUMN

Now is the stately c. broke, 148.7

The Fifth C., 116.9

COMMERCE

C. is the grand panacea, 39.4

C. is the greatest of all political interests, 32.3

the prostration of agriculture at the feet of c.,
75.4

the spirit of c. has a tendency to soften the
manners of men, 70.9

The very essence of competitive c. is waste,
117.8

We have arrived at the epoch of c., 41.8

COMMERCIALISM

C. is laying its greasy paw, 8.1

COMMON

Did something for the c. good, 107.11

'Each of us places his person and power in
c. ...', 142.10

He nothing c. did or mean, 109.8

I will govern according to the c. weal, 84.5

COMMONPLACE

the c. mind ... has the assurance to proclaim
the rights of the c., 124.2

COMMONS

a talking, corrupt and impudent set, whom
they call the House of C., 38.9

The c. ... remained in a wise and masterly
inactivity, 104.12

the House of C. ... an elaborate conspiracy,
16.4

The House of C. ... is a Palace of
Illogicalities, 22.13.

The House of C. lives in a state of potential
choice, 9.5

COMMONWEALTH

the Empire is a *C. of Nations*, 142.1

The principal mark of a c., 20.2

COMMUNISM

C. is exploitation of the strong by the weak,
136.1

C. is successful fascism, 153,5

C. is the logical consequence of Christianity,
27.12

C. is the necessary development of Socialism,
118.3

C. ... is the solution of the riddle of history,
109.10

c. is Tsarist autocracy turned upside down,
77.1

c.'s claim ... has ended by turning individual
human beings into sheep, 137.13

everything progresses towards C., 90.3

if we lose the war to C. in Asia the fall of Europe is inevitable, 103.1

May God preserve C., 92.1

The confrontation between a man . . . and C. is always over in two rounds, 153.2

The more C., the more civilization, 149.8

COMMUNIST

A C. has no right to be a mere onlooker, 89.7

A C. is no more a left wing member of the Labour Party, 38.5

Between capitalist and c. society lies the period of . . . transformation, 110.16

One cannot be a C. and preserve . . . one's personal integrity, 49.12

There will never . . . be a C. government, 10.4

What is a c.?, 53.3

COMMUNISTS

I would not be just if I did not send the C. to hell at last, 65.15

If ever I have trouble with the C., 13.4

We C. are like seeds, 109.4

COMPACT

this *original* C., whereby he and others incorporates into *one Society*, 100.8

COMPETITION

So long as the system of c. . . . goes on, 117.6

COMPLAIN

Never c. and never explain, 11.2

CONFLICT

the never-ending din of political c., 12.2

CONNECTIONS

In our Parliamentary government c. are absolutely necessary, 34.1

CONQUERED

I came, I saw, I c., 27.2

CONSCIENCE

C. has no more to do with gallantry than it has with politics, 150.13

I do not believe any nation ever entered into a great controversy with a clearer c., 91.1

I will not cut my c. to fit this year's fashions, 74.13

CONSCIOUSNESS

It is not the c. of men that determines their existence, 110.10

CONSCRIPTION

C. is repugnant to the British character, 94.4

CONSENT

·full-hearted c. of the parliament, 74.3

In the field of politics, force and c. are correlative terms, 42.8

no one can be . . . subjected to the Political Power of another, without his own *C.*, 100.7

CONSEQUENCES

to try to prevent it, and to damn the c., 115.9

CONSERVATIVE

A C. Government is an organised hypocrisy, 47.10

A c. is a man . . . who has never learned to walk forwards, 140.15

A C. is only a Tory who is ashamed of himself, 58.10

consistent with true C. policy to promote so much happiness, 129.15

the C. Party . . . have a grand sense of where the votes are, 134.7

the C. Party . . . is the party of non-politics, 3.11

The healthy stomach is . . . c., 25.8

the whole art of C. politics in the twentieth century, 16.2

When a nation's young men are c., 12.13

CONSERVATIVES

Men are . . . c. after dinner, 53.8

The C. . . . the stupidest party, 115.6

CONSERVATISM

c. . . . adherence to the old and tried, 97.3

C. goes for comfort, 53.7

C. is distrust of the people tempered by fear, 64.2

C. . . . is mainly due to want of imagination, 2.10

C. . . . makes no preparation for the future, 47.7

The great political want . . . is a capitalist c., 8.9

The principle of C. has always appeared to me to be . . . felo da se, 5.8

CONSIDERABLE

This is a c. event, 64.10

CONSTANTINOPLE

that C. in the hands of Russia would be a European danger, 18.12

The Russians shall not have C., 80.8

CONSTITUTION

fundamental principle of the English c., 19.11

Our c. is founded upon common sense, 33.10

Your c. is all sail and no anchor, 104.6

CONSTITUTIONAL

an honest observance of c. compacts, 83.2

CONSUL

C. . . . a person who having failed to secure an office, 17.13

CONSULTATION

the customary processes of c., 105.11

CONSUMERS

Nothing is so easy as to make c., 160.3

CONSUMPTION

leisure and conspicuous c. of goods, 166.4

CONTINENTAL

We always catch C. diseases, 11.11

CONTRACT
Society is indeed a c., 24.12
the fundamental problem to which the Social
C. gives the solution, 142.9
The Socialists would drag men back from c. to
status, 106.10
You have only to mention a social c., 113.7

COOK
This c. will give us nothing but spicy dishes,
95.13

CO-OPERATION
C. is power, 102.3
The instinctive appeal of every successful
political movement is . . . never to the need
for c., 143.7

CORAL
slower . . . than the insect which raises the c.
reef, 141.13

CORDIAL
the c. understanding (*entente cordiale*) . . .
between my government and hers, 100.4

COST
they go straight for it without counting the c.
to themselves, 93.11

COTTON
King C. . . . is riding on, 34.8

COUNTERVAILING
power to beget c. power, 60.6

COUNTRY
Ask not what your c. can do for you, 88.15
my soul to my God and my cause to my c.,
85.12
our c. right or wrong!, 46.2
The citizen who criticizes his c. is paying it
an implied tribute, 59.8
The love of c. is the first virtue, 120.6
Who saves his c. violates no law, 120.11

COWBOY
that damned c., 71.2

CREEPING
climbing is performed in the same position
with c., 156.8

CRIMES
His c. are the only great things about him,
151.1

CROCODILE
Like Sidmouth, next, Hypocrisy On a c. rode
by, 150.8

CROWN
for the first time the C. would have an
Opposition returned, 112.11
The C. is . . . the 'fountain of honour', 8.12
The c. signifies a nominal office of a million
sterling a year, 126.11

The influence of the C. . . . ought to be
diminished, 51.4
upon the brow of labour this c. of thorns, 23.2

CROWNED
There is not a single c. head in Europe, 85.2

CRUCIBLE
America is God's C., 177.2

CRUEL
rather be c. than counted cold, 33.5

CUBA
I say that the United States is ninety miles
from C., 30.10

CULT
the c. of the individual, 89.8, 89.9

CULTURE
a c. which is above classes, 163.5
C. and State . . . are antagonists, 122.15
There would be no c. without kitchen maids,
162.8

CUNNING
c. men do pass for wise, 8.2

CURRENCY
no surer means of overturning the existing
basis of society than to debauch the c., 89.5

CUSS
the rest . . . do not matter a tinker's c., 151.5

DANCE
This d. will no further go, 169.7

DEAD
I am d. . . . but in the Elysian fields, 49.4
standing between the d. and the living, 42.7
unless we would be governed by them after
they are d., 73.6

DEAL
every individual, has a right to expect . . . a
Fair D., 164.7
good enough to be given a square d.
afterwards, 141.7
I pledge . . . myself, to a new d. for the
American people, 140.11

DEATH
d. . . . the only fact we have, 10.3
nothing can be said to be certain, except d.
and taxes, 58.6
The angel of d. has been abroad throughout
the land, 22.1

DEBATES
he fights d. like a war and a war like a debate,
15.7

DEBATING
What makes a man minister? D. power, 72.10

DEBT
a national d. . . . is calculated to raise . . . a
moneyed aristocracy, 83.1

A national d. . . . will be to us a national
blessing, 70.2
'a public d. as a public blessing.', 38.8
DEED
the foulest and most atrocious d., 131.13
DEFENCE
the huge industrial and military machinery of
d., 52.8
DEGREE
Take but d. away . . . And hark what discord
follows!, 149.2
DELUGE
After us the d.!, 133.3
DEMAGOGUE
D. . . . A political opponent, 17.14
DEMOCRACIES
In D. there is a . . . disposition to make
publick opinion stronger than the law, 42.4
This is ordained for d., 3.7
DEMOCRACY
A d. . . . becomes easy prey for the demagogue
and the charlatan, 59.3
A d. . . . oppressive for the conscientious and
licentious for the rest, 52.9
All the ills of d. can be cured by more d.,
152.2
Conservatives do not worship d., 63.5
D. and tyranny . . . may be the Cholera, 5.7
D. . . . goes with Bridge, and Women and
Champagne, 13.2
D. has arrived at a gallop, 10.6
D. is a political *method* . . . incapable of being
an end in itself, 148.6
D. is . . . a self-cancelling business, 29.8
D. is a truth in America, 114.7
D. is an abuse of statistics, 20.10
D. is Lovelace and the people is Clarissa, 1.11
d. . . . is necessarily a *despotism*, 87.5
D. . . . . requires me to sacrifice myself *for* the
masses, not *to* them, 27.6
D. . . . tends to separate men, 114.6
If d. is so stupid as to give us free tickets, 65.5
In a d. dissent is an act of faith, 59.5
In a pure d., 155.3
Man's capacity for justice, makes d. possible,
122.8
Of all despotisms, a d. . . . is the most violent,
3.8
So Two cheers for D., 57.3
Social D. is the moderate wing of fascism,
154.9
the country was doomed to run the full
length of d., 94.12
The enemies of d. . . . grow daily more
insolent, 151.10
the imprudence of d., 70.4
Voting . . . is not to be identified with d., 40.2

What *is* D., this huge inevitable product of
the Destinies, 29.15
when d. shall elevate itself to the position of a
religious party, 112.2
where the poor rule, it is d., 4.4
DEMOCRATIC
A d. constitution, not supported by d.
institutions, 115.2
All d. parties should . . . hand over power to
the people, 121.5
the d. interest, 14.3
the D. Party is like a mule, 49.13
the D. party, which has always supported
God, 115.8
the foundation of d. . . . liberty to believe that
other people may perhaps be wiser, 7.1
The increasing discredit into which d.
government has fallen, 73.1
We have not got d. government today, 52.1
DEMOCRATS
If they [Republicans] will stop telling lies
about the D., 155.8
the D. believe that the whole people should
govern, 140.10
DESICCATED
a d. calculating machine, 16.7
DESPOTIC
We must . . . seek first to secure government,
even though d., 144.7
DESPOTISM
a system of d. tempered by casualness, 2.5
d. tempered by epigrams, 29.4
the history of men under a d. . . . a collection
of anecdotes, 32.9
who adopt as their symbol a sabre and d., 93.5
DESTINY
checking the fulfilment of our manifest d.,
124.13
DESTROYERS
D. rightlier call'd and Plagues of men, 116.1
DESTRUCTIVE
the d. forces . . . of the soulless mechanical
civilisation, 89.4
DETERRENT
a credible d. out of an incredible action, 106.2
DIALECTIC
No other d. is admissible save the d. of fists
and pistols, 135.11
DICTATOR
The man who is born to be a d. is not
compelled, 77.8
there are greater risks in not stopping a d.,
159.9
DICTATORSHIP
A d. is a regime in which people quote
instead of thinking, 151.7

DIE
Better to d. on one's feet than to live on one's knees, 82.1
If a man hasn't discovered something that he will d. for, 90.6
let us d. to make men free, 79.9
The d. is cast, 27.1
The greatest mistake I made was not to d. in office, 1.2

DIGNIFIED
the d. parts, 8.11

DIN
A dictator ... who can stand all the din ... gets elected, 121.10

DIPLOMACY
D. is letting someone else have your way, 129.1
D. is to do and say The nastiest thing in the nicest way, 66.5
D. without armaments is like music without instruments, 58.9
The old-world d. of Europe, 9.3
unsuitable ... as a sanction of d., 88.7

DISCONTENT
Every new civilization began as d., 98.12

DISEASE
A desperate d. requires a dangerous remedy, 56.5

DISEASES
We always catch Continental d., 11.11

DISORDER
d. will give them but an incommodious sanctuary, 100.2

DISSENT
In a democracy d. is an act of faith, 59.5

DITCH
I shall die in the last d., 173.2

DIVIDED
I do expect it [Union] will cease to be divided, 96.13

DIVISION
such a dreadful Spirit of D. as rends a Government into two distinct People, 2.4

DOMINATION
any d. which did not appear natural to those who possessed it?, 115.7

DOMINIONS
his Majesty's d., on which the sun never sets, 174.4

DOMINOES
You have a row of d. set up, 52.7

DOWNFALL
only to end with every weakness disclosed and every error compounding the d., 90.13

DREAM
I have a d. that one day this nation will rise up 90.8

DRIFTING
d. towards war, 36.17

DUBLIN
What D. says today Ireland will say tomorrow, 128.11

DUKE
A fully equipped d. costs as much to keep up as two Dreadnoughts, 99.3
To stop the D., go for gold, 132.6

DUTCH
So we clap on D. bottoms just 20 per cent, 28.11

DYNASTIC
protectors of d. rights, 23.7

EACH
From e. according to his abilities, 19.14
to each acording to his needs, 9.13

EAST
it has always been wise to try something in the E., 148.8

ECCENTRICITY
No society in which e. is a matter of reproach, 115.1

ECONOMISTS
there are no e. now, 71.8

ECONOMY
political e. is not in my line, 118.4

EDITORS
a government of bullies tempered by e., 53.10

EDUCATION
The project of a national e. ought uniformly to be discouraged, 65.3

EFFICIENT
the e. parts, 8.11
Whenever you have an e. government you have a dictatorship, 164.10

EGG
The King regarded me as a kind of e., 19.5

EGGHEADS
E. of the world, arise, 155.9

EGOISM
The only healthy foundation for a great state is e., 18.3

ELDON
like E., an ermined gown, 150.7

ELECTED
the e. leader says: 'Now shut up and obey me.', 171.2

ELECTIONS
More is done ... in politics whilst ignoring e. and parties, 170.8

We cannot have free government without e., 97.9

ELECTRIFICATION
Socialism is . . . e. of the whole country, 95.12

ELOQUENCE
immunity to e. is of the utmost importance to the citizens of a democracy, 144.9

ELYSIAN
in the E. fields, 49.4

EMPIRE
a great e. and little minds go ill together, 24.3
All E. is no more than Pow'r in Trust, 50.6
England without an E.!, 32.6
Great Britain has lost an E. and has not yet found a role, 1.3
great responsibility administering an E., 10.5
I shall have the E. of the two Worlds, 120.4
lies are one of the central pillars of the E., 121.3
neither Holy, nor Roman, nor an E., 167.3
The British E. seems to be running out, 36.10
the disintegration and dismemberment of the E., 64.8
the great Mother E. stands splendidly isolated in Europe, 57.4
There has never been anything so great . . . as the British E., 44.12
To found a great e. for the sole purpose of raising up a people of customers, 152.1
to preside over the liquidation of the British E., 36.4

EMPIRES
The day of E. has come, 32.5

EMPLOYMENT
Something ought to be done to find these people e., 52.4

ENCOURAGE
it is good to kill an admiral . . . to e. the others, 167.4

END
But it is, perhaps, the e. of the beginning, 36.5
how it will e. no one can foresee, 45.8
no other rule . . . than . . . that the e. justifies the means, 91.3

ENDS
These are the [four] e. for which the associated peoples of the world are fighting, 174.9

ENEMIES
To rule with the help of one's e., 19.8

ENEMY
I do not approve the extermination of the e., 52.10
plotting a trap into which your e. in the party is bound to fall, 154.14

We should support whatever the e. opposes, 108.7

ENFRANCHISEMENT
The demand . . . for economic freedom . . . is the natural outcome of political e., 71.11

ENGINEERS
e. of the soul, 67.4

ENGLAND
E. alone employs . . . an unwritten law and custom, 21.5
E. has been the most . . . essentially political, 117.1
E. is . . . the last ward of the European madhouse, 164.5
E. is the mother of parliaments, 22.3
E. . . . will, as I trust, save Europe by her example, 132.2
I know E. cannot, nay will not endure it, 116.11
If E. does not want something to happen, Russia will not do it, 114.1
Speak for E., Arthur!, 20.9
The Continent will not suffer E. to be workshop of the world, 47.5

ENGLISH
I am anxious . . . that the E. supremacy shall last till the end of time, 104.11
insolence which we E. show only to little or weak races, 170.2
No man . . . is equipped for the battle of life unless he has an E. education, 94.5
The E. have all the material requisites for the revolution, 110.14
The German general staff fought against the E. parliament, 68.6
The mass of the E. people are politically contented, 9.6
The whole life of E. politics, 9.4
why an E. interest must become a European interest, 18.12

ENGLISHMAN
an E. . . . does everything on principle, 149.3
an E. ought not to despise all nations of the world, 38.7

ENIGMA
a mystery inside an e., 35.10

ENJOYING
the next greatest pleasure consists in preventing others from e. themselves, 144.1

ENTHUSIASTS
so few e. can be trusted to speak the truth, 12.1

EQUAL
e. division of unequal earnings, 53.3
some animals are more e. than others, 124.8

those who . . . are refused e. participation, must be discontented, 127.2

We hold . . . that all men are created e., 84.8

You are e. in right to obey, 156.10

EQUALITY

e. . . . an absolutely necessary condition for freedom, 10.1

e. . . . as primordial condition of liberty, 9.13

E., like Liberty, appears . . . to be a big name for a small thing, 155.4

liberty without e. is a name of noble sound and squalid result, 78.13

no broad political idea which has entered less into . . . the political system . . . than the love of e., 64.13

Socialism means e. of income or nothing, 150.3

The gradual development of the principle of e. is . . . universal, it is durable, 161.6

the idea of e. should now be regarded as out of date, 53.13

the red banner of economic e., 9.14

the theory of e. represents a mistake found in all ages, 42.9

The yearning after e. is the offspring of covetousness, 156.4

ERIN

Dabbing its sleek young hands in E.'s gore, 26.2

ESTABLISHMENT

By *them* he meant not the English, but . . . the E., 159.1

nothing more agreeable . . . than to make peace with the E., 159.2

ESTATE

He is a king of *fourth e.*, 73.11

in the Reporters' Gallery . . . sat a *Fourth E.*, 29.11

The gallery . . . has become a fourth e. of the realm, 103.2

What is the Third E.? – Everything, 151.6

ETON

Probably the battle of Waterloo *was* won on the playing fields of E., 124.6

EUROPE

A new disease is spreading over E., 116.14

knock the heads of the Kings of E. together, 30.2

my business to . . . maintain the balance of E., 30.3

the crucial year of a great New Order in E., 78.3

this vague and deceptive theory of a Republican United States of E., 61.1

Those who live in . . . E. are wanting in intelligence and skill, 4.8

EUROPEAN

The state forms of . . . E. countries are . . . compatible with neither liberty, equality, nor fraternity, 76.2

EUTOPIA

a vain *E.* seated in the brain, 107.12

EVENT

How much the greatest e. it is that ever happened, 57.9

EVENTFUL

What an e. period this is!, 135.5

EVILS

the elimination of concrete e. rather than for the realisation of abstract goods, 133.10

EXECUTIVE

An e. is less dangerous . . . when in office during life, 70.5

EXERCISE

a just and honourable war is the true e., 8.6

EXPANSION

When great nations . . . shrink from e., 141.3

EXPLOIT

To e. and to govern mean the same thing, 9.15

EXPRESSION

if he permits his freedom of e. to be abolished, 153.9

EXTREME

I have invariably objected to all violent and e. measures, 172.3

EXTREMISTS

just a few e. are doing all the harm, 62.8

EYES

Mine e. have seen the glory, 79.8

FABIUS

For the right moment you must wait, as F. did, 132.13

FACTORY

that part that F. Acts alone can cure!, 150.2

FACTS

There seem to me very few . . . ascertainable f. in politics, 130.3

FAGGOTS

I set fire to the f., 16.14

FAITH

The ascendancy of f. may be impracticable, 121.11

FALKLANDS

nothing we do in the F. makes it more or less easy for any other nation, 134.8

FALLS

no need of recovery because they are not subject to f., 113.12

FAME
when the love of f. shall cease to be the ...
  passion of our public men, 48.14

FANATICISM
From f. to barbarism is only one step, 47.3

FASCISM
F. is ... a new way of knowing the
  phenomena of our epoch, 135.13
F. is Capitalism plus Murder, 151.14
F. is *nonsense*, 39.10
F. is not defined by the number of its victims,
  148.4
F. was a counter-revolution against a
  revolution that never took place, 151.8
Under the species of Syndicalism and F. there
  appears ... a type of man, 124.4
we are the first victims of American F., 142.6

FASHION
in a very corrupt age f. is very formidable,
  168.5

FATHERLAND
Everything belongs to the f. when the f. is in
  danger, 45.3
exile is our f., our f. exile, 165.1
When it is a question of saving the f., 106.3
workers of all countries shooting at each other
  in the name of the 'Defence of the F.', 95.5

FEAR
the only thing we have to f. is f. itself, 140.12

FEATHERBED
translated from despotism to liberty in a f.,
  85.4

FELLOW
her artist 'f.-travellers', 163.7

FETTERS
their passions forge their f., 25.2

FEW
Never ... was so much owed by so many to
  so f., 36.1

FIFTY-FOUR-FORTY
Fifty-four-forty or fight!, 3.1

FIGHT
f. and f. again, 60.2
We shall f. on the beaches, 35.13
you must be sure to f. for what is just, 169.10

FIGHTING
the Italian character has to be formed through
  f., 119.11

FIGURES
They give you the f., 46.11

FINAL
This is the f. round, 65.12

FINEST
'This was their f. hour.', 35.14

FINGERS
one f. on the trigger, but ... fifteen f. on the
  safety catch, 105.10

FIREBELL
This momentous question, like a f. in the
  night, 85.9

FIRM
As long as the old f. was Townshend and
  Walpole, 169.4

FIRST
powers of a f.-rate man, 8.8

FISH
A man who tosses worms in the river isn't ...
  a friend to the f., 107.8

FIST
the good old English f., 118.8

FLAG
The people's f. is palest pink, 6.11
We'll keep the red f. flying here, 41.3
With a blood-red f. ahead, 19.17

FLAME
Though the f. of liberty may sometimes cease
  to shine, 126.3

FLOWERS
letting a hundred f. blossom, 108.8

FOOLISH
never said a f. thing, 140.9

FOOLISHEST
it was the f. thing ever done, 113.1

FORCE
an implied willingness and ability to use f.,
  41.5
anything of great value that ever changed
  hands was taken by f. of arms, 83.7
F. is not a remedy, 22.6
F. ... is the midwife of every old society, 54.2
In the field of politics, f. and consent are
  correlative terms, 42.8
people considered ... it possible so to unite
  men by f., 162.5
We will meet your physical f. with soul f.,
  90.5

FOREIGN
Time is the ... commodity which the F.
  Office is expected to provide, 166.3
The politician who will refuse the F. Office is
  not yet born, 155.11

FOREST
The f. laments, in order that Mr Gladstone
  may perspire, 34.10

FORTUNATE
*The f. must not be restrained in the exercise
  of tyranny*, 144.2

FOURSCORE
F. and seven years ago, 97.7

FRANCE
F. . . . a despotism tempered by epigrams, 29.4
F. is revolutionary or she is nothing at all, 93.6
F. plays the part of protectress of nationalities, 23.7
I speak in the name of F., 46.4
I was F., 46.5
the atmosphere between ourselves and F. . . . to have been of the glacial epoch, 68.1
The modern history of F. is the substitution of one crisis for another, 130.5
The real Turkey in Europe is F., 32.10

FRAUD
Next came F., and he had on, like Eldon, an ermined gown, 150.7

FREE
A f. nation is a being that thinks before it acts, 160.8
a f. society is . . . where it is safe to be unpopular, 155.7
A people are f. in proportion as they form their own opinions, 40.5
As a nation of f. men, we must live through all time, 96.7
He who would be f., 50.3
If a f. society cannot help the many who are poor, 88.12
Man is born f. 142.8
Men are not born f., 56.9
No kingdom can be secure . . . that is not f. in spirit, 73.5
the abstract right of the human race to be f., 73.10
while there is a soul in prison, I am not f., 45.13

FREEDOM
a right to f., because the Englishmen of Alfred's reign were free, 105.3
f. is something people take, 10.2
F. is the recognition of necessity, 154.3
f. outside of equality can create only privilege, 10.1
F. remains still the wisest cure for f.'s temporary inconveniences, 92.5
F. suppressed . . . bites with keener fangs, 36.14
He who dies for f., dies . . . for the whole world, 21.2
In giving f. to the slave, we assure f. to the free, 97.6
It is the land that . . . sober-suited F. chose, 159.3
People demand f. only when they have no power, 122.14
The dagger plunged in the name of F., 109.7
Those who expect to reap the blessing of f., 126.4

What f. is a f. which doesn't provide anything in the stomach?, 139.3
wind of nationalism and f., 10.11

FREEDOMS
We look forward to a world founded upon four essential human f., 140.17

FRENCH
F. Canadianism entirely extinguished, 22.12

FRENCHMAN
a F. respects authority & despises the law, 32.11

FRIENDS
I have f. in this House, 31.8
that he lay down his f. for his life, 160.14

FRONTIER
We stand today on the edge of a New F., 88.9

FURROW
I must plough my own f. alone, 142.4

FUTURE
I have been over into the f., and it works, 155.1
The f. smells of Russian leather, 74.11

GAEL
The G. is not like other men, 128.12

GAINED
We have g. everything that we would have lost, 132.1

GALLERY
The first play to the g.; the second usually bore it, 113.12

GANDHI
Mr G., a seditious Middle Temple lawyer, 35.6

GARAGE
The slogan of progress is changing from the full dinner pail to the full g., 79.5

GARTER
But he ended PM . . . and a knight of the g., 7.5

GENERAL
I usually try to kill someone – a g. if possible, 38.2

GENIUS
Jealous mediocrity will ever wish to bring g. to the scaffold, 146.6

GENTLEMAN
rather a plain russet-coated captain . . . a 'g.', 43.4

GEORGE
G. the Third Ought never to have occurred, 14.10
The blood and dust of both – to mould a G., 26.1

GERMAN
a vendetta against every G. in Britain, 21.3
I cannot make him an object of G. policy, 18.13
'The G. army was stabbed in the back.', 77.2

GERMANS
The G. are shockingly bad politicians, 170.2

GERMANY
Communism fits G. as a saddle fits a cow, 154.13
G. must be either the hammer or the anvil, 23.6
If G. is to become a colonising power, 64.9
Let us put G. . . . in the saddle, 18.6

GESTAPO
some form of G., 36.7

GIN
We have been borne down in a torrent of g. and beer, 63.15

GLACIAL
the atmosphere between ourselves and France . . . to have been of the g. epoch, 68.1

GLOBALONEY
Much of what Mr Wallace calls his global thinking is . . . g., 101.4

GNOMES
all the little g. of Zurich, 173.6

GO
In the name of God, g.!, 43.10

GOD
a public crime to act as though there is no G., 96.3
G. has erected two forms of government among men, 101.7
G. has made of you a little g., 84.6
G. is always on the side of the big battalions, 167.9
G. is usually on the side of the big squadrons, 25.3
I am one of those whose heart G. has drawn out, 43.5
I came, I saw, G. conquered, 33.8
It matters not who is our Commander-in-Chief if G. be so, 43.7
the chief and ultimate end of human society . . . that men . . . should serve G., 17.2
the only thing that was killed was belief in G.., 27.13
The providence of G. hath cast this upon us, 43.6
this country supports G., 115.8

GODS
It was to the stronger that the g. gave their aid, 158.2

GOLD
saying good-bye to the g. standard, 118.9

the great cities are in favor of the g. standard, 23.2
You shall not crucify mankind upon a cross of g., 23.2

GOOD
most of our people have never had it so g., 105.16
The g. of the people is the supreme law, 36.16

GOODS
how many g. we can send abroad for foreigners to consume, 118.7

GOOSE
balance: . . . leave that to Mother G., 14.4

GOVERN
Even though counting heads is not an ideal way to g., 71.1
Let the people think they g. and they will be governed, 130.6
To exploit and to g. mean the same thing, 9.15
Whoever puts his hand on me to g. me is . . . a tyrant, 136.3

GOVERNED
that the Kingdom shall be g. by King, Lords and Commons, 169.9

GOVERNMENT
a free g. is . . . what the people think so, 24.6
A g. is *not* in power, 11.9
A g. that is big enough to give you all you want, 66.11
All g. is . . . absolute, 86.7
bad enough having to behave like a G. when one is a G., 105.8
Every country has the g. it deserves, 106.11
G. is a contrivance . . . to provide for human *wants*, 24.9
G. . . . is the badge of lost innocence, 126.2
G. is very limited in its powers of making men . . . virtuous or happy, 64.14
g. of the people, by the people, for the people, 97.7
g. . . . the greatest of all reflections on human nature, 106.8
G. was intended to suppress injustice, 65.1
good intention . . . no mean force in the g. of mankind, 24.4
I would not give half a guinea to live under one form of g. rather than another, 86.5
If g. be founded in the consent of the people, 65.2
in the machine of g., immobility . . . is wanted, 14.4
Must a g. . . . be . . . too weak to maintain its own existence?, 97.5
Objections . . . against a standing army . . . may also . . . be brought against a standing g., 160.10

Popular g. is inconsistent with the reticence which official etiquette formerly imposed, 31.12

The best form of G. ... is one where the masses have little power, 146.13

the first end of g. is to give security to life and property, 117.3

the history of g. is one of the most immoral parts of history, 64.12

the principal spring of our actions was to have the g. ... in our hands, 20.4

The whole duty of g. is to prevent crime and to preserve contracts, 112.13

There are no necessary evils in g., 83.3

This g. cannot endure ... half slave and half free, 96.13

This is the negation of God erected into a system of G., 63.9

we are the g., you and I, 141.6

What is a G. for except to dictate?, 99.9

Without you the g. would have been ridiculous, 71.9

GOVERNMENTS
G. are more the *effect* than the cause of that which we are, 40.7

Perpetuity is implied ... in the fundamental law of all national g., 97.4

When the ground shakes under g., 114.2

GOVERNOR
the G. of the Bank of England goes on for ever, 20.8

GRADUALNESS
the inevitable g. of our scheme of change, 170.9

GRAPES
He is trampling out the vintage where the g. of wrath are stored, 79.8

GRAPESHOT
It begins with national workshops, and ends with ... 'a whiff of g.', 71.5

'with ... a whiff of g.', 29.5

GRATITUDE
G. is not an active sentiment in politics, 114.8

GREAT
a good many g. men must have been frauds, 94.8

All rising to g. place is by a winding stair, 8.4

behave like a g. man, 12.7

G. men are almost always bad men, 1.6

g. men are like g. mountains, 32.7

G. men are the guide-posts and landmarks, 23.10

history of the world is but the biography of g. men, 29.10

Nations are not g. solely because the individuals composing them are numerous, free, and active, 5.2

The g. appear g. to us only because we are on our knees, 46.14

The renown of g. men should ... be measured by the means, 93.10

GREATEST
the g. happiness for the g. numbers, 81.2

GREEN
Wherever g. is worn ... A terrible beauty is born, 176.2

GRINDING
nine-tenths of mankind have been g. the corn for the remaining one-tenth, 99.6

GROUND
The first man who, having enclosed a piece of g., 142.7

GUERRILLA
G. warfare ... is invincible, indestructible, 111.12

G. warfare is to peasant uprisings what Marx is to Sorel, 45.12

GUILTLESSLY
No one can rule g., 146.2

GUN
Every g. that is fired ... a theft from those who hunger and are not fed, 52.6

'Political power grows out of the barrel of a g.', 108.5

GUNFIRE
I intend to march my troops towards the sound of g., 68.5

GUNPOWDER
G., Printing and the Protestant Religion, 29.3

HABITS
In politics h. ... rule humanity, 111.6

HAMMER
the h. or the anvil, 23.6

HANG
we must all h. together, 58.4

HAPPENED
Everything that h. once can happen again, 161.4

HAPPINESS
H. is a new idea in Europe, 146.1

The good and h. of the members ... of any state, 135.6

the greatest h. for the greatest numbers, 81.2

the greatest h. of the greatest number, 14.7

HARVEST
we must h. the wheat when it is still green, 7.6

HAT
the h., the headgear worn by the whole civilised world, 6.10

HATE
Let them h. me, so they but fear me, 27.7

HATRED
Mankind in the mass is not moved by h., 72.2

HAVE
a struggle between those who h. . . . and those who h. not, 147.2

HAWK
In a contest between a h. and a dove the h. has a great advantage, 59.7

HE
the poorest H. . . . hath a life to live as the greatest H., 139.1

HEAD
But bow'd his comely H., Down as upon a Bed, 109.8
He who makes jokes as the h. of a government, 146.7

HEADS
the hardness of our h. and the largeness of our hearts, 11.4
h. are the best judges as to the course to be taken, 130.2

HEALTH
the first consideration of a Minister should be the h. of the people, 48.17

HEARD
I will be h., 62.3

HEARSE
Their h. is ordered, 128.9

HEARTLESS
Judicial decrees . . . can restrain the h., 90.7

HEARTS
the hardness of our heads and the largeness of our h., 11.4

HEAVEN
every man must get to h. in his own way, 58.7
the national account with H. must some day . . . be settled, 126.6

HEBRAISM
these two forces . . . we may call . . . H. and Hellenism, 4.13

HELL
I never did give anybody h., 164.8

HELLENIC
the H. race . . . is . . . high-spirited and also intelligent, 4.8

HELLENISM
these two forces . . . we may call . . . Hebraism and H., 4.13

HENRY
H. V cannot give up the flag of H. IV, 32.8

HERESY
H. is a spiritual thing, cut with no iron, 101.6

HEROES
To make Britain a fit country for h. to live in, 99.10

HISTORY
h. is on our side, 90.1
I shall not fail before the bar of h., 160.5
Only the h. of free peoples is worth our attention, 32.9
Politics are vulgar when they are not liberalised by h., 148.11
There is nothing new . . . except the h. you do not know, 164.11

HITLER
It takes a bomb under his arse to make H. see reason, 65.10

HOLY RUSSIAN
fire swept over the H. R. land, 92.6

HOMOSEXUALITY
a celebration of individual freedom, not of h., 22.15

HONEST
an 'H.' politician, 143.9

HONOR
we mutually pledge . . . our Lives, our Fortunes and our sacred H., 84.9

HOOLIGAN
I am what you call a h., 128.1

HORSE
One could go h.-stealing with them!, 65.7

HORSES
Men are not hanged for stealing H., 69.14

HOST
Tory and Whig in turn shall be my h., 152.5

HOT
H.-air propaganda in mean streets, 170.4

HOUSE
get his bread by voting in the H. of Commons, 130.14
I have friends in this H., 31.8
keep us in the H. of Commons, the land of Pensions and Plenty, 79.3
nor tongue to speak in this place but as this H. is pleased to direct me, 96.1
the H. of Commons . . . does not like to be driven, 127.10
the H. will NEVER forgive . . . if a Minister misleads it, 11.1
there is a corrupt influence in the Crown which destroys the influence of the H., 123.7

HUMAN
a society in which they can feel h. among h. beings, 50.13

HUMANITY
God has given you your country as cradle,
and h. as mother, 111.13
H. is only I writ large, 155.5
HUMBUG
the . . . new Jerusalem of h., 135.1
Vox populi, vox h., 151.2
HYPHEN
the most un-American thing . . . is a h.,
174.11

IDEA
To die for an i., 57.11
IDEALISM
I. is the despot of thought, 9.17
I. is the noble toga, 81.5
ILLEGITIMATE
Men are . . . corrupted by . . . the exercise of a
power which they believe to be i., 161.7
ILLOGICALITIES
The House of Commons . . . is a Palace of I.,
22.13
IMPATIENCE
I. is fatal in politics, 111.2
IMPERIALISM
i. is monopolist capitalism, 95.8
I., is nothing but this – a larger patriotism,
142.2
that real . . . universal enemy is precisely
Yankee i., 30.8
IMPERIALLY
Learn to think i., 32.4
IMPOSSIBLE
never colliding with the i., 114.13
IMPRISON
if two men . . . i. you, that is freedom, 147.3
INACTIVITY
a wise and masterly i., 104.12
INDEPENDENCE
She [America] is the well-wisher to the
freedom and i. of all, 2.1
we have this day assumed our sovereign i.,
152.3
INDIA
I. alone . . . represents the aspirations . . . of
the disinherited, 121.4
The British Government in I. is like a tooth
that is decaying, 121.8
the key of I. is London, 49.7
The loss of I. would mark . . . the downfall of
the British Empire, 35.4
INDIAN
The only good I. I ever saw is a dead I.,
150.12

INDIFFERENCE
i. . . . which might squander the accumulated
wealth of tradition, 134.1
INDIVIDUAL
In politics the i. does not count, 139.2
the i. counts but as one among many, 74.7
the liberty of the i. is the greatest thing of all,
75.11
The power of this community is then set up
as 'right' in opposition to the power of the
i., 58.11
We must abolish the cult of the i. decisively,
89.9
INDIVIDUALISM
i. . . . threatens to spread in the same ratio as
equality of condition, 161.12
the American system of rugged i., 79.4
The recognition of private property has really
harmed I., 172.10
INDUSTRIAL
the military-i. complex, 52.8
INDUSTRIALISTS
the i. . . . are always inclined to support the
existing government, 146.10
INDUSTRY
Captains of I. are the true Fighters, 29.13
INEQUALITY
I. . . . leads to the misdirection of production,
158.6
i., like absolutism, thwarts a vital instinct, 5.1
INFAMOUS
crush the i. thing, 167.5
INFLATION
There is only one cure for i., 59.1
INJUSTICE
Man's inclination to i. makes democracy
necessary, 122.8
INSTITUTIONS
an understanding of the English i., 8.11
i. alone fix the destinies of nations, 120.8
INSURRECTION
I. is the most sacred of duties, 93.4
INTEREST
connecting the notion of right with that of
private i., 161.10
INTERESTS
We have no eternal allies . . . Our i. are
eternal, 127.7
INTERNATIONAL
The I. Party shall be the human race, 133.11
this is a breach of i. law, 15.5
INTERNATIONALISM
i. . . . is a luxury which only the upper classes
can afford, 119.6

INVISIBLE
led by an i. hand, 151.15

IRELAND
Believing that the British government has no
    right in I., 41.6
If . . . there is still to be fought a final conflict
    in I., 64.7
I., I.! that cloud in the west, 63.7
I. is in your hands, 124.1
My mission is to pacify I., 63.14
The government of I. by England rests on
    restraint, 30.4
The Six Counties . . . are part of I., 46.16
Till I., a nation, can build him a tomb, 45.11

IRISH
I will not barter English commerce for I.
    slavery, 57.6
on I. ground No poisonous reptiles ever yet
    were found, 72.11
That is the I. question, 47.6
The I. Prostestant can never be free, 67.9
there is no remedy that we can apply for the
    I. hatred of ourselves, 147.7

IRON
an i. curtain has descended across the
    Continent, 36.9
An i. curtain is drawn down upon their front,
    36.6
An i. curtain would at once descend on this
    territory, 65.11
an i. hand in a velvet glove, 120.19
great questions of the day [will] be settled . . .
    by i. and blood, 18.4
I stand before you . . . the I. Lady of the
    Western World, 159.7
We were behind the 'i. curtain' at last!,
    152.11

ISLAM
He who forsakes the Law of I. should be
    fought, 82.2

ISLAMIC
By socialism we mean above all an I.
    socialism, 137.1

ISOLATED
I. man is an abstraction, 146.12
splendidly i. in Europe, 57.4

ISOLATION
I dislike i., 51.1
our splendid i., 67.6

'ISMS'
the 'i.' that currently bedevil the world, 112.6

ISRAEL
I. . . . was . . . one of the consequences of
    imperialism, 121.6
The security of I. is a moral imperative, 90.11

ITALIAN
My only ambition is to be the first soldier of
    I. independence, 166.9

ITALY
How splendid were your Thousand, O I.!, 62.2
I. has need of a blood bath, 119.2
I. is a geographical expression, 114.10
I. is made, all is safe, 31.3

JACKSON
J. standing like a stone wall, 12.12

JACOBIN
Whoever builds on social rights . . . is an anti-
    J., 40.8

JACOBINISM
Culture is the eternal opponent of . . . the
    signal marks of J., 4.10

JEFFERSON
when Thomas J. dined alone, 88.17

JESUS
J., not Caesar, is the meaning of history, 111.4

JEW
by defending myself against the J., I am
    fighting for the work of the Lord, 77.5
no peace in Europe until every J. has been
    eliminated, 65.9

JEWISH
a national home for the J. people,, 11.12

JEWS
O Believers! take not the J. or Christians as
    friends, 138.2

JINGO
We don't want to fight, but by j. if we do,
    80.8

JOB
the state is obliged to find a j. for him, 19.3

JUDAISM
Whenever he [the German] finds his life
    sullied by the filth of J., 163.1

JUNGLE
This is not a j. war, but a struggle for
    freedom, 85.16

JUST
nothing is j. save what is honest, 139.10

JUSTICE
a democracy cannot possibly support j., 3.9
God is just; . . . his j. cannot sleep forever,
    84.10
If powerful men will not write j. with black
    ink, 128.8
J. must not become the mistress of the state,
    65.14
render the observance of j. the immediate
    interest, 80.3

The greatest problem ... is that of attaining a civil society which can administer j. universally, 87.2

The sword of j. has no scabbard, 107.1

The three fundamental rules of j. ... are duties of princes as well as of subjects, 80.4

When j. has spoken, humanity must have its turn, 166.6

KENTUCKY

I owe allegiance ... to the sovereignty of the State of K., 37.4

KEYNES

there are few halts between K. and Marx, 79.2

KEYS

the k. of the kingdom of heaven, 17.10

KING

a good K. will frame his actions to be according to the Law, 84.2

a k. on whom the eyes of a whole people are fixed, 20.5

he will recognise no authority, and that he has become his own k., 135.15

I prefer the individual whom chance, birth ... have given us for a K., 140.1

interfere between a K. and his mistress, 10.12

the K. can do no wrong, 19.11

The K. reigns and does not govern, 160.2

the law makes the k., 21.4

The people's silence is the k.'s lesson, 12.6

There can be only one K. of France, 100.11

There's such divinity doth hedge a k., 149.1

wash the balm from an anointed k., 148.12

KINGDOM

I will give unto thee the keys of the k. of heaven, 17.10

KINGS

By me K. reign, 17.4

How small ... that part which laws or k. can cause or cure, 86.11

K. are justly called Gods, 84.4

K. are the publick Pillars of the State, 50.8

K. will be tyrants from policy, 24.10

my business to make k. and emperors, 30.3

The Book of K. is fast closing, 86.12

the grand conspiracy of k., 73.10

the misfortune of k. that they will not listen to the truth, 84.1

the palaces of k. are built upon the ruins of the bowers of paradise, 126.2

the People have a Right Supreme to make their K., 50.6

The RIGHT DIVINE of K. to govern wrong, 133.9

That k. should philosophise, 87.7

To honour God and to wage war on k., 140.4

vain and trivial is the power of k., 29.2

KNAVE

every man must be supposed a k., 80.5

KNEES

To kick over an idol, you must first get off your k., 158.12

we are on our k., 46.14

KNIFE

instead war to the k., 101.10

KNOWLEDGE

equality of k., producing unity of feeling, 102.5

the reign of k. is impossible, 121.11

KREMLIN

Until we stop pushing the K. against a closed door, 88.6

LABOUR

a convenient belief to those who live on the l. of others, 117.10

Capital ... lives the more, the more l. it sucks, 110.11

If the L. Party is not ... a Socialist Party, 16.8

L. ... has become the camp-follower of the capitalist class, 121.4

L. ... has its natural and its market price, 139.9

L. ... is the only universal ... measure of value, 151.16

L. may be likened to a man waylaid by a series of robbers, 63.1

political leader for the L. party ... a desiccated calculating machine, 16.7

The L. Party ... aims at the establishment of a single-party system, 69.1

The L. Party is a moral crusade, 173.9

The two most important emotions of the L. Party, 44.2

to try to construct the L. Party without Marx, 13.11

Vote L. and you build castles in the air, 59.2

We shall have L. governments in every country after this, 68.3

What harm have I ever done the L. Party?, 158.11

LAISSER FAIRE

Socialism and l. f. are like north and south poles, 11.3

LAISSEZ

L. faire, 138.1

LAMB

better if the l. consented ... to lie inside the lion, 32.2

LAMPS

The l. are going out all over Europe, 68.2

LAND
all great political questions end in the tenure of L., 48.11
L. of Hope and Glory, 14.1
Private ownership of l. is the nether millstone, 62.9
To buy and sell l. is an immorality, 53.11

LANDSLIDE
'I'll be damned if I'm going to pay for a l.', 88.8

LANSBURY
L. . . . waiting for martyrdom, 16.14

LANTERN
People look on me as a kind of l., 113.9

LATIN
don't quote L., and sit down, 172.4

LAW
all the paraphernalia and folly of l., 125.2
Man in Society is not free where there is no l., 40.1
More l., less justice, 36.13
The l. is reason free from passion, 4.7
The l. . . . is the infallible rule of moral goodness, 78.11
The natural l. of any society is either tradition . . . or religion, 137.6
the spirit and credentials of a l.-giver, 40.9
when the land lacks l. and order, 41.1
Where-ever L. ends, Tyranny begins, 100.9

LAWMAKER
the l. has to ascertain . . . the common belief, 47.1

LAWMAKERS
we are here in our efforts to become l., 127.13

LAWS
How small . . . that part which l. or kings can cause or cure, 86.11
method to secure the repeal of bad or obnoxious l., 67.8
not the best possible l. but the best which they will bear, 71.7
They have l. . . . and I broke them . . . Who is wrong?, 177.3
where l. end, there tyranny begins, 131.6

LEADER
Do not weaken the hand of . . . your L., 31.9
harder for a l. to be born in a palace than . . . in a cabin, 174.6
the first function of a political l. is advocacy, 16.5
The king presupposes subjects; the l., followers, 151.12

LEADERS
Great l. of parties are not elected, they are evolved, 135.4

I feel a want of many essential qualifications which are requisite in party l., 129.7
The efforts and plans of . . . l. . . . reveal themselves as *vaticinatio ex eventu*, 111.9

LEADERSHIP
consultation . . . within the party about its future l., 105.11
place their hopes of political salvation in *l. of any description*, 101.1
The art of l. consists in consolidating the attention of the people, 77.4

LEAP
a sudden l. forward, from capitalism into socialism, 15.3
taking a l. in the dark, 46.13
The l. which the House of Commons is taking . . . is a l. . . . in the dark, 147.1

LEARNING
it is always those with little l. who overthrow those with much l., 108.10

LEFT
our inside l. has scored against his own side, 7.4
The definition of the L., 44.4

LEGISLATURE
The tyranny of the l. is really the danger most to be feared, 85.10

LEISURE
Millions of well-fed bumptious citizens with plenty of l. for argument, 150.4
The l. class stands at the head of the social structure in . . . reputability, 166.4

LENIN
The works of L., Marx and Engels are meaningless now, 137.2

LENINISM
L. is a combination of . . . religion and business, 89.6
Stalin's terror . . . foreshadowed by L., 49.11

LEPER
a Member who . . . will serve his time here as a Parliamentary l., 173.10

LESSON
The people's silence is the king's l., 12.6

LEVEL
Those who dread a dead-l. of income or wealth, 158.8

LIBERAL
being a L. today . . . is not a . . . remunerative career, 6.6
calling myself an advanced conservative l., 163.3
The German L. . . . neither as German nor as a L., 19.4
the L. party is the party of promise, 10.7

The L. State is a mask behind which there is no face, 119.8

LIBERALISM
L. always prospers more than its supporters desire, 19.1
L. is trust of the people tempered by prudence, 64.2
Politics without ideology . . . equals L., 153.10
That is not l.; it is degeneration, 79.6

LIBERATE
If only people wanted to . . . l. themselves instead of liberating humanity, 76.6

LIBERATOR
'Europe's L.' – still enslaved, 26.4

LIBERTY
A man cannot part with his l. and have it too, 100.4
abridging . . . a non-Englishman's assertion of his l., 4.11
anyone . . . who has done nothing for l. . . . deserves to be counted an enemy to it, 56.6
extremism in the defence of l. is no vice, 66.10
give me l., or give me death, 75.3
harder to preserve than to obtain l., 27.4
I am the son of l., 31.1
I pardon something to the spirit of l., 24.5
I would curtail . . . it [liberty] . . . that men may learn to value it better, 75.6
lean l. is better than fat slavery, 59.9
L. and monopoly cannot live together, 98.7
L., and *Necessity* are consistent, 78.8
L., by itself, is Protestantism in religion, 112.3
L. cannot be established unless the heads of scoundrels fall, 140.8
L. is not a means to a higher political end, 1.4
L. has never come from the government, 174.5
L., misunderstood by materialists, 111.15
L. . . . must remould our institution of wealth into the Commonwealth, 98.9
L. produces wealth and wealth destroys l., 98.8
L. recast the old forms of government into the Republic, 98.9
L. without learning is always in peril, 89.1
Licentiousness is the alloy of l., 33.11
Life, L. and the pursuit of Happiness, 84.8
Political l. is . . . the diffusion of power, 69.2
prefer poverty with l. to gilded chains and sordid affluence, 131.9
The cause of L. is a cause of too much dignity, 47.2
the despotism of l. against tyranny, 140.5
the Friends of L. Who preach up Freedom, 25.11
The love of l. is the love of others, 73.9

The manna of popular l. must be gathered each day, 130.9
The more a regime claims to be the embodiment of l., 63.3
the more l. is given to everything . . . in a state of growth, 135.7
The people of France . . . find their cap of l. a soldier's helmet, 3.5
the seal of l., the genius of republicanism, 45.10
The tree of l. must be refreshed . . . with the blood of patriots and tyrants, 85.1
The tree of l. will not grow, 12.3
They that give up their . . . l. to obtain . . . safety, 58.1
Three millions of people, so dead to all the feelings of l, 131.5
to seek power and to lose l., 8.3
we shall pay any price . . . to assure the survival and success of l., 88.11
Whether in chains or in laurels, l. knows nothing but victories, 130.11
Where the State begins, individual l. ceases, 9.9
you cannot create l. when it has gone, 16.12

LIE
the people . . . will more easily fall victim to a big l., 77.6
The rulers . . . may be allowed to l. for the good of the state, 132.7

LIES
All political parties die . . . of swallowing their own l., 4.1

LION
If a l. lies on its back waving its paws, 88.3

LISTEN
patience to l. to the sentiments of individuals, 129.7

LITERARY
The cultivation of l. pursuits, 133.2

LIVES
Great . . . changes begin to be possible as soon as men are not afraid to risk their l., 111.7

LIVING
Government is for the l., and not for the dead, 126.7

LOCAL
the best thing to do was to settle up these little l. difficulties, 105.7

LOCOMOTIVE
For myself, I prefer the l., 136.6

LORDS
converts the House of L. into a kind of plebiscitory organ, 6.1
that Hospital of Incurables, the House of L., 34.5

The House of L. is the British Outer
  Mongolia, 13.6
while the House of L. retains such power, 9.2

LOSE
If I l., I l. only myself, 96.6

LOST
Never came man to so l. a business, 155.15

LOUIS
L. must die that the country may live, 140.3

LOUSE
either the l. defeats socialism or socialism
  defeats the l., 95.10

LOYALTY
l. is a sentiment, not a law, 30.4

LUNATIC
Every reform movement has a l. fringe,
  141.12

LUXURIES
How should we ... procure the l. of life in a
  socialist society?, 118.1

LYBERTIES
other L. ..., depend on the Silence of the
  Law, 78.9

MAD
even a m. dog does not tie a can to its own
  tail, 158.10

MAGNA CHARTA
M. C. ... will have no sovereign, 39.7

MAGNANIMITY
M. in politics is not seldom the truest
  wisdom, 24.3

MAHOMETANISM
I had rather that M. were permitted amongst
  us, 43.9

MAIDS
There would be no culture without kitchen
  m., 162.8

MAINE
As M. goes, so goes Vermont, 56.4

MAJORITIES
Great innovations should not be forced on
  slender m., 85.11

MAJORITY
as a rule the m. are wrong, 46.1
the great silent m. of my fellow Americans,
  123.2
The tyranny of the m., 161.11

MALICE
With m. toward none, 98.1

MAN
m. is by nature a political animal, 4.3
She is so clearly the best m. among them, 30.5

MANIPULATED
the Deity would not tolerate the presumption
  that all can be m. 90.13

MANKIND
'm.' ... seems to me a good word for a Foreign
  Secretary to have firmly fixed, 155.10

MANNERS
in a democracy m. are the only effective
  weapons against the bowie-knife, 101.3

MANY
Ye are m. – they are few, 150.9

MAO TSE-TUNG
the greatest fighting force is the man armed
  with M.-T. thought, 98.3

MAP
Roll up that m., 132.3

MARTYR
I am the m. of the people, 33.4
the dagger of the conspirator ... sharpened
  upon the tombstone of a m., 111.10

MARX
M.'s *Capital* is ... a collection of atrocity
  stories, 143.8
to try to construct the Labour Party without
  M., 13.11

MARXISTS
M. do not believe in persuasion or dialogue,
  27.11

MASS
The m. of the people have nothing to do with
  the laws but to obey them, 79.7
the psychological chart of the m.-man of
  today, 124.3

MASSES
I will back the m. against the classes, 64.11
It is difficult to impregnate the m. with ideas,
  76.4
The m. must for ever remain the m., 162.8
What the m. vote or do not vote for is not
  important, 121.2
Your huddled m. yearning to breathe free,
  94.11

MASTER
As I would not be a *slave*, so I would not be a
  m., 97.1

MASTERS
Let us be m. of the Straits for six hours, 120.2
prevail on our future to learn their letters,
  101.2
We are the m. at the moment, 150.6

MATCHSTICKS
I do my sums with m., 79.1

MATERIALISM
a wave of m. will sweep over the land, 99.8
the banner of theoretical m., 9.14

MATERIALIST
According to the m. conception of history, 54.4

MEASURES
Not men, but m., 23.9
'M., not men!', 28.9

MECHANICS
The proletarian state must bring up thousands of . . . 'm. of culture', 67.4

MEDDLE
'M.' and 'muddle', 46.12

MELTING
America is God's Crucible, the great M.-Pot, 177.2

MEMBER
The first duty . . . of a private m. of the House of Commons, 5.9

MEMORY
how often men are ruined by having too good a m., 162.2

MEN
'Measures, not m.!', 28.9
Not m., but measures, 23.9
politics has taught me . . . that m. are not a reasoned or reasonable sex, 159.5

MERCIFUL
You have no right to be m. or compassionate where traitors are concerned, 146.4

MERCY
We shall show m., but we shall not ask for it, 35.15

METAPHORS
Half the wrong conclusions . . . are reached by the abuse of m., 127.5

MIDDLE
The m. man governs, 170.6

MIDDLEMAN
a m. . . . bamboozles one party and plunders the other, 47.11

MILITANCY
The m. of men . . . has drenched the world with blood, 128.2

MILITARY
the m.-industrial complex, 52.8

MIND
The most potent weapon . . . is the m. of the oppressed, 17.19

MINISTER
M. of England . . . one of a lofty line, 63.11
No m. ever stood . . . against public opinion, 43.2
one could as easily replace an old tree as an old m., 113.14
The m. exists to tell the Civil Servant, 71.10

MINISTERS
if we were not partisans we should not be m., 49.9
Very shining M., . . . are apt to scorch, 34.3

MINISTRY
a quarrel between two states . . . generally occasioned by some blunder of a m., 48.9

MINORITIES
we are all m. now, 160.15

MINORITY
So long as a m. conforms to the majority, it is not even a m., 61.4

MISFORTUNES
governments attribute m. to natural causes, 144.4

MOB
the turbulence of the m. is always close to insanity, 2.7

MOBILISED
Each sovereign keeps m. all the divisions he would need, 116.14

MOBS
The m. . . . add just so much to the support of pure government, 84.12

MODERATE
Tell a man whose house is on fire, to give a m. alarm, 62.3

MODERATION
Any plan conceived in m. must fail, 113.8
chill m. on the Treasury Bench, 170.4
Conservative m. brings its own reward, 63.4
M. in the affairs of the nation is the highest virtue, 85.18
m. in the pursuit of justice is no virtue, 66.10
M. is fatal to factions, 114.5

MONARCH
Adam was an absolute M., and so are all Princes, 56.9

MONARCHICAL
the *m.* . . . interest, 14.3

MONARCHY
A m. is a merchantman, which sails well, 3.4
M. alone trends to bring men together, 114.6
M. is only the string which ties the robbers' bundle, 150.11
sovereign power, can hardly be established except in a m., 20.2

MONEY
a hard m. party, 15.1
An organised m. market . . . is not a school of social ethics, 158.7
M. is . . . considered as the vital principle of the body politic, 70.11
m. is like muck, 8.5

MONEYED
a m. aristocracy, 83.1

MONIED
To erect . . . and perpetuate a large monied interest, 75.4
'M. Interest' . . . that blood-sucker, that muckworm, 131.8

MONOPOLIST
I shall leave a name execrated by every m., 130.1

MONOPOLISTIC
Patriotism is one of the M. Instincts, 2.9

MONOPOLY
Liberty and m. cannot live together, 98.7

MONSTER
We will not leave this m. to prowl the world unopposed, 131.15

MONSTERS
She [America] does not go abroad in search of m. to destroy, 2.1

MOOSE
I am as strong as a bull m., 141.4

MORALISED
It is impossible that all persons can be equally m., 170.7

MORALITY
periodical fits of m., 103.4
politics and m. do not mix, 89.4
social m. . . . will . . . take the place of theological m., 117.11
The principles of public m. are as definite as those of private m., 1.7
Those people who treat politics and m. separately, 142.13

MORALS
the King's Court as . . . guardian of the public m., 108.3

MOSCOW
Do people in Britain . . . feel the same about M. or Leningrad?, 112.8
M. will be the sponge to suck him [Napoleon] dry, 92.7
The flames of M. were the aurora of the world's liberty, 41.7

MOTHER
I would not have the m. country become a stepmother, 34.4

MOTORS
What's good for the country is good for General M., 173.4

MUCK
only if they know when to stop raking the m., 141.9

MUGWUMP
A m. is a person educated beyond his intellect, 128.4

MULE
the Democratic Party is like a m., 49.13

MUSIC
m. . . . affects your nerves, 95.15
m. . . . is politically suspect, 108.4

MUSICAL
Any m. innovation is full of danger to the whole state, 132.8

MUSTAPHAS
your M. have no idea of any traffic beyond rhubarb, figs and red slippers, 127.3

MYTHS
disabuse ourselves of old m., 59.4

NAKED
You will send a Foreign Minister . . . n. into the conference chamber, 16.9

NAPOLEON
N. stands by himself, 5.10

NATION
a portion of the territory . . . is separated from the N., 111.14
I . . . will remain at the disposition of the n., 46.6
no greater than to expect . . . real favors from n. to n., 169.14
The n. is a power hard to rouse, 64.5
To me the n. is the ultimate political reality, 134.5

NATIONAL
The n. task that has been incumbent upon me for eighteen years, 46.7
the n. will . . . commands, and we obey, 30.12

NATIONALISM
a wind of n. and freedom, 10.11
Nations whose n. is destroyed are subject to ruin, 137.9
The American people are right in demanding that New N., 141.10

NATIONALITY
lawful separation between one n. and the other . . . is a reactionary idea, 95.6

NATIONHOOD
n. is not achieved otherwise than in arms, 128.13

NATIONS
N. touch at their summits, 9.3
the day of small n. has long passed away, 32.5
the grand adventure of n. has become a sordid scramble for the microphone, 166.8
Two n., 48.2
You may roughly divide the n. of the world as the living and the dying, 147.10

NATURAL
The N. Liberty of Man is to be free from any Superior Power on Earth, 100.5

NAZI
I cannot trust the N. leaders again, 31.6

NECESSITY
Freedom is the understanding of n., 109.1
N. . . . is the argument of tyrants, 131.11

NECK
Some chicken! Some n.!, 36.3
Who saving his own N. not sav'd the State, 50.10

NEED
In n. freedom is latent, 137.7

NEGATION
the n. of God erected into a system of Government, 63.9

NEGLECT
a wise and salutary n., 24.5

NEGOTIATE
Let us never n. out of fear, 88.13

NEGRO
The N. revolution is controlled by foxy white liberals, 107.3
the N. . . . will plunge even deeper into the philosophy of non-violence, 90.5
When I hear of the sufferings of a N. in China, 18.13

NEGROES
the loudest *yelps* for liberty among the drivers of n., 86.6

NEIGHBOUR
I would dedicate this nation to the policy of the good n., 140.13

NEUTRALITY
Just for a word – 'n.', 15.4

NEW SOUTH WALES
Go out and govern N.S.W.!, 13.3

NEWCASTLE
I borrowed the Duke of N.'s majority, 131.2

NEWSPAPERS
n. . . . engines of propaganda, 10.9
War is never brought about by n., 18.9

NOBILITY
N. . . . is the intermedium between the king and the people, 116.5

NOBLEMAN
A n., a gentleman and a yeoman, 43.13

NOTHING
Nothing (*Rien*), 100.13

NOMINATED
I will not accept if n. and will not serve if elected, 151.4

NORMALCY
not nostrums, but n., 72.4

NUM
Do not run up your nose dead against the Pope and the NUM, 11.8

OBEDIENCE
o. . . . does not of itself make a man a slave, 153.11
O. to the laws and to the Sovereign, is o. to a higher Power, 166.10

ODER-NEISSE
The O.-N. frontier is a frontier of peace, 90.2

OFFICE
no worse heresy than that the o. sanctifies the holder of it, 1.6
Upon every other plan, o. is shabbiness, labour, and sorrow, 152.7
when a man receives the seals of o. from his Sovereign, 142.3

OLD
All . . . is in favour of the employment of . . . young men instead of o. ones, 129.6
not allowing men to grow o. in their jobs, 120.17

OLIGARCHIES
an accidental feature of o., 4.4

OLIGARCHY
What we have done . . . is to broaden the basis of o., 52.1

OMNIBUSES
six o. abreast through Temple Bar, 22.5

OPINION
If all mankind minus one were of one o., 115.4
In Democracies there is a . . . disposition to make publick o. stronger than the law, 42.4
that great compound of folly . . . and newspaper paragraphs, which is called public o., 129.2

OPINIONS
If we cannot yet reconcile all o., 125.3
No human government has a right to enquire into private o., 57.8
O. become dangerous to a state, 57.10
the instrument of carrying other men's o. into effect, 129.12
We are at war with armed o., 131.15

OPIUM
Religion . . . is the o. of the people, 109.11

OPPONENT
One must, if one can, kill one's o., 114.9
one's o. . . . must be weaned from error by patience and sympathy, 61.7

OPPOSITE
whichever way you decide you will . . . wish you had done the o., 80.2

OPPOSITION
Don't say in Power what you say in O., 60.11
for the first time the Crown would have an O. returned, 112.11
it is much more hard on His Majesty's o. to compel them [his ministers] to take this course, 78.12
lead an o. on a certain plea, 63.10
the duty of an O. . . . to oppose everything, 46.10
When the Government . . . and the O. . . . take the same side, 144.10

OPPRESSED
We . . . should plead *for* the o., not *to* them, 40.3

OPPRESSING
he hates the o. few, 14.9

OPPRESSIVE
O. government is more terrible than tigers, 41.2

OPPRESSOR
The most potent weapon in the hands of the o., 17.19

OPPRESSORS
only the blood of the o. can fertilise the soil, 154.5

OPULENCE
private o. and public squalor, 60.9

ORATORY
rarity of great political o. 8.10

ORDER
a great New O. in Europe, 78.3
the honey-bees, Creatures that . . . teach the act of o. to a peopled kingdom, 148.13
The o. maintained by any state is called political, 154.1
The word O. . . . a cloak for tyranny, 14.5

ORIENTAL
three things that the O. certainly will not do, 68.4

OUTPUT
I am all for o., 99.8

OWNERSHIP
the extent of man's o. of his needs, 137.8

OXFORD
keep him in O. and he is partially muzzled, 127.11

PACIFISM
a doctrinaire faith in p., without facing its consequences, 44.2

PAIN
two sovereign masters, p. and pleasure, 14.2

PALACES
Peace to the hut, – war to the p., 23.3

PALE
every man . . . within the p. of the constitution 63.12

PALESTINE
the establishment in P. of a national home for the Jewish people, 11.12

PANTHEON
as for my name, you will find it in the P. of History, 45.9

PANTHER
I suggested that we use the p. as our symbol, 122.2

PANTS
I fly by the seat of my p., 173.12

PAPACY
The *P.* is . . . the *Ghost* of the deceased *Roman Empire*, 78.10

PARADISE
a P. . . . which has . . . angels with swords, 135.12

PARIS
P. wealth and P. luxury must also pay, 45.6
When P. sneezes, Europe catches cold, 114.3

PARLIAMENT
For us p. is . . . merely a means to an end, 77.12
No man can make a figure . . . but by P., 34.2
not member of Bristol, but . . . member of p., 23.12
P. . . . a dignified, not an effective, element in the Constitution, 44.3
When . . . words are to be discussed P. wakes up, 118.6
You are no P., 43.11

PARLIAMENTARY
the party and p. systems become becalmed, 63.2
The perfection of P. style is to utter cruel platitudes, 144.11
'We are a P. nation.', 135.2

PARLIAMENTS
England is the mother of p. 22.3
Long p. are . . . fatal to sound business, 93.2

PARSON
The P. leaves the *Christian* in the Lurch, 25.10

PARTIES
All p. . . . are varieties of absolutism, 136.4
maintain the line of demarcation between the p. 48.4
Most p. . . . go through a fit of cold feet, 10.8
p. are formed, more with reference to controversies that are gone by, 147.4

P. . . . generally, like *Freebooters*, hand out *False Colours*, 69.8

P. must ever exist in a free country, 24.2

p., which are a natural offspring of Freedom, 106.7

political p. were like snakes, guided not by their heads, but by their tails, 112.12

things must be done by p., not by persons using p. as tools, 48.1

PARTINGTON

Gentlemen . . . You will beat Mrs P., 152.4

PARTY

A furious P.-Spirit . . . exerts itself in Civil War, 2.4

a hard money p. against a paper p., 15.1

A p. to *be* strong, should always *appear* strong, 102.4

A sect or p. is an elegant incognito, 53.4

acquiring influence in a political p. in England, 172.3

All free governments are p. governments, 62.1

He serves his p. best who serves his country best, 73.3

I am sure that the P. System is right and necessary, 75.9

I had to . . . educate our P., 48.16

I have always acknowledged myself to be a p. man, 57.5

I shall never join any p., 19.15

Ignorance maketh most Men go into a P., 69.13

in the place of the . . . will of the nation the will of a p., 170.1

no p. is . . . better than another, 11.5

p. attachments . . . in the first class of a statesman's duties, 43.1

P. is a body of men united, 23.8

P. is . . . a survival . . . of the primitive combativeness of mankind, 106.9

p. is . . . bone of its bone, 9.5

P. is in England a stronger passion than love, 42.11

P. is organised opinion, 48.13

P. is the contemporary dictatorship, 137.5

P. loyalty lowers the greatest men, 93.3

principles are fitted to p., p. degenerates into faction, 33.12

take care never to speak or act . . . in a p. spirit, 54.9

The best P. is but a kind of Conspiracy against the rest of the Nation, 69.12

the existence and maintenance of a great p., 130.1

The Heat of a P. is like the Burning of a Fever, 69.11

The p. in the last instance is always right, 163.10

The p. lash and the fear of ridicule, 96.9

the unhappy divisions of mankind by p.-spirit, 133.4

There are some of us . . . who will fight and fight again to save the P. we love, 60.2

There is nothing so bad for the Face as P.-Zeal, 2.3

to p. gave up what was meant for mankind, 66.9

unless he believes that p. represents his own highest . . . ideas, 173.5

You cannot influence a Political P. to do Right, 13.5

Your p. man . . . regards himself as the next in succession, 41.9

PASSIONS

The agents that move politicks, are the popular, p. 3.6

PASSIVE

I do not like the term 'p. resistance.', 61.13

P. resistance is a sport for gentlemen, 87.9

P. resistance is an all-sided sword, 61.12

Satyagraha differs from p. resistance, 61.7

PAST

Those who cannot remember the p. are condemned to fulfil it, 148.2

PATRIA

The old Lie: Dulce et decorum est Pro p. mori, 125.4

PATRIOT

A P. is a Fool in ev'ry age, 133.8

Never was P. yet, but was a Fool, 50.9

P. – A candidate for place, 56.8

PATRIOTISM

I realise that p. is not enough, 30.13

No money, no p., 158.5

one thing worse than the cant of p., 145.2

Our country is . . . too sordid for p., 3.7

P. . . . . is a necessary link in the golden chains of our affections, 40.11

P. is the last refuge of the scoundrel, 86.8

the p. of the deracinated, 124.5

There is no word so prostituted as p. 141.14

To strike freedom of the mind with the fist of p., 155.6

PATRIOTS

P. rise up like mushrooms, 116.6

the loudest p. are the greatest profiteers, 12.8

Why, p. spring up like mushrooms!, 169.2

PATRONAGE

No one knows better than a former p. secretary, 74.2

PAY

They deserve the shortest hours and the highest p., 60.10

PEACE
A quarter of a century of p. does not pass over a nation in vain, 127.4
determined on p. when all the other Powers . . . are at war, 133.1
Fascism . . . believes neither in the possibility nor the utility of perpetual p., 119.9
For the p., that I deem'd no p., is over and done, 159.4
I believe it is p. for our time, 31.5
If p. cannot be maintained with honour, it is no longer p., 145.1
Let him who desires p. prepare for war, 166.5
one [current of opinion] wanting war and the other p. 119.13
p. does not pass over a nation in vain, 127.4
p., I hope, with honour, 49.5
P. is indivisible, 98.5
P. to the hut, 23.3
There never was a good war, or bad p., 58.5
There never was a time . . . when . . . we might not more reasonably expect fifteen years of p., 131.12
They make a wilderness and call it p., 158.1

PEACEMAKERS
Blessed are the p., 17.9

PEASANTS
A great Country of hardy P. is not to be subdued, 58.3

PEEL
P. . . . so near our definition of a constitutional statesman, 8.8

PENDULUM
a p. movement in history, swinging from absolutism to democracy, 91.4
The p. swung furiously to the left, 104.1
the so-called swing of the p., 25.5

PENSIONS
P. . . . pay given to a state hireling, 86.3

ʾEOPLE
A government is . . . put there by the will of the p., 11.9
a government of all the p., by all the p., and for all the p., 128.5
A p. which is able to say everything, 120.21
an indictment against an whole p., 24.1
the bludgeoning of the p. by the p. for the p., 172.11
the despot who tyrannizes over soul and body . . . is called the P., 172.3
the Legislators . . . put themselves into a state of War with the P., 100.10
The p. are turbulent and changing, 70.3
the p.'s government, made for the p., made by the p., and answerable to the p., 171.4
The p.'s silence is the king's lesson, 12.6

We are here . . . not to obey the will of the p., 129.8

PERMANENT
a p. revolution, 164.4

PERMISSIVE
P. legislation is the characteristic of a free people, 49.3

PERPETUITY
P. is stamped upon the constitution by the blood of our Fathers, 83.4

PERSECUTION
The doctrine of p. for cause of conscience, 173.3

PHILOSOPHERS
The p. have only interpreted the world differently, 110.1

PHILOSOPHY
unless political power and p. meet . . . there can be no rest from troubles, 132.10

PIGS
We began to show policeman as p. in our cartoons, 122.3

PILATE
Was P. right in crucifying Christ?, 155.2

PILL
I have got no Morrison's P. for curing the Maladies of Society, 29.12

PILOT
turn to the p. who weathered the storm, 28.8

PIN-PRICKS
avoid the p.-p. which precede cannon-shots, 120.3

PINK
well-meaning ambassadors . . . who belong to . . . the p.-tea type, 141.8

PIPS
I will squeeze her until you can hear the p. squeak, 62.6

PITY
P. is treason, 140.7

PLANNED
The idea that a completely p. . . . economic system could . . . bring about distributive justice, 72.12

PLATFORM
the p. . . . one of the most powerful . . . instruments of government, 31.12

PLEASURE
two sovereign masters, pain and p., 14.2

PLOUGH
The p. is not a political machine, 152.6

PLUTOCRACY
the oldest and toughest p. in the world, 158.13

PLUTOCRATIC
a people half democratic and half p. cannot . . . endure, 98.10

POETS
P. and philosophers are the unacknowledged legislators of the world, 150.10

POLAND
P. will never lose her national character, 92.4

POLES
For two hundred years the P. sold nothing but freedom, 139.3

POLICE
If . . . citizens are to be protected against unjust persecution by the p., 144.8
We Americans have no commission from God to p. the world, 72.9

POLICIES
sticking to the carcass of dead p., 147.9

POLICY
A p. is a temporary creed, 61.10
My [foreign] p. . . . to take a ticket at Victoria Station, 17.1
Refined p. ever has been the parent of confusion, 24.4
the only good p. is to pursue no p., 113.11
To render it agreeable to good, p. 70.1

POLISH
no Russian regime can abide a P. state, 148.9

POLITIC
In our body p., . . . what can be . . . assimilated is nutrition, 161.1
The body p. is like a tree, 116.8
the word *p.*, which . . . has signified cunning, 53.9

POLITICAL
A declining p. class has all the infirmities of old age, 151.11
circumstances render every . . . p. scheme beneficial or noxious, 24.11
custom . . . authorises a certain latitude in p. matters, 34.6
P. action is not moral action, 62.4
p. genius, . . . the identification of an individual with a principle, 74.6
P. language . . . is designed to make lies sound truthful, 124.9
P. thinking consists in deciding on the conclusion first, 43.16
The true end of p. action is . . . to affect the deeper convictions of men, 88.7
to accept the status of a p. robot, 15.9

POLITICIAN
A p. crystallises what most people mean, 135.3
A p. will do anything to keep his job, 74.1
An honest p. . . . will stay bought, 27.8

easier . . . for a rich man to enter the kingdom of heaven than for a p. to lay aside disguise, 32.14
No man can be a p. except he be first a historian, 72.8
The distinction between a statesman and a p., 44.9
the rudiments of a p.; the world must be your grammar, 33.13
When I want to buy up any p. 166.2

POLITICIANS
P. are ambitious not to *make* important decisions, 44.7
P. are like the bones of a horse's fore-shoulder, 130.13
P. neither love nor hate, 50.5
P. . . . promise to build a bridge even where there is no river, 90.4
They should certainly not get it [sense of purpose] from their p., 105.12
timid and interested p., 104.5
We cannot safely leave politics to p., 62.10

POLITICS
A gentleman will blithely do in p., 142.5
A man who is not interested in p. is not doing his patriotic duty, 164.12
all p. seem like provincial struggles for booty between dusky tribes, 153.8
Are not Religion & P. the Same Thing?, 19.12
English p. . . . reaction between the Ministry and the Parliament, 9.4
Finality is not the language of p., 48.10
I am not made for p. 27.14
I taste no p. in boiled and roast, 152.5
In p., guts is all, 30.7
In p. one must take nothing tragically and everything seriously, 160.6
In P. . . . the public ought to have the means of checking those who serve it, 103.6
In p. there is no use looking beyond the next fortnight, 32.1
In public p. . . . character is better than brains, 6.5
Make p. a sport, as they do in England, 154.15
Most mistakes in p., 117.4
Only he has the calling for p. who . . . will not crumble, 170.10
P. . . . a means of livelihood affected by . . . criminal classes, 17.16
P. . . . a means of rising in the world, 86.9
P. are an ordeal path among red-hot ploughshares, 1.12
P. can be relatively fair in the breathing spaces of history, 91.3
P. . . . has always been the systematic organisation of hatreds, 1.8
p. in the presence of social dangers . . . a luxury, 114.11

p. is a matter for tact, study, observation and precision, 61.3

P. is a systematic effort to move other men, 86.13

P. is the art of the possible, 18.7

p. is the despot of will, 9.17

P. is war without bloodshed, 109.3

P. is who gets what, when, how, 93.12

P., like religion, hold up the torches of martyrdom, 85.7

P. ruin the character, 65.13

P. – the art of getting [a place], 56.8

P. . . . The conduct of public affairs for private advantage, 17.15

P. would become an utter blank to me, 63.8

Practical p. consists in ignoring the facts, 1.9

The field of p. always presents the same struggle, 12.10

The man who puts p. first is not fit to be called a civilised being, 69.3

though p. is . . . a highly competitive profession, 45.2

PONTIFF

It is an error to believe that the Roman P. can . . . agree with progress, 132.4

POODLE

It is Mr Balfour's p., 99.2

POOR

everywhere man, the heir of nature, is p., 98.6

Give me your tired, your p., 94.11

It is not revenge we want for p. people, but happiness, 117.12

Laws grind the p., 66.8

the perennial and unfailing kindness of the p. to the rich, 34.7

uphold the p. against the rich, 100.12

where the p. rule, it is democracy, 4.4

POPE

Do not run up your nose dead against the P., 11.8

If you're not made P. in the Roman Catholic Church, 25.6

The P.! How many divisions has *he* got?, 154.10

POPULAR

rarely an ambitious man who does not try to be p., 123.6

The doctrine of p. sovereignty . . . will produce perfect anarchy, 158.4

We do not veto p. initiatives, 137.12

POPULARITY

I . . . never . . . do anything for the sake of p., 42.10

governments have nothing to do with seeking p., 160.4

POPULIST

A p. politician . . . says things because he believes them to be popular, 134.6

POSSESSION

Where p. has no stability, there must be perpetual war, 80.4

POSSESSIONS

the people's wants do not exceed their p., 16.11

when in the course of war any nation acquires new p., 131.14

POSTERITY

never to think of p. when making a speech, 113.4

POUND

It does not mean . . . that the p. here in Britain . . . has been devalued, 174.1

POVERTY

In other countries p. is a misfortune, 102.2

P. has many roots, but the tap root is ignorance, 86.1

P. is the parent of revolution and crime, 4.6

P. is the symptom; slavery the disease, 39.9

p. will use democracy to win the struggle against property, 16.1

This administration . . . declares unconditional war on p. in America, 85.14

POWER

a classic example of p. without responsibility, 20.8

a perpetuall . . . desire of P., that ceaseth onely in Death, 78.5

absolute p. corrupts absolutely, 1.6

An honest man can feel no pleasure in . . . p. over his fellow citizens, 85.8

even an angel becomes a whore . . . when he enters the church of p., 139.4

Every high degree of p. . . . involves . . . freedom from good and evil, 122.13

excessive love for the balance of p. 22.2

his happier hour of Social Pleasure, ill-exchanged for P., 133.7

In a social system in which p. is open to all, 144.6

Men of p. have no time to read, 57.2

No reason can be assigned why one man should exercise any p. . . . over his fellow-creatures, 69.16

Only he deserves p. who every day justifies it, 70.14

Political p. grows out of the barrel of a gun, 108.5

P. and *Liberty* are like *Heat* and *Moisture*, 69.9

P. is so apt to be insolent, and Liberty to be saucy, 69.15

P.? It's like a dead sea fruit, 106.1

P. tends to confuse itself with virtue, 59.6

P. vegetates with more vigour after these
gentle prunings, 105.2

p. without responsibility, 10.9

the love of p. is the love of ourselves, 73.9

the love of p. . . . requires the sacrifice of
principle, 73.7

the possession of p. . . . corrupts the
untrammelled judgement of reason, 87.7

The principle in mechanics is by the smallest
p. . . . to produce the greatest possible effect,
67.15

The purpose of getting p., 16.10

the tendency for p. to beget countervailing p.,
60.6

The use of p. in the extension of American
institutions, 38.4

There is no man . . . that lusts for p. . . . that
does not rue it in the end, 75.7

there is nothing but p. that can restrain p.,
139.5

to distinguish . . . between P. and *Right.*, 58.2

to seek p. and to lose liberty, 8.3

Unlimited p. is apt to corrupt, 131.7

We have given the prize of p. to the strong,
the cunning, the arithmetical, 98.11

Whoever has p. in his hands wants to be
despotic, 167.7

PRAYER
the Conservative Party at p., 143.3

PRAYS
he who p. best will fight best, 43.8

PRECEDENT
A p. embalms a principle, 48.6

from p. to p., 159.3

PRESERVATION
confusing the duty of p. with inactivity,
114.14

PRESERVE
that . . . most deadly error . . . that our
business is to p. and not to improve, 5.5

PRESIDENCY
carry out of the P. the reputation which
carried him into it, 85.5

Extremism in the pursuit of the P. is an
unpardonable vice, 85.18

it isn't for you. It's for the P., 164.13

PRESIDENT
that damned cowboy is P. of the United
States, 71.2

the office of P. will never fall to the lot of any
man . . . not . . . endowed with the requisite
qualifications, 70.13

PRESS
In old days men had the rack. Now they have
the p., 172.12

The p. is . . . a chartered libertine, 131.3

this is my last p. conference, 123.1

PRETENDER
But who P. is, or who is King, 25.9

PREVENTIVE
A p. war is always evil, 122.7

PRICE
All these men have their p., 169.6

PRIDE
there is no p. where there is distress, 146.3

PRIESTS
P. have . . . been remarkable for . . .
unrelenting cruelty, 38.11

P. have nephews, 129.14

PRIMA
P. *facie* is not meant for serious politics, 117.5

PRIME MINISTER
A p.m. governs by curiosity and range of
interest, 173.13

A P.M.'s position brings meanness to his feet,
57.1

great talents . . . are not to be wished for in a
p.m., 102.1

P.M. . . . loneliness of that position, 11.6

such power as every modern British P.M. has,
13.8

the P.M. has to be a butcher, 25.7

'would you rather be a country gentleman
than a P.M.?', 104.9

PRINCE
A p. . . . should learn from the fox and the
lion, 106.6

No p. is so Great, as not to . . . give an
outward . . . worship to the laws, 69.7

PRINCES
all the p. of the earth are subject to the laws
of God, 20.1

PRINCIPLES
Political p. . . . are usually designed for a war
which is over, 158.9

PRISON
the true place for a just man is also in p.,
160.13

the walls of the p. remained standing, 75.13

PRIVATE
P. opulence and public squalor, 60.9

PRIVILEGE
The accursed power which stands on P., 13.2

PRIVILEGED
the P. and the People form two nations, 48.3

PROFITS
Civilisation and p. go hand in hand, 42.2

PROGRAMME
Our p. is simple: we wish to govern Italy,
119.7

PROGRESS
Every jump of technical p. causes a fall in the political-maturity thermometer, 91.4

PROHIBITIONS
P. can ruin only weak parties, 65.6 ·

PROLETARIAN
A p. church is impossible, 163.6
moral grandeur of the p. revolution, 163.5
one nation more unfortunate than the Polish ... the nation of p., 169.11
What the p. lacks is capital, 19.13
without the preliminary victory of the p. revolution in other countries, 154.6

PROLETARIAT
class struggle ... leads to the dictatorship of the p., 110.9
Dictatorship of the P., 54.6
The dictatorship of the p. is an historically regressive idea, 72.7
The judge is history, the executioner is the p., 111.1
The p. alone is a really revolutionary class, 110.4
The p. has its reasons to rejoice, 95.2
that pentasyllabic French derivative, 'p.', 10.4

PROMISED
I've looked over, and I've seen the P. Land, 90.9

PROMISES
Where p. are not observed, there can be no leagues or alliances, 80.4

PROPERTY
a sword pointed at the heart of p. power, 16.3
Democracy is not possible except in a nation where there is so much p., 128.7
Government has no other end but the preservation of P., 100.6
If we women are wrong in destroying private p., 128.3
Next to the right of liberty, the right of p. is the most important, 158.3
P. is a god, 9.16
P. is theft, 135.14
p. ... should share its political supremacy, 1.5
p. ... will destroy democracy, 16.1
save p. divided against itself, 103.3
the horrible evils that result from ... private p., 172.7
The right to p. ... alone stands, an isolated privilege, 162.1
Where p. is not transferred by consent, there can be no commerce, 80.4
You cannot divorce p. from power, 139.6

PROPERTYLESS
Civilisation cannot survive if it rests upon a p. proletariat, 16.13

PROSPERITY
the tropical growth of p., 99.7

PROTECTION
P. and patriotism are reciprocal, 27.3

PRUSSIA
In P. it is only kings who make revolutions, 18.5
P. is rather stout, 19.9
Should P. perish, the art of government would return to its infancy, 116.2

PSYCHIATRY
Institutional p. is a continuation of the Inquisition, 157.1

PSYCHOLOGY
Any political party whose leaders knew a little p., 144.3

PUB
this place is like a p. to a drunkard, 100.1

PUBLIC
every action of his life ... the fair subject of
He speaks to me as if I was a p. meeting, 167.2
P. bodies are ... worse than the individuals composing them, 73,12
P. opinion is the ... result of the intellect of the community acting upon general feeling, 73.13
What we call p. opinion is generally p. sentiment, 49.6

PUBLICITY
I have none of the qualities which create p. 7.2

PUNISHMENT
The ... ultimate instrument of political power is capital p., 112.10

PURSE
the longest p. finally wins, 61.5
solving every difficulty ... by thrusting the hand into the public p., 129.9

PURSES
Long p. make strong swords, 156.9

QUARREL
trying on gas-masks because of a q. in a faraway country, 31.4

QUIXOTES
Are we to be the Don Q. of Europe, 39.6

RABBIT
about to be trampled to death by a r., 87.8

RACE
I ... am in favour of the r. to which I belong having the superior position, 97.2

RACIAL
There are no revolutions except r. revolutions, 77.11
unwholesome weeds that grow in the morass of r. hatred, 99.12

RACIALISM
The flag of r. . . . hoisted in Wolverhampton, 13.7

RADICAL
A r. is a man with both feet firmly planted – in the air., 140.15

RADICALS
Few r. have good digestions, 25.8

REACTION
There is no middle way between R. and Revolution, 136.6
to seek refuge in the almshouse of r. 75.10

REACTIONARY
A r. is a somnambulist walking backwards, 140.15
I shall adopt a r. line throughout my speech, 119.5

REALITIES
the new r. of our time, 59.4

RE-ARM
supposing that I had . . . said we must r., 10.13

REASON
Great public measures cannot be carried by . . . mere r., 130.4

REBEL
The r. is careful to preserve the abuses from which he suffers 148.3

REBELLION
a little r. now and then, is a good thing, 84.13
I will always side with him . . . who endures r., 101.5
r. demands that one *rise or exalt oneself*, 155.13
R. is as the sin of witchcraft, 17.3
R. is justified, 109.2

RECONCILE
to r. is perhaps a more amiable virtue . . . than to reform, 168.8

REFERENDUM
a device so alien to all our traditions as the r., 6.12

REFORM
A slender r. amuses and lulls the people, 105.2
Conservatism goes for comfort, r. for truth, 53.7
Every r. was once a private opinion, 53.6
If you try to make a big r. you are told you are doing too much, 75.5

R., that you may preserve, 103.3
the people in power were against reform, 14.6

REFORMATION
The heart makes a revolution, the head a r., 56.7
the glorious principles and the immortal martyrs of the R., 144.13

REFORMERS
Public r. had need first act in private, 33.6
r. . . . lay down the pontoons, 76.1

REGISTER
The advice which I give to the Conservatives is this – r., r., r., 129.10

REIGN
R., but do not govern!, 177.1

RELIEF
gigantic system of outdoor r., 22.2

RELIGION
An Empire without r. is like a house built upon sand, 167.1
It is not socialism but capitalism that is opposed to r., 41.4
R. . . . the centre of gravity in a realm, 40.13
the discovery that we were mistaken in maintaining their [politics'] association with r., 63.8
the introduction of politics into r. is the prostitution of true r., 69.4

RELIGIONS
All r. . . . are more or less inimical to liberty, 37.3
All r. have based morality on obedience, 76.8

REMEDY
A desperate disease requires a dangerous r., 56.5

RENT
down with everything, and up with r.!, 26.5

REPRESENTATION
R. is fraud, 137.4
the system of r. possess[es] the full . . . confidence of the country, 171.11

REPRESENTATIVE
no statesman . . . with greater right than I can say that he is the r. of his people, 78.2
The benefits of the R. system are lost, 114.17

REPRESENTATIVES
the r. of the people are . . . candidates for tyranny, 41.10

REPRESSION
Applying legal methods to r. eliminates . . . the illegal nature of r., 161.2

REPUBLIC
a r. is a raft, which will never sink, 3.4
'A R.?' said the Seagreen . . . 'What is that?', 29.6

the r. has no mystical saving-clauses, no Divine Right, 75.12

We are unfit for a r.; we cannot breathe under a despotism, 160.1

REPUBLICAN

R. despotism is more fertile in acts of tyranny, 120.14

The r. is the only form of government . . . not . . . at . . . war with the rights of mankind, 85.3

To *rule* autocratically and . . . *govern* in a r. manner, 87.6

REPUBLICANISM

the seal of liberty, the genius of r., 45.10

What has r. ever done for freedom?, 22.10

REPUBLICS

R. . . . . appeal to the understanding, 8.13

The genius of r. is pacific, 70.9

REPUTATIONS

Over even the greatest r. it closes with barely a bubble, 18.2

RESIGNATION

Ministers have a great deal of patience, but no r., 152.8

RESPONSIBLE

Being r. I *will* direct, 131.4

RESTORATION

The worst of revolutions is a r., 57.7

RETREAT

In the Soviet Army it takes more courage to r. than to advance, 154.12

REVISIONISM

only one answer to r.: smash its face in!, 95.4

REVOLT

arming for r. the wicked and the revolutionary, 54.10

Every successful r. is termed a revolution, 135.10

REVOLUTION

a great democratic r. is taking place amongst us, 161.5

A nation in r. is like boiling bronze, 45.5

A r. is a misfortune, 74.12

A r. is opinion backed by bayonets, 120.15

A r. such as ours is . . . a clap of thunder for the wicked, 146.8

A r. that does not continue to grow deeper is a r. that is retreating, 68.7

Better to perish with the r., 75.10

do you want a r. without r.?, 140.2

I have heard it said each year that we are going to have a r., 32.13

my forte is r., 49.10

Progressiveness is an absolute condition for a Modern R., 156.3

R. . . . . an abrupt change in the form of misgovernment, 17.17

R. is the festival of the oppressed, 67.14

R. or dictatorship can sometimes abolish bad things, 111.2

The heart makes a r., 56.7

the third [way] is by social r., 9.18

The R. . . . . eats its own children, 23.4

The r. is incapable of . . . burying its dead, 154.6

The spirit of r. . . . . is . . . radically opposed to liberty, 68.8

REVOLUTIONARIES

The city is the cemetery of r., 30.9

the baseness which makes conservatives and the envy which makes r., 67.2

REVOLUTIONARY

A r. against the revolution, 77.7

A r. idea . . . expresses . . . popular instincts, 9.12

A r. party is a contradiction in terms, 44.6

The duty of every r. is to make a revolution, 30.11

the r. politician should know when to make his exit, 176.5

To separate himself from the society . . . will lead the r. . . . . to death, 70.15

REVOLUTIONS

Do you demand . . . that r. be made with rose-water?, 32.12

Great r. are the work rather of principles than of bayonets, 111.11

In Prussia it is only kings who make r., 18.5

In r. those who want everything always get the better, 114.4

People's r. are born from the course of events, 9.11

R. are as a rule not made arbitrarily, 164.2

R. are like the most noxious dunghills, 120.16

R. are never waged singing 'We Shall Overcome', 107.4

R. do not go backward, 96.11

R. have never lightened the burden of tyranny, 149.4

R. . . . . spring from trifles, 4.5

Ten or a hundred Cultural R. are needed, 80.1

without this purpose there may be riots . . . but no r., 112.4

RHINE

the R. . . . is where our frontier lies today, 10.10

RICH

In the interest of the r. we must get rid of it [property], 172.8

the r. are r. because they rob the poor, 118.4

The r. . . . . consume little more than the poor, 151.15

Two nations ... the r. and the poor, 48.2

RIGHT
Every civil r. grows out of a natural r., 126.8
There is only one r. . . . and that r. is one's own strength, 77.10
What is r. must be unavoidably politic, 129.3

RIGHTEOUSNESS
R. exalteth a nation, 17.5

RIGHTS
Natural r. . . . nonsense upon stilts, 14.8
out of the shadow of states' r. and into the sunlight of human r., 80.7
rational abstraction in the place of the r. of the people, 66.1
r. . . . : not open to all alike would be no r., 36.15
the abstract r. . . . of woman . . . will not shrink from the same test, 175.2
the miserable sophism of the R. of Man, 40.14

RING
My hat's in the r., 141.11

RISES
No man r. so high, 43.14

RISING
All r. to great place is by a winding stair, 8.4

ROAR
I had the luck to be called upon to give the r., 36.11

ROMANTICISM
The only healthy foundation for a great state is egoism, not r. 18.3

ROME
R. alone must be the capital of Italy, 31.2
Today it [the world] is filled with the memory of R., still prophesying liberty, 146.5

RORSCHACH
it was like a R. ink blot, 123.4

ROYAL
this puling R. Great Grand-child, 71.12

ROYALTY
R. . . . appeals to diffused feeling, 8.13
to shake that decent respect for the living symbol of the State . . . r., 93.1

RULE
No one can r. guiltlessly, 146.2
To r. with the help of one's enemies, 19.8

RULERS
R. are a scourge, 1.1
r. are much the same in all ages, 40.6

RULING
every r. class has at its disposal . . . the necessary material means with which to defend itself, 151.9

revolution always starts from . . . dissension in the r. class, 132.11

RUSSET
a plain r.-coated captain, 43.4

RUSSIA
All the small nations . . . need a strong R., 111.8
Autocracy is the main condition of R.'s political existence, 165.2
Give Holy R. a taste of shot, 19.16
If England does not want something to happen, R. will not do it, 114.1
in R. they are slaves to the future, 15.6
R. is . . . a comet of eccentric orbit, 47.4
the distance between R. and British India is not to be measured by the finger and thumb, 147.8
They are fighting for Mother R., 154.11

RUSSIAN
I don't know a good R. from a bad R., 141.1
Invasion is second nature to the R. Empire, 113.13
The R. people . . . does not aspire to political power, 2.6
the R. people have moved forward . . . through revolution, 112.7
That key is R. national interest, 35.10

SACRIFICE
The willing s. of the innocents, 61.11

SAFE
The world must be made s. for democracy, 174.7

SALVATION
a S. Army which took to its heels, 118.11

SANCTIONS
There were two kinds of s., effective and ineffective, 52.2

SANITAS
s. sanitatum, omnia s., 48.17

SANS-CULOTTISM
s.-c., which has devoured them, will . . . end by devouring itself, 45.7

SATYAGRAHA
s. differs from passive resistance, 61.7

SAVAGE
Remember that the rights of the s., as we may call him, 64.3

SAVAGES
We are not ignorant s. any more, 89.10

SAVE
I can s. this country and . . . no one else can, 131.1

SAVED
A country will never be s. by the best men in it, 168.6

SAY
If you do not s. what you think, soon you will dare to s. what you do not think, 128.6

SCAFFOLD
Every step of progress . . . has been from s. to s., 130.8

SCHOOLMASTER
The s. is abroad, 22.7

SCIENCE
the *dismal s.*, 29.14

SCIENTISTS
Statesmen must learn to live with s., 118.10

SCOUT
He was the nation's number one Boy S., 88.5

SCRUM
All cannot be fly halves; there must be a s., 75.9

SCUTTLE
s. is the only word, 36.10

SEAGREEN
O s. incorruptible, 29.6

SECESSION
S., like any other revolutionary act, may be morally justified, 83.5

SECOND-RATE
creed of a s.-r. man, 8.8

SECRETARY
the former future S. of State, 51.2

SEDITION
I have . . . snapped my squeaking baby-trumpet of s., 40.4

SEDITIOUS
better for a Government to be *hard of hearing* in respect of s. language, 129.13

SEGREGATION
S. now, s. tomorrow and s. forever!, 168.2

SELF
objections . . . to the extension of s. government amongst the people, 31.10
s.-determination is not a mere phrase, 174.8

SELFISHNESS
Socialism proposes no adequate substitute for the motive of enlightened s., 158.3

SELSDON
S. Man is designing a system of society for the ruthless, 174.2

SERPENT
The s. may as well abandon . . . obliquity of his motion, 150.14

SERVANTS
Men in great place are thrice s., 8.3

SERVILITY
They aspire through s.; they repose in insignificance, 73.14

SHADOW
I am running a Bolshevik Revolution with a Tsarist S. Cabinet, 173.7

SHITTERS
We have always been shooters, but never s., 66.4

SHOES
If you rebel against high-heeled s., 150.1

SHOPKEEPERS
A nation of s. are very seldom so disinterested, 2.2
fit only for a nation of s., 152.1

SHOW
the s. often wins the battle, 102.4

SICK
The 's. man of Europe' today, 60.3
We have on our hands a s. man, 122.4

SIDMOUTH
like S., next, Hypocrisy, 150.8

SILENCE
a period of s. on your part would be welcome, 6.14
The people's s. is the king's lesson, 12.6
the s. of the people is a lesson for kings, 116.3
the s. reverts to patriotism, 161.3

SILLIES
if the s. can always be sure of re-election, 25.5

SLAVE
Let us draw a cordon . . . round the s. States, 96.12
the suppression of the s. trade, and the reformation of manners, 172.5

SLAVERY
If s. is not wrong, nothing is wrong, 97.8
S. is founded on the selfishness of man's nature, 96.8

SLAVES
S. cannot breathe in England, 42.6

SLAY
not one, nor thousands must they s., 118.2

SLEEP
to break this s. of a century, 129.4

SLEEPWALKER
I got the way . . . with the assurance of a s., 78.1

SLIP-SHOD
a nation who . . . pass the whole of their lives s.-s., 127.3

SMALL
S. nations have . . . ever been the cradle of political liberty, 161.8

SMILE
S. without Art, 133.7

SMITHS
We S. want peace so bad we're prepared to kill . . . the Joneses, 155.14

SNAILS
S. are a wise generation, 70.6

SNOUTS
those with the biggest s. get the largest share, 171.6

SOCIALISE
We s. human beings, 78.4

SOCIALISM
a sudden leap forward, from capitalism into s. 15.3
anti-semitism is the s. of fools, 12.9
can the final victory of s. be achieved in one country . . .?, 154.7
Give s. back its human face, 50.12
Schopenhauer and suicide or s. and struggle, 67.12
S. and *laisser faire* are like the north and south poles, 11.3
S. and rationalism are . . . the touchstones of humanity, 76.9
s. becomes a science, 54.7
the entire programme of revolutionary s., 10.1
This is not s. It is Bolshevism run mad, 153.1
This is S. pure and simple, 71.5
We cannot outline s., 95.14

SOCIALIST
a common problem and concern of all S. countries, 21.7
Defeat is not in the S. dictionary, 72.1
In one country it is impossible to accomplish . . . a s. revolution, 95.11
No S. can be a law-abiding citizen, 73.4
No s. system can be established without a political police, 36.7
. . . not a S. society, 16.11
The saying has been attributed to me that everyone is a s. now, 71.8
The s. revolution . . . is completed in the world arena, 164.4
The sun of the world s. revolution has already risen, 95.7
the word S. is one I could never well stomach, 13.1

SOCIALISTS
The s. talk first, then act, 114.15
The s. would drag men back from contract to status, 106.10

SOCIETY
I do not believe that the Great S. is the ordered . . . battalion of the ants, 86.2
S. is produced by our wants, and government by our wickedness, 126.1

the great lazar house of s., 153.7
the mortal enemy of existing s., 12.11
we have the opportunity to move . . . upward to the Great S., 85.15

SOLIDARITY
S. was needed in Poland, 139.4

SOULS
our s. contain exactly the contrary of what they wanted, 168.1

SOUTH
The S. is avenged!, 20.7

SOVERAIGNE
Judgments of the S., 78.6

SOVEREIGN
A subject and a s. are clean different things, 33.3
's. power' is no parliamentary word, 39.7
the s. has . . . three rights, 9.1

SOVEREIGNTY
S., being nothing more than the exercise of the general will, 142.11
The s. of each socialist country cannot be opposed to the interest of the socialist world, 91.6
The s. of the people can only be a fictitious idea, 114.12

SOVIET
The S. regime is not the embodiment of evil as you think, 177.3

SPEAK
Let other people s. out, 108.11

SPECTATORS
no reason why we should be anything more than s., 6.4

SPECTRE
the s. of Communism, 110.2

SPECULATION
This is the essence of *politics*; all the rest is *s.*, 71.7

SPINNING
in losing the s. wheel we lost our left lung, 61.9

SPIRITUAL
We are the s. reserve of the western world, 57.13

SPONGE
Paris a s. which must be squeezed, 45.6

SQUALOR
private opulence and public s., 60.9

SQUEAKS
the hinge that s. that gets the grease, 107.5

STABILITY
in order to preserve s. in government, 80.6
s. and experiment. The former is Tory, and the latter Whig, 43.3

STABLE
we don't know how bad the s. is going to smell, 50.2

STAGE
I cannot fail to be . . . in the centre of the s., 46.3

STAIR
All rising to great place is by a winding s., 8.4

STALIN
even S. himself begins to seem only a blind . . . agent, 153.2
It would be too much to say that I liked S., 52.5
my friend S., 13.4
S. himself . . . supported the glorification of his own person, 89.8

STATE
a free Church in a free S., 31.2
A s. without the means of some change, 24.8
Every S. must conquer, 9.10
If the s. is strong, it crushes us, 166.1
in the declining age of a s., mechanical arts and merchandise [flourish], 8.7
No s. can pledge its future to another, 162.7
the inner essence of the s., 74.10
The man who is guided by reason is more free in a S., 154.4
The mystery of the S. is become . . . ineffable, 33.9
The S. is a collection of officials, drawing comfortable incomes, 143.6
the s. is a creation of nature, 4.3
the S. is a trick, 53.9
The s. is embodied morality, 74.9
The s. is nothing but an instrument of oppression, 54.5
The S. is still . . . a collective despot, 79.10
The s. is the divine idea as it exists on earth, 74.8
The s. lies in all languages of good and evil, 122.11
the S. . . . makes them men, 40.10
The s. owes to every citizen an assured subsistence, 116.13
The S. . . . the most flagrant negation of humanity, 9.8
the s., . . . the poor man's bank, 19.13
The s. . . . withers away, 54.1
The word s. is identical with the word *war*, 92.2
this will be the century . . . of the S., 119.10
What has always made the s. a hell on earth, 78.14
Where the S. begins, individual liberty ceases, 9.9

STATES
the problem of a law-governed *external relationship* with other s., 87.3

STATESMAN
A constitutional s. is . . . a man of common opinions, 8.8
A s. should be possessed of good sense, 159.10
The heart of a s. should be in his head, 120.20
The vice most fatal to the s. is virtue, 57.12

STATUS
The Socialists would drag men back from contract to s., 106.10

STATUS QUO
Metternich and Guizot . . . became the guardians of the s.q., 76.2

STEAM
the loom and s.-engine are furiously political, 152.5

STERLING
s. should be above politics, 173.14

STICK
'Speak softly and carry a big s. . . .', 141.5

STIR
do not s. them up – it is a fearful responsibility, 172.1

STOCK
Of all the mysteries of the s. exchange, 60.7

STOMACH
the s. governs the world, 120.22

STONE
Jackson standing like a s. wall, 12.12

STREET
Whoever can conquer the s. will one day conquer the state, 65.4

STRENUOUS
I wish to preach . . . the doctrine of the s. life, 141.2

STRIKE
An occasional s. . . . manifestation of the continued health of the system, 60.8
There is no right to s. against the public safety, 42.1

STRIKES
With . . . general s. and Bolshevism . . . I have nothing to do at all, 104.8

STRUGGLE
politics is in essence 's.', 171.1
S. is the father of all things, 77.9

SUBSTITUTE
no s. for victory, 103.1

SUFFRAGE
Universal s. is counter-revolution, 136.5

SUICIDE
I found eternal life. Revolutionary S., 121.12

SUMMER
The s. soldier and the sunshine patriot, 126.5

SUMMITS
Nations touch at their s., 9.3

SUN
his Majesty's dominions, on which the s. never sets, 174.4
The s. never sets upon the interests of this country, 127.6
We have fought for our place in the s. and won it, 172.14
we want our place in the s., 23.5

SUPERMAN
the rainbow and the bridges to the S., 122.12

SUPERSTITION
the mummeries of s., 144.13

SURRENDER
No terms except unconditional and immediate s., 67.7

SWAMP
in the middle is the S., 12.10

SWORD
that intolerable slavery of a s. government, 116.11
The great strides which civilisation makes . . . are only made actual by this s., 162.10
when a nation that lifts up the s. against a nation, 99.1

SWORDS
they shall beat their s. into plowshares, 17.7

TARIFFS
T. . . . assist the struggle of capitalist *producers* against *consumers*, 101.9

TARTAR
sometimes they catch a T., 50.11

TARTARS
the *T*. . . . presently fall upon the *Baggage*, 69.8

TAX
The greatest . . . power entrusted to the government is the right to t. the citizens, 146.11
To t. and to please . . . is not given to men, 23.11

TAXATION
T. without representation is tyranny, 125.1
The result . . . is the perpetual increase of t., 116.14

TAXED
no subject of England shall be t. but by his own consent, 131.9

TAXER
Allegiance . . . bond of duty between t. and taxee, 17.12

TAXES
a direct and simple transfer of t. from one class of the community to another, 147.2
nothing can be said to be certain, except death and t., 58.6

TEEMING
The wretched refuse of your t. shore, 94.11

TERROR
T. is . . . justice, prompt, secure and inflexible, 140.6
T. is the homage that the malignant recluse finally pays, 27.15
t. the order of the day, 12.4

TERRORISM
the selective brutality of t., 88.1

THEATRE
made me quit that splendid t. of pitiful passions, 168.7

THEORY
A gram of experience is worth a ton of t., 146.14
Is it a recommendation to have no t.?, 70.8

THIN
The Russians dashed on towards that t. red streak, 145.3

THING
The feeling towards the T., 39.1

THIRD
it happeneth there is a t. Opinion, 69.6
we must try to find a 'T. System', 137.13

THISTLES
National ideals without imagination are but as the t. of the wilderness, 99.8

THOROUGH
And for the State . . . I am for T., 94.1

THOUGHT
t. is harder to tame than passion, 76.9

THOUSAND
How splendid were your T., O Italy!, 62.2
Nor will it be finished in the first one t. days, 88.14

THRONE
the crash of the proudest t. of the Continent, 103.3
What Prudent man a settled T. would shake?, 50.7

TIBER
I seem to see 'the river T. foaming with much blood.', 134.2

TICKET
take a t. at Victoria Station and go anywhere I damn well please, 17.1

TIGER
The people is a t. when it is loosed from its chains, 120.24

TIGERS
All the . . . reactionaries are no more than
  paper t., 108.9
Dictators ride to and fro upon t., 35.7

TIME
T. . . . my most useful colleague, 21.8

TIMES
the t. that try men's souls, 126.5

TITLE
Who gain'd no T., and who lost no Friend,
  133.5

TITLES
bring our t. to the market-place and make a
  bonfire of them, 94.7
T. had in all nations denoted *offices*, 105.1

TOLERANCE
T. is . . . of little worth in politics, 175.1

TOLERATION
T. is the cause of many evils, 4.2

TONGUE
if my life will not speak for me, my t. cannot,
  139.7

TOOLS
Give us the t. and we will finish the job, 36.2

TORIES
an idle schoolboy's dream to suppose that T.
  can legislate, 44.13
T. own no argument but force, 23.1
the rising hope of those stern and unbending
  T., 104.4

TORY
A T. government may do very well without a
  policy, 71.4
I hate the T. party, their men, their words,
  and their methods, 35.2
I was born a T., am a T. and shall die a T.,
  134.3
Keep on voting T. Till Eternity, 25.4
the T., and which might . . . be called the
  Conservative, party, 42.12
The T. Democracy . . . has embraced the
  principles of the T. party, 34.11
The T. party . . . lower than vermin, 15.8
The T. party, unless it is a national party, is
  nothing, 49.2
T. men and Whig measures, 47.8

TORYISM
a great deal in Villa T. which requires
  organisation, 34.9
T. . . . like the serpent sheds its skin, 94.6

TOTALITARIAN
a t. state [contradicts] the needs of a thriving
  industrial community, 15.9

TRADE
To make war upon those who t. with us,
  126.10

T. and commerce, if they were not made of
  India rubber, 160.11

TRANQUILITY
No important political improvement was ever
  obtained in a period of t., 105.2
To model our political system upon
  speculations of lasting t., 70.12

TREASON
For if it prosper, none dare call it t., 72.5
If this be t., make the most of it, 75.1

TREASURY
Our Lord who art in the T., 79.3
the T. is the spring of business, 8.12

TRIFLE
The outcome of the greatest events is . . .
  determined by a t., 120.1

TRIMMER
this innocent word T., 69.6

TRIUMPH
Injustice, arrogance, displayed in the hour of
  t., 99.11

TROUGH
get your snouts in the t., 171.7

TRUDEAU
T. . . . a political leader worthy of
  assassination, 94.10

TRUMPET
if the t. gives an uncertain sound, 169.9

TRUTH
Political t. is a libel, 73.8
The ministry of T. – Minitrue, 124.11
throwing love of t. and accurate reasoning
  into a secondary place, 117.2
T. can stand by itself, 84.11

TRUTHS
We hold these t. to be self-evident, 84.8

TUNISIAN
I think the T. pear is now ripe, 18.11

TURK
I should not be sorry . . . to see the T. kicked
  out of Europe, 127.3

TURKS
Let the T. now carry off their abuses, 64.1

TURNING
This lady's not for t., 159.8

TWENTIETH
I ought to . . . have had the t. century before
  me, 113.6

TYRANNISING
an equal chance to everybody of t., 115.2

TYRANNY
Democracy and T. . . . may be the Cholera,
  5.7
T. is a habit, 49.14
Where laws end, there t. begins, 131.6

TYRANT
a pulling down of one T., to set up another, 169.8

TYRANTS
watered by the blood of t., 12.3

ULSTER
U. . . . supported by the overwhelming majority of the British people, 94.9
U. will fight, and U. will be right, 35.1

UNBELIEVERS
Rid the sanctuary of God of the u., 165.1

UNCARING
a system of society for the ruthless and the pushing, the u., 174.2

UNEMPLOYED
An army of u. led by millionaires, 124.7

UNILATERALISM
the vast majority of Labour Members of Parliament are utterly opposed to u., 60.2

UNION
I considered it at once as the knell of the U., 85.9
sentiment, dear to every true American heart, – Liberty *and* U., 171.3
The Trade U. Movement has become . . . an avenue to political power, 170.3
trade u. for the nation, 74.5
We are not a Nation, but a U., 27.5

UNIONIST
the great U. party shall still control . . . the destinies of this great Empire, 11.10

UNIONISTS
the Party that betrayed the U., 30.1

UNITE
WORKING MEN OF ALL COUNTRIES, U.!, 110.8

UNITED STATES
All that is valuable in the U.S. constitution is one thousand years old, 130.12
North Vietnam cannot . . . humiliate the U.S., 123.3
The Constitution of the U.S., then, forms a *government*, 83.5

UNMUZZLED
I am come among you u., 63.13

UNPOPULAR
it is safest to take the u. side in the first instance, 113.2

UNSOCIALIST
Socialist production and U. distribution, 150.5

UNTHINKABLE
We must dare to think about 'u. things', 59.4

UPPER
only the u. echelons who are licked, 13.9

UTOPIA
An acre in Middlesex is better than a principality in U., 104.2
For other nations, u. is a blessed past never to be recovered, 90.12

VANITY
I . . . subtract the man's v. from his other qualities, 19.6

VEGETARIANS
There are certain people like v. and communists whom one cannot answer, 124.12

VENDETTA
I call for a V. . . . against every German in Britain, 21.3

VESUVIUS
We live as in a villa on V., 149.9

VICE
So v. is beneficial found, 107.13

VICES
Men are more easily governed through their v., 120.18

VICTORY
One more such v. . . . and we are utterly undone, 136.7
V. – v. at all costs, 35.11

VIGILANCE
Eternal v. is the price of liberty, 130.10
The condition . . . is eternal v., 44.11

VIOLENCE
Non-v. is the law of our species, 61.8
Socialism could not continue to exist without an apology for v., 153.6
the power which established a state is v., 87.8
there is a difference between v. practised by the oppressed and by the oppressors, 109.5
Victory attained by v. is tantamount to a defeat, 61.6
V. is man re-creating himself, 56.3

VIOLENT
answer a v. action with another action still more v., 130.7
turn political crisis into armed crisis by performing v. actions, 109.6

VIRGINIAN
I am a V., so naturally I am a politician, 6.9

VIRGINIANS
rally on V., 12.12

VIRTUOUSLY
A man who wishes to act v. . . . comes to grief, 106.5

VOICE
Governments will never be awed by the v. of the people, 135,8
'The v. of the people is the v. of God', 2.7

VOLCANO
two icy geniuses in a v., 67.1

VOLCANOES
You behold a range of exhausted v., 49.1

VOLTAIRE
One does not arrest V., 46.9

VOTING
All v. is a sort of gaming ... with a slight
moral tinge, 160.12
V. ... is not to be identified with democracy,
40.2

WAGES
Till your labour wax fat on its w., 156.9

WAIT
I'm afraid we must w. and see, 6.2

WAR
a just and honourable w., 8.6
A long w. ... reduces nations to ... ruin ...
or to despotism, 161.9
A w. more unjust in its origins ... I do not
know, 63.6
Always, everywhere, I wage w., 37.8
angry Heaven unto W. had sway'd, 109.9
As long as w. is regarded as wicked, 172.6
'balance of power' ... always an argument for
w., 21.9
England ... has chosen shame and will get
w., 35.8
far easier to make w. than to make peace, 38.3
For a war to be just, three conditions are
necessary, 3.13
He ... will think twice before beginning a
war, 19.7
I detest this [English Civil] w. without an
enemy, 168.4
In w. one sees one's own difficulties, 120.5
It is a phoney w., 45.1
It is magnificent, but it is not w., 21.1
It is politics which begets w., 37.2
it is the good w. that hallows every cause!,
122.10
It is well that w. is so terrible, 95.1
Mankind must put an end to w., 88.16
many a boy here to-day who looks on w. as
all glory, 151.3
No sane enemy ... would destroy the W.
Office, 119.1
ridiculous to associate ... w. with an earth
covered with railroads, 81.1
The blood-red blossom of w. with a heart of
fire, 159.4
The majority has usually no inclination for
w., 18.9
The perfecting of instruments of w., 119.3

these were the real reasons which moved me
to w., 58.8
To be prepared for w. is ... means of
preserving peace, 169.13
to make future w. improbable, 147.5
to prepare for w. in a capitalist country,
155.12
W. can be abolished only through w., 108.6
W. is just like a bush-clearing, 88.2
W. is never brought about by newspapers,
18.9
W. is only a regrettable expedient for
asserting one's rights, 87.4
W. ... is the breakdown of policy, 148.10
W. is the faro table of government, 126.9
W. is to man what childbirth is to woman,
118.12
w. ... *the continuation of politics by other
means*, 37.1
We are drifting towards w., 36.17
We have sustained a defeat without a w., 35.9
When is w. not w.?, 27.9
when you enter upon a w. purely ... for the
purposes of plunder, 98.13
Wisdom is better than weapons of w., 17.6
Without w. no state could exist, 162.9
Without w. the world would sink into
materialism, 116.10

WATER
Our future is on the w., 172.14

WATERLOO
it is W. which has deposed me, 120.10

WEAK
the West would say we were either stupid or
w., 89.11

WEAKNESS
Let w. learn meekness, 156.9
W. is not treachery, but it fulfils all its
functions, 173.1

WEALTH
A society cannot hold w. in honour, 132.12
As w. is power, 24.7
Liberty produces w. and w. destroys liberty,
98.8
Men of w. and influence, who act upon the
principle of virtue and religion, 135.9
People say law, but they mean w., 53.5
persuade poverty to use its political freedom
to keep w. in power, 16.2
There are three ways by which an individual
can get w., 62.11

WEAPON
The suicidal nature of this w. [atomic bomb],
88.7

WELFARE
the executive power as steward of the public
w., 141.10

WESTERN
We are the spiritual reserve of the w. world, 57.13

WESTMINSTER
W. is a place where moderation thrives, 44.5

WHEAT
we must harvest the w. when it is still green, 7.6

WHIG
The first W. was the Devil, 86.10
W. The name of a faction, 86.4

WHIGGISM
the glorious spirit of W., 131.9

WHIGS
caught the W. bathing, 47.9
Except the W. not getting into place, 26.3
The great enemies of real liberty have always been the W., 39.2
W. allow no force but argument, 23.1
W. . . . are an unnatural party standing between the People and the Tory aristocracy, 128.9

WHISPER
that the w. of a faction shall prevail against the voice of a nation, 144.12

WHITE
For the w. man to ask the black man if he hates him, 107.7
Take up the W. Man's Burden, 90.10
The Britain . . . to be forged in the w. heat of this [scientific] revolution, 173.8
the preservation of the w. man and his state, 166.7
the w. man is sitting at our table, 18.1
the w. people are chosen for the leadership of the world, 66.2
The w. race is the cancer of human history, 153.4
there are no 'w.' or 'colored' signs on the . . . graveyards of battle, 89.2
why did you allow us to worship at a w. altar?, 83.8

WIDOW
the departing world leaves behind it not an heir, but a pregnant w., 76.7

WILBERFORCES
Think of that! No W., 38.10

WILL
what makes the general w. general is . . . the common interest uniting them [the voters], 142.12

WIND
a w. of nationalism and freedom, 10.11
The w. of change is blowing through the continent, 105.9

WINE
put new w. into old bottles, 7.3
the route of the w.-shop, 9.18

WINNING
a w. cause has always pleased the gods, 151.13

WIREPULLERS
the ruling men will be the w. and their friends, 155.3

WISDOM
W. is better than weapons of war, 17.6

WISE
He never said a foolish thing, nor ever did a w. one, 140.9

WITCHCRAFT
I would rather that the people believe in w., 39.3

WOLF
As the w. bursts into the flock, so we come, 65.5

WOMAN
a w. politician who looks as if her hair has just been permed, 30.6
Discrimination between man and w. is a flagrant act of oppression, 137.10
I never knew a Party-W. that kept her Beauty, 2.3
let him despise w., if she do not share it [freedom] with him, 175.3
Life in the House is neither healthy, useful nor appropriate for a w., 6.8
materialistic conditions hindering w. from performing her natural role, 137.11
not alwayes that difference of strength . . . between the man and the w., 78.7
the body of a weak and feeble w., but . . . the heart and stomach of a king, 53.2
To promote a w. to bear rule . . . is repugnant to Nature, 91.2

WOMEN
There is no occupation . . . which belongs either to w. or men, 132.9
We are here to claim our rights as w., 127.12
W., and Champagne and Bridge, 13.2
W. . . . ought to have but little liberty, 143.1
w., their rights and nothing less, 3.12
W.'s liberation . . . will abolish a necessary substructure of the authoritarian state, 67.13

WOODEN
The w. walls are the best walls of this kingdom, 42.5

WOOLWORTH
We shall have to . . . live a W. life hereafter, 122.6

WORDS
If you use w. for political purposes, they soon
  lose whatever meaning they may have had,
  152.10
WORKERS
let the w. go hungry when business was slack,
  53.12
you, the organised w. of the country, are our
  friends, 151.5
WORKING
a real, democratic party is impossible unless it
  be a w. men's party, 54.3
Between them . . . the w. classes are being
  ground, 62.0
It will take the British w. man twenty years
  to . . . elect his equals, 72.3
The w. class is for Lenin what ore is for a
  metal-worker, 67.3
the w. world to whom the future belongs,
  61.2
those who would ameliorate the conditions of
  the w. classes, 141.13
w.-class bees without a sting, 118.5

WORKSHOP
w. of the world, 47.5
WORLD
I called a New W. into existence to redress
  the balance of the Old, 29.1
We are a w. power . . . or we are nothing,
  173.11
WRETCHED
ye w. of the earth, 133.11
WRINGING
before long they will be w. their hands, 169.1

YOUNG
When y. people grasp a truth they are
  invincible, 108.10

ZION
the Lord hath founded Z., 17.8
ZOMBIES
I have no wish to lead a party of political z.,
  174.3

Supplementary Index

Addison, Joseph, 133.5
Anarchism, 9.7, 9.8, 92.2, 92.3, 136.3
Aristocracy, 4.9, 99.3, 105.1, 116.5

Black Power, 17.18, 18.1, 37.6, 37.7, 83.7,
  88.10, 107.2, 107.3, 107.6, 122.2

Capitalism, 16.1, 29.13, 41.4, 42.2, 42.3, 60.8,
  60.9, 60.10, 73.2, 95.8, 101.9, 110.11, 117.6,
  117.8, 121.4, 121.7, 144.2, 149.9, 164.1
Castlereagh, Viscount, 26.2
Censorship, 57.10, 115.4, 115.10, 129.13,
  156.7, 163.9
Charles I, 109.8
Charles II, 140.9
Churchill, Winston, 15.7, 118.9, 118.13
Class and Class War, 13.9, 54.4, 72.2, 110.3,
  110.9, 116.7, 147.2
Communism and Marxism, 13.10, 95.4, 109.2,
  124.5, 124.12, 136.1, 137.2, 154.13, 155.2,
  163.10, 168.1
Conservatism, 3.10, 5.5, 12.13, 24.12, 50.7,
  56.1, 63.4, 63.5, 66.8, 76.2, 80.6, 113.11,
  114.14, 129.5, 134.3, 172.2
Conservative Party, 15.8, 30.1, 42.12, 44.1,
  74.5, 143.3, 148.1
Constitution (English), 8.11, 9.1, 12.2, 14.4,
  21.5, 38.9, 44.3, 52.3, 117.3
Contract, 1.5, 24.13, 50.6, 65.2, 78.6, 83.2,
  100.5, 100.7, 100.8, 100.10, 142.10
Crime, 4.6, 28.3, 45.13, 102.2, 112.13, 162.11
Cromwell, Oliver, 109.9

Democracy, 1.5, 3.9, 5.2, 8.1, 16.1, 16.3, 28.7,
  31.12, 54.3, 61.1, 73.2, 91.4, 101.3, 114.12,
  120.12, 120.13, 121.7, 128.5, 128.7, 135.2,
  143.6, 144.9, 158.13, 161.5, 172.11
Despotism and Tyranny, 3.8, 17.19, 24.10,
  41.2, 41.10, 42.4, 63.3, 70.7, 85.10, 87.5,
  120.14, 125.1, 127.2, 131.6, 131.11, 146.7,
  146.9, 147.3, 157.2, 157.3, 158.4, 161.7,
  161.11, 164.10, 167.7, 172.13

Education, 22.7, 101.2, 102.5, 128.7
Eisenhower, Dwight, 88.5
Elections, 3.1, 22.9, 23.12, 25.5, 31.12, 36.7,
  36.8, 40.2, 56.4, 62.3, 63.12, 63.15, 70.13,
  71.1, 72.3, 96.10, 103.6, 121.2
English, the, 4.11, 4.12, 7.3, 9.6, 12.2, 15.6,
  27.10, 32.11, 49.8, 117.1, 118.13, 124.5,
  170.2

Fascism and Nazism, 6.12, 65.4, 65.5, 65.7,
  119.9

Freedom, 5.2, 16.2, 22.10, 22.15, 25.2, 33.3,
  37.5, 40.1, 58.12, 58.13, 62.1, 71.11, 109.1,
  127.2, 147.3, 152.10, 153.9, 154.4
Foreign Relations and Diplomacy, 1.3, 2.1, 9.3,
  10.10, 11.12, 12.5, 15.4, 15.5, 16.9, 17.1,
  17.13, 18.10, 18.12, 18.13, 19.2, 19.10, 21.7,
  22.2, 23.5, 23.7, 28.10, 29.1, 30.2, 30.3, 31.5,
  31.6, 31.7, 32.2, 35.8, 35.9, 35.10, 37.8, 47.4,
  48.9, 51.1, 51.3, 52.2, 60.4, 62.6, 64.12, 68.1,
  68.4, 85.6, 87.3., 88.6, 88.7, 88.11, 88.13,
  90.11, 91.5, 95.6, 100.14, 101.4, 106.2, 113.3,
  114.1, 119.12, 120.3, 122.4, 122.5, 127.6,
  127.7, 127.9, 140.13, 141.3, 141.8, 147.5,
  147.8, 147.10, 148.8, 148.9, 155.11, 159.11,
  162.7, 169.14, 169.15, 175.5

Gladstone, William, 104.4, 127.11, 167.2
Government, 4.9, 11.8, 14.5, 19.8, 40.8, 40.11,
  47.11, 70.1, 71.10, 72.10, 73.12, 80.2, 83.5,
  84.8, 85.10, 85.11, 87.6, 100.5, 100.6, 101.8,
  116.4, 120.17, 120.18, 120.19, 120.22, 126.1,
  126.7, 129.9, 133.6, 135.8, 144.4, 144.7,
  146.2, 146.7, 146.9, 146.10, 146.11, 160.4,
  161.10, 170.1, 174.5

Hastings, Warren, 150.14, 151.1
House of Commons, 5.9, 6.8, 11.1, 18.2, 20.3,
  100.1, 168.7, 172.4
House of Lords, 49.4, 99.2, 99.4, 158.10,
  158.11

Imperialism and Colonialism, 14.1, 18.11,
  23.6, 34.4, 35.4, 35.6, 37.5, 64.9, 90.10, 94.3,
  104.11, 107.9, 108.9, 112.5, 120.3, 120.6,
  123.5, 126.6, 142.1
Individualism, 15.2, 115.1, 115.3, 115.4,
  119.10

Labour Party, 10.5, 31.9, 44.1, 45.2, 71.11,
  113.3, 153.1, 158.10, 158.12
Law, 15.5, 21.4, 21.5, 22.8, 36.15, 39.7, 39.8,
  42.4, 53.5, 61.5, 65.14, 66.3, 66.10, 69.7,
  69.14, 78.9, 79.7, 80.4, 84.2, 90.7, 106.4,
  108.1, 108.3, 113.5, 120.11, 125.2, 129.4,
  131.14, 137.6, 144.8, 154.2, 170.1
Leadership, 11.7, 31.9, 73.15, 93.11, 120.18,
  120.19, 121.10, 171.1, 172.2
Liberty, 7.1, 9.13, 12.3, 22.7, 33.3, 37.3, 41.7,
  41.10, 44.11, 52.8, 68.8, 69.15, 70.5, 78.13,
  94.11, 98.6, 98.7, 98.9, 111.15, 112.1, 115.3,
  126.3, 130.10, 146.5, 155.5, 158.3, 161.8,
  168.9

Macdonald, Ramsay, 35.5, 170.5, 118.11
Mill, James, 14.9, 79.2

Monarchy, 9.1, 20.1, 20.5, 21.4, 33.3, 51.4,
71.12, 84.6, 86.12, 93.1, 116.3, 126.11, 134.1,
140.4, 160.1, 166.10

Nixon, Richard, 90.13

Parliament, 9.4, 9.5, 11.1, 16.6, 34.1, 48.1,
72.10, 96.1, 123.7, 163.2
Parnell, Charles Stewart, 5.10
Party, 4.1, 11.7, 20.4, 27.7, 49.9, 130.1, 130.2,
146.12, 147.6, 160.4, 170.8
Patriotism, 2.9, 27.3, 46.2, 66.7, 74.1, 79.11,
99.7, 120.6, 125.4, 161.3, 164.12
Peace, 18.10, 38.3, 51.3, 120.3, 127.4, 147.5,
155.15, 158.1
Peel, Robert, 47.9, 48.1, 48.5
Pitt, William, 28.8, 148.7
Politics, 1.6, 3.6, 3.10, 3.11, 9.15, 11.2, 14.4,
25.10, 38.6, 42.8, 67.15, 71.7, 80.5, 81.3,
89.4, 91.4, 105.3, 111.6, 114.8, 114.11, 117.2,
117.5, 118.6, 120.17, 120.18, 120.19, 120.21,
120.23, 121.9, 129.3, 130.3, 130.4, 132.10,
133.10, 139.10, 142.13, 143.9, 146.3, 146.11,
147.7, 147.9, 148.11, 150.13, 158.9, 162.2,
162.5, 163.2, 174.1, 175.1
Power, 8.3, 8.4, 11.9, 13.8, 20.1, 20.4, 81.5,
110.6, 112.10, 139.6, 142.3, 144.1, 146.2,
149.2, 152.7, 159.6, 161.7, 162.6
Property, 48.11, 53.11, 62.9, 63.1, 112.13,
137.1, 141.10, 142.7, 172.8, 172.10
Poverty and Wealth, 4.4, 16.2, 16.3, 34.7, 45.6,
48.3, 60.9, 70.3, 88.12, 99.6, 116.7, 117.9,
117.12, 118.4, 120.22, 132.12, 133.10, 146.9,
172.9
Public Opinion, 42.4, 43.2, 129.2

Race and Racism, 17.18, 66.11, 81.4, 134.2,
161.1, 166.7, 168.2, 173.10
Religion, 1.1, 5.3, 9.7, 9.14, 19.12, 20.1, 20.6,
21.4, 25.10, 27.12, 33.8, 38.11, 43.5, 43.6,
43.7, 43.8, 46.17, 58.7, 59.6, 64.3, 74.8, 77.5,
82.2, 89.6, 101.6, 101.7, 107.3, 109.11, 110.7,
111.4, 112.7, 115.8, 117.11, 121.11, 132.5,
137.3, 137.6, 137.14, 138.2, 143.3, 144.13,
151.13, 163.6, 165.1, 167.5, 172.5
Revolution, 4.6, 5.5, 12.3, 92.3, 112.7, 132.11,
135.10, 136.6, 146.4, 163.8
Revolution (American), 1.10, 34.4, 58.2, 58.3,
58.4, 75.1, 84.8, 84.9, 86.6, 125.1, 126.5,
131.5, 131.9, 131.10

Slavery, 9.7, 22.14, 34.8, 50.4, 59.9, 62.3, 76.5,
84.10, 85.9, 97.6, 108.2, 128.13, 153.11

Socialism, 9.14, 41.4, 43.15, 50.13, 53.13, 60.1,
91.6, 93.9, 95.12, 110.7, 118.3, 118.4, 119.6,
137.1, 137.8, 137.13, 149.7, 150.3, 150.4,
150.5, 153.6, 158.3, 162.4, 164.3, 170.7
State, the, 5.2, 8.2, 8.7, 9.8, 9.9, 9.10, 18.3,
29.9, 40.14, 87.8, 106.3, 106.4, 122.15

Taxation, 38.8, 75.8, 116.14
Thatcher, Margaret, 30.5
Trade Unions, 41.11, 42.1, 53.12, 60.8, 118.5,
171.6, 171.7

Walpole, Robert, 133.7
War and Militarism, 16.9, 27.1, 27.2, 31.4,
31.7, 33.8, 35.11, 35.12, 35.13, 35.14, 35.15,
36.1, 36.2, 36.12, 39.6, 41.8, 51.3, 52.6, 52.7,
52.8, 52.10, 58.5, 59.7, 60.2, 61.5, 65.8,
66.12, 68.2, 68.3, 68.6, 77.2, 77.3, 80.8, 88.4,
88.7, 88.16, 91.1, 116.1, 116.2, 116.14,
118.12, 119.3, 119.4, 119.11, 119.13, 120.5,
122.7, 124.6, 125.4, 126.6, 126.10, 127.9,
128.2, 128.13, 131.14, 131,15, 132.1, 133.1,
134.8, 136.7, 147.10, 153.6, 155.15, 162.9,
164.6, 164.9, 169.1, 171.8, 174.7
Wellington, Duke of, 26.4
Women, 67.13, 127.13, 128.1, 128.2, 128.3,
149.5, 159.6, 175.2